STANDING GUARD

Written under the auspices of
the Center for International Affairs,
Harvard University

STUDIES IN INTERNATIONAL POLITICAL ECONOMY

Edited by Stephen D. Krasner
Department of Political Science
Stanford University

STANDING GUARD

Protecting Foreign Capital
in the
Nineteenth and Twentieth
Centuries

Charles Lipson

University of California Press
Berkeley • Los Angeles • London

University of California Press
Berkeley and Los Angeles, California

University of California Press, Ltd.
London, England

Copyright © 1985 by The Regents of the University of California.
First Paperback Printing 1985

Library of Congress Cataloging in Publication Data
Lipson, Charles.
Standing guard.

Includes index.
1. Investments, Foreign—Law and legislation—History.
2. Eminent domain (International law)—History.
3. International economic relations—History.
4. United States—Foreign economic relations. I. Title.
K3830.4.L56 1984   346'.07   83–24260
ISBN 0-520-03468-6   342.67
ISBN 0-520-05327-3 (ppb.)

Printed in the United States of America

08   07   06   05   04   03   02   01   00
        9   8   7   6   5   4   3

The paper used in this publication meets the minimum requirements
of ANSI/ NISO Z39.48-1992 (R 1997) (*Permanence of Paper*). ∞

For my family

Contents

CHAPTER THREE

The Interwar Challenge to Traditional Rules   65

CHAPTER FOUR

"The American Century": The Revival and
Decline of International Property Rules   85

CHAPTER FIVE

The Sources of International Property Rules   140

Tables

Figures

Preface and Acknowledgments

Studying the multinational corporation is a relatively new business, but one that has grown enormously over the past decade. The first important work was not completed until 1960: Stephen Hymer's MIT thesis on the international operations of national firms.[1] For Hymer, the central issue was not why capital flows took place (which might be related to interest-rate differentials), but rather why some investments involved direct operational control. His approach was grounded not in international economic theory but in the theory of the firm. The problem was to explain why firms undertook horizontal and vertical integration across national boundaries. This approach firmly situated the study of multinational corporations (MNCs) in the more general study of industrial organization[2] and pushed aside the political issues associated with multinational investment.

Over the next few years, as American firms continued their worldwide growth, more economists were moved to consider the sources of this expansion, its impact on balances of payments, welfare, and economic efficiency, and its relationship to national economic policies. The best of this early work is collected in Charles Kindleberger's edited volume, *The International Corporation* (1970).[3] Subsequent studies are surveyed in Richard E. Caves, *Multinational Enterprise and Economic Analysis* (1982).[4]

Sustained empirical inquiry dates from the 1971 publication of Raymond Vernon's *Sovereignty at Bay*.[5] This book advances a number of inventive hypotheses on the international transfer of production processes, on the changing bargains between multinational corporations and foreign governments, and on the serious problem of controlling these global firms at the national level. It marks the first real effort to collect and interpret data relevant to these questions. Equally important, Vernon's work pushes the study of international investment beyond its roots in industrial organization theory to address explicitly political issues, as its exaggerated title indicates.

Sovereignty at Bay stimulated a number of detailed studies of multinational investment, all of them concentrating on economic and organizational issues. They range from Louis Wells and John Stopford's work on the management of these enterprises,[6] to Mira Wilkins's histories of their slow emergence and maturation;[7] from M. Y. Yoshino's and Yoshihiro Tsurumi's pioneering studies of Japanese multinationals to Lawrence Franko's work on their European counterparts.[8] The cumulative contribution of these works is their illumination of the organizational dynamics of multinational investment. The most recent extension (and variant) of this organizational perspective centers on the idea that all firms, including multinationals, internalize market transactions. The point is to understand when these market failures occur, when transactions within the firm are more efficient than transactions at arm's length or by long-term contract or licensing.[9]

Except for Vernon's, virtually all of these works downplay the political issues, often ignoring them entirely. There are a few exceptions, most notably Theodore Moran's sophisticated analysis of Chilean copper firms,[10] but most authors focus on intracorporate behavior. When political issues are introduced, they are typically limited to the erosion of state economic controls in an interdependent world economy.

The dependency literature, by contrast, *does* treat political issues quite explicitly in relationship to international capital. These studies, however, are rarely concerned with multinational firms in detail or with the political context of international capital flows.[11] Their real focus is on the evolving international division of labor and its impact on class alliances, state structure, and economic development in peripheral areas.[12]

These limitations leave a great—and unnecessary—gap between the study of multinational enterprise and the study of political issues in the world economy. This book is, in part, an effort to bridge that gap.

Until recently, political scientists were uninterested in integrating these two topics, preferring to pass over the "low" politics of economic relations in favor of the "high" politics of strategic interaction. Take, for example, the clearest statement of the Realist position: Hans Morgenthau's first edition of *Politics among Nations* (1948). Morgenthau only briefly discusses geography, natural resources, and industrial capacity, and he does so all under the rubric of "elements of national power."[13] This approach, widely followed, effectively restricted the study of international politics to strategic, military, and diplomatic relations—the "pole of power," in Arnold Wolfers's phrase.

Over the past decade, however, the study of international relations has taken on a significant new dimension: the sustained analysis of international political economy. This shift in focus was undoubtedly spurred by events: the basic institutional arrangements of the postwar world economy were in obvious turmoil. Although the world economy remained essentially open, political disputes were rife in international trade, money, and investment. Two shocks to world oil supplies and prices, a deep and prolonged recession, and the slow ebbing of American power raised the most fundamental questions about the sources of international order and disorder.

If international order was the underlying issue, the research itself focused on a wide variety of topical questions, particularly monetary affairs, trade relations, and policy coordination. The extensive spread of equity investment and of its novel organizational forms have not been studied extensively by political scientists in spite of the controversies they generated and the theoretical issues they suggested.

An important exception to this dominant research agenda is the work of Robert Gilpin. His *U.S. Power and the Multinational Corporation* (1975) is a serious inquiry into the international transfer of production and its impact on the U.S. economy and polity. He particularly stresses its adverse effects on U.S. economic development and its immediate costs to American workers. Gilpin's conclusion, strongly argued, is that public policy should curtail this transfer of productive facilities engineered by multinational firms.

Gilpin's work is also the first to examine systematically the relationship between the international political order and the multinational spread of capital. He raises many of the questions addressed in Part I of this book and, even though my methods and conclusions differ from his, I am very much in his debt.

Where earlier studies of economic interdependence and

multinational investment had neglected their political context, Gilpin argues convincingly that corporate expansion requires political backing. But what kind of political backing? Here Gilpin's conclusions parallel those of Charles Kindleberger, who claims that international order is what economists term a public good.* According to Kindleberger (and, by implication, Gilpin), the public good of world economic order must emanate, if at all, from a single world leader.

Following this line of reasoning, Gilpin concludes that a stable, liberal economic order is the historic creation of successive hegemonial powers: Great Britain in the last century, the United States after World War II. Acting in their own security interests, they created a favorable environment for economic interdependence. The decline of these hegemonial powers inevitably undermines the global order they created.[14]

Stephen Krasner makes a similar point and tests it with equivocal results in "State Power and the Structure of International Trade."[15] Krasner has also studied U.S. investments in raw materials, but his *Defending the National Interest* is really about the goals of foreign policy rather than the sources of international order. (Krasner's principal conclusion is that support for foreign investments is largely a by-product of policies aimed at wider national objectives.)[16]

As interesting as the hegemonial approach is, it nevertheless leads to serious problems in explaining the changing security of foreign capital. Consider foreign direct investments during the interwar period. British power had declined substantially by then, but America's had not fully risen. Hence, according to a model based on hegemonial power, foreign investments should have been markedly less secure. They were not.

---

*This claim is a contentious one. True public goods are characterized by jointness of supply and by the impossibility of exclusion. A good is jointly supplied if one's consumption does not diminish the amount available for others to consume. The "impossibility of exclusion" simply means that there is no way to stop relevant people from consuming the good—whether they pay for it or not. Yet few international arrangements wholly lack the capacity to exclude nations that do not contribute to their upkeep. While some benefits of an open, liberal system of trade and investment are, in fact, generally available to all nations, many trade and monetary arrangements permit discrimination. East-West trade is thoroughly laced with discriminatory provisions. Another example comes from the Tokyo Round trade agreements, where the nontariff barrier codes apply only to trade among the signatories. The point is not that discrimination is pervasive (the world economy is rather more liberal than that), the point is that discriminatory arrangements are almost always possible. This threat of discrimination may be used to ensure reciprocal contributions by the beneficiaries of international agreements.

A more general problem with the public goods approach to international order is its tendency to confuse all acts of cooperation with public goods.

Their relative security not only casts doubt on the hegemonial model, it also suggests an important feature of the international economic order: differences among issue areas. International trade and payments were, of course, seriously disrupted by the Depression. But the security of foreign capital remained relatively stable. Robert Keohane and Joseph Nye observe that the politics of ocean use were equally stable from 1920 to 1945, with no departure from the cardinal principle of freedom of the seas.[17] Their conclusion is that no matter how important hegemonial power may be, it still cannot fully account for the varied structure of international issues or for the varied pace of change.

A recent example might clarify the point. Some would argue that the decline of U.S. power accounts for the wave of expropriations during the 1970s. If that were the whole explanation, though, then other forms of foreign capital such as portfolio loans should be equally insecure.* That prediction, however, would be incorrect.

Syndicated bank credits, the dominant form of modern portfolio lending, have been remarkably secure against renunciation. Only a few states, all of them communist, have declared unilateral suspensions of debt payments. Default or persistent arrears in the face of severe impoverishment is another matter. Some states may simply be unable to meet their payment schedules given their foreign exchange earnings and limited capacity to attract new capital. Like it or not, creditors may be forced to postpone their collections because of the debtor's weakness.[18] Equally noteworthy, however, is the extent of economic contraction that debtor states have been willing to endure rather than suspend repayments unilaterally.[19]

These differences between direct and portfolio investment suggest once again that the decline of hegemonial power is not a comprehensive explanation.

---

*According to the usual definition, portfolio investments do not involve control over the enterprises in which the investments are made. Rather, they simply add to the investor's asset portfolio of bonds, loans, and equity investments. Direct investments, by contrast, carry with them operating authority. This customary distinction between portfolio and direct investments is difficult to make in practice because "control" is difficult to define in a nonarbitrary way. As an example, consider the problem of determining the extent of foreign direct investments by the United States. The immediate problem is that many foreign affiliates have widely dispersed ownership. The Commerce Department, which compiles U.S. statistics on investments abroad, has simply drawn a line: a U.S. foreign affiliate is a foreign business enterprise in which a single U.S. direct investor owns at least 10 percent of the voting securities, or their equivalent. Using this definition, the department's 1977 Benchmark Survey reported that 3,500 U.S. parents owned some 35,000 foreign affiliates. U.S., Department of Commerce, *Survey of Current Business* 61 (April 1981), 29.

Indeed, a closer examination indicates that *investment security is not exclusively a matter of state power.* Private actors, ranging from nineteenth-century bondholders to modern corporations, have played a crucial role in protecting their own investments. In the most recent period, they have been joined by international institutions such as the International Monetary Fund (IMF). Including these organizations in an account of investment security is not simply a matter of descriptive completeness. It is, more importantly, a matter of predictive validity and convincing explanation.

Thus, despite the appealing parsimony of Gilpin's and Krasner's approach, their hegemonial models are fraught with difficulties. To begin with, they incorrectly specify the unity of international issues. Investment security, at least, is organizationally distinct from trade and monetary relations. Second, these models seem to overstate the consequences of hegemonic decline for investment security, both in the interwar period and more recently. Finally, their exclusive focus on state power ignores the vital role of private transnational actors in securing their own capital.

This brief discussion indicates that issues such as investment security may have distinctive patterns. On this point, in particular, I share the general conclusions of Keohane and Nye.[20]

The central topics in this study are the security of foreign capital and the process of international rule making. *Standing Guard* is, above all, an analysis of long-term changes in investment security and the factors underlying them. Part I examines the *regime for foreign investment,* including the political rules, norms, and institutions that have characterized investment security during the nineteenth and twentieth centuries. I consider the convergent (and divergent) expectations about the proper treatment of foreign capital, as they are revealed in various national policies and articulated in international forums.

Fundamental changes in investment security are explained in terms of the changing distribution of economic and military resources, the capacity to manipulate international institutions (such as the IMF), and the evolving character of state bureaucracies in less developed countries. This work is summarized in chapter 5, which situates the security of foreign capital in its international context. This chapter can be read alone, for those who wish to skip over the preceding historical analysis.

Part II examines the foreign policy of investment protection since World War II. It shows how the evolution of U.S. anti-expropriation policy is closely related to the evolution of multinational investment. Chapters 6 and 7 evaluate hypotheses predicting investment-security policy on the basis of corporate preferences, which in turn are related to corporate strategies. The concluding chapter links these issues of foreign policy to those of international rule making.

This work carries with it many debts—improvements large and small that I can trace to discussions with friends and colleagues. I am especially grateful to Joseph Nye for his sustained support, guidance, and criticism. I benefited considerably from the efforts of Bruce Andrews and Robert Keohane, who read several drafts and offered valuable comments all along the way. Peter Cowhey, Jorge Domínguez, Peter Gourevitch, Ernst Haas, Stanley Hoffmann, Miles Kahler, Stephen Krasner, James Kurth, Theodore Moran, Kenneth Oye, Robert Paarlberg, Robert Pastor, Tony Smith, Raymond Vernon, Tony Walters, and Mary Yeager all gave me careful readings and useful advice.

Most have been associated, at one time or another, with Harvard's Center for International Affairs. The Center, under Raymond Vernon and Samuel Huntington, generously provided me with office space, research funds, and a lively forum for considering the basic issues of international relations.

My colleagues at the University of Chicago have provided years of vigorous and fruitful debate on these issues and more. They particularly stimulated my thinking about general processes of rule making and their international setting. I wish to thank Brian Barry, Russell Hardin, John Ikenberry, Morton Kaplan, Lloyd Rudolph, Susanne Rudolph, Philippe Schmitter, Duncan Snidal, Tang Tsou, Aristide Zolberg, and my colleagues in the Program on Interdependent Political Economy.

I also wish to thank Princeton University Press and the University of Wisconsin Press for permission to use, in revised form, materials published earlier in *World Politics* and *International Organization.* *

I am grateful most of all for the constant support of my family. As always, they have been there for me.

C. L.

*An earlier version of chapter 6 was published in *World Politics* 27 (April 1976), 396–421, © 1976 by Princeton University Press. An earlier version of chapter 7 appeared in *International Organization* 32 (Spring 1978), 351–375, © 1978 by the Regents of the University of Wisconsin. Both are reprinted by permission.

INTRODUCTION

CHAPTER ONE

An Unruly World?
Anarchy, Rules, and
International Capital Flows

"'This dog is mine,' said those poor children; 'that is my place in the sun.' Here is the beginning and the image of the usurpation of all the earth," according to Pascal.[1] Rousseau, who understood the point well (he cites it in the *Second Discourse*), considers this usurpation the founding myth of modern civilization. "The first person who, having fenced off a plot of ground, took it into his head to say *this is mine* and found people simple enough to believe him, was the true founder of civil society."[2]

Rousseau's image is at once compelling and penetrating. Property, like the related but distinct notion of contract, is indeed fundamental to modern economic life and to the complex civil society in which it is embedded. By the same token, the very meaning of property is socially constructed and is therefore subject to constant revision as social relations and expectations change. Because the idea of property has these social, cultural, and phenomenological aspects, its meaning is not a settled matter. It must be reestablished continually—in political theory and in political practice.

Ian Macneil, a legal theorist, has written that contracts without social structure and stability are rationally unthinkable.[3] Otherwise, how could promises be projected effectively into the future?[4] The same point applies with equal force to the idea of property and to the stability of possessions. They must be understood as elements of a more inclusive normative order that is itself socially constituted and culturally inscribed.

3

Precisely for these reasons, stable property rights and contractual relations are exceedingly difficult to establish across national boundaries. Although collective evaluations and expectations are an important feature of international relations,[5] these normative properties are weaker because political, social, and cultural communities are constituted primarily at the domestic level, where they typically overlap and reinforce one another (as the term *nation-state* suggests). Thus, while it is difficult to establish the meaning and value of property rights domestically, it is far harder internationally.

Yet, by the mid-nineteenth century, when foreign investments began to increase dramatically, international property rights were well established in Europe, codified as international law, and imposed on a global basis from China to Latin America. The central idea was that, at the very least, all foreign-owned property should be accorded some internationally approved minimum standard of treatment. Knowing these standards, investors could then assess the various commercial risks and decide for themselves whether to buy foreign bonds or build a railroad in some remote locale. By establishing this minimum code of conduct and promoting stable expectations about future interactions, these international laws and property rules served, as many laws do, to facilitate social transactions.[6] Certainly, they served as "shapers and enablers" of international capital flows.[7]

Changing Forms of International Capital

Even with clear rules, the extension of capital across national boundaries is an inherently problematic activity. It requires the ability to manage events at a distance, to gain accommodations from foreign governments, and perhaps to secure support from one's home government in difficult situations. Despite all these risks, international capital flows and multinational corporations have become a characteristic feature of the modern world economy.

That capital has been internationalized on such a wide scale over the past two centuries is closely related to two fundamental developments in Western history: the rise of industrial capitalism and the continued growth of the modern state. The conjuncture of these two developments not only produced the capacity to organize production on a worldwide basis but also to protect it with effective rules signaling the proper treatment of foreign capital in all countries. In recent years, however, the meaning and significance of these international property rules have shifted markedly. This work is about their origin and evolution.

By the mid-nineteenth century, capital markets had become efficient and well institutionalized, most notably in the city of London. Deep enough to finance large-scale enterprise, they incorporated information about foreign opportunities and offered broad markets for exotic securities. In these respects, London resembled its immediate predecessor, Amsterdam, which had been Europe's economic capital in the seventeenth and eighteenth centuries.[8] Significantly, though, Amsterdam's capital market represented the golden age of international *merchant* capitalism, while Victorian London financed not only long-distance trade and foreign government debt but also *industrial* enterprise and the establishment of economic infrastructure on a global scale.

The risks were high, but so were the rates of return. As a result, foreign bonds became fixtures on Victorian London's stock exchange, and to a lesser extent in Paris, Berlin, and (later) New York. The resulting investments were seldom directly managed or controlled from abroad. The same could be said for many foreign equity offerings. They were simply added to investors' asset portfolios.

Such portfolio investments are still commonplace, although their institutional form has changed considerably. The most creditworthy European states may still sell some international bonds, but most debt financing is done through banking syndicates, which arrange floating-rate loans from their own deposits and other assets. In the nineteenth century, by contrast, banks served mainly as underwriters, selling fixed-rate bonds to the general public.

If foreign bonds were the most common form of international investment in the late nineteenth century, direct investments had also begun to increase sharply by then. Decreasing costs for communication and transportation allowed formerly domestic corporations, which were already operating in consolidated national markets, to begin extending their operations abroad. These were not simply more old-line trading houses, like those that had imported and exported furs, spices, precious metals, and foodstuffs for centuries. They were, instead, international *producers:* companies that mined, farmed, generated electricity, and even manufactured in far-flung locations.[9] They were followed by truly multinational companies, whose global operations were both extensive and tightly integrated. Their prototype was the major international oil company, which developed along with the internal combustion engine after World War I. These integrated multinational companies explored and produced in the Middle East and Latin America—wherever they could find oil—and then transported, refined, and sold the final products throughout Europe and North America. These corporations simultaneously extended international markets and internalized them within individual firms.

This dual process of market extension and internalization accelerated substantially after World War II. The older oil companies were joined by aggressive national firms from Western Europe and by formerly domestic U.S. companies (the so-called independents). At the same time, many large and technologically advanced companies, in both the manufacturing and service sectors, were establishing their own elaborate networks of foreign subsidiaries.

The aims and strategies of these manufacturing and service companies differed from those of extractive firms. Oil and mining companies, for example, were usually seeking secure oligopoly control over critical factors in their production processes. Their goal was to maintain tight market control by incorporating the entire production and distribution process within the firm, from minerals in the ground to final sales.

In contrast to this *vertical* integration (up and down the chain of production), manufacturing and service companies tended to establish foreign subsidiaries similar to those in the headquarters country. Their *horizontal* integration had several potential advantages. By producing abroad instead of exporting, they could avoid trade barriers and minimize their transportation costs. And because they were now closer to foreign markets, they could tailor their products and processes more easily to fit local conditions.

The diversity of these investments obscures what is common: all require years to be amortized fully and so will be undertaken only if local political conditions seem to permit stable, profitable operations. Commercial calculations and the assessment of political risks are thus inextricably intertwined in the foreign investment decision. Naturally, the prospective investor must assess his capacity to organize production abroad and to sell it profitably in changing markets around the world. At the same time, he must evaluate not only the existing terms on which his investment is permitted, but also the likely future terms. War, revolution, or civil strife may render the investments worthless. More commonly, host states could unilaterally change the arrangements under which multinational firms operate, sometimes overriding earlier contracts. For example, taxes and royalty schedules may be increased, more exports or local purchases required, or profit remittances blocked because of foreign exchange shortages.

The array of national policy instruments is complex and increasingly variegated. In export sectors, where many countries compete for low-wage production facilities, subsidized loans and tax waivers may be used to attract electronics assembly or apparel manufacture. Yet the same countries often restrict entry or prevent expansion by foreign firms in other, more sensitive sectors, notably raw-materials extraction.*

Of all the risks facing multinational firms, one of the most serious is a direct challenge to their ownership or managerial control. A foreign-owned firm may be required to take on an unwanted local partner (which may be the host state itself) as a majority owner. It may even be forced to sell out entirely, with or without compensation for the enterprise's market value.

In all these ways and more, the political context directly affects the value of foreign investments. The host state can, in effect, alter the property rights of foreign investors, either prospectively or retrospectively. The likelihood that they will do so increases as states take on more extensive responsibilities for economic planning and management.

It is these risks and uncertainties that make international property rules so important. They furnish a common baseline for the expectations of both host states and foreign investors. In particular, they point to the acceptable limits on national treatment of foreign capital.

---

*In recent years many host states have established standards for new foreign investment, usually in the form of entry contracts. Devised by Indonesia and Colombia in 1967, these screening techniques have spread to much of Asia and Latin America. Typically, they specify the extent of foreign ownership, prospective local employment, target rates for growth and exports, requirements for transferring technology and operational control, and, in some cases, procedures for eventual divestiture. Richard D. Robinson, *National Control of Foreign Business Entry: A Survey of Fifteen Countries* (New York: Praeger Publishers, 1976), and François J. Lombard, *The Foreign Investment Screening Process in LDCs: The Case of Colombia, 1967–1975* (Boulder, Colo.: Westview Press, 1979).

The Development of
International Property Rules

The ground rules for foreign capital were well defined by the mid-nineteenth century. They grew out of numerous commercial treaties among European states, treaties whose provisions ultimately hardened into general principles of international law. These principles are discussed in detail in the following chapter; their basic features, however, can be stated simply here. Foreigners were deemed subject to local laws, as they had been since the Middle Ages, but national jurisdiction over aliens and their property had to comply with a variety of international standards. Interference with foreigners' property was permissible, but only in exceptional cases involving a clear and limited public purpose. Both independent judicial review and full compensation had to be provided. Without these procedural and substantive remedies, any taking was an illegal confiscation and an international tort. In such cases, the investor's home state could choose whether or not to pursue the claims of its nationals once local remedies had been exhausted.[10]

These principles are still enunciated by major capital exporting states, including the United States. The United States embraced them most forcefully when it challenged Mexico's expropriations in the late 1930s.[11] They were reaffirmed when the United States last codified its foreign relations law (*Restatement, Second, Foreign Relations Law of the United States* [1965]).[12] An official comment, included in the *Second Restatement*, is worth quoting because it states so clearly the broadest, and most contentious, principle underlying international property rules—that of international minimum standards:

> Some states maintain that an alien is not entitled to a higher standard of justice than a national. . . . This Section [of U.S. law] follows the prevailing rule that such national treatment is not always sufficient, and that there is an international standard of justice that a state must observe in the treatment of its own nationals, and even if the standard is inconsistent with its own law.[13]

These minimum standards for the proper treatment of foreigners and their property developed initially within Europe. Beginning with the Treaties of Westphalia (1648) and Paris (1763), the major trading states effectively secured the economic rights of their subjects abroad through a network of treaty provisions. Britain, France, Holland, and Spain all played important roles. The German Empire, Sweden, and Russia were involved to a lesser extent. Their aim was to protect not only the personal safety and tangible property of their nationals, but all their assets, including private debts.[14]

The freedom and security of foreign persons and their property was guaranteed by every important European state, and by the United States soon after its independence.* During peacetime, at least, foreigners could acquire and transfer debts, demand repayment of loans, and use local courts to enforce claims.[15] Equally important, host states were not permitted to interfere with foreigners' assets. Seizure and confiscation were prohibited in peacetime. In wartime, belligerents could seize enemy assets, but many treaties required later restitution.[16] The overall result was an extensive web of treaties that "provided the legal security necessary for international enterprise and investment."[17]

This security for foreign capital was essentially the legal expression of reciprocal interests among European states.[18] They had extensive, ongoing economic ties with one another, along with local procedures for guaranteeing property against arbitrary seizure or confiscation, as well as the capacity to conclude treaties as sovereign equals. Taken together, these relations formed the basis for international economic rule making. Devised initially to protect merchants and long-distance trade, these rules later provided an effective framework for the international extension of industrial and financial capital.

By facilitating capital transfers, these rules have encouraged international specialization and economic interdependence and, as a consequence, have rationalized the international division of labor. The same can be said of rules dealing with trade relations and foreign exchange—all are important aspects of interstate relations.

---

*United States acceptance of these general principles was reflected in article 6 of the 1795 treaty between the United States and Spain. Some years later, Secretary of State John Quincy Adams wrote of that provision: "There is no principle of the law of nations more firmly established than that which entitles the property of strangers within the jurisdiction of another country in friendship with their own to the protection of its sovereign by all efforts in his power. This common rule of intercourse between all civilized nations has, between the United States and Spain, the further and solemn sanction of an express stipulation by treaty." Mr. Adams to Mr. de Onis, Spanish minister, March 12, 1818, in U.S., Congress, *American State Papers. Foreign Relations*, vol. 4 (Washington, D.C.: Gales and Seaton, 1834), 476.

Unfortunately, their importance—indeed, their very presence—is obscured by the dominant metaphor of international relations: international anarchy. Derived from Thucydides and Hobbes, central to the Realist tradition, this metaphor is both profound and misleading. It points, quite rightly, to the lack of an international sovereign and therefore to the inescapable problems of national "self-help" as the generative grammar of international relations.[19] States lack, as Hobbes put it, a "common power to keep them all in awe." As a consequence, no state's security can be guaranteed, and organized violence is an ever-present danger.* Given the risks, the benefits of cooperation among nations are potentially great, but so are the dangers of betrayal. For all these reasons, cooperative rule making in security issues is, at best, difficult and the results unreliable.

Even so, states can and do establish some effective joint controls over the international environment, especially in economic issues. As Brian Barry observes, "International affairs are not a pure anarchy in which nobody has any reason for expecting reciprocal relations to hold up. In economic matters particularly, there is a good deal of room for stable expectations."[20] Extensive, ongoing exchange relationships can give rise to stable, complementary expectations about interactions. These can serve as the basis for international rules and conventions.**

*This is Hobbes's "State of Warre," which has long been considered the most basic characterization of international relations. It refers not to actual combat but to circumstances in which the disposition to fight is general and the resort to force legitimate. For "Warre," as Hobbes says,

> consisteth not in Battell only, or the act of fighting; but in a tract of time, wherein the Will to contend by Battell is sufficiently known: and therefore the notion of *Time,* is to be considered in the nature of Warre; as it is in the nature of Weather. . . . So the nature of Warre, consisteth not in actual fighting; but in the known disposition thereto, during all the time there is no assurance to the contrary. All other time is *peace. (Leviathan,* Part I, chap. 13)

In such times "every man is enemy to every man."

Snyder and Diesing have recently objected that it is hyperbolic to call international relations "a state of war." They prefer a less exaggerated, less memorable phrase, saying that crises reveal the distinguishing feature of international politics: "the pervasive expectation of potential war, which follows from the 'anarchic' structure of the system." This does indeed highlight a unique and fundamental feature of international relations. But the overemphasis on anarchy (every state is *not* every other's enemy) systematically obscures the possibilities for cooperation, rule making, and stable expectations among sovereign states. Glenn H. Snyder and Paul Diesing, *Conflict Among Nations* (Princeton, N.J.: Princeton University Press, 1977), 3–4.

**Stable expectations often arise among actors with long-term exchange relationships. Stewart Macaulay explores this point in his study of noncontractual relations in modern business. Businessmen with ongoing relationships often avoid formal con-

These rules are inherently fragile, and adherence to them is uncertain because they lack (1) the continuous backing of coherent sanctions; (2) agreed procedures for dispute resolution; and (3) ancillary cultural and ideological support. Moreover, in international relations, as in some societies, order and regularity must be secured, if at all, against a background of significant conflict.[21] And yet, as Georg Simmel notes, social conflict can be constitutive of social order, at least in conjunction with some unifying forces.[22]

Important baselines for interaction have, in fact, developed in some areas of international relations, as our earlier discussion of property rules indicates. Robert Keohane and Joseph Nye stress these possibilities for international reglementation in their analysis of economic interdependence: "By creating or accepting procedures, rules, or institutions for certain kinds of activity, governments regulate and control transnational and interstate relations."[23] They call these governing arrangements *international regimes*, a term I shall also use (without, however, confining the process of rule creation or maintenance to states alone). Convergent expectations are also an important feature of regimes, and recent studies have gone beyond Keohane and Nye's initial formulation to emphasize them.[24]

In the case of foreign investment, expectations about appropriate treatment developed, as I have said, among European trading powers

---

tracts and seldom resort to litigation. They rely instead on the convergence of expectations (which may be reinforced by professional standards), the implicit sanctions inherent in the bilateral relationship, and the likely impact of noncompliance on reputation. Some international rules may arise in the same way.

The legal theorist Lon Fuller develops a similar argument to explain the growth of domestic customary law, which (he claims) grows out of stable, complementary expectations and serves as a "language of interaction" and a "base line for human interaction."

These arguments are ultimately derived from Hume. They posit that contractual norms arise internally from contractual relations themselves. They complement Durkheim's position (which Hume accepts) that contractual norms also have cultural and social roots reaching well beyond any immediate relationship between the contracting parties.

Stewart Macaulay, "Non-Contractual Relations in Business: A Preliminary Study," *American Sociological Review* 28 (February 1963), 55–69; Lon L. Fuller, "Law and Human Interaction," in *Social System and Legal Process: Theory, Comparative Perspectives, and Special Studies,* ed. Harry M. Johnson (San Francisco: Jossey-Bass Publishers, 1978), 61, 76. Fuller adds that legal sanctions "reinforce interactional expectancies and facilitate a respect for them." Ibid., 76. David Hume, *A Treatise of Human Nature,* ed. L. A. Selby-Bigge, 2d ed., P. H. Nidditch (Oxford: Clarendon Press, 1978), Bk. III, Sec. III: "Of the rules, which determine property." William C. Charron, "Conventions, Games of Strategy and Hume's Philosophy of Law and Government," *American Philosophical Quarterly* 17 (October 1980), 327–334; Emile Durkheim, *The Division of Labor in Society,* trans. George Simpson (New York: Free Press, 1933), chap. 7.

before the advent of industrial capitalism. Their self-restraint regarding foreign investors, pledged in treaty form, was supported by their self-interest. Their own nationals were abroad and therefore vulnerable. In addition, they knew that any arbitrary seizures would likely disrupt their own commercial relations. As a result, the emerging rules were supported less by the threat of coercion than by the potential withdrawal of normal reciprocities, a powerful sanction indeed.[25]

Extending these rules beyond Europe, however, involved few reciprocal relationships, considerably more coercion, and constrained bargaining among radically unequal states.* It is the history of colonial annexation, capitulation treaties, treaty ports, and ad hoc diplomatic intervention, backed up by gunboats when necessary.

Extending Property Rules to Africa and Asia

Relations between the Ottoman Empire and the West illustrate one important way that property rules were extended and defended beyond Europe in the nineteenth century.

The Ottomans had, of course, granted commercial privileges to European merchants for centuries, receiving similar privileges in re-

---

*It is sometimes suggested that the rules protecting foreign investors were developed specifically to constrain poor countries. That is simply wrong. It is certainly true that LDCs played no role in developing the traditional rules and were, in fact, constrained by them. But the rules were developed and applied first within Europe, where they were widely accepted. Only later were they extended to Africa, Asia, and Latin America.

That these rules were accepted in Europe is evident from a 1913 arbitration. The new Portuguese government had decided to expropriate all properties belonging to religious associations. The British, French, and Spanish governments immediately protested on behalf of their nationals, who were affected. What is crucial about this case is the underlying agreement of *all* four governments on the rights of aliens. They all agreed, at the very outset, that foreigners were owed compensation as a matter of principle, regardless of how host states treated their own nationals. Naturally, the British, French, and Spanish governments asserted this traditional point in their presentations to the arbitration tribunal. Significantly, the Portuguese government, in its response, approved these traditional principles without reservation and based its defense on much narrower grounds (that the religious property in question belonged not to the individual claimants but to their religious associations). The issues were finally resolved by compromise, but that is less important for our purposes than the convergent sense among all the parties of the proper scope of state responsibilities for injuries to aliens. Alexander P. Fachiri, "Expropriation and International Law," *British Year Book of International Law* 6 (1925), 167–169; Rudolph Dolzer, "New Foundations of the Law of Expropriation of Alien Property," *American Journal of International Law* 75 (July 1981), 558 fn.

turn. These "capitulation treaties," as they were called, stretched back to the early 1500s. Freely made by Ottoman authorities, they were calculated to obtain scarce goods for the empire, increase its customs revenues, and win it political allies in Christendom. These treaties had always been premised upon foreign pledges of "friendship, peace, and sincerity." In practice, that meant the extension of similar protection to Muslim merchants and other Ottoman subjects abroad.

This principle of reciprocal protection was written directly into Ottoman treaties, such as that with Venice in 1540. Typically, both sides pledged to compensate for damages inflicted at sea, to protect victims of shipwrecks, to safeguard their goods, and to seize fugitive debtors, among other things. These pledges allowed Ottoman subjects (including Jews, Armenians, Greeks, and Slavs) to conduct business in Europe under the Sultan's diplomatic protection. "Reciprocity was therefore a reality, from which the whole Empire benefited," according to historian Halil Inalcik.[26]

Although these reciprocal treaties opened the Ottoman Empire to more extensive trade, they still had major limitations. They offered no relief, for example, from the regulations on internal trade and travel that hampered foreign merchants. Nor did they relieve the burdens of high tariffs, price fixing, or government monopolies. Thus, by 1830, as the industrial revolution was starting and foreign trade expanding, the Western powers, and particularly Britain, felt that the markets of the Levant "should become more accessible, secure and stable."[27]

In addition to this avowed interest in greater trade and investment, Britain had a growing security stake in the eastern Mediterranean. It particularly wanted to halt Russian expansion in the region and to secure its own lines of communication to the Middle East and South Asia.[28]

These aims were embodied in the 1838 Anglo-Turkish Convention, a one-sided agreement that gave new meaning to the term *capitulation*. In place of genuine reciprocity, the treaty pried open the now-feeble Ottoman Empire to European manufactures and investments. Tariffs were drastically lowered and internal barriers removed.

By mid-century, foreign capital had extensively penetrated Ottoman territories. Europeans were granted extensive concessions for mining, railroad and port construction, coastal navigation, banking, and public utilities.[29] When disputes arose between foreign investors and Ottoman authorities, as they did with bondholders in 1876, the Sultan was forced to accept the creditors' interpretation of the capitulations and commercial treaties.[30]

Ottoman control over foreign enterprises simply disintegrated. Foreign firms "conserved their nationality," in the words of one U.S. report, and were governed according to the laws of their own country.[31] In cases of conflict between foreigners and Ottoman subjects, trials had to be conducted in special courts, where Ottoman judges were joined by consular delegates. Proceedings of this mixed court were not considered valid without approval from the foreigner's own consular representative.[32] Under these arrangements, international property rights were effectively guaranteed by the extraterritorial application of European and American laws.[33]

This system of foreign concessions and extraterritorial laws was developed most fully in the treaty ports of the Far East. Once again, Britain took the lead, pressing China and Japan for open, nondiscriminatory access for all commercial powers.[34] Indeed, the Anglo-Chinese wars of 1839–1842 and of 1856–1860 were fought mainly to open China to world trade.[35] The unequal treaties that ended the first of these Opium Wars established a network of treaty ports, free-trading zones that were effectively ruled by Europeans. They were characterized by most-favored-nation treatment, opium traffic, and extraterritorial jurisdiction. According to John King Fairbank, the whole system was "designed to revolve around the British Consul," who was vested with nearly all the powers of government.[36] He could, for example, hear grievances against both Chinese and British subjects, punish British criminals, and furnish security to British merchant ships and property.[37] Diplomatic means were preferred, but he could (and did) call in the gunboats when necessary to maintain order or punish disorder.[38] This Chinese model was later used in the Anglo-Japanese treaties of 1854 and 1858, which limited Japan's tariff autonomy and gave Britain the power to appoint consuls and exercise extraterritorial rights.[39]

These consular arrangements, which were also used in Africa, guaranteed both commercial penetration and a modern structure of property rights. The two were complementary since the right to acquire and alienate property was essential if the new commerce was to flourish. One reason was that as trade grew, so did the diversity and anonymity of commercial transactions. Merchants, who supplied credit to the growing army of traders, needed security that went beyond personal trust. "The introduction of acceptable impersonal forms of security for advances of cash and goods was an essential precondition of the success of legitimate commerce," according to Antony Hopkins in his study of British West African policy. That entailed radical changes in local property rules—changes accomplished by treaty agreements: "Obtaining payment for commercial debts was a serious and persistent problem, and it featured prominently in the various trade agreements which were used to exert informal influence over the indigenous authorities during the consular period."[40]

Where local legal structures were adequate and political arrangements stable, Britain could accomplish its commercial expansion through less direct intervention. By relying on local protection (where it was sufficient), Britain could minimize one of its most serious diplomatic problems: the progressive erosion of local authority in the face of European commercial expansion.

The dangers of destroying local rule were real and recurrent. Lagos offers a good example. There the power and prestige of tribal chiefs was undermined by the piecemeal imposition of Western economic and legal arrangements. The external slave trade, on which the chiefs had a valuable monopoly, was abolished by the British in 1851. An onslaught of Western exports and the establishment of a European system of land tenure further weakened the chiefs' position.[41] As the sinews of local rule collapsed and political unrest grew, Britain was drawn increasingly into direct intervention, culminating in the formal annexation of Lagos in 1861.

It was a sequence that the Foreign Office and Lord Palmerston understood well but could not always avoid. Their task, essentially, was to manage the articulation between once-remote agricultural regions and a dynamic, expanding industrial capitalism. This industrialism had its own logic of growth, well beyond British control, and was premised on a legal system that ensured certain forms of property rights and contractual relations. Providing this political and legal structure on the periphery was an enormous struggle that presented mid-Victorian policymakers with difficult choices. Their policies naturally aimed at a vast, global extension of commerce. At the same time, they tried to limit the direct imposition of political and military controls, which were expensive and difficult to manage.[42]

This balancing act was a difficult one, at best. It became even less tractable as Continental states increased their competition on the periphery for political control and economic opportunity. Where local governments were weak and vulnerable, and where property relations had to be radically restructured, the balancing act was seldom successful. The result—in Africa and much of Asia—was the inexorable extension of imperial rule in the late nineteenth century.

Extending Property Rules to Latin America

Whether it was for formal annexation or extraterritorial jurisdiction, the protection of foreign capital in Africa and Asia was accomplished through the direct intervention of colonial powers. Their policies were developed and implemented gradually but, taken together, they comprised a far-reaching program for the extension of modern capitalism to backward regions. To do that, these policies not only had to protect investors against predations, they often had to realign the very structure of local property rights. As Britain's governor of The Gambia, MacDonnell, remarked in 1849:

> On what do the English capitalists rely for their security? Of course on the prestige of English power. On the knowledge that English troops and guns are stationed in different positions along the Gambia—and also I am happy to add on the more civilized and juster notions of the rights of property which the continued presence of Europeans and the spread of legitimate commerce is producing.[43]

Latin America was different. MacDonnell's idea of "more civilized and juster notions of the rights of property," still embryonic in Africa and Asia, was embedded in the basic laws of the new Latin American states.*

---

*Frederick Dunn makes this point in his still-valuable 1932 study of *The Protection of Nationals*. In the nineteenth century, he notes, European norms of conduct were extended to the wider international arena. Based on capitalist individualism, these ideas included "notions of individual liberty, of the sacredness of private property even as against the actions of governments, and the sanctity of contracts" (p. 54).

Dunn then goes on to differentiate Latin America from the regions that were to become colonies or treaty ports.

> "The new nations in the western hemisphere embodied these concepts in their fundamental laws (which they had borrowed largely from outside sources), and hence there was, in theory at least, a common basis of ideas on which relations could be established. Where that was not the case, as in the Far East and certain countries of the Near East, relations were conducted on the special basis of extra-

In Buenos Aires, for instance, one of the first acts of the revolutionary junta was to meet with British merchants and to assure them of equal protection under the law. Immigration was permitted, import and export duties were slashed, and they were allowed, for the first time, to buy local property.[44]

These policies were designed partly as a counterweight to Spanish influence, but they also reflected a broader strategy by landed elites and international borrowers. In both Argentina and Brazil, according to Hopkins, the emerging class of large landowners rapidly adopted "British ideas of property as the basis of agricultural progress, sound money, and political stability."[45] These European-style property rights, and their local political guarantees, facilitated the integration of these elites into the world economy as high-volume, low-cost producers of staples, including beef, grains, coffee, and nitrate.[46]

Even so, there were conflicts with foreign investors, who then sought (and often won) the support of their home governments. There were occasional outbreaks of disorder, changes of government, clashes of interest, and fundamental differences over the ultimate ownership of subsoil rights.[47] Defaults on foreign bonds were a persistent source of trouble, one that is discussed at length in the next chapter.

When these difficulties breached the rights of foreign investors, as their home governments understood them, they generated diplomatic protest and even military action. In many cases, however, the investors were able to protect themselves through concerted economic action, principally their stranglehold over credit.*

These direct sanctions were obviously an important source of protection to foreign capitalists, but they should not be confused with the application of extraterritorial laws or the more radical transformation of property rights and legal structures that characterized European commercial expansion in Africa and Asia. Instead, Britain's extensive trade and investment in Latin America was protected mainly by local laws and institutions, commercial treaties, and international

---

territoriality. But the conditions of order and stability that were required to make the European system work satisfactorily had not yet been established in many countries of the new world. Hence we find continual clashes of interest and charges of unjust treatment of foreigners."

Dunn, *The Protection of Nationals* (Baltimore: The Johns Hopkins Press, 1932), 54.

*Later chapters consider the ability of foreign investors to protect themselves—the means they have used, their effectiveness, and the persistent problems of coordinating investors whose immediate interests may differ.

legal rules. If the methods used in Africa are now extinct, those developed in Latin America are still very much alive today.

This continuity means that Latin America is particularly important for the study of international property rules. It is there, after all, that foreign investors have faced independent, less developed countries since the early 1800s. While most other regions were still colonies, foreign investments in Latin America were subject to international law and diplomacy. This long history of independence thus allows us to examine the international property rules as they have evolved over a century and a half.

For much of this period, Latin American states have welcomed foreign investment. The railroads and port facilities, built with foreign capital, complemented a strategy of export-led growth.[48] But to welcome foreign investment is not always to welcome its local influence or its protection by foreign powers. In fact, a number of Latin American states have raised these issues since the late nineteenth century. They have led the struggle, now widespread among less developed states, to curb foreign investors' dominance in national economic development. And they were the first to dispute the investors' traditional legal privileges, particularly the right to call on outside powers for diplomatic and military assistance.[49] It is these broad challenges in the face of extensive foreign investments in the region that have made Latin America the focus of international efforts to protect foreign capital.

These challenges are especially pointed for the United States. Of all U.S. investments in less developed countries (LDCs), about 70 percent are in Latin America.[50] They have been threatened repeatedly over the years and have stimulated aggressive U.S. anti-expropriation policies. Congressional debates over investment protection customarily begin with a Latin American example, and often never move beyond it. The idea of using foreign aid to protect investments, for example, arose immediately after the Cuban Revolution and was debated mainly with reference to Latin America. (The evolution of these foreign aid sanctions is treated in chapter 6.)

While such debates are often framed in regional terms, by both North Americans and Latin Americans, they raise larger issues affecting all foreign investors and all host states. The Calvo Doctrine (1868)[51] and the Mexican Constitution (1917) were among the earliest and most important dissents from traditional legal forms. The Calvo Doctrine challenges the very basis of international tribunals.[52]

The Mexican Constitution contained strict, and unprecedented, restraints on foreign corporations. Drafted by the Revolution's most radical elements, the Constitution guaranteed free land to every landless peasant and allowed the government to carry out expropriation at any time for the nation's welfare. It also reasserted the old Spanish principle, abandoned by the Díaz government in 1884, that landowners did not possess the subsoil mineral rights.[53]

In principle, at least, these constitutional provisions drastically restricted foreigners' rights within Mexico and explicitly rejected basic international legal norms concerning diplomatic protection and property rights. This visionary language, however, did not control subsequent state practice. Mexico's agrarian structure remained essentially the same, and there were no large-scale expropriations of foreign property. Indeed, the displacement of European interests during the revolution and World War I actually left American capital with an unaccustomed economic supremacy in Mexico.[54]

Mexico did not challenge that position openly until 1938, when it seized control of its oil fields from foreign companies. This bold act, like the earlier constitutional provisions, was among the first expressions of what was to become a central issue in the North-South debate: the assertion of national sovereignty over natural resources.*

The Shifting Challenges to Foreign Capital and the Changing Meaning of Expropriation

The Mexican nationalizations, and those in the Soviet Union just after the revolution, signaled a new phase in the status of foreign capital. The challenges were novel.

Before World War I, there simply were no large-scale takings of foreign property.[55] There were only limited expropriations and confiscations, which were vigorously (and successfully) repulsed by Great

---

*Since World War II, less developed states have used the United Nations General Assembly as a forum to debate and ultimately pass a series of resolutions on "National Sovereignty over Natural Resources." The earliest of these resolutions were really a compromise with more developed states. Although they pressed national rights to control raw materials, they also acknowledged international legal standards. By the early 1970s, as U.N. voting power shifted toward LDCs, and as the LDCs pushed for a broader and more radical agenda, the character of these resolutions changed. They no longer acknowledged any international legal obligations regarding compensation, due process, or investors' rights to international adjudication, even if their case was espoused by their home government. These resolutions are discussed in chapter 4.

Britain and other European states. Before the era of massive nationalizations, the most profound impediment to foreign capital was the
political turbulence of the frontier and the uncertain political and
legal status of foreign investments there, if they were permitted
at all.*

As a result, one of the principal problems of international commerce in the nineteenth century was to propagate Western standards
of individual ownership around the world and to secure these standards in the face of considerable social, cultural, and political diversity.** That sometimes meant, as I have stated, a radical revision of
local property relations. Collective forms of ownership and shared
use-rights (with ambiguous ownership) were either overturned entirely or confined to the native sectors of dual economies, as in In-
donesian sugar cane production.† Capital-exporting states established

---

*In the first half of the nineteenth century, much of the Orient was still closed to
foreigners, and, in the Near East, the Ottoman Empire retained its restrictive regulations. These obstacles had been cleared away by the latter part of the century.
**This underscores my earlier observation that property is a variable social construct
whose meaning must be continually re-established. Fixing that meaning, and ration-
alizing its legal expression, was a central issue of nineteenth-century jurisprudence.
As the great Italian legal historian, Paolo Grossi, has written:

> If there is an order that the limpid, monodic nineteenth-century juristic culture
> found repellent, it was precisely collective property in its various forms or, more
> accurately, any communitarian or communistic order that might arise to corrupt
> the direct, immediately sovereign relationship between [an individual] subject and
> his goods.

Grossi, *An Alternative to Private Property: Collective Property in the Juridical Consciousness
of the Nineteenth Century*, trans. Lydia Cochrane (Chicago: University of Chicago Press,
1981), 5.
Like Grossi, Hannah Arendt emphasizes the centrality of individual possession to
modern ideas of property:

> ... remember the sharply polemical aspect of the modern age's concern with prop-
> erty, whose rights were asserted explicitly against the common realm and against
> the state.

Arendt, *The Human Condition* (Chicago: University of Chicago Press, 1958), 109; see
also, C. B. MacPherson, *The Political Theory of Possessive Individualism: Hobbes to Locke*
(Oxford: Oxford University Press, 1962), and C. B. MacPherson, ed., *Property* (Toronto:
University of Toronto Press, 1978), 199–207.
†In tribal areas, the issue of who "owned" the land or resources was a complicated
one, varying naturally from place to place, but always differing from modern Western
practice. Families, not individuals, were usually the basic economic unit, and they
held only usufructuary privileges over farmland, pasture, or natural resources. Subject
to local modes of exchange, they could control their use and consume their products.
But even though the family had use rights, the real proprietor was usually a lineage
or village, and the family's privileges hinged on their membership in this larger corporate body.

enforceable claims to property as an individual right, superseding diverse local standards for use, possession, and exchange. Property was thus privatized as part of a politically guaranteed international legal order.

The means varied, ranging from colonialism to extraterritorial laws to informal commercial empire. But whatever the means, the major European powers assured the juridical dominance of individual possession *on a worldwide basis*. That, in turn, assured the hegemony of individual appropriation, the very basis of modern capitalism.

For those standing guard over foreign capital in the *twentieth* century, the fundamental problem was first to constrain, and later to cope with, Third World nationalism. The very success of foreign firms in penetrating Africa, Asia, and Latin America, and the firms' centrality in national economic life, often made them appear as obstacles to autonomous growth and development. They were inviting targets, conspicuously controlling the nation's natural resources as well as its main sources of export earnings. As such, they graphically illustrated national dependence on foreign markets, foreign technology, and foreign managers.

In spite of this dependence, or perhaps because of it, Third World states were increasingly willing to confront foreign firms. By doing so, the state could represent itself as the standard-bearer of national grievances—a unifying position—and as the legitimate director of national development. Many states were actually taking on these larger economic functions and were not only willing to confront foreign firms, but felt themselves increasingly able to do so. What Friedrich Katz has written of Mexico is also true more generally: "One of the main transformations effected by integration into the world market was a strengthening of the centralized power of the state. The state now had sufficient revenues to organize, maintain,

---

In some cases, these tribal and village economic systems were maintained alongside large-scale colonial agriculture. In Indonesia, for example, villagers raised sugarcane that was processed and sold by heavily capitalized Dutch mills. A whole network of laws was established to preserve village agriculture and, according to Clifford Geertz, it succeeded. This conservation of traditional land-tenure systems was quite unusual, however, and contrasts sharply with the Lagos example cited earlier. Few land-tenure systems could survive the transformation associated with incorporation in modern world commerce. That commerce, with its beachheads in the port cities, required credit, rights of alienation, and procedures to determine contractual rights—the whole panoply of modern property rules and procedures. Geertz, *Agricultural Involution* (Berkeley and Los Angeles: University of California Press, 1963), chaps. 4, 5; Marshall Sahlins, *Tribesmen* (Englewood Cliffs, N.J.: Prentice-Hall, 1968), 74–80.

and buy the loyalty of a reinforced army and police, as well as a more efficient bureaucracy."[56] But if the state had become stronger in many cases, especially in Latin America, its place in the international division of labor was all too often dependent upon one or two basic exports. Foreign capital was a visible reminder of this national dependence, especially in such prominent sectors as raw materials, public utilities, and, in one-crop countries, agriculture. The politics of nationalization, up through the early 1970s, was dominated by this symbolically charged relationship between multinational firms, with their networks of wholly owned subsidiaries, and less developed countries, with their growing state responsibilities for national economic management.

In recent years, as more states have developed sophisticated tools for economic management, the frontal challenges of nationalization have been supplemented by much more detailed efforts to regulate foreign investments. Once again, Latin American states have led the way. They have been among the first to push for more local ownership, joint ventures, and other forms of technology transfer that do not require extensive foreign ownership and control.

These measures form a new and complicated regulatory context for international business, one that varies from country to country and from sector to sector. *Business Week* has written that "the new rules require a basic rethinking by multinational companies of their investment strategies, not only in Latin America but also in other parts of the developing world. Asian and African countries are adopting Latin models."[57]

Most multinationals have done this rethinking and have adapted successfully to the complex new environment. They have assessed their exposure to political risks,* acquired local partners when necessary, and tried to meet the host country's various economic targets,

---

*Corporate demand for political risk assessment took off after the Iranian revolution, which caught many firms completely off guard and heavily exposed. The prevailing attitude is expressed by Robert O. Anderson, the chief executive at Atlantic Richfield (Arco), which sustained "some rather substantial losses" in Iran. "You can't be complacent about investments anywhere," says Anderson. "Mexico is the latest case in point. Two or three years ago it looked like a sure financial success, but now it's just the opposite." *New York Times*, 7 August 1983, Sec. 3, p. 1.

Political risk consultants have stepped forward to provide "customized" assessments and data bases to multinational firms and international banks. Many are quantitatively oriented social scientists. Others are regional specialists, quite a few of them retired CIA intelligence officers. Ibid., 1, 23.

To complement these consultants, many MNCs (and all large banks) have set up their own in-house groups. They have even formed a professional association, the Association of Political Risk Analysts, founded in 1980. Their tasks are summarized

such as local purchasing. They have been forced, at times, to replace equity holdings with management contracts and licensing agreements.[58] At other times, they have simply chosen these nonequity alternatives because the prospective payback on invested capital was too slow and the associated risks too great.

Nearly all multinational firms now plan, quite self-consciously, to diminish their exposure to political risks.[59] The basic strategies are not especially complicated. It is axiomatic, for instance, that investments should be spread across many countries rather than concentrated in a few. Equally important, local branches should be made dependent upon the parent corporation rather than independent and self-sufficient. Research and development can be concentrated in the headquarters' country. A single, worldwide trademark, which can be legally protected, can be used instead of local brand names. The parent company can either supply critical materials in the production process or purchase most of the finished goods. A sophisticated strategy thus takes on some local coloration (through joint ventures and a low profile), while carefully integrating local subsidiaries into a global network.[60] Because the subsidiaries cannot stand alone, they are less inviting targets for nationalization.

Of course, investors can neither foresee nor protect against every contingency. They are particularly vulnerable when their projects require heavy initial expenditures but are relatively straightforward and profitable to run. That is why U.S. and European mining companies have shown less interest in the Third World over the past decade, and why they have concentrated instead on the United States, Canada, and Australia.[61]

If the mining companies have been cautious, other industries have continued to go abroad in search of profits. In many ways, they have found the climate for foreign investment more receptive in recent years, in spite of greater regulations and investment screening. Certainly the virulent attacks on foreign capital, so common in the late

---

in Theodore H. Moran ed., *International Political Risk Assessment: The State of the Art*, Landegger Papers in International Business and Public Policy (Washington, D.C.: Georgetown School of Foreign Service, 1981).

The literature on political risk assessment seems to be expanding about as rapidly as the consulting opportunities. Most of it is worthless. One important exception is the work of Stephen J. Kobrin. Kobrin is primarily concerned with the firm's institutionalized capacity to assess its external environment and to incorporate these assessments in its decision making. Kobrin, *Managing Political Risk Assessment: Strategic Response to Environmental Change* (Berkeley, Los Angeles, London: University of California, 1982).

1960s and early 1970s, have subsided for a while. They have been replaced by more focused efforts to encourage certain kinds of foreign investment and to regulate all kinds.*

These more sophisticated efforts to both attract and regulate foreign capital, and the success of corporate adaptation to this new environment, should not obscure the more fundamental point: the rules dealing with foreign investment have changed significantly and irreversibly. Regardless of the incentives for new foreign investment or the existing regulations, there are no real long-term guarantees. That is what traditional property rules, backed by public and private sanctions, once promised. What has been lost, perhaps irretrievably, is a sense of certainty about the way investments will be treated in the future.

A century ago, there was a settled international law governing expropriation of foreign investments. It embodied clear values, imposed strict minimum standards of conduct upon all states, and required full compensation for expropriation. "At the high tide of this version of international law," notes Detlev Vagts, "breaches by host countries might be avenged by any number of plagues ranging from gunboats to arbitration."[62]

In the past decade, by contrast, it is not unusual to find equity assets expropriated with only partial repayment. Long-term contracts, involving substantial commitments and sunk costs, have been renegotiated with no payment at all. And whatever the settlement, the expropriating states always claim the right to determine it themselves, just as they claim the right to regulate foreign investments within their borders.

The most attractive targets, such as the rich oil concessions of the Persian Gulf, have now been nationalized at little cost to the host states. As a result, the toughest bargaining is now over the terms that will govern future management contracts and new investments in selected areas.

---

*Historically contingent circumstances have, as always, played a role in this shifting environment. LDC debt problems, in particular, have helped sweeten the incentives for foreign direct investment. For several years, when the Euro-credit markets were eager lenders, the largest (and most creditworthy) LDCs could fund their development programs without direct investments. They could rely heavily on state-owned corporations, which borrowed abroad to finance their expansion. But the combination of heavy borrowing, high real interest rates, and a global recession changed all that. Export earnings simply stopped growing just as annual interest payments soared. The result was predictable: most LDCs were forced to reschedule their debts. No longer able to borrow freely, they have tried to attract direct investments as an alternate source of long-term capital.

But these terms, once negotiated, could still be overturned later. The risks are serious, and investors understand them: host states can use their laws and regulations to coerce investors if they wish, seize their assets, or deprive them of the value of their contracts. The process is less noisy than outright nationalization but no less effective. That is why Vagts has said that expropriations today "proceed more suavely than in the past."[63]

> Straightforward seizure, to be sure, still has devotees. However, an increasingly favored approach is to induce the foreign investor to convey his property (or an interest therein) by an instrument that on its face represents an ordinary sale. That sale may be accompanied by a revision of the terms of some underlying contract between the investor and the government.[64]

This renegotiation of existing contracts, in line with changes in the parties' relative bargaining power, is now commonplace.[65] It can be as costly as outright expropriation since the investor, having relied on the contract, may have put substantial funds into the project only to be deprived of the ultimate revenues.

These new policy tools require a basic rethinking of what expropriation is. J. Frederick Truitt, in his statistical study of postwar expropriations, defines the term as "an official taking by a sovereign state of a [foreign] direct investment."[66] That is surely the core of the matter, and the central topic of this book. Yet, taken alone, this definition obscures as much as it resolves. Not only are foreign investments "officially taken" (with or without compensation), but foreign firms are also acquired by forced sale, told to hire more local managers, denied permission to take profits out of the country, told to take in local partners, and required to export. There is, in sum, a whole range of state actions that affect foreign equity and profits, a range where regulation and expropriation overlap. In practical terms, it is hard to distinguish a forced sale from a freely negotiated one, even if all the pertinent records are available. Likewise, it is hard to tell whether an administrative action discriminates against foreigners (a criterion sometimes used to define expropriation) if foreign firms control an entire sector of the economy. And, finally, it is unreliable to depend upon the government's "expropriatory intent," as some do, when different bureaucracies and political factions may have different goals and when the outcome may not match anyone's intentions exactly.

Were I constructing a statistical profile, these problems would confound the data.* Since I am examining international property rules and anti-expropriation policies, I can be more sanguine. First, the burgeoning regulation of foreign investments expands the scope of anti-expropriation policy. The new agenda includes "fade-out formulas" and "local-content requirements" as well as confiscation. Equally important, the new regulations modify corporate demands on the U.S. government. In the early sixties, when outright seizures were the chief issue, companies could ask for diplomatic help with a single, overriding problem. The issue was unmistakable and clearly set off from normal business operations. Today, the issue is much broader. It includes not only appropriation of capital but also control of the production process. Diplomatic issues are imbedded in daily work routines and are much more clouded. Instead of a crisis, a company is more likely to face a briefcase full of major problems and minor hassles. To seek diplomatic help on more than a few would be impractical and a self-defeating approach to economic nationalism. The trend toward more state regulation thus complicates and blurs the meaning of expropriation and reinforces the independent efforts of corporations to protect their capital and their profits.

The Protection of Foreign Capital: Research Strategies

In response to these shifting challenges, the policies of the U.S. government and most multinational corporations have been formulated and reformulated, negotiated and renegotiated. One byproduct is an extensive public record and an extensive scholarly literature, one especially rich in Latin American case studies.

---

*Stephen Kobrin has made the most serious effort to cope with these issues statistically. His data cover not only formal expropriation, which he defines narrowly and legalistically, but also several other types of "forced divestment." These include contractual renegotiations and sales, whenever they appear to be coerced, and extralegal forced transfers of ownership. Including these categories means that considerable information needs to be collected about each event and careful judgment made about its final coding.

Even though this approach is more comprehensive than previous studies, Kobrin has chosen to limit himself to actual transfers of ownership. To do more—to try to cover the regulatory issues discussed above—would create intractable problems of data collection. Stephen J. Kobrin, "Foreign Enterprise and Forced Divestment in LDCs," *International Organization* 34 (Winter 1980), esp. 68–69.

This work draws on that literature, while trying to avoid its most serious methodological problems. The case studies are full of generalizations, more often implied than revealed, without adequate empirical foundation. To accept these generalizations, even tentatively, we need to know how the particular case is significant and instructive. It need not be typical, but its value for a more general account and for theory building does need to be shown. What candidate hypotheses, if any, are being tested, and how does the case study relate to them? Can the findings be extended to other cases? Which ones? Unfortunately, these critical questions are seldom asked.[67]

There are several strategies to avoid these problems. It is especially important for theoretical propositions to be explicit. This work develops and tests several hypotheses and compares each with plausible alternatives. It also analyzes major policies dealing with investment security rather than specific expropriation disputes. This approach has several advantages. First, it sidesteps the vexing diplomatic issues that affect all expropriation controversies, allowing a more precise concentration on trends in anti-expropriation policy. Second, it permits one to deal comprehensively with the shaping of these policy tools—their specific aims, their evolution, and their use. There are, of course, dozens of expropriation disputes, each with its idiosyncratic details, and still more cases of stringent regulation that approximate confiscation. But there are only a few general policies designed explicitly to deal with these issues. Two policies are clearly the most important: foreign-aid sanctions and investment-guaranty insurance. Both have been the subjects of extensive public debates and many congressional hearings. Both span several U.S. administrations and touch on numerous diplomatic quarrels. Part II of this book will examine their evolution.

If it is tricky to generalize from the experience of International Telephone and Telegraph (ITT) in Chile or Exxon in Peru, it is flatly wrong to assume that all foreign policy resembles anti-expropriation policy. Where issues are better known and more controversial—trade policy, for instance—one expects large corporations to have a less coherent and less influential voice.[68]

That limits generalizations from the data and raises another methodological question. Isn't anti-expropriation policy precisely the issue where one would expect major foreign investors to play a central policymaking role?[69] The case is not biased against my hypotheses, but in their favor. *But that is a damning flaw only if the case studies were intended to develop propositions that applied to all foreign policy.* This study has other aims.

First, it examines changes in corporate and state strategies to protect foreign investments. It is precisely the closeness between corporations and the state, and the open character of most American political debate, that makes these strategies so accessible. Corporate demands for specific policies are frequently matters of public record, giving us a clear picture of shifting corporate responses to political risk. Sometimes the demands are surprising. One would expect, for example, that companies facing expropriation would try to get all the diplomatic help they could. Sometimes they do, but certainly not always. There are other, crosscutting pressures on the companies. They want to maintain their independence and to control their own negotiations.* They usually prefer to keep the issues out of public view, not to publicize them through diplomatic disputes. Nor do they want to be seen as mere satellites of their home governments. Given the sensitivities of foreign governments, that would only create more problems for their operations abroad. They have investments spread around the world and are necessarily concerned about fueling other nationalist conflicts. At the same time, they recognize that their home governments can frequently add weight to their claims. The debates over anti-expropriation policy reveal these conflicting pressures and highlight their policy implications.

The formulation of anti-expropriation policy also raises the thorny issue of political legitimacy within capital-exporting states. Policies to protect foreign investment, like any other public policy, must either be justified in terms of popular political values or obscured from public view. But both are potentially difficult in this case since they are highly visible *public* policies to assist *private* capital accumulation.

---

*In confidential interviews, executives repeatedly stressed that an appeal for diplomatic assistance could lead to a loss of corporate control over the negotiations. U.S. government officials agree. Their basic point has been stated by David A. Gantz, an assistant legal adviser to the State Department and a member of the team that negotiated a settlement between Marcona Corporation and Peru. According to Gantz:

> No company is likely to favor a direct U.S. Government role without being guaranteed a substantial say in how the negotiating team can operate effectively without the company's cooperation in providing financial data, technical advice, and it may be hoped, creative suggestions. . . . On the other hand, the U.S. Government cannot properly assure the company that it will have an absolute veto over the settlement, as such assurances might lead to an unreasonable attitude on the part of the firm and place the U.S. negotiators in a difficult position vis-a-vis the foreign government.

Gantz, "The Marcona Settlement: New Forms of Negotiation and Compensation for Nationalized Property," *American Journal of International Law* 71 (July 1977), 492.

Moreover, because the capital is abroad, its contribution to overall national welfare must be considered problematic.[70] The debates are revealing. Again and again they show how corporate objectives are woven into larger diplomatic ones. As a result of this intermeshing, private rewards are at once publicly justified and eclipsed by more far-reaching issues. The debates over investment protection thus underscore the problem of political legitimacy and provide an excellent setting for studying it.

Investment protection also plays a vital role in relations between advanced and less developed countries. As such, it offers an important vantage for understanding that larger relationship. Investment issues have surfaced repeatedly in North-South discussions, often as highly contentious matters.[71] LDCs typically frame the issues in terms of sovereign economic rights, while advanced states and MNCs depict them as matters of contractual reliability and the security of possessions.

These issues naturally bear on the flow of international capital. They point to the very real risks of investing abroad and to the political ambivalence of the recipients, who generally want more long-term capital and new technology but who want it on their own terms. These risks affect not only the level of investment but also its institutional form and its sectoral composition. Investments in high-technology industries, for instance, are rarely taken over.[72] They are insulated because they need constant modernization and close technical supervision by the parent company. To seize them is to seize only physical assets that will soon be outmoded. The heart of such firms is their proprietary knowledge—not only their patents but also their organizational capacity to generate new products and processes. These institutionalized resources are the essence of successful high-technology companies. They cannot be usurped by fiat.[73] At the other end of the spectrum lie the standardized industries that can be operated easily and efficiently after a takeover. These characteristics help explain why foreign-owned public utilities are now virtually extinct, and why natural-resource companies are so vulnerable. Their vulnerability makes new extractive projects exceptionally risky and difficult to finance. That, in turn, leads some analysts to worry about long-term shortages in basic metals such as copper, nickel, iron ore, and aluminum.[74]

The study of investment protection also touches on the close relationship between expropriation and stringent regulation, which remains a serious problem for multinational business. Indeed, businessmen frequently call restrictive regulations "creeping expropriation" since they can lessen both the value of their assets and their ability to control them. At least a dozen researchers have found that these political risks play a decisive role in multinational investment decisions.[75] A sustained study of investment protection can shed light on how corporations have adapted to these risks.

It can also illuminate some of the symbolic structures of economic dependence. Expropriation, after all, is more than just the assertion of state control over some portion of the domestic economy. It is a powerful and evocative expression of sovereign authority against outside powers and, most often, a rejection of subordinate status within an international hierarchy. Action and representation are thus interlaced.

Seizing a well-known foreign firm usually has broad nationalist appeal.* It is often considered a significant step toward economic independence—indeed, toward a new economic order. Depending on the government's strategy and its capabilities, expropriation can either build popular support for more extensive investment regulation or divert attention from its absence. Although this study does not concentrate on the social origins of expropriation, its symbolic meaning in most less developed countries again underscores the subject's importance.

Expropriation also has symbolic significance in the United States. In the aftermath of Cuba's communist revolution, for instance, virtually any action against American firms was seen as a telling indicator of that country's diplomatic intentions. Expropriations thus took on a larger encoded meaning. To Senator Bourke Hickenlooper, a conservative Republican, they suggested a "prairie fire," a spreading evil that could be stopped only by resolute American action. To Sen-

---

*To say that expropriation appeals to nationalist values is not to say that it has only symbolic significance. It has often been used to achieve effective control over key economic actors, either as a substitute or supplement for more extensive regulation. It is, in other words, a policy instrument designed to achieve larger political and economic objectives. This point is emphasized by Kobrin and contrasts with Harry Johnson's treatment of economic nationalism as a form of psychic income. Kobrin, "Foreign Enterprise and Forced Divestment in LDCs," 85; idem, "Political-Economic Factors Underlying the Propensity to Expropriate Foreign Enterprise," unpublished paper, Sloan School of Management, MIT, 1979; idem, "Expropriation as a First Attempt to Control Foreign Firms in LDCs: Trends from 1960–1979," unpublished paper, Graduate School of Business Administration, New York University, 1982; Harry G. Johnson, "A Theoretical Model of Economic Nationalism in New and Developing States," in *Economic Nationalism in Old and New States*, ed. H. G. Johnson (Chicago: University of Chicago Press, 1967), 3.

ator Hubert Humphrey, a liberal Democrat, they were acts of "reckless abandon" requiring firm countermeasures.[76]

In their view, and that of their colleagues, expropriation was contagious, with ramifications well beyond investment security. It represented the most inflammatory evidence of U.S. policy setbacks, especially in Latin America. It thus stood for a broader challenge facing the United States in its relations with less developed countries. The overriding issue, said one senator, was "a trend of events which had its beginning with the Castro expropriation of American property."[77] While this shared meaning did not dictate the appropriate response, it did reinforce the importance that foreign investors attached to the issue and assured it a prominent place on policymakers' agendas.

It is important to remember that the social meaning of expropriation is neither intrinsic nor immutable. Its meaning, and that of investment protection, must be continually reestablished.[78] "Actors compete to contrive and propagate interpretations of social behavior and relationships," according to A. P. Cohen and J. L. Comaroff. "The management of meaning is an expression of power, and the meanings so managed a crucial aspect of political relations."[79]

In the nineteenth century, the meaning of expropriation was determined hegemonically, at least as far as Africa, Asia, and Latin America were concerned. The limitations on host-states and their responsibilities toward foreign investors were well established in international law (which, in turn, had developed from reciprocal relations within Europe). Confiscation amounted to little more than robbery—an interpretation that was not effectively challenged on the periphery.

In the twentieth century, by contrast, the meaning of expropriation has not been imposed so much as negotiated.* Certainly the declining

---

*Expropriation's status as a "deviant act" has long been central to its political meaning, and hotly disputed by LDCs. The literature on deviance may be helpful in understanding this status. Pat Lauderdale, writing about the creation of deviance, insists that the actors' intentions are always established interactively. Intentionality is thus negotiated and should be understood in its broader social context.

This interactive approach is a useful corrective to "labeling theories" of deviance, which focus on stigmatization and its effects. But it says nothing, unfortunately, about the actors' negotiating capacities. These may be asymmetric, perhaps decisively so. It is important, then, to examine the specific cases to understand the various actors' resources, their incentives, and the negotiating process itself.

In the case of expropriation, my argument is that the deviant label was established hegemonically (with respect to LDCs) in the nineteenth and early twentieth centuries.

coercive capacities of investors and their home states have been important here. But two other, less obvious factors have also been significant. One is the changing role of the state in less developed countries. Under earlier legal theories, if expropriation was acceptable at all, it was only if its public purpose was clear and limited. Today, however, the state not only mediates many market relationships but is frequently a direct producer itself (through state-owned corporations). The point here is that "public purposes" have been expanding steadily, along with state capabilities. Equally important, the whole question of investment protection has been opened up for genuine international debate. In the United Nations and its agencies, the LDCs have found attractive forums to denounce traditional property rules.

These challenges are important because international property rules, like expropriations themselves, do not have fixed meanings or decontextualized significance. Rather, they are continually reproduced and redefined in the dispute process as the actors use or resist existing standards.[80]

My interest, then, is not in some static treatment of deviance and compliance, of seizure and sanction, but in the evolution of both standards and practices. Both are important. Throughout this analysis, I am concerned simultaneously with *regularized patterns* of investment security (what Friedrich Hayek calls "descriptive rules") and with *evaluative standards for action and associated expectations* (what he calls "normative rules").[81]

This emphasis on recurrent events and rule-guided action differs notably from the dominant metaphor of international relations, that of "international anarchy." It does not, however, minimize its most

---

Its shifting characterization since then—a political act in itself—is related precisely to the negotiating process that Lauderdale emphasizes.

To say that "deviance" is socially negotiated, however, is not to say that all actors agree on its meaning. In the case of expropriation, there are still significant differences of interpretation. Capital-exporting states now concede that foreign investments can be taken for a wide variety of public purposes and no longer insist on full compensation at market value. But they do still see the issue fundamentally in terms of contractual reliability and investment security. Expropriation without procedural remedies and full compensation is still a marked departure from Anglo-Saxon and Continental legal practice—and a challenge to the foundations upon which business transactions are built. For LDCs the same issues are framed in different normative categories, notably that of sovereign rights.

See Lauderdale, "A Power and Process Approach to the Definition of Deviance," and other articles by Lauderdale and James Inverarity in *A Political Analysis of Deviance*, ed. Pat Lauderdale (Minneapolis: University of Minnesota Press, 1980), and Edwin Lemert, "Beyond Mead: The Societal Reaction to Deviance," *Social Problems* 21 (1974), 462–463.

significant elements: the independence of national decision making and the conflictual character of international affairs. To focus on expropriation is to focus squarely on hard national choices and contentious diplomatic issues. But it should be recognized, at the same time, that extensive economic intercourse does produce regularities and often convergent expectations, and that these can be reinforced by sanctions.*

In the final analysis, these property rules are important because they promote—or impede—the internationalization of capital. By protecting foreign investments, advanced states have supported traditional property rules and provided essential political support for the multinational accumulation process.

Part I of this book, on international property rules, examines this state role. Its empirical focus is on Great Britain and the United States in Latin America, but its concerns are obviously larger. It looks at how the rules have been enforced and the limits of state action. It looks at the changes in the rules and the reasons for them. And it examines the adaptations that all actors have made in light of these changing circumstances and expectations.

There is a common theme to this research agenda, and a larger significance. The underlying questions are:

- How does the leading industrial state protect and defend the internationalization of capital?
- What are the domestic sources of its policies?
- How important is the international context?

Investment protection is worth studying closely because it touches these fundamental issues.

---

*Lon Fuller offers a subtle argument about the inner connection between sanctions and rule maintenance. "The law's sanctions," he writes, "reinforce interactional expectancies and facilitate a respect for them." Along the same lines, he entitles part of another essay, "Preserving the Integrity of the Law at the Point of Enforcement." Fuller, "Law and Human Interaction," 76; and Fuller, *Anatomy of the Law* (New York: Praeger, 1968), 19.

PART I

International Property Rules
in the
Nineteenth and Twentieth Centuries

CHAPTER TWO

Expropriation and the Great Powers Before World War I

The history of states' efforts to protect foreign capital and commerce is long and embattled, but its main features before World War I are clear. It begins in the seventeenth century with the diplomacy of Europe's rising nation-states and culminates two centuries later in customary international law. All the while, the rights of foreign traders and investors were being spelled out with increasing clarity.

During most of the Middle Ages, itinerant merchants could rely only on the protection of local municipal laws. As national economies developed, states began to take a more comprehensive interest in foreign commerce. Many states moved to reduce the risks and uncertainties of such commerce by signing bilateral commercial treaties that protected alien property.[1] A 1667 treaty between Great Britain and Spain is typical: it prohibited the mistreatment or seizure of ships and merchandise in each other's territory.[2] Similar provisions can be found in commercial treaties throughout the seventeenth and eighteenth centuries. Their protection was amplified when states began to defend private claims against foreign governments.[3]

Despite these efforts, treaty standards were not fully elaborated or hardened into international law until the nineteenth century. The law reflected the basic inequality between industrialized, well-armed capital exporters and weak, underdeveloped capital importers. Not surprisingly, the legal norms emphasized the extensive responsibilities of all states toward foreign capital. The core principle was that the property of foreigners could not be taken without prompt, full compensation. That principle was frequently evident in diplomatic notes by European powers and was politically secure. According to two prominent international lawyers, Henry Steiner and Detlev Vagts, "Prior to World War I, there appeared to be a consensus among the principal nations of the world—those whose nationals were trading with and investing in the less developed countries or European colonies—that the taking of an alien's property required a state to pay prompt and adequate compensation."[4]

The political content of these norms and their evolution cannot be understood if one approaches them, as too many legal scholars do, as ahistorical, universal rules setting forth a transcendental moral code. They were created, like so much other international law, in the orderly climate of European diplomacy after the Congress of Vienna. They were elaborated and sustained by the expansive foreign policies of the Great Powers, particularly Great Britain. Their function, as Frederick Dunn noted over forty years ago, was to maintain

> a unified economic and social order for the conduct of international trade and intercourse among independent political units of diverse cultures and stages of civilization, different legal and economic systems, and varying degrees of power and prestige.[5]

British Policy, British Power, and the Security of Foreign Capital

The development of anti-expropriation rules in the nineteenth century is closely linked to the changing international role of Britain. Because the rules defined the minimum conditions for the internationalization of capital at that time, they became deeply embedded in the foreign policy of the largest capital exporter.

During the first half of the nineteenth century, after Britain had fully exploited nearby markets for its textiles, its industry turned to untapped regions such as Latin America. James Kurth has called this shift the "motor behind the British foreign policy of free trade" and the source of Britain's occasional intervention in Latin America's Wars of Independence.[6] In its early stages, this intervention was direct, blundering, and sometimes self-defeating. Sir Home Popham, returning with his soldiers from Cape Colony in 1806 and aware that the Spanish had been defeated in the Rio de la Plata region, decided to occupy Buenos Aires. When his impulsive maneuver was turned back by local militia, the British government dispatched another 10,000 men to occupy Montevideo and move against Buenos Aires. The defeat and withdrawal of this augmented force led to a critical reassessment of British policy in Latin America.

In 1807, Castlereagh issued a cabinet memorandum outlining the new British policy. Its central points were to become Britain's longstanding policy in Latin America. First, Castlereagh rejected territorial ambition and resolved not to intervene in the region's internal politics. As secretary for war and the colonies, and later as foreign secretary, he understood full well the dangers of intervention. They would *not* stabilize Latin America's politics; they would only compel more intervention. The keynote of his policy was its minimalist, economic definition of British objectives. Its principal goal was the maintenance of equal, open access to Latin America's markets. That policy was later embodied in a series of commercial treaties, which, appropriately enough, constituted Britain's recognition of Latin American independence from Spain.[7]

The creation of equal and relatively open access for British trade and investment in world markets was a central and continuous strand in British foreign policy.[8] While Britain's policies were naturally designed to consolidate its leadership in international commerce and finance, they were hardly mercantilist. They pushed for open access not for special privilege. A good example was Britain's reliance on most-favored-nation treaties. The widespread use of these treaties, which Britain encouraged, was important for two reasons. First, they helped crystallize international commercial law.[9] Second, they opened up to all foreign merchants the benefits first won by the British. Yet, because Britain's superiority in foreign markets was economically secure, its policy of "fair field and no favor" was also a minimal restatement of the political conditions for economic hegemony.

The British government acknowledged its responsibility to assist British trade but, as a rule, limited itself to opening new areas to economic intercourse and to ensuring continued free access. When local legal structures were inadequate for modern commerce, the British also established extraterritorial jurisdiction. Significantly, though, British traders in hazardous markets such as Latin America, the Levant, and China *opposed* more far-reaching government interference under ordinary circumstances. Their reasoning was strikingly similar to that of modern multinational corporations: persistent, excessive interference "endangered . . . property and persons and broke . . . carefully constructed contacts with local traders, officials, and politicians."[10]

According to David McLean (whose analysis is supported by D. C. M. Platt and W. M. Mathew), that limited conception of diplomatic responsibility became embedded in the fundamental bureaucratic values of the Foreign Office:

> Where the universal benefits of free trade seemed to be obstructed by the forces of ignorance or backwardness the British government might exert itself to open up new areas for mercantile endeavor. . . . But once new openings for trade, commerce, and finance had been made the government sought only to retire from the scene. "Official" abstention from commercial and financial affairs overseas was the basis for Foreign Office thinking in the mid-nineteenth century. Whatever the role of discreet intervention within the context of informal imperialism, freedom from formal obligation was the undisputed rule.[11]

Backed by Britain's considerable naval and financial power, this policy of equal, open access was applied almost universally. It expressed Britain's economic superiority in spare, effective terms. Britain refused to discriminate against other countries' goods, either in its home market or in its diplomacy. These nondiscriminatory policies coincided neatly with Britain's leading role in organizing world trade and investment. The Foreign Office recognized the requirements of its global role even when it (occasionally) assisted its nationals directly. Its transgressions were rare and, where possible, discreet. They did not accelerate diplomatic competition or set a pattern for others to follow.[12]

Over the course of the nineteenth century, Britain's economy became increasingly tied to the expansion of foreign trade and investment. A substantial surplus of capital led to an aggressive search for higher yields in newly emerging areas. Manufacturers and merchants became more interested in foreign markets and long-trade routes.

The growth of foreign investments is particularly striking. Much of it came in three spurts: in the late 1860s and early 1870s, in the late 1880s, and in the decade before World War I.[13] In fact, British foreign investment quadrupled between 1854 and 1874, and quadrupled again before the war (see table 1).

TABLE 1

TOTAL BRITISH FOREIGN INVESTMENT
1854–1913

(Millions of pounds sterling)[a]	
1854	235
1874	1014
1894	2155
1913	3990

SOURCE: Albert H. Imlah, *Economic Elements in the Pax Britannica* (Cambridge, Mass.: Harvard University Press, 1958), 72–75.

[a] Figures rounded to nearest million pounds.

Until the 1850s, foreign trade and related investments were held down by Britain's slack demand for noncolonial imports. That limitation eased as Britain's industry grew, demanding more raw materials and agricultural products.

Eric Hobsbawm has suggested another, less obvious source of foreign economic expansion—Britain's industrial decline. By the time of the Great Depression (1873–1894), the slow process of industrial senescence had already begun. Once the world's most efficient producer, Britain was losing its lead in many fields to new industries in Germany and the United States. Instead of innovating, British firms stayed with their old equipment and archaic organizations. At the same time British financial institutions were effectively promoting overseas investments, with their promise of high returns. As Hobsbawm states:

> The British economy as a whole tended to retreat from industry into trade and finance, where our service reinforced our actual and future competitors, but made very satisfactory profits. Britain's annual investments abroad began actually to *exceed* her net capital formation at home around 1870. What is more, increasingly the two became alternatives.[14]

Following the sequence generalized by Raymond Vernon's model of the product cycle, British manufacturers were exploiting the international rents made possible by their previous innovations.[15] But, as Hobsbawm suggests, this profitable strategy was replacing innovation.

If Britain's economic hegemony was no longer secured by its industrial superiority, then its foreign policy of "fair field and no favor" no longer seemed so appropriate. Its exports faced stiff competition from local producers in traditional markets throughout Europe and North America. They faced new political obstacles as well. High tariffs were closing formerly international markets on the Continent and even in the now-autonomous dominions of Canada and Australia. In some underdeveloped markets such as China, European governments, notably Germany, were conducting active financial diplomacy, threatening informal partition or preemptive annexation.[16] Britain's overall production continued to climb—in spite of the political barriers, the new competition, and the diffusion of industrial technology. But market shares and profit margins started to fall.

The rise of Continental protectionism and interventionist economic diplomacy challenged the basic premise of Britain's earlier policies. Mid-Victorian governments had practiced a kind of international laissez-faire. British foreign policy, like its domestic counterpart, had limited aims. But those aims were crucial to the global extension of modern capitalism. They sought to secure a politically stable environment for trade and investment, not to regulate or promote it at the "micro" level. They sought contractual freedom among buyers and sellers of commodities and labor power, not pervasive control over foreign economies. Their policies were vigorous, but they were carefully limited. They proved harder and harder to sustain as France and Germany moved abroad more aggressively in the 1880s and 1890s and backed their individual merchants in head-to-head competition with the British. These increasingly competitive conditions necessarily transformed the British government's role and influenced the Foreign Office's conception of its proper functions.[17] According to D. C. M. Platt:

> Quite apart from the competition of the emergent industrial nations, revived Protectionism was a new and dangerous element which threatened the exclusion of British trade from existing and prospective markets. This, and the transformation in the character of Continental financial diplomacy, could often find no satisfactory answer other than "significant acquisitions of land." It was in the name of equal favor and open competition that H. M. Government was compelled on occasion simply to apply diplomatic pressure, at others to colonize, and at others still to reach an international compromise whereby underdeveloped nations were divided into spheres of interest or influence.[18]

Under new conditions Britain reassessed its long-established diplomatic practice and began assuming wider responsibility for its trading and commercial interests in Turkey, Persia, West Africa, Japan, and China. As Ronald Robinson and John Gallagher note, active interventionist policies were novel means, but they pursued traditional goals.[19] Thus, formal imperialism can be understood, at least partially, as *both* an aggressive and defensive response to the failure of less elaborate methods.*

Even so, departures from earlier practice were generally reluctant and, when possible, temporary. In China, for instance, the Foreign Office quickly returned to its traditional function of maintaining an open commercial and financial system after German diplomatic intervention had been frustrated.[20]

In Latin America, where British trade and bond investments were extensive, the Foreign Office's role was carefully confined. Early in the nineteenth century, British goods had secured a virtual monopoly. That experience, plus the size of the region's markets and its vast natural wealth, led to extensive investments in government loans. The first boom came in the 1820s, when British investments in Latin America came to nearly £25 million, almost all of it in government bonds.[21] There was no public regulation of these securities, and fraud was as widespread as the defaults. Virtually all Latin American loans from the 1820s went into swift default. Despite efforts by a few states to resume payments, they stayed in arrears for decades.**

---

*Britain's role as the leader of an open system of international trade and investment was related to formal imperialism and interventionist diplomacy in another, more complex way. To preserve that system Britain had to avoid manipulating its own tariffs. Yet such manipulation might have assisted its bargaining to maintain nondiscriminatory terms for British trade in protected colonial markets. The alternative to this "tariff bargaining" was active diplomatic intervention in these markets, sometimes including preemptive annexation. See Platt, "Economic Factors in British Policy," *Past and Present* 39 (April 1968), 126. For the social sources of Britain's tariff policy, see an excellent article by Peter Gourevitch, "International Trade, Domestic Coalitions, and Liberty: Comparative Responses to the Great Depression of 1873–1896," *Journal of Interdisciplinary History* (August 1977); see also Benjamin Brown, *The Tariff Reform Movement in Britain, 1884–1895* (New York: Columbia University Press, 1943).

**Rippy, *British Investments in Latin America, 1822–1949* (Hamden, Conn.: Archon Books, 1959), 26–27.

These were full-blooded defaults—failures to pay contractual interest and amortization—not technical quibbles. Many bonds remained in default for years awaiting renegotiation with the Corporation of Foreign Bondholders. I have found no "rollovers" (where maturing bonds are replaced with new ones) and no refunding (where debt relief operations are undertaken to prevent outright default). Although there are substantial risks (and costs) in both operations, they can still blunt the impact of a major default on the security of all foreign capital.

At least one generation of investors learned their lesson, and British capital did not flow back into the region until a second boom in the 1860s. This time the figures were considerably larger: £62 million in government bonds and £19 million in industrial enterprises by 1865, and double that ten years later. British investments in the region continued to grow despite periodic debt crises. (The most spectacular was the 1890 collapse of Baring Brothers, which came after Argentina failed to meet its debt payments because of falling commodity prices.) Even so, British investments in Latin America grew to around £1 billion by 1913, mostly in railways and government bonds.[22]

The totals are difficult to measure precisely, but it is clear that investors were eager to buy exotic securities, which promised high yields, even though most of them knew nothing about the debt instruments beyond their names. Sometimes they even got that wrong. One audacious promoter introduced a London merchant bank to a fictitious Latin American country. The bank had already decided to float the bonds before the hoax was discovered.[23] With risks like that, it is not surprising that so many investors met disaster.

The defaults were often serious, and they posed a serious question for British policymakers: When should they intervene?

Bond Defaults and Intervention

In spite of the defaults, the British government stuck to its policy; interventions in Latin America were highly circumscribed. The attitude of the Foreign Office was summed up by Viscount Palmerston in a celebrated 1848 circular: "The British Government has considered that the losses of imprudent men who have placed mistaken confidence in the good faith of foreign Governments would prove a salutary warning to others."[24] That policy was sorely tested—indeed, Palmerston himself questioned it in the circular—but it was retained, though slightly relaxed. Through a succession of prime ministers and foreign secretaries, the policy remained Castlereagh's.

That policy confronted a difficult choice throughout the less developed, noncolonial world. Britain's naval capacity and its diplomatic network were formidable. Direct and frequent interventions promised immediate and tangible gains. Yet such a course was both risky and costly. It was costly, even in the short run, if the desired results could be won diplomatically. It was risky in the long run because direct interventions undermined the basis of local political authority and social control.

British policy in Latin America demonstrated a clear understanding of these alternatives. It was founded on the idea that it was cheaper to bear the immediate costs of occasional bond defaults than to risk sabotaging local governments by frequent interventions. In general, those governments provided a political and legal framework that protected foreign trade and investment.

As the greatest trading and investing nation in the region, Britain principally sought to maintain the independence of those nations that promised continued economic opportunities.* It maintained this policy even after U.S. and German economic competition grew during the latter part of the century. The Foreign Office refused to quash market competitors by its diplomacy or to preempt them by annexation. As a result, British policy coincided with the Monroe Doctrine and with basic United States commercial policy.

By carefully limiting its intrusions into local politics, Britain signaled other capital exporters that it intended to maintain an open, multilateral order for trade and investment. It was trying to avoid an escalating cycle of mercantilist reprisals. At the same time, the Foreign Office was signaling British investors about the risks they had to bear. Then, as now, there was no bright line separating "commercial" and "political" risks. To draw that line was, and is, an inherently political act. And that was just what the Foreign Office was doing. It was defining the risks the state would bear for foreign investors, and it was defining them narrowly. This definition not only conformed to laissez-faire principles, it also recognized some important long-term consequences of state intervention in the bond market. By extricating the owners of defaulted securities, Her Majesty's government would only be encouraging still more imprudent investments in the future. As Herbert Spencer once said, "The ultimate result of shielding men from the effects of folly is to fill the world with fools."[25]

The bond losses of the 1820s ensured that very little British capital

---

*Platt, *Finance, Trade, and Politics* (Oxford: Clarendon Press, 1968), 348. Indeed, the United Kingdom's major intervention in the Rio de la Plata region in 1806 can be understood, in part, as a response to the potential exclusion of British interests from a Bourbon monarchy, which would probably have had a special relationship with France and Spain.

flowed into Latin America over the next quarter-century. The next major influx came between 1860 and 1890, when investors purchased substantial amounts of bonds issued by previously defaulted governments. According to calculations made by J. Fred Rippy (using nominal values), those investments totaled more than £123 million in 1880, over two-thirds of all British investments in Latin America. Once more, these bonds proved to be very poor investments; by 1880 more than half were in default.[26]

What kinds of remedies did bondholders attempt? How successful were they? *Aggrieved bondholders in the nineteenth century, like multinational corporations in the twentieth, usually relied on their own collective resources.* After 1868, they coordinated their efforts through the Corporation of Foreign Bondholders which, in turn, relied on British dominance of international credit markets. Short of active government intervention, their most powerful weapon was the denial of further credit. This sanction generally took one of two forms. The first was an informal boycott of a defaulted nation's bonds, an everyday event in late nineteenth-century London. A more formal, and more severe, punishment was the suspension of a bond's quotation on the stock exchange. Suspension seriously wounded a nation's credit and effectively disrupted its international financial operations. Even though these suspensions inevitably hurt existing investors, they furnished "invaluable long-term assistance to the Corporation of Foreign Bondholders."[27] Typically, the Corporation sought to exert additional pressure by linking the credit of other Latin American governments to that of the defaulted state—a self-interested manipulation of the centralized transnational financial system.

These private acts had mixed results. Their incomplete success was due mainly to the incomplete monopoly exercised by the London Stock Exchange and, to a lesser extent, to conflicts of interest within the financial community. Conflicts of interest, which weakened demands for full restitution, persisted in spite of efforts by the Corporation of Foreign Bondholders. Brokerage firms, like speculators, stood to profit from new listings. The original owners had usually sold out long ago. The new owners found that investors in other securities did not always see a unity of interests. Even the Corporation itself faced internal divisions. If a settlement was reached, even a very modest one, it received a share; if default continued, it got nothing.

Even when the creditors were united, their capacity to apply effective financial sanctions was problematic. It was possible to punish a nation by denying it credit only if it needed to raise new capital and was unable to do so elsewhere. But the need for new capital was only intermittent and sometimes could be met on Continental exchanges. Those exchanges did manage some coordination with British investors. They required some sort of settlement with defaulted bondholders. The stringency of that demand and the effectiveness of private British sanctions were both related to London's control of financial markets, which varied secularly and cyclically. Access to continental Europe's capital markets was closely tied to short-term market conditions:

> When times were good on the European exchanges, virtually any government could come to an arrangement with its creditors and float a new loan; when times were bad nobody, however virtuous, could get money.[28]

Though defaulted nations may have occasionally obtained access to continental financial markets, that avenue gradually declined in importance as London's dominance of foreign lending grew. That growth is attributable mainly to Britain's industrial preeminence and to its expanding trade. Financial institutions became more experienced, aided after the 1860s by the greater reliability of sterling. London's growth far outstripped competing financial centers. Its lead was widened further when its major rival, Paris, was permanently crippled by the Franco-Prussian War.[29]

The best comparative figures are for 1914 (see table 2). They show that except for Venezuela, where German loans slightly exceeded British ones, London was the leading creditor of every country in Latin America. It held over two-thirds of Latin America's public debt. Paris was a distant second with about 14 percent.

London's near monopoly of international capital markets ensured at least the slow settlement of Latin American defaults in the late nineteenth century. In 1880, ten Latin American governments had defaulted on obligations totaling over £71 million. By 1890, only four remained. Amounting to £7.6 million, these defaults comprised less than 4 percent of British-owned government securities in the region.[30]

As I have already argued, the British government was usually reluctant to intervene in support of individuals who faced foreign competition or who lost investments through default. It steadfastly resisted committing itself in advance to safeguarding any loan.[31] The Foreign Office's traditional policy was justified by a well-established

TABLE 2

LATIN AMERICAN EXTERNAL PUBLIC
DEBT AT THE END OF 1914

	Millions of dollars	Percentage
Great Britain	1,481	68
France	302	14
Germany	47	2
United States	93	4
Others	262	12
Total	2,185	100

SOURCE: United Nations, Department of Economic and Social Affairs, Economic Commission for Latin America, *External Financing in Latin America* (New York, 1965), 16.

network of banks, agencies, and import-export houses that were well able to defend themselves.

The government's policy was not entirely consistent, however. The crucial problem was that default possessed an inherently ambiguous character. As Palmerston observed, a defaulted investment had usually been an imprudent one. But if the creditor had freely contracted that imprudent obligation, so had the debtor state. The debtor's obligation implied some responsibility for the British government, since it organized and led the international system of investment finance and was its major beneficiary. In case of widespread or important defaults, it was impossible to differentiate a risky investment environment from a more generalized assault on international property relations.

Laissez-faire policies thus confronted a profound tension. The Foreign Office wanted to support investors' general rights, but it also wanted to stay out of private commercial transactions. This distinction, however, was easier to announce as policy than to draw in practice. It offered diplomats little day-to-day guidance in cases of major bond defaults.

Had the legitimacy of international property rules been directly at issue, the choice would have been simple. It seldom was. Most cases were murky and complex. If defaults violated international rules and norms, they usually did so quietly. Was it mere commercial risk if a default severed the most important economic link between the debtor and Europe? Or was it really cheating on the international regime—trying to escape the penalties without challenging the rules themselves? Except for outright fraud (which the British government stood ready to punish), these questions had no clear answers.

Instead, each case demanded policy judgments without explicit criteria. There were two central dilemmas. The first, suggested above, was the difficulty in operationalizing the policy distinction between political risk and commercial risk. This hypothetical distinction was the crux of laissez-faire economic diplomacy, yet it was elusive and ambiguous in practice. A second problem was the inherent contradiction in global laissez-faire norms. In extreme cases, the norm of corporate autonomy conflicted with the norm of open, liberal access to politically stable markets. The Peruvians, for example, sold their guano to Great Britain through a monopoly contract with a London firm. British farmers were outraged by the prices they had to pay and insisted their government break the monopoly. The Foreign Office tried and failed to persuade the Peruvians to allow more competition, but it was never willing to restrict its own merchants.[32]

In spite of these problems, there does seem to be a systematic relationship between the actions of foreign governments and the sanctions applied by the British. Foreign governments could harm British investors in many ways, some that obviously violated international property rules and others that did not. Some acts, such as gross fraud or robbery, and some kinds of inaction, such as the failure to maintain civil order, clearly violated norms that specified secure access for foreign investors. Others, such as default because of state insolvency, were much more ambiguous and might not be violations at all. *In general, the more direct and clear the rule violation, the more likely an overt, forceful, and purposive British response.*

Of course, other considerations also affected policy. The size and scope of the investment and its strategic location were sometimes important. So was the local government's capacity to restore order after rioting. But often the most critical obstacle to intervention was its uncertain consequences. Every intervention risked prolonged involvement in local affairs. Thus, the British refused to quell disorders in Peru in 1844, despite the heavy impact on foreign commerce. The Foreign Office understood that diplomatic threats and naval gestures would scarcely touch the causes of Peruvian instability, and the dangers were obvious.[33] The Peruvian case is only one example, but by no means an unusual one. The Foreign Office was not entranced by a narrow vision of foreign investors' rights or its own responsibilities. But unless property rights were obviously abused and other remedies were lacking, it was usually unwilling to intervene.

Since most commercial problems did not affect the legitimacy of property rights, the Foreign Office could usually avoid open intervention. Instead, it offered investors informal and unofficial aid, almost always hewing to its policy of "fair field and no favor." Such diplomacy offered a practical, though imperfect, means of reconciling a limited diplomatic role with the global assurance of investors' rights. David McLean, for instance, has written that unofficial contacts were the most important aspect of British commercial policy in China. W. M. Mathew observes that unofficial support helped achieve a restoration of Peruvian credit in 1849. Yet Mathew's research also suggests the clash of policy norms and ambivalence about proper diplomatic procedures. Prior to the Peruvian settlement, the Foreign Office had seriously considered joining with the French to coerce the Peruvians. Joint naval forces were even maneuvered into the vicinity, a display that probably hastened the voluntary settlement.[34]

Sometimes the issue was simplified because the default resulted from a nation's deception or from its bald refusal to fulfill international legal obligations. According to Platt, the Foreign Office considered Peru's default in 1879 to be the result of a "gross Public Fraud": the misappropriation of funds meant to pay off bondholders. Britain was not reluctant to intervene diplomatically in such cases.[35] Similarly, it joined with France, Italy, Holland, Belgium, and Spain in refusing to acknowledge Chile's conquest of Peruvian territory in 1883 unless Chile simultaneously assumed certain Peruvian bond obligations.[36] When the issue was clear, Britain was ready to enforce investors' rights. When other capital exporters were also involved, it was ready to lead concerted action.

The Growth of British Direct Investment

Thus far my analysis of British investment protection has concentrated on that state's policies concerning defaulted foreign bonds. Government loans were, after all, the chief form of British capital exports to noncolonial underdeveloped areas for more than half the nineteenth century. Creating a relatively secure framework for this internationalization of capital without simultaneously enlarging the scope of colonial rule was an unprecedented achievement by the British.

That achievement also extended to direct equity investments, which increased sharply after 1875. Until then, almost all foreign capital was invested in government bonds. As late as 1885 they accounted for two-thirds of Britain's investment in Latin America.[37] A few stock companies had been organized in the 1820s, but nearly all had failed by mid-century. The real beginnings of British direct investments came in the 1860s, when commercial banks were organized in Argentina, Brazil, Peru, and Mexico. A few shipping lines had already begun operations.[38] Around 1870, foreign direct investments began to come in quantity. Investors turned away from unprofitable government securities toward activities where they held distinct advantages over local producers. Latin America's metallurgical and engineering industries were not yet adequate to build railways, ports, and public utilities.[39] Britain's industries were. They had the know-how, and they had the access to the substantial sums of surplus European capital that were needed.

The returns were handsome. Although more than twice as much capital was invested in government bonds in 1880, direct investments produced a larger profit. The impact was swift. More than £174 million in direct investments flowed into Latin America over the next decade, much of it for railway construction. By 1890, Great Britain's direct investments exceeded its bondholdings in the region, and the lead continued to grow (see table 3).

Comparative figures are available only for 1914 (see table 4). They must be considered estimates, since undistributed investments account for about one-fifth of the total.

Most of this investment was in the largest Latin American countries: Argentina, Brazil, and Mexico. Its sectoral composition varied considerably, depending on the recipient and the investor. The United States, for example, was the leader in agriculture, mining, and oil; Great Britain concentrated its capital in railways and public utilities.[40] Despite these variations, one pattern was unmistakable: the investments were closely tied to the industrial needs of Europe and the United States. Miguel Wionczek maintains that the investments formed enclaves within Latin America but were well integrated into a global, Europe-centered system of production:

TABLE 3

SECTORAL COMPOSITION OF BRITISH INVESTMENT IN LATIN AMERICA, 1880–1913
(MILLIONS OF POUNDS STERLING)[a]

Sector	1880 Total	1880 Percent of total	1890 Total	1890 Percent of total	1900 Total	1900 Percent of total	1913 Total	1913 Percent of total
1. Government	123.0	68.6	194.3	45.6	228.0	42.2	316.5	31.7
2. Private	56.4	31.4	231.4	54.4	312.0	57.8	682.9	68.3
Railways	34.4	19.2	166.9	39.2	200.0	37.0	457.8	45.8
Utilities	11.1	6.2	19.9	4.7	30.0	5.6	—	—
Mining	3.4	1.9	12.6	3.0	10.4	1.9	22.5	2.2
Nitrate	—	—	5.4	1.3	9.2	1.7	—	—
Real Estate	0.5	0.3	7.9	1.9	10.8	2.0	—	—
Banking	3.0	1.7	3.6	0.8	11.7	2.2	18.5	1.8
Others	4.0	2.1	15.1	3.5	39.9	7.4	184.4	18.5
3. TOTAL	179.4	100.0	425.7	100.0	540.0	100.0	999.4	100.0

SOURCE: ECLA, *External Financing* (as for table 2), p. 10.

[a] Figures correspond to nominal values of Latin American securities issued on the London Stock Exchange.

NOTE: While these figures are a useful guide to British investments in Latin America, they are hardly precise. Some additional investments were held privately, and the figures above are only nominal values, which must be treated carefully. Still, the figures amply bear out the trends discussed in the text: the growth of direct investments, especially in railways, and the relative decline (but absolute growth) of government securities. The same trends are evident in recent empirical studies by Irving Stone. (Stone's figures are similar but do show slightly higher government lending.) Stone, "British Direct and Portfolio Investment in Latin America Before 1914," *Journal of Economic History* 37 (September 1977), table 1, p. 694.

TABLE 4

PRIVATE FOREIGN INVESTMENTS IN LATIN
AMERICA, DECEMBER 1914
(MILLIONS OF DOLLARS)

	Total	Percent of total[a]
Great Britain	3,585	47.3
United States	1,394	18.4
France	711	9.4
Germany	320	4.2
Others	1,559	20.6
Total	7,569	100.0

SOURCE: ECLA, *External Financing* (as for table 2), 17.

[a] Percentages do not total due to rounding.

After the opening of the Mexican economy to external economic influence in the final quarter of the past century, foreign private capital directed itself primarily—as elsewhere in Latin America—into sectors which largely served the needs of the European industrial countries that had excess capital for export and were witnessing at the same time rapidly increasing demand for industrial raw materials and tropical foodstuffs. By being directly or indirectly linked with the Mexican export economy, all foreign investment activities of that period constituted small but powerful enclaves within the traditional society that had changed very little from colonial times.[41]

British Investment Protection and International Law

Because these investments formed enclaves along the seacoasts of weak countries, they were easily protected by European, primarily British, naval power. If Britain was reluctant to intervene widely in Latin American politics or to offer strong official support to every aggrieved bondholder, it was still quite prepared to use coercion and armed force to protect persons and property. According to nineteenth-century international law, interference with alien property was permitted only in exceptional cases of expropriation for narrowly defined public purposes, and even then had to be accompanied by prompt, adequate, convertible compensation. Because the law implicitly assumed a narrow scope for public property, its strict principles generalized a laissez-faire conception of domestic government.

Enforcement was unilateral. If a state chose to espouse the private claims of its nationals, it could use diplomacy, arbitration, or force.[42] Britain customarily used force only to save its citizens' lives or to protect their direct investments from seizure, a fact confirmed by the famous Argentine jurist, Luis Drago:

> Britain's normal, if not absolutely invariable practice has been to take coercive military or naval measures, or to threaten them, in defense of her citizens, only when these were wronged by the seizure of their property or by personal injuries.[43]

Since European powers considered uncompensated seizure robbery, force was often threatened and sometimes used. In addition to innumerable threats of force, Platt has discovered at least forty examples of British armed intervention in Latin America between 1820 and 1914. Twenty-six of these episodes were to "enforce claims of British subjects for outrage and injury" or to restore order and protect property.* Typical among them were port-city interventions in Uruguay in 1868 and Chile in 1891. In the former, sailors landed at the request of Uruguay's government to protect the important customs house in Montevideo. Lord Stanley observed that he had found it difficult, as prime minister, to specify general rules about applying such force, but he agreed that it "should only be resorted to under circumstances of the greatest urgency" for the protection of British lives and property. In Chile, a revolution threatened British interests in trade, banking, railroads, and nitrates—investments amounting to about £15 million. The British Navy did intervene, but the admiral in charge was ordered to confine his action strictly to the protection of those interests.[44]

---

*Platt, *Finance, Trade, and Politics,* 330. Of the other interventions, ten were concerned with "offenses against national honor," which, according to Platt's classification, also included unspecified "unsettled claims." Furthermore, an offense against national honor usually meant a riot in which the mob tore down the consulate's flag. Hence, to restore honor was to restore civil order. One effect was to protect foreign property endangered by the breakdown of order. Three more interventions were to safeguard nations under British protection, and one was to erect a telegraph station on an uninhabited island.

It is correct to argue, as both Platt and Mathew do, that these British policies were grounded in the stern, extensive requirements of international law. On issues such as government fraud and robbery, Platt maintains, the British government was not only entitled to intervene under the law, it was actually obliged to do so.[45] (This last point goes too far, since a state could always decline to espouse a private claim.) Mathew also points to the important role of international law in British foreign economic policies:

> In refusing to honor her obligations to British bondholders in the 1850s, however, [Peru] was committing what could be legitimately regarded as an offense. It would seem likely, in short, that *insofar as the British government took action against Peru, or contemplated such action, the object in view was more the correction of injustice than the general advancement of national economic interests.*[46]

Yet it is incomplete to argue that British policy was based squarely on international law without also noting the functions served by that law and their relationship to British economic interests.

A central feature of all law, domestic and international, is the rationalization and maintenance of social relations, including, most significantly, property relations. The most effective legal systems do this with the least coercion, stimulating support for some political claims and hiding others from public view.

The symbolic role of international law is particularly noteworthy, since it can sometimes turn questionable claims into approved obligations or prerogatives. Mathew's own statement—that Britain was more interested in "the correction of injustice than the general advancement of national economic interests"—inadvertently illustrates the point. By equating illegality with injustice, he shows how legal symbols, by abstracting from and disguising material relations, can serve to authenticate them ethically across nations and social classes. The law, Bentham once said, "shews itself in a mask."

The best-known symbol in international property law is the requirement of "just" compensation. Its meaning is not to be found in some exegesis of Plato. It refers to full, prompt convertible repayment for expropriations. It is, in essence, a cloak for the interests of foreign investors.

The term went unchallenged until the first quarter of the twentieth century. Even then, it was not rejected outright. Who, after all, favors "unjust compensation"? Less developed countries have generally argued that *just* should be replaced by *adequate,* a code word for partial compensation. But they have shrewdly stressed another issue and a different symbol—*sovereignty.*

"Sovereign rights" and "just compensation" may begin as debating points, but they have diplomatic consequences. Symbolic legitimation can turn possession into ownership, domination into dominion.[47] It slowly and indirectly affects the capabilities of states and their willingness to undertake particular actions. Illegitimate policies are harder to enforce and more costly to defend.

Legitimation is especially difficult in an international setting. Despite important hierarchical relations and significant functional linkages, most historic systems of nation-states have succeeded only partially in integrating their fragmented and competitive elements. This fragmentation frustrates the integrative function of political symbols, including their capacity to legitimate political claims, while making it all the more vital.

If it is often difficult to legitimate national policies through international law, it is even harder to use the law to obscure those policies and their consequences. Here, too, international law differs from its domestic counterpart. One important feature of domestic law is its capacity to hide particularist claims in general—and obscurantist—language. Precise, technical language is often necessary, of course, but it also serves as an inaccessible code masking the structural relationships it defines. In this sense, law is the fine print of social structure and political relations. The best example, not surprisingly, is the tax code. International law, however, cannot perform this function well. To begin with, there is a lot less fine print in which to hide its demands. It is built on treaties and custom, not detailed statutes, regulations, and opinions. Moreover, it is inherently controversial, since it confines national policies in a nationalist world. In the twentieth century especially, it has proved nearly impossible to obscure the demands of international law on nation-states. And nowhere are the demands more exposed than in cases of expropriation.

Finally, international law, like modern civil law, defines the political and regulatory environment. Again, civil laws are much more elaborate, specifying complex liabilities precisely. To permit decentralized economic decisions they must be exact. Moreover, future rules must seem sufficiently predictable for investors to undertake substantial long-term commitments. International law has never matched this precision or detail, or facilitated such stable expectations about the future. It has served mainly to coordinate national laws and to limit their scope in certain areas.

The failures of international law in all these areas are familiar. Clearly, it performs few functions as well as (most) domestic law. Yet nineteenth-century international property law, developed in Europe and enforced elsewhere mainly by the British, was undeniably successful in its central task. It legitimated, regulated, and obscured well enough to permit the internationalization of capital. Its triumph was the massive export of loans and direct investments to independent, underdeveloped regions such as Latin America.*

United States Investment Policy at the Turn of the Century

If international laws protecting foreign capital had profited only the British, they would probably have faded as British power did, the victims of inter-imperial rivalries. But, as I have shown, the laws were strongly supported and sometimes enforced by other European states. In the case of Latin America, however, the most important support came not from continental Europe but from the United States.

The United States, as I noted in the last chapter, endorsed traditional property rules soon after its independence. It strongly reasserted that position as it matured economically in the nineteenth century. In particular, it signed a number of treaties that included expropriation-compensation clauses.[48] This policy took on special importance to all foreign investors as the U.S. began its diplomatic, military, and economic expansion in the late 1800s.

*These features of international law, plus Britain's preference for an open economic system, dissolved much of the contradiction between Britain's national economic interests and its role in preserving international property rules. The distinction suggested by Mathews is unfounded: "the correction of injustice" was, as a rule, the same as "the general advancement of British national economic interests."

A more intriguing question is whether this perception of national economic interests, which was realized through an open system of foreign investment, detracted from Britain's capacity to innovate and to renew its industrial plant. See Robert Gilpin, *U.S. Power and the Multinational Corporation* (New York: Basic Books, 1975), 88–98; D. E. Aldcroft, ed., *The Development of British Industry and Foreign Competition, 1875–1914* (London: Allen and Unwin, 1969); and D. E. Aldcroft and Harry W. Richardson, *The British Economy, 1870–1939* (London: Macmillan, 1969), esp. 119–122.

That the United States would expand had long been clear. Since mid-century the United States had edged southward by fits and starts, hemmed in by its regional compromise with Great Britain. The vehicle of that compromise was an agreement to share control of any Central American canal. The same device was used to overturn it. At the turn of the century, Britain agreed that the United States would control any canal exclusively.[49]

The push south began in earnest in 1889, when the United States convened the first Inter-American Conference. But it took several years and an economic depression (1893–1897) to consolidate domestic support for the new policy. When lower tariffs failed to stimulate manufacturing and quell widespread labor unrest, leading congressmen and businessmen settled on a course of foreign economic expansion.[50] The richest markets, those in Britain and on the continent, were certainly the most attractive. But their size was offset by the advantages of entrenched local producers.[51] Latin American markets, by contrast, were not only close by and almost untapped by U.S. producers, they also involved a much less direct challenge to European industry.[52]

As trade grew, so did foreign investments. Figures are not precise, but they indicate about $300 million in U.S. investments in 1897. That figure tripled in a decade and continued to grow rapidly (see table 5). Between 1897 and 1914, U.S. corporations made nearly one billion dollars in direct investments in Latin America, a figure that equals America's direct investments throughout the rest of the world.[53]

The United States' rising economic stake in Latin America and its bright prospects elicited strong corporate support for a more active regional diplomacy. Quite naturally, one of its aims was to offer political support to U.S. trade and investment. At the same time, anxiety over military security was building. It found forceful expression in the works of Alfred Thayer Mahan. As Mahan himself understood, economic and military interests are interwoven and had broadly similar implications for U.S. policy in the Caribbean. According to Walter LaFeber, Mahan's position was shared by the most important architects of U.S. policy:

To Mahan, William McKinley, Theodore Roosevelt, and Henry Cabot Lodge, colonial possessions, as these men defined such possessions [that is, as strategic naval bases rather than as markets] served as stepping

TABLE 5

U.S. INVESTMENTS IN LATIN AMERICA, 1897–1914
(MILLIONS OF DOLLARS)

	1897	1908	1914
Portfolio investments[a]	—	334.1	365.6
Direct investments[b]	304.3	748.8	1275.8
Total	304.3	1062.9	1641.4

SOURCE: ECLA, *External Financing* (as for table 2), 14.

[a] Portfolio investments are defined here to include noncontrolling shares in foreign corporations, as well as bonds issued by foreign governments and private firms.

[b] Direct investments are defined as those in which U.S. interests have a controlling share, usually 25 percent or more of equity capital. All investments are shown at book value.

stones to the two great prizes; the Latin-American and Asian markets. This policy much less resembled traditional colonialism than it did the new financial and industrial expansion of the 1850–1914 period. These men did not envision "colonizing" either Latin America or Asia. They did want both to exploit these areas economically and give them (especially Asia) the benefits of western, Christian civilization. To do this, these expansionists needed strategic bases from which shipping lanes and interior interests in Asia and Latin America could be protected.[54]

To push south, however, was to confront Great Britain—with all its risks. Especially in the Caribbean, where the Royal Navy potentially threatened U.S. military security, there was a serious risk of collision.

Tension ran high at times, especially in the mid-1890s, and probably affected investment security in the region. British and U.S. power overlapped in Mexico, Central America, and the Caribbean, and it was there that foreign investments were least secure. Burns Weston has surveyed all "foreign-wealth deprivations" before World War I and found that they occurred "almost exclusively within the comparatively weak and usually fragmented communities of Latin America, especially 'Middle America' (i.e., Central America, Mexico, and the Caribbean)."[55] Weston's own conclusion (with which I agree) is that "this was largely the result of the coincidence of newly won

Latin American political independence on the one hand, and of geographically proximate and increasingly expansive United States commercial interests on the other."[56]

Yet both governments managed to temper the conflict and moderate its effects. A number of circumstances contributed to this result, and it is hard to avoid the problem of overdetermination. Still, three factors seem especially important: the pattern of foreign investment, the absence of territorial ambitions, and careful, prudent diplomacy.

First, economic conflict was minimized because the economic interests of the two nations were largely segregated. In 1897, 87 percent of U.S. investment in Latin America was in the Caribbean, Mexico, and Central America. The figure for Britain was only 22 percent. Both figures remained stable until World War I.[57] Country-by-country comparisons are available for 1914. They show significant overlaps only in Chile, Mexico, and Cuba.[58] The sectoral differences are just as important. U.S. capital was concentrated in agriculture, mining, petroleum, and railways; Britain's was overwhelmingly in railways and public utilities.[59] There was still room for competition—Mexican oil is the most famous example[60]—but far less than there might have been. As a rule, U.S. and British investments followed different patterns.

The chances for serious conflict were further minimized because both countries had sharply restricted territorial ambitions. Except for the Falkland Islands off southern Argentina, Great Britain had not acquired any territory in Latin America since the Wars of Independence. Naval bases and fueling rights were far more important than colonial protectorates, for it was the navy that secured British power in the Americas. Until the end of the century, that same naval superiority deterred a direct challenge from the United States. By then, however, Great Britain was ensnared by its colonies and was fighting the Boer War. Admiral Mahan's strategy of naval expansion could proceed without real opposition from the British. The two navies passed in the night.

There was more than fortuitous circumstance and investment strategy at work. Conflict was averted by careful diplomacy as well. When Great Britain was dominant in the Caribbean, it actively deflected potential confrontations by protecting United States interests. As noted earlier, Britain signed the Clayton-Bulwer Treaty at mid-century, renouncing exclusive control over any future canal and neutralizing Central America. Britain also withheld its diplomatic pressure when the United States began expanding its regional trade after 1870. Likewise, the United States maintained British economic interests through its own open commercial and investment policies and through its defense of traditional international law. The British formula of "fair field and no favor" had been congenial to new, competitive U.S. exports, and the United States continued to support it long after the British had withdrawn their navy.

For both Great Britain and the United States, "fair field and no favor" held attractions beyond simple profits and cheap diplomacy. It implied a fundamental consistency between the domestic and international character of both states. Each had sustained its domestic market without developing an extensive administrative apparatus and without intruding on the autonomy of individual firms. Similarly, each wanted to support open international markets without intruding into its firms' private activities. The United States departed from that course more often than Great Britain did, probably because America was disadvantaged by its late start. But its economic diplomacy seldom matched the aggressive, persistent intervention of the Germans. In general, the State Department, like the British Foreign Office, allowed its nationals to win their own prizes and suffer their own defeats. In this respect, foreign investors were very much at home abroad.

At several crucial points, then, British and United States policies in Latin America converged. Neither wanted more territory and neither attempted to trample the other's commerce by aggressive state action. In Arnold Wolfers's famous phrase, both countries pursued milieu goals, and they desired very much the same milieu. The two countries differed on some important issues, to be sure, but each acted to assure the other's vital interests in the region. Britain's Caribbean policy was especially sensitive to U.S. military and economic interests there. Later, the United States reciprocated. Its expansive diplomacy was not aimed at British commerce. Good luck followed good sense. When the United States finally did achieve hemispheric dominance, Britain was absorbed by other battles. But even here U.S. diplomacy played a role. The British decision to withdraw to its colonies was fostered by the U.S. commitment to protect foreign commerce and investment. These multiple junctures of events and interests, as well as the relative coherence of local Latin American governments (compared with those in Africa), prevented a preemptive scramble to partition the region.

United States Policy and International Law

Although U.S. strategy aimed at competing (peacefully) with European economic and military interests in Latin America, it was confounded by a major contradiction. The United States wanted to expand its regional influence while still adhering to international law. These dual aims could not be reconciled easily. To achieve regional hegemony, the United States tried to exclude European powers from the Caribbean. At the same time, the United States reluctantly recognized that customary international law permitted European intervention on behalf of injured investors.

Existing law permitted economic sanctions, the display of naval force, even port-city occupation. If defaults continued, it allowed the assignment of customs revenue or the direct control of mortgaged assets, usually railways and mines. Given the shaky economies of the region, the scope for European intervention was vast—and threatening to the United States.

As a nation with its own stake in global commerce and investment, America recognized the legitimacy of international laws to protect investors' interests. But the United States was exceptionally edgy about other states enforcing these laws so close to its borders. Kicking the Europeans out of the Caribbean was the essence of the United States' new expansionism; letting them come in was the essence of international property rules. Ironically, a reconciliation was possible only after the United States expanded its regional power still further.

At first, the United States tried to subordinate European claims to its own immediate interests, as defined by the Monroe Doctrine. After a revolution broke out in Venezuela in 1870, Secretary of State Hamilton Fish told Germany that it could intervene on its own to protect its nationals, but it could not seek the aid of other European powers.[61] This kind of ad hoc restriction collapsed completely after a turn-of-the-century arbitration involving Venezuelan bondholders. The Hague award gave priority to claimants from countries that had intervened to win the settlement. After that, joint receiverships were inevitable. The law had joined the interests of European bondholders. Unless the United States wanted to confront the Europeans head on, it had to choose between intervening alongside them or intervening by itself to ensure their legal rights.[62]

The decision was never in doubt. The United States would intervene on behalf of all foreign investors. This policy was anticipated by the Platt Amendment and made explicit in the Roosevelt Corollary, issued soon after the Germans and British blockaded Venezuela in 1902–1903. If the United States wanted to prevent European intervention, said Roosevelt, it had to assume ultimate responsibility for Caribbean finances. It had to protect the rights of all foreigners there. Dana Munro has called that policy "the basic idea that inspired the Caribbean policy of the United States in the first two decades of the twentieth century."[63]

Preventing European entanglements in the area ultimately entangled the United States. The instability of local governments was endemic and constantly threatened foreign interests. It was not unusual for civil-war factions to seize customs houses to finance their battles or for anarchy to threaten foreign lives and property. To preempt the rebels and stabilize financial conditions, the United States began to collect customs in some countries. Quite logically, customs control soon had to be extended to all phases of financial management. Since even that drastic step could not ensure social stability, the Roosevelt Corollary eventually trapped the United States in a jungle of coastal landings, civil wars, and armed interventions lasting until the 1930s.

It was a chain of consequences that more careful British diplomacy managed to avoid in Latin America, if not in Africa. The British, along with other European creditor nations, had not been reluctant to see the United States pick up the burdens of system-maintenance in the Caribbean. They were well aware that international law, strictly enforced, would adequately safeguard their investors' interests, no matter who enforced it. For that reason, all major European powers assented to American regional hegemony, as Samuel Flagg Bemis has noted:

> Thus there was adequate reason to believe that Great Britain would welcome intervention by the United States alone, to clear up the bad finances of these shaky republics in case of another lapse of justice, and that Germany would not object to it. It proved that France and Belgium, too, were ready to acquiesce in such a procedure. To the United States such a course was preferable to participation in a joint receivership as proposed at various times by representatives of the European powers, which would have meant an "ottomanization" of the strategic Caribbean area. The events of the previous five years [since 1897], together with the European

situation, had induced—we will not say reconciled, unless in the case of Great Britain—the powers tacitly to accept the hegemony of the United States in that region.[64]

International law thus served a dual function as the United States turned aggressively southward. Because the United States acknowledged, however haltingly, European rights to protect lives, property, and debentures,[65] it was finally impelled to intervene throughout the Caribbean *instead of simply preventing European interventions*. Equally important, international law served as a lowest common denominator of *all* capital exporters' interests, facilitating the smooth transition from British hegemony. Through all this change, the international rules protecting foreign property remained the same. And so did the ultimate remedy—local military intervention.

CHAPTER THREE

The Interwar Challenge to Traditional Rules

The first really serious challenges to international property rules came after World War I, primarily on the edge of Europe but also in Mexico. If the Congress of Vienna had forged an interstate order among the Great Powers capable of regulating itself and others by an elaborate code of conduct, then the crash of that order was bound to strain the code.

Earlier, I argued that even though international law supersedes individual states and may constrain even the most powerful, it still embodies fundamental social and economic relationships. As such, the laws are premised on a variety of metalegal assumptions about the political requirements of maintaining and justifying those relationships, or, in the case of more radical politics, changing them. Like other, less formalized rules, international law can be seen as providing an intersubjective definition of situations, thereby structuring expectations, guiding inferences, and providing warrants for action.[1] Customary international property law was undermined during the interwar period because larger political relationships were in flux and corresponding assumptions and expectations had become more problematic.

Britain had always been the key. Now its naval preeminence was fading, and its economic attention was turning toward home and empire. Between 1911 and 1913, for example, nearly 80 percent of London's new loans went overseas; in 1934, 80 percent stayed at home. Why such a dramatic change? "The primary cause," writes Derek Aldcroft, "must be the fact that the surplus on current account was insufficient to support a volume of lending of pre-war dimensions."[2] On top of that there was an unofficial embargo on foreign loans during the early 1920s and even tougher controls in the 1930s. When foreign investments were made, they were made mainly in colonial areas. That, too, was a significant change from the prewar era. Before the war, non-empire investments (including those in developed countries) had accounted for nearly half of all issues. By the 1930s, the figure was less than 3 percent. At the same time, investments within the empire dropped from 34 percent to about 15 percent, reflecting the tendency to invest at home. As a site for foreign investments, however, the empire and dominions were increasingly favored, rising from 47 percent to 59 percent of all British foreign investments. The relative preference for the Empire reflected the difficult trading conditions of the Depression and the renewed ties forged by imperial preference.[3]

Meanwhile, the United States had become the world's leading creditor, and Wall Street the world's banker. From the start of World War I until 1929 (when all international lending dried up), New York was easily the largest foreign lender. Total U.S. foreign investments increased sixfold during that period. The result was a stock of foreign investments that nearly equaled Britain's.[4]

These dramatic shifts had important implications for the enforcement of long-standing international rules. Before the war, the United States had assumed responsibility for enforcing property rules only in Latin America. Elsewhere, sanctions were either British or collective. Now, however, Europe was weak and divided, and Britain was unable to act alone. The most obvious solution was condominium between the two largest investors, the United States and Great Britain. Yet President Wilson's defeat excluded that hypothetical solution. Even though U.S. economic interests continued to expand, the state flatly refused to assume commensurate political and military responsibilities outside the Western Hemisphere. That refusal and Britain's shrunken power diminished the capacity of advanced capitalist states to enforce traditional property rules.

New Issues: The Soviet Revolution

If the capacity to enforce international rules was declining, the need to do so was not. In 1918, the new Soviet government repudiated its inherited debt and began to socialize industry systematically. They made no distinction between foreigners and nationals. From 1921 onward the Soviet Union acknowledged a legal obligation to pay foreign claims but also demanded that the Allies pay for damage they inflicted during the civil war.* Soviet recognition of foreign claims was an important ratification of existing international legal principles, but its socialization of private property constituted the most significant attack ever waged on foreign capital. Linking counterclaims to obligations created a model for later expropriations, where retroactive taxes are sometimes demanded as reparations for decades of profits. Even more important was the Allies' inability to override the counterclaims and enforce their own.

The Allies first tried and failed to break Soviet socialism militarily. The next step was collective financial sanctions. That project was equally complicated and no more successful. To be effective, economic sanctions needed to be applied consistently and uniformly. Even so, their leverage depended partly on Soviet calculations. How much did they value contact with the West? If the Soviets were willing and able to disentangle themselves from international commerce and investment—and they were—then financial sanctions were a much weaker threat. Equally important, the Allies were not much allied in their policies. No single nation could adequately punish the Soviets for violations. And no state could command general agreement about a proper course of joint action.

To resolve their differences, the major national creditors met with the Soviet Union at Genoa and at The Hague in 1922. The meetings ended as they had begun—in stalemate. Britain wanted to lead the process of Soviet reconstruction. Economic development, they believed, would require foreign investments, and they hoped to capitalize. To succeed, they needed cooperation from nearly everyone: the Soviets, the Europeans, the United States, and a large group of anxious investors. To reassure the investors, the British first had to settle the inflamed issue of Soviet nationalizations. They proposed a simple reassertion of traditional legal rules: any nation could nationalize private property, but it must pay full compensation.[5]

The British plan did not confront the unprecedented character of the Soviet acts. The very meaning of property had been transformed, and the old rules were unsuited to the new issues. Under customary law, expropriation was considered a rare means to an exceptional end. But the Soviet decrees had systematically abolished private prop-

---

*Damages were estimated at 39 million rubles; debts at 9.6 million.

erty. Moreover, they were an integral aspect of that state's social and economic policies. Classical expropriations were *isolated* seizures for *limited* purposes. The USSR aimed to socialize the means of production. To reduce the revolutionary Soviet acts to simple violations of international law was to miss their meaning and misunderstand their challenge. They opposed the whole tradition on which international property rules were founded.

The United States gave a stiff answer to the Soviets, refusing even to attend the European conferences. Yet its unofficial role was crucial, since it adamantly opposed the British policy of seeking special concessions for economic development. The United States wanted the Europeans to approve the general principle of open economic development, including equal and liberal opportunities for all foreign investors. In practice, that meant the Soviets must restore Standard Oil's expropriated property, not simply compensate the company before parceling out its property to the British. Likewise, restitution, not compensation, was far more valuable to French and Belgian companies whose large investments had also been seized. By skillfully manipulating the French and Belgian delegations at Genoa, the United States prevented a settlement that would have acknowledged a Soviet right to nationalize foreign property.[6]

At first glance, these negotiations appear to redeem traditional international standards. When the old rules had been challenged, they were reasserted with even more stringent interpretations. Yet this ideological reiteration was doomed when the major powers failed to develop a coherent positive position. Too many states were involved; their interests were too disparate; and they lacked any real diplomatic leadership. Having lost on the battlefield and in the conference hall, the Allies broke apart.

The Soviets responded logically. They exploited the diplomatic stalemate by actively pursuing bilateral commercial treaties. Nations that had once written the laws now faced the Prisoner's Dilemma. Almost immediately the Germans broke ranks. One by one, the other major powers concluded separate agreements reopening the Soviet market to their own corporations.

Even before the agreements were signed, individual companies were straining to conclude their own pacts. Oil firms led the way. They, too, had tried to sustain a united policy. In 1922, sixteen producers formally agreed to refuse individual deals until full restitution was granted. This proved to be a seriously flawed effort to overcome divergent interests. "It almost immediately began to disintegrate," notes Joan Hoff Wilson, "as the Soviets continued to play upon the self-interests of the larger firms. By the end of 1922 . . . the Open Door position of the United States had produced a temporary stalemate over Russian oil reserves that major international companies almost immediately tried to break."[7]

Whatever the firms' common interest on restitution (and it was uneven), it collapsed before more immediate goals. The new Soviet concessions looked profitable. Furthermore, in a competitive world, it is always risky to ignore profitable opportunities, since others may have different ideas or less fortitude. Each company thus faced the age-old problem of conspiracy: Can my partners be trusted? Moreover, even if they could be, might not the Soviets themselves become a potential competitor in Europe and the Middle East?

The solution in this case was modest collusion. If the oil companies found it hard to cooperate in the early 1920s, they found it much easier by the end of the decade. In 1928, faced with overproduction and ruinous competition, the major companies agreed to maintain their global production shares on an "as is" basis. The Achnacarry accord, as it was known, facilitated collusion for just over a decade.[8] In the Soviet case, the biggest companies simply joined together to buy Soviet crude and eliminate it from independent competition.

As important as this joint action was, the Soviet expropriations were not opposed by a set of unified sanctions. No one state, and no one group of companies could effectively discipline the others, so none could effectively enforce the traditional law of property. Sooner or later, everyone scrambled to grab their own piece of the Soviet market. But in pursuing their short-run interests, they seriously compromised the legal principles that defined permissible expropriation and demanded full, immediate compensation.[9]

The Soviet expropriations were significant not only because they succeeded but because they redefined the potential relationship between the state and private property. This was the first direct challenge to international property rules. Until then, those rules were based on a nearly absolute right of property, subject only to narrowly bounded eminent domain procedures. As enforced by the major European powers, traditional international law guaranteed foreigners complete property rights and protected them from the breakdown of local government or isolated acts of expropriation-by-fiat. Practice and expectations were thus convergent. The Soviet expropriations were unique because they resulted from neither turmoil nor executive decree, but from the redefinition of the social character of the state. They were fundamental acts, general and impersonal, embodied in organic laws. So novel was the issue they posed that some legal scholars were temporarily confounded. They were unsure whether international law even covered such nondiscriminatory expropriations.[10] They quickly regained their composure and determined that it was definitely illegal. But legal or not, massive expropriations were clearly unprecedented—and unanticipated by traditional law. They defied the crucial metalegal assumption that all states governed by international law were themselves committed to limited state control over the economy.[11]

New Issues:
The State and Economic Development

The metalegal problem was posed most sharply in the Soviet case because the reorganization of state functions was most extensive there. But it is also noticeable in other, much less far-reaching expropriations. Yugoslavia, Rumania, Czechoslovakia, Poland, and Latvia all redistributed some land to peasants. It is easy to overlook these modest reforms. They were, after all, strictly limited and were intended to preserve basic social relationships, not to transform them. They did *not*, in fact, overturn the drastically unequal distribution of land and did not affect industry at all.[12] Indeed, the Polish reforms went hand in hand with a vigorous effort to attract foreign capital.* Even so, the agrarian redistribution departed from traditional legal assumptions about eminent domain. These were general and impersonal acts, elements of a centralized social policy, not isolated cases of classical eminent domain. As such, they contradicted traditional legal assumptions about the social control of property.

The reforms did not attack foreign capital. That limitation is especially noteworthy because no foreign power was able to supervise the political security of investments in Eastern Europe. The prime candidate for the job was France, the major diplomatic force in the

---

*The influx of foreign capital never materialized, but that was due mainly to Poland's serious inflation and its international insecurity. It was not because of domestic political risks. Piotr S. Wandycz, *France and Her Eastern Allies, 1919–1925* (Minneapolis: University of Minnesota Press, 1962), 371.

region until Germany's revival in the 1930s. Yet French foreign policy after the war was preoccupied with its usual problem, Germany, not with foreign trade or investment security. Its overwhelming priority was to repair an alliance structure crippled by the October Revolution. A pact with Poland and Czechoslovakia was the only available replacement for the earlier one with Imperial Russia, but it was hardly adequate.

For our purposes, it is crucial that France never played a hegemonial role in Eastern Europe and that its economic ties to the region remained weak. Its role was limited by its own economic weakness, the product of war damage, inter-Allied debts, and more. French investors played only a minor role in the region's long-term development, although some swept in for swift profits. In addition, French policies discouraged foreign trade. The result was that France could offer its allies military guarantees and occasional loans, but not stable, open markets for their industrial and agricultural production. France, then, was a major power in Eastern Europe after World War I, but its influence was always limited to diplomatic and military issues. It did not extend to commerce and investment.[13]

For the most part, foreign investments in Eastern Europe were protected by the conservatism of local governments. That conservatism, as we have already noted, did not preclude modest agrarian reforms with a larger metalegal meaning.

The changes in Turkey were more far-reaching. Often overlooked because foreign investments were not treated harshly, the new republic's policies are important for several reasons. They marked a significant departure from the long-standing assumption (so important to nineteenth-century property rules) that the state would not take an active role in production. Equally important, they raised issues of nationalism, autonomous development, and state authority which would dominate multinational investment for decades to come.

The Turkish state was founded after World War I on the ruins of the Ottoman Empire. Led by Mustafa Kemal Atatürk, it made one of the first comprehensive efforts to modernize.[14] This process, which involved both state building and economic development, was essentially one of an "emerging state trying to become national."[15]

From the very outset that meant overturning the Ottoman Empire's subordinate relations with foreigners. The new state sought to cancel the earlier capitulations, liquidate the imperial debt, and diminish the status of foreign concessions. It was only partially successful. The

Treaty of Lausanne, which granted Turkey its independence in 1923, did abolish the capitulations but said nothing about the imperial debt. (A compromise was subsequently reached on that issue, keeping most of the debts intact.) Meanwhile, foreign investors turned skittish over the nationalist pretensions of the new state, an attitude that frustrated Turkey's initial efforts to attract long-term capital.[16]

Turkey's policies in the 1920s were designed primarily to recover from the war and to foster more lasting economic development. The state played an active role, but it did so in support of private capital accumulation. International trade was basically open, foreign capital was invited in, and state intervention in the economy was limited.* As the world slipped into the Depression, however, Turkey turned protectionist and began to replace imports with domestic production.[17] It found, as much of Latin America would in the 1950s and 1960s, that sheltered industries are often extremely inefficient and require continued protection.

The difficulties with import substitution, and the deepening world depression, only drew the state more deeply into economic affairs. The most important changes came in 1932–1933 as state-owned banks took over the financing and direction of productive investments. This policy of state-led industrialization was known as *devletçilik* (statehood), or *étatism*, and was embodied in a series of five-year plans drawn up with Soviet assistance.[18]

These policies directly affected foreign investments. While capital imports were never excluded in principle, the new state banks moved quickly to purchase key foreign-owned companies. Most were public utilities—telephone, water, public transport, and electric power— although some foreign-owned coal mines were also taken.[19] None were confiscated. "Apparently fair prices were paid," according to one study. "Their previous record of service was not good enough to warrant objection on the part of their private owners."[20] Indeed, some

---

*Atatürk's early attitude toward new foreign investment is reflected in his 1923 statement:

> Do not suppose that we envy foreign capital. No, our country is extensive. We require great effort and great capital. Therefore, we are always prepared to provide the necessary security to foreign capital on the condition that its profits be regulated by law.

Few investors were persuaded. They well remembered the troubles of the dying Ottoman Empire and were worried by the emergence of militant Turkish nationalism. Richard D. Robinson, *The First Turkish Republic* (Cambridge, Mass.: Harvard University Press, 1963), 106.

foreign-owned railroads had been allowed to deteriorate in expectation of government purchase.[21]

Foreign investors may have escaped real harm, but there were larger issues at stake here. The evolving Turkish economic program prefigured the dilemmas that would face foreign capital in other less developed areas. What is crucial here is the conjuncture of nation building and state-led development of import substitution and national capitalism. The state apparatus was being used—quite self-consciously, if not always effectively—to direct economic growth and to mediate between national and international markets. This implied a more precarious role for foreign capital, and a more carefully monitored one. It also implied a new standard for the justification of foreign investments: *their contribution to national development.* These issues were just surfacing during the interwar period, most notably in Turkey and Mexico, but they would be critical to investment protection worldwide after World War II.

International Organizations: The Stalemate over Property Rights

In addition to these emerging national controls and occasional expropriations, the global investment-protection regime was weakened in another, more diffuse way. For the first time, the fundamental principles of property law were attacked in international forums.

Before World War I these norms had gone largely unchallenged. No one publicly doubted that states should treat foreign investments according to minimum international standards, and no one disputed the content of those standards. What *was* contested, especially by some Latin American states, was the right to enforce these rules unilaterally.

The issue was tested at the Hague Peace Conference of 1907. The conference touched on international property law because the delegates took up the sensitive question of debt collection. Shortly after the first Hague Conference (in 1899), Great Britain, Germany, and Italy blockaded and bombarded Venezuela. They demanded satisfaction of a number of claims, including bond defaults. Luis Drago of Argentina replied that foreign debts were not a proper cause for war and that their forcible collection should be outlawed. He raised the point again at the 1906 Pan American Conference, observing that European bombardment and occupation violated the Monroe Doctrine. Secretary of State Elihu Root seemed to agree, but managed to steer the issue to the upcoming Hague Conference, where more fellow creditors would be in attendance.

The Hague Conference produced a false compromise, the Porter Doctrine. Creditors agreed not to collect contract debts by force *if debtor states would accept binding arbitration.* That condition, however, was unacceptable to most Latin American states. Almost all entered major reservations to the Hague Treaty, and only Mexico's Porfirio Díaz finally ratified it.[22]

This abortive compromise was the only challenge to customary property norms before World War I, and it was hardly serious. The authoritativeness of the prewar norms is particularly evident at the Hague Conferences because they should have been congenial forums for debtors to dispute them. Both conferences were widely attended (the second had forty-four participants), and Britain had no more votes than Uruguay. Yet, as legal historian Konstantin Katzarov points out, "The Hague Convention of 1899 passed very quickly over the question of protection of private property, almost without discussion. At that time, respect for private property was accepted as self-evident—as self-evident as honor, life and religious convictions. At the Hague Conference of 1907, the problems relating to the inviolability of private property were in the same way the subject of no particular discussion."[23] Direct investments were never mentioned, and neither was the question of compensation. Only enforcement procedures were discussed.

Still, hidden within the objections to binding arbitration lies a deeper division. Binding arbitration was unacceptable to most Latin American states because it would limit an essential aspect of their sovereignty—control (at least hypothetically) over foreign investments. That position, dating from the Calvo and Drago doctrines, could never be reconciled with the opposing norm of "international minimum standards."

Yet this division was not made explicit before World War I. The developed capitalist states, led by Great Britain, were able to sustain a unified system of enforceable rules and publicly accepted norms. What mattered most was not the secret opposition to those norms. What mattered was the effective suppression of the challenge.

After World War I, suppression began to fail. Besides the expropriations mentioned earlier, a number of European states had abandoned old standards of "equal and equitable" treatment for foreigners. Significantly, these obstacles to commerce were confronted in multilateral forums where challenges to traditional norms were finally made explicit. Contention had replaced custom.

Throughout the 1920s the League of Nations held economic conferences, culminating in an attempt to codify international property law.[24] The major European powers, who called the conferences, were really attempting to restore the old standards. Their purpose was to clarify the obligations of host states to foreign capital. They foundered, as the Law of the Seas conferences did in the mid-1970s when less developed and peripheral states asserted their own rights.

The first codification conference met in Paris in 1929 and quickly boiled down to a fight over compensation standards. The major capital exporters wanted a clear statement that foreign capital had to be treated according to international minimum standards. The League's draft treaty explicitly rejected that approach. It asked only for "national treatment," or equality between foreign and domestic investments. The British led the fight for stronger language and got support from nearly all major European states. They were consistently defeated by a combination of Latin American, East European, and ex-colonial states.[25]

The same issues were debated the next year at The Hague, with the same results. Once again, the conference was supposed to concentrate exclusively on *imposing* responsibility and ignore areas where sovereignty could be asserted or responsibilities disclaimed. That plan miscarried because it was rejected by Latin American and East European states, a group large enough to veto the proposed convention. Their counterproposals were swiftly dismissed, and the conference ended without tangible results.[26]

Considering the extensive representation of economically less developed states at the conferences, their outcome is less surprising than the fact that they were held at all. That they were illustrates the decline of traditional norms and enforcement capacity during the interwar period. Major European states could no longer legitimate the old standards, and they could no longer substitute effective force for agreement. To revive the rules they needed sustained agreement among themselves and significant approval from a wide number of peripheral states. In the nineteenth century, European diplomatic practice had been approval enough.

If traditional norms were to be reestablished, truly international conferences were essential. Yet the outcome of those conferences paradoxically accelerated the decline of traditional norms. All League members were invited, and each had the same voting rights.* These procedures made it especially difficult for capital exporters to ratify old and favored principles since vast differences in wealth and power were formally ignored. In contrast, prewar conferences had used similar voting rules for equally large memberships without confronting traditional anti-expropriation norms. The organizational arrangements, then, may have been a necessary aspect of the normative challenge, but they were hardly a sufficient condition. The diffusion of nationalism and anticolonialism was equally important. So was the declining ability of advanced capitalist states to protect their investments bilaterally. By the late 1920s several states had already limited foreign investors' rights unilaterally. Now they saw the chance to win collective approval for their individual acts. They certainly did not want them condemned, even implicitly. For other less developed countries, the League conferences provided a unique chance to gain approval for their sovereign aspirations. In both cases, League rules granted poor countries the power of numbers. They used that organizational power to prevent an exclusive focus on their obligations to foreigners.

The resulting stalemate contrasts markedly with prewar outcomes. In 1907, Latin American states had added one important item to the agenda (forcible debt collection) and slightly modified one normative aspect of property protection. In 1929 and 1930, the same states, joined by India and several East European countries, were ultimately able to veto the conference agendas.

The Pan-American Regime

As the conferences indicate, Latin American states had old and deep concerns about foreign investments. As early as the 1860s, some had rejected the claim that foreign states could properly

*The United States and Soviet Union attended as observers.

intervene to protect their nationals. In addition, their legal systems often incorporated the Spanish principle that the state was the ultimate owner of subsoil rights. Still, it was not until the 1920s and 1930s, when Mexico began its land reforms, that the first important Latin American expropriations took place.

Mexico's reforms were inspired by revolutionary ideals, boldly expressed in the Constitution of 1917. Asserting that the nation alone owned the land within its borders, the new constitution broke with traditional ideas about private property and anticipated the reform of agriculture and the nationalization of oil. It reserved the right to convey land titles and to control land use.

Although few foreign properties were initially affected, the United States government was concerned about the long-range implications of Mexico's investment laws. It withheld recognition until 1923, when it reached an agreement protecting foreign investments and assuring compensation for any expropriated land. U.S. property rights remained secure until the pace of land reform quickened in the mid-1930s.

Most expropriated property belonged to Mexicans, but the reforms were general and some American citizens were affected. Mexico obviously lacked the money to pay immediate compensation; it promised instead to pay foreign owners as funds became available. The United States protested but reluctantly accepted the situation.

Compensation came slowly. A preliminary agreement to pay the landowners was worked out in 1938, in the wake of Mexico's more important expropriation of foreign oil companies. An overall settlement, covering both land and oil, was finally signed in 1941.

At about the same time, a lesser dispute with Bolivia was resolved. Charging Standard Oil with fraud, the Bolivian government had expropriated some minor concessions in 1937. Although the properties were much less valuable than oil holdings in Mexico ($1 to 2 million versus $24 million or more), the dispute festered for several years before a compensation agreement was signed in 1941.

In all these cases the State Department took the same legal position: no principled objections to the confiscations, but strong, careful arguments for traditional standards of compensation. Its diplomatic pressure achieved partial compensation in each case. But diplomacy had to be cautious and sanctions measured. World war was again on the horizon. Thus, the oil expropriations in Mexico and Bolivia forced a basic choice between the need to protect particular investments and the more pressing need to conserve political resources and strengthen hemispheric solidarity.

Nevertheless, the State Department did try to prevent Bolivia from exploiting or exporting its confiscated oil and refused to grant any loans or technical assistance until Standard Oil was paid. In the end, very modest compensation was agreed upon and, literally the next day, the U.S. government announced a $25 million dollar development program for Bolivia.[27]

In Mexico, the companies themselves tried to prevent the sale of their oil, but the U.S. government imposed economic sanctions for only a brief time. Not that effective coercion would have been difficult. Silver was the basis of Mexico's currency and its second biggest export; the main customer was the U.S. Treasury. According to historian Howard Cline, "To have suspended purchases of silver in reprisal for the expropriation of American oil would have brought the Mexican economy crashing."[28]

The question of sanctions against Mexico was debated extensively within the Roosevelt administration. Curiously (in light of recent debates), it was the State Department that backed the oil companies most vigorously. Secretary of State Cordell Hull and his economic adviser, Herbert Feis, urged a link between silver purchases and an expropriation settlement. They were sharply opposed by the U.S. ambassador to Mexico, Josephus Daniels, and Treasury Secretary Henry Morgenthau. Morgenthau was convinced that Mexico's economy was precarious and that the country might collapse into another Spanish Civil War. Under the circumstances, he thought sanctions extremely risky. Similarly, he stressed the risks to larger foreign policy goals, including economic ones. The companies' oil boycott had already forced Mexico to deal with the Axis. More sanctions could only worsen the situation. Ultimately, Morgenthau's views prevailed.[29]

Two considerations were paramount. First, the United States discovered, as Britain had in the nineteenth century, that the very weakness of less developed states sometimes protected them. Because tough, external sanctions threatened internal chaos (not just a change of policies), they were often self-defeating. Moreover, the issue was acute because the approach of global war demanded secure and stable allies, especially among neighbors. The threat of war made manifest the latent hierarchy of military and economic goals.

That hierarchy was reinforced by the confusion of economic interests. Economic relations with Mexico were extensive and profitable—and they were not immediately endangered by the expropriations. Mexico, for example, was the United States' sixth largest trading partner "in a world threatened by bilateralism and Nazi trade drives."[30] Besides threatening trade, rigid sanctions would strike directly at the sizable American investments remaining in the country. Ambassador Daniels complained that if harsh sanctions were applied, Mexico and U.S. silver miners would have to pay for "the sins of the oilmen."[31]

This transnational network of trade and mining interests, coupled with their bureaucratic allies, restricted the State Department's discretion and limited its ability to sanction Mexico's violation of existing anti-expropriation rules. According to Cline:

> Seventy percent of the silver producers in Mexico were [North] American; they, not the Mexicans, were being penalized, and the Washington silver lobby was as powerful as the oil. Further, if Mexicans had no dollars, they could buy no American goods. And beyond that, silver producers employed Mexican labor, too; if pushed at all, Cárdenas was quite likely to expropriate American mining as well as petroleum enterprises. So the chief weapon—withdrawal of silver purchases from Mexico by the United States government—remained sheathed.[32]

All U.S. investors had a vital stake in upholding the rights of foreign capital. But beyond that, their interests diverged. Some, such as the silver producers, wanted to avoid a diplomatic clash. The expropriated oil producers, by contrast, wanted a settlement that vindicated their rights and recouped their investments. They demanded vigorous action. Thus, complex transnational relations fostered ambivalent class interests, a situation repeated in later cases of selective expropriations. This division among U.S. investors was the ironic price of U.S. dominance in Mexico's mining, oil, and foreign commerce.

The combination of conflicting economic interests and grand diplomatic purpose led to prolonged negotiations instead of swift sanctions. The State Department never renounced the traditional international rules requiring full compensation. But in Mexico, as in Bolivia, it was willing to settle for something less.

All the interwar expropriations, but especially the Soviet and Mexican ones, revived the old, formerly hypothetical issue of compensation standards. Actually, two compensation questions were muddled together. One was whether full compensation was required by international law. What was the content of international law? What was required by treaty, custom, and practice? In several interwar cases, compensation was partial and long delayed. The settlements thus departed from traditional legal standards and might be considered cheating on the old rules. A second issue was whether international law demanded minimum standards of conduct toward foreigners, *regardless of how local citizens were treated*. By raising the issue directly, Mexico challenged the basic assumptions of international law. It disputed the legitimacy of the entire international regime protecting foreign investments. The United States could not budge the Mexicans from their position in bilateral talks, and they have maintained it ever since. Yet it is significant that during the interwar period this practical challenge to international minimum standards was confined to Mexico.

To support its position, the Mexican government cited a half-century of Latin American jurisprudence. As early as 1889, when the American states held their first international conference, some Latin Americans had recommended that foreigners be treated like local citizens. Eminent jurists such as Carlos Calvo and Rafael Seijas had already developed the legal basis of that claim. If foreigners were to be admitted to local commerce on an equal basis, they contended, then they should not be granted the advantage of appealing to their home governments. Contractual clauses to that effect were actually included in many concessions, so-called Calvo clauses. This practice, although disapproved of by European states, may have "practically inhibited diplomatic intervention except in the most flagrant cases."[33] The United States responded like the Europeans: minimum standards, not just equal ones, were required by international law and could be enforced if necessary. This is sometimes called the Hull Doctrine but, as I have noted, it is far older than Hull's 1938 notes to the Mexicans. The United States, for example, had voted against Latin American proposals in 1889 and at later international conferences, arguing each time that diplomatic protection of aliens was a legal concept even older than territorial sovereignty. Again in 1933, the United States specifically reserved its rights under international law after the Seventh Inter-American Conference had approved a Calvo clause.[34]

The earliest inter-American conferences anticipated issues that were not raised in Europe until the League conferences of 1929 and 1930.

To secure approval first for its aggressive policies and then for its hegemony, the United States had created an international forum that gave nominal equality to much smaller states. That gave Latin Americans an opportunity unique among less developed areas. They could advance their legal position collectively and at least claim for it the legitimacy bestowed by a regional conference.

Despite this long-running battle and the recent expropriations in Mexico and Bolivia, the pan-American regime for investment security was still a tight, de facto one between the wars. The United States, like Great Britain earlier, was still able to protect foreigners from acts considered illegal under customary international law.

The Global Regime between the Wars

To summarize, the global regime governing expropriation came under unprecedented challenge between World War I and World War II. Before World War I, foreign investment was generally treated with circumspection. Sporadic violations were overturned without serious or lasting damage to the overall security of foreign capital. These observed regularities alert us to the existence of guiding rules. There were, in fact, widely shared standards regarding the proper treatment of foreign capital and a coercive structure sufficient to sanction departures from those standards. These standards were still widely observed during the interwar period, but there was somewhat more variation in the treatment of foreign capital and sharper rhetorical dissent by some states. The expropriations in the Soviet Union, Turkey, and Mexico, while dramatically different from one another, were all departures from traditional property rules. So, too, were the much more modest acts in Bolivia and Eastern Europe.

Alongside these expropriations, there was an explicit (but far from widespread) attack on the normative premises of investment security. It had been assumed that host states were properly limited in two important ways when dealing with foreign investors. First, although it was acknowledged that states could purchase private property (subject to full compensation and procedural guarantees), this right of eminent domain was considered a highly circumscribed one. Second, the treatment of foreign investment was supposed to meet certain minimum standards, regardless of how domestic investments were treated. The enforcement of foreign investment security was justified by recourse to these values. The profit-seeking behavior of foreign nationals was recast as a basic right and embodied in international law. To a considerable extent, these values were accepted by capital-importing states. In the prewar period there was little ideological opposition on the periphery—no redefinition of individual property rights, no assertion of the state's role in steering the economy and directing economic development.* True, Latin American states had long asserted their right to treat foreign investments according to their own standards. But this assertion did not evolve into a full-fledged attack on international legal principles. In international forums, at least, it was largely confined to a protest over military enforcement of investors' privileges. The turn-of-the-century Hague conferences easily ratified the rights of investors and the obligations of host states. They glided over questions about sovereign rights and investor obligations. The stalemate over those same questions in 1929 and 1930 signaled a dramatic change from the prewar consensus.

In spite of these challenges, most foreign investments were still secure and major expropriations still isolated acts. The prevailing standards were the customary legal ones, despite notable exceptions. The overall regime is best characterized as a relatively strong one, even though property rules were obviously more controversial and conformity more problematic than before World War I.

Enforcement during the interwar period was an odd patchwork. In the Western Hemisphere, the rules were sustained by the United States. Elsewhere, they were still maintained chiefly by colonial rule. In the few noncolonial areas of Africa and Asia, the rules were supervised by interested colonial powers. Aside from Turkey (where no single European state was dominant), there were few major disputes. Thailand, for instance, was trying as usual to assure its independence from the neighboring French and British empires and prudently avoided antagonizing their merchants and investors. Iran, while not formally a colony, was dominated by the British. Before World War I, it had been a scene of Anglo-Russian rivalry. The revolution drew the Russians homeward while the Royal Navy pulled the British in. At Churchill's insistence, the British government bought a controlling interest in the Anglo-Persian Oil Company. Besides saving the navy

---

*In parts of Africa and Asia, the establishment of individual property rights was itself a radical change from local forms of possession, exchange, and usufructory privilege. These issues are discussed in chapter 1.

millions in fuel costs, the arrangement freed Britain from exclusive reliance on Shell and Standard Oil. The British purchase and the Russian withdrawal, writes Fereidun Fesharaki, "enabled the British government and APOC [Anglo-Persian Oil Company] to dominate Persia completely, though no formal colonization took place."[35]

The expropriations came not in Iran, or Thailand, or Ethiopia, or Afghanistan, but on the underdeveloped periphery of Europe. Several East European states redistributed privately owned land to peasants. The policies were modest and basically conservative in their aims, but they advanced the idea that expropriations need not be confined to the strict Anglo-Saxon notion of eminent domain. They could be legitimate acts of social policy. Previously, expropriation had been limited to rare and isolated instances with an overriding public purpose. While that limit was inherently ambiguous, it was never meant to cover general, impersonal acts of redistribution, even if compensation was paid. Under the old order, writes Konstantin Katzarov, private property was understood as a personal right, not as a social relation subject to state manipulation. Even modest acts of agrarian redistribution contradicted this once-shared premise. It was called into question still more seriously in Turkey and Mexico. In Turkey, the expropriations, though compensated adequately, were part of a state-led industrialization strategy. In Mexico, they were a nationalist expression of state control over subsoil rights.

But by far the most serious challenge to customary rules and norms came from the Soviet Union. That country's sweeping acts redefined the social meaning of property. The scope of its expropriations, their resolution, and their domestic and international meaning were all unique. Even though the Soviets finally acknowledged a legal responsibility to compensate foreign investors, the damage to customary rules was already done.

But if the Soviet expropriations were a serious challenge to traditional property rules—and they were—they also served, paradoxically, to reinforce the consensual basis of traditional property rules among capital-exporting states. Because the Soviet expropriations were embedded in a larger program of anticapitalist revolution, they italicized the politically deviant character of expropriation. They framed the meaning of expropriation in a particular way. In the process, large-scale expropriation came to be associated vaguely with communism, with a radical antagonism to capitalism in general (even though it was more often part of a state-led program of national capitalism). This association clearly informed America's postwar policies of investment protection.

The Soviet expropriations (and, to a much lesser extent, the ones in Turkey and East Europe) showed how difficult it was to enforce property rules in the absence of a hegemonic power. In East Europe, France was the most important political power among the capital exporters. Its influence, however, was far from hegemonic and was confined largely to military-alliance issues. Britain had once been supreme in the eastern Mediterranean, but no foreign power tried seriously to limit Turkey's étatist program. In the Soviet Union, where the interests of capital exporters were clear and widely shared (at least in the beginning), condominium was tried and failed.

The overall regime governing foreign investments was still relatively strong, the rules reasonably coherent. Most investments in most countries were completely secure. But the major expropriations and the stalemated conferences constituted an unprecedented challenge to the rules and norms dealing with foreign investment.

CHAPTER FOUR

"The American Century": The Revival and Decline of International Property Rules

If the 1930s were a time of stalemate and drift, the late 1940s and 1950s were a time of purpose and reconstruction. Economic and military power were consolidated in the United States, resolving the interwar problem of rule enforcement. The strengthening of property rules, at least from the investors' point of view, was assured.

But the recovery was only partial. The United States was well equipped to police the rules, but the problems were mounting. As decolonization proceeded, international property rules had to cover a much wider area. Not surprisingly, the perpetuation of old standards was a contentious issue for new states, as was the whole concept of "international minimum standards." Finally, the social character of property continued to evolve. State economic responsibilities continued to grow and were central to state building in less developed countries. These new state functions, combined with anticolonial ideology, guaranteed a tough fight to legitimate anti-expropriation rules.

Multilateral Forums

The United States faced the devastation of war and depression with an overriding economic goal: the reconstruction of an open, multilateral world economy. This purpose ensured that investment policy would parallel trade policy, as it had in nineteenth-century Britain. The link between trade and investment runs deeper still, since America's new investment proposals were first announced as part of the planned International Trade Organization (ITO).

Trade, money, and investment—the principal issues of the world economy—were knotted together by the failures of the Depression. As the crash spread from Wall Street to London, Paris and beyond, states hastily threw up what barriers they could. Many passed steep tariffs. Even the British, the model free traders, claimed new preferences in their colonies. The sharp, swift contraction of global trade and investment was accelerated by chaotic national controls over foreign exchange. To protect domestic production and currency reserves, states universally adopted beggar-thy-neighbor policies. The result, aside from beggared neighbors, was a jumble of national regulations and segmented markets. To overcome these obstacles in the postwar years the United States turned repeatedly to multilateral solutions.

The first, partial step toward reviving world commerce came at Bretton Woods, where the World Bank and International Monetary Fund were set up. Once the multilateral payments scheme was in place, the next step was a charter for world trade. First, the United States reached general agreement with Britain over the charter. Then, it invited several Continental powers to join the talks. Finally, after the United Nations created a Preparatory Committee on Trade and Employment in 1946, the United States broadened its invitation to include all U.N. members. This wide membership ensured a serious debate over economic development, including the treatment of foreign investment.[1]

Curiously, it was the United States, not the Latin American states, that first raised the problem of foreign investment at the trade negotiations. The reason it did so is instructive. The draft charter produced at the London conference made only vague references to the rights of investors and the obligations of host states. It said nothing specific about investment security. The State Department soon heard about its sin of omission. The chairman of the U.S. delegation, Clair Wilcox, described the process briefly: "In response to suggestions made by such bodies as the National Foreign Trade Council and the National Association of Manufacturers, the inclusion of an additional article on international investment was therefore proposed by the American delegation at Geneva."[2] In Geneva, and again in Havana, the U.S. delegation argued for traditional legal principles, including the old rule of "prompt, adequate, and effective compensation."

The U.S. proposals were self-defeating, as they were bound to be in such a forum. After long debates and stiff opposition (primarily from Latin American, Indian, and Australian delegations), the United States could salvage only a tepid compromise.

Whatever advantages that compromise may have held for foreign investors, they were more than offset by the lack of positive guarantees and the strong emphasis on sovereign rights. Disturbed by these and other provisions, many strong proponents of multilateral trade and investment began to back away from the ITO. Some contended that it did not adequately safeguard American interests. Others said it ratified economic planning, which they equated with economic nationalism and considered incompatible with an integrated world economy.[3] It was the defection of these free traders, together with the steady opposition of old-fashioned protectionists, that sunk the International Trade Organization.

The ITO conferences clearly demonstrated the lack of broad international approval for traditional investment laws. The scene was soon repeated in Bogotá at the Ninth International Conference of American States, where the final clause on foreign investment was subject to formal reservations by almost all participants.[4] The trend in later international meetings, particularly those at the United Nations, has been to stress sovereign rights and to depreciate the international status of foreign investments.

Organizational rules and procedures have played a vital role in this normative challenge. While voting procedures in the General Assembly cannot shut out external sources of influence, they nevertheless define a universe of organizational power that is formally independent of wealth, population, and military strength. In other words, voting procedures can create organizationally specific power. This power can be used by otherwise weak states to ratify principles they favor and to discredit principles they reject.

On salient issues such as foreign investment, the effect has been to undermine the legitimacy of older international property rules. Significantly, this erosion was true even at the height of United States military and economic power. In 1952, for example, the General Assembly passed its first resolution on Permanent Sovereignty over Natural Resources. Introduced by Uruguay and Bolivia, the resolution endorsed the right of all states to nationalize and freely exploit their natural resources. The compensation question was handled delicately and, as far as the United States and Great Britain were concerned, unsatisfactorily. The word "nationalization" was dropped from the final version, along with any reference to compensation or international law. The resolution merely recommended that member states "have due regard, consistent with their sovereignty, to the need for maintaining the flow of capital in conditions of security."[5]

Sporadic U.S. debates have consistently reaffirmed the resolution on Permanent Sovereignty and slowly expanded the claims of less developed states. The 1962 Resolution on Permanent Sovereignty, for instance, diluted compensation standards. Instead of "just compensation," it urged only "appropriate" payments. The turn of phrase signified an important shift in prevailing attitudes. Even so, it was a compromise of sorts. An earlier Soviet draft had ignored international compensation standards entirely and required only municipal ones. The Soviet proposal was rejected in favor of one that referred vaguely to both international and municipal law.[6] In 1966, the General Assembly reaffirmed the right of member states to nationalize natural resources but significantly deleted all references to international legal principles.[7]

This trend was consolidated and extended in the 1970s. In 1972, the General Assembly overwhelmingly passed a resolution asserting that nationalization was "the expression of sovereign power . . . in virtue of which it is for each state to fix the amount of compensation and the procedure for these measures." The conditions that might justify nationalization were simply omitted as irrelevant, and any disputes were said to fall "within the sole jurisdiction" of the nationalizing country's courts.[8] This position was spelled out further in U.N. reports and in additional resolutions passed by the General Assembly, the U.N. Conference on Trade and Development (UNCTAD), and the Economic and Social Council (ECOSOC).

The most vivid and strident expression of this position came just after the 1973–1974 oil crisis, as less developed countries began demanding a new international economic order. To launch this larger agenda, the General Assembly passed the Charter of Economic Rights and Duties of States, in December 1974. The rights belonged to LDCs, the duties to multinational firms and advanced states. One hundred twenty nations voted for it; ten abstained; and six voted no (the United States, United Kingdom, West Germany, Denmark, Belgium, and Luxembourg). The charter effectively endorsed national efforts to restrict and control foreign capital throughout the Third World, including expropriations, contract abrogation, and the exclusive use of municipal courts to settle disputes.[9] While subsequent rhetorical claims have not always been so openly hostile to multinationals, there has been no rollback of this fundamental assertion of national control over foreign investments. And no rollback is likely.

These U.N. resolutions expose the cumulative shift in international values. Through the 1920s at least, those norms unambiguously expressed the values of capital-exporting states. They marked off clear limits to expropriation and endorsed full compensation. Countervailing claims were advanced during the interwar period but were largely stymied until the 1950s, when the first U.N. Resolutions on Permanent Sovereignty were passed. Those U.N. resolutions were aimed directly at the older standards; indirectly they rebuked capital-exporting states for enforcing them.

The distinguished international lawyer Richard Lillich sees an even larger purpose in the U.N. resolutions. He thinks they attack the basic procedural principle of diplomatic protection for nationals abroad. "While the doctrine of diplomatic protection admittedly has its imperfections," Lillich says, "weakening or abolishing it under present conditions would effectively undercut the substantive norms developed by state practice over the past 150 years."[10]

Of course, passing a resolution at the United Nations is not the same as passing an international law. Some lawyers, however, maintain that a *series* of widely accepted U.N. resolutions can achieve legal status. Others point to additional, sometimes conflicting, sources of law. International law has traditionally been based on treaty practice, customary interstate behavior, broadly approved principles, and the commentaries of accepted authorities. These are still important sources of law, as are the rulings of international tribunals.[11]

The courts, however, have done little to resolve expropriation disputes or to develop international property law in the postwar era. Severely restricted by its own rules, the International Court of Justice (ICJ) has heard only two expropriation cases,* and one of them had to be thrown out when Iran challenged the court's jurisdiction.[12] The ICJ's meager role in property law merely highlights the importance of U.N. resolutions on the subject.

If these resolutions are not quite law, what are they? Basically,

---

*Anglo-Iranian and Barcelona Traction. Anglo-Iranian Oil Company v. Jaffrate (United Kingdom v. Iran), *ICJ Reports, 1952*, p. 11ff.; and Case Concerning the Barcelona Traction, Light, and Power Co., Ltd. (Belgium v. Spain), *ICJ Reports, 1961*, p. 9ff. and *ICJ Reports, 1970*, p. 3ff.

they are an expression of prevailing international values and rhetorical claims—mainly non-Western ones, given the voting procedures of the United Nations and the salience of investment issues to LDCs. They are, in Inis Claude's phrase, less a matter of lawmaking than of "affixing the stamp of political approval or disapproval."[13] This stamp is most meaningful when the language is forceful, the votes overwhelming, and the resolutions repeated. In the case of multinational investment, no one could mistake the meaning of repeated U.N. resolutions.

The United Nations' function of collective legitimation further corrodes the ability of major capitalist states to assure investment security. In the nineteenth century, when the prevailing rules were legitimated mainly by treaties and customs, their approval ultimately derived from the military and financial strength of Europe. In the years since World War II, however, institutions such as the United Nations have increasingly assumed the task of justifying or condemning international behavior. To be fully accredited now, international rules must be approved by institutions whose memberships and voting rights have nothing to do with military or economic power. The powerful can still try to enforce behavioral conformity (with uneven results), but they can no longer secure approval by fiat. Nor can they silence the opposition. One result is that the diplomatic costs of enforcement have escalated markedly. Thus, the rise of broad-based international organizations has undermined the legal status of diplomatic protection for foreign investments.[14]

Despite the important role of the United Nations, no single international institution has exclusive jurisdiction over foreign investment. Nor does any major institution concentrate primarily on that subject. As a result, it is not clear in advance which institutions (if any) will help shape international rules.

Ever since the ITO experience, advanced capitalist states have prudently favored institutions such as the World Bank (International Bank for Reconstruction and Development, or IBRD) and the International Monetary Fund (IMF), which they jointly control. Voting in these institutions is determined mainly by capital contributions, not by sovereign equality.[15] That is also true at the World Bank's affiliate, the International Development Association, which makes heavily subsidized loans to poor states (see table 6). As a consequence of these voting arrangements and the institutions' mission of stim-

TABLE 6

VOTING POWER AT THE WORLD BANK

	International Bank for Reconstruction and Development		International Development Association	
	Voting power	Percent of membership	Voting power	Percent of membership
U.S.	20.61	.7	18.97	.7
EEC	24.67	7.0	25.64	7.6
OECD	56.91	16.2	62.82	16.9

SOURCE: World Bank, *Annual Report, 1982*, 154–155, 172–173.

ulating capital flows, both the Bank and the Fund have favored open economies and have consistently supported the rights of foreign investors.

The IBRD and its affiliates have helped protect foreign investors and have averted interstate clashes by applying the quiet authority of a moneylender. According to the Bank's "Blue Book," these anti-expropriation policies fulfill its chartered obligation to expand international investment:

> The Bank is charged, under its Articles of Agreement, to encourage international investment. It has, therefore, a direct interest in the creation and maintenance of satisfactory relations between member countries and their external creditors. Accordingly, the normal practice is to inform governments who are involved in such disputes that the Bank or IDA will not assist them unless and until they make appropriate efforts to reach a fair and equitable settlement.[16]

Edward Mason and Robert Asher, the Bank's official historians, have confirmed the "Blue Book" statements, citing a number of loans that were barred by expropriation controversies or by the absence of negotiations toward an "equitable settlement."[17]

The IMF is typically less involved in expropriation disputes, but its policies and voting procedures are similar to the World Bank's. The United States controls about 20 percent of the votes; Great Britain, Germany, France, and Japan another 20 percent. By contrast, the executive director for most of Africa controls 3.17 percent.[18]

The Fund is generally hospitable to foreign investment and has affected investment security in two important ways. First, it has worked to abolish restrictions on capital mobility—restrictions that diminish the value of investments and that some consider "creeping expropriation." Second, it has played a critical role in protecting troubled commercial loans (the modern form of portfolio lending) through its key role in debt reschedulings.

Perhaps the most important restriction on capital mobility is the sudden limitation of profit repatriation. Governments strapped for foreign exchange will often order foreign investors not to convert their local profits into hard currencies. Brazil did just that during its 1962 exchange crisis, to take one of many examples. At other times, they will permit only a fraction of profits (or loans from the parent company) to be repatriated. And additional restrictions may be put on that. In 1982, debt-burdened Mexico carefully doled out its scarce foreign exchange, and it placed a very low priority on profit repatriation. Even if a firm could acquire dollars, it could send home only a designated fraction of the company's invested capital.[19] Likewise, in 1983, Brazil made little hard currency available to foreigners and then slapped a 25 percent tax on all transfers out of the country. Most multinationals responded by keeping their subsidiaries as illiquid as possible and reinvesting profits locally. Extra funds were often put into real estate.[20]

The IMF opposes such restrictions, which distort local economies and weaken their external links. The IMF Articles of Agreement aim at the elimination of national controls over foreign exchange,[21] and its loan agreements sometimes include that demand. They often prevent additional restrictions from being imposed.[22]

Even more important, as far as investment protection is concerned, is the IMF's central role in protecting foreign loans. From its earliest days, the IMF has staunchly opposed debt renunciation and has assisted impoverished or illiquid debtors in rescheduling the claims against them. The debts themselves are mostly from private banks or foreign-aid donors, but the IMF's role in rescheduling them is absolutely central.

When debtors have trouble repaying their obligations and cannot find new sources of private financing, they typically turn to the IMF for stand-by credit. The IMF, in turn, imposes political and economic conditions on its larger loans—progressively tougher deflationary requirements for increasing amounts. By agreeing to these conditions, and then meeting the target standards of performance, the debtor can secure IMF credit. Much more important, its gets the IMF's "seal of approval." This approval is an essential prerequisite for the rescheduling of other, much larger loans made by private banks and public-aid donors.[23]

Setting conditions for the debtor is essential to rescheduling and crucial to creditor cooperation. Until recently, the IMF's role in co-ordinating creditors was limited to this stamp of approval. In response to larger debt crises in Brazil and Mexico, however, the IMF moved aggressively to expand its leadership role. The crucial problem was that hundreds of private lenders were involved in each case—with billions at stake. Without some tough-minded discipline, the creditors might not be able to reach agreement among themselves. That, in turn, would throw both creditors and debtor into chaos. The main problem was that some smaller creditors, who lacked extensive ties to the debtor and to other creditors, were reluctant to stretch out their debt maturities and were even more wary about shelling out new cash. The IMF effectively resolved this coordination problem by announcing each bank's share of the rescheduling packages and then threatening not to sign any stabilization agreement with the debtor until every bank met its share. The pressure on outliers was tremendous, and effective. The regional banks grumbled but paid up. The big money-center banks in America and Europe, who normally co-ordinate the creditors, were profoundly grateful.

In general, the IMF's lending policies embody the political and economic requirements of prudent foreign lending, public or private. At the same time, the IMF provides a buffer for private banks. As long as the IMF arranges and supervises the debtor's stabilization program, private lenders can avoid direct involvement in the internal politics of the borrowing country.* Thus, in spite of a competitive

---

*Direct bank involvement in the management of stabilization programs is a very risky affair, and they are loathe to accept it. They are organizationally ill equipped for the task and for the political demands that go with it.

If commercial banks had any doubts on this point, they were resolved in 1976 in Peru. That country was facing a debt crisis, having exhausted its reserves and its bank credits. It continued to run huge deficits on current account—over $1 billion annually. When a deadlock developed over the terms of new bank lending and the amount, the Peruvian government imposed an austerity program designed to conserve foreign exchange. The announcement of higher taxes and devaluation led to riots in Lima, a declaration of national emergency, and a reshuffling of government officials. Still, the government adhered to its austerity program and, on that basis, negotiated a new $220 million loan from a consortium of U.S. banks. The Peruvians had convinced the banks that the usual arrangement—first, an IMF stabilization agreement, then a re-market for foreign lending, the international financial system is institutionally well-coordinated in cases of near-default.

This intertwining of public and private and financial institutions has become increasingly important. The most recent impetus has been the vast debt burden acquired by the largest LDCs—those most significant in the world economy. By the early 1980s, after a decade of borrowing, their debts had reached crisis proportions. Some, such as Brazil, had gone to the Euromarkets to finance rapid growth in the face of high oil import bills. Others, such as Mexico, were oil exporters who borrowed to finance rapid industrialization based, unfortunately for them, on overly optimistic forecasts of future oil prices. Both kinds of borrowers were hit hard by high real interest rates and a prolonged recession in key export markets.

Refinancing this debt has proved to be a complex and delicate matter, drawing together the leaders of international banking syndicates and the IMF's staff. The key to their cooperation has been the IMF's continuing ability to maintain its strict lending conditions, which offer creditors their only real control over the debtor's public policies. Today, as in the past, "most governments, central bankers, and com-

---

scheduling of debts and continued IMF surveillance of government policies—would bring down the government and lead to a more radical successor. Hence, both the bankers and the existing Peruvian government reached for an unusual arrangement.

The loan terms were unique. To secure the loan, Peru pledged to maintain certain austerity measures and to report periodically on their success. But instead of reporting to the IMF, they would report directly to the private lenders. This made the banks highly visible and involved them directly in Peru's daily political life—an increasingly uncomfortable position. As David Beim of the U.S. Export-Import Bank notes:

> Not in recent memory had the banks been so fully drawn into the policymaking process within an LDC. . . . The real risk in LDC lending is not that the countries will walk away from the banks, but rather that they will draw the banks too deeply into their own internal affairs, making them a target of popular resentment over conservative economic policies. . . . This carries a clear political risk to the banks and to the United States generally.

The earlier riots in Lima prefigured these risks of direct bank involvement in Peru's austerity program.

In most cases, however, private banks have not intervened directly to set the policy conditions that accompany their loans. Rather, the IMF has established tough conditions for its credits (at least those in the higher credit tranches), and private banks have accepted these terms as the necessary (if not sufficient) condition for their own debt rescheduling. The net effect has been to insulate the banks from direct political involvement in less developed countries.

For a general discussion of bank lending to LDCs, see Charles Lipson, "The International Organization of Third World Debt," *International Organization* 35 (Autumn 1981), 603–631. David O. Beim's comments are in "Rescuing the LDCs," *Foreign Affairs* 55 (July 1977), 725.

mercial banks, who have lent billions of dollars to countries with balance-of-payments deficits, have welcomed and even encouraged . . . intervention by the IMF. It has helped government officials impose politically unpopular measures on their economies, and it has helped make bank loans more secure."[24]

If the IMF has moved aggressively to coordinate debt reschedulings, its sister institution, the World Bank, has moved more slowly and cautiously to work with private investors. Its main effort in this area is its cofinancing program: loan packages that include credits from both the World Bank and private lenders.

The exact terms of these loan packages are crucial. Of special concern to private investors is the relationship between a default on their portion of the loan and one on the World Bank portion. Deterrence is the issue. No state has ever defaulted on a loan from the World Bank, and none is likely to. The Bank, after all, is a vital source of concessionary aid and technical advice. Knowing this, private investors want any default against their portion of the loan to be considered *automatically* a default against the World Bank. "What bankers want," according to the *Economist*, "is cross-default clauses that force the World Bank to turn off its taps if the borrower fails to keep up payments to the commercial banks."[25] The World Bank, however, wants to control its own taps and its relations with troubled debtors. It has instituted cross-default clauses in its cofinancing program, but these give each creditor the option of calling a default in case the debtor fails to pay either portion of the loan.[26]

Despite these limitations, the cofinancing program does highlight an important point about modern investment protection. Private investors recognize the perils they face abroad, and they are willing to explore new institutional forms to minimize them. It is no secret that international financial institutions such as the IMF and the World Bank are uniquely situated to supervise foreign investments and, as I have noted, they have done so in many ways. Private investors understand the point and are seeking closer ties to these institutions and new forms of collaboration.

They do not always succeed. International financial institutions have their own operating procedures and insist on preserving their decision-making autonomy. Some of their information comes confidentially from member states and cannot easily be shared with private investors. So there are important limits to cooperation.

Still, as I have already shown, these institutions do collaborate with private investors and, in doing so, reduce the risks of investing abroad. As lenders themselves, the World Bank and the IMF have been directly involved in securing international debts. Less directly, each has added to the safety of direct investments as well. To take another example now on the public record, a 1965 IMF loan to Ceylon included a typical provision "to review the moratorium on [profit] remittances and take steps to improve the climate for the inflow of foreign official and private capital into Ceylon."[27] This clause was directed specifically at an expropriation dispute: the 1962 seizure of foreign-owned gas stations. The combination of multilateral and bilateral sanctions ultimately led to a settlement of that long-standing dispute.

As important as such sanctions and collaborative actions have been, they have one crucial limit. The same weighted voting that is so useful for enforcing international property rules also precludes their legitimation. Legitimation, I have argued, is increasingly the function of organizations such as the United Nations—with its universal membership and equal voting rights.[28]

Bilateral Policies

Having failed to certify the privileges of foreign investors in multilateral forums, the United States pursued the same policy bilaterally. Starting in the late 1940s, the State Department began to negotiate new treaties of "Friendship, Commerce, and Navigation" (FCN). These treaties had been used for over two hundred years to ensure reciprocal commercial rights, but their usage was now changing. With the signing of the General Agreement on Tariffs and Trade (GATT) in 1947, most trade questions could be dealt with multilaterally. Thus, the new bilateral FCN treaties could concentrate on other issues, particularly the rights and privileges of foreign investors. The State Department negotiators hoped that the treaties would stimulate international capital flows by creating a general regulatory framework for foreign commerce and investment. An explicit purpose of these treaties, according to Dean Acheson, was to "provide that the property of investors will not be expropriated without prompt, adequate, and effective compensation."[29]

This approach was consistent with earlier U.S. policy and with international legal rules, but as a diplomatic strategy it was deeply flawed. Where treaties would have been most valuable to investors, they could never be obtained. In Latin America and elsewhere, there was very little principled agreement with the United States over foreign investors' legal rights or host-states' obligations. Since World War II, fewer than two dozen FCN treaties have been signed, and not all of them have been ratified. None has been concluded since 1966.[30]

In 1982, after years of stalemate, the U.S. trade representative unveiled a prototype bilateral investment treaty. It was designed to protect and encourage capital investments and to address some of the new uncertainties surrounding them. It protects against entry barriers, performance requirements, foreign-exchange blockage, and unfair competition from state-owned enterprises.[31] It also provides for dispute resolution.

The problem, of course, is getting LDCs to sign. Few seem willing. Some states, it is true, have been willing to update the FCN treaties they signed earlier. Egypt, for instance, has already signed a bilateral investment treaty, and other negotiations are underway. But securing many such agreements on a truly worldwide basis will surely run into the same obstacles that the Friendship treaties did. This inability to negotiate important areas of agreement regarding foreign investment simply reconfirms its shaky legal basis.

The Pattern and Meaning of Postwar Expropriations

If the law protecting investments had withered, the investments themselves seemed secure enough until the late 1960s. According to one study of U.S. foreign affiliates, at least 170 companies were taken over between 1946 and 1973—but only 12 of these seizures came before 1961. A really sharp increase does not occur until the late 1960s (see table 7).

The same general conclusions hold for *all* foreign investments, not just U.S. companies. Available data do not cover the entire postwar period, but, according to a U.N. study, expropriations were twice as frequent in the 1970s as in the 1960s.[32]

The same pattern is evident—indeed, more pronounced—if one considers all types of forced divestment, not just expropriation. These include forced sales, contract renegotiations (when they effectively

TABLE 7

FOREIGN TAKEOVERS OF U.S. FIRMS,
1946–1973

Period	No. of expropriations	Expropriations per year
1946–1960	12	0.8
1961–1966	22	3.7
1967–1971	79	15.8
1972–1973	57	28.5

SOURCE: Robert G. Hawkins, Norman Mintz, and Michael Provissiero, *Governmental Takeovers Of U.S. Foreign Affiliates: A Postwar Profile* (Washington, D.C.: Center for Multinational Studies, Occasional Paper no. 7, 1975), table 1. The periodization is presented in Hawkins, Mintz, and Provissiero, without further breakdown of the data.

NOTE: The takeovers include expropriations, intervention/requisition, contract renegotiation, and forced sales. Expropriations were the most common by far, accounting for 103 out of the 170 cases.

transfer ownership), and other forms of seizure. Beginning in the late 1960s, these, too, increased sharply (see table 8).

These data have obvious limitations. Most importantly, they do not cover the size or relative importance of expropriations, either to the host countries or to the companies. Still, they do present a reasonably clear picture of investment security in the 1950s and 1960s, and of the substantial changes since then.

Several trends stand out. First, until the mid-1960s, most expropriations were directed broadly at all foreign investors. These sweeping expropriations, like those in Cuba, gave way to more selective expropriations directed at single industries or at particular foreign firms.[33] These more discriminating policies often entailed the expropriation of some firms and the simultaneous recruitment of others, as well as the cultivation of new relationships with foreign investors (licensing agreements and joint ventures, for instance). Second, this new selectivity was accompanied by a diversification of policy instruments in host states. The means of forcing divestment and regulating foreign firms have become more varied, better articulated, and more effectively institutionalized. Third, as the variety of expropriations and regulations grew, and as their selectivity became apparent, the social meaning of expropriation began to change. Investors,

TABLE 8

ACTS OF FORCED DIVESTMENT,
ALL FOREIGN FIRMS, 1960–1976

Period	% of total acts
1960–1967	19.3
1968–1972	37.7
1973–1976	43.0

SOURCE: Stephen J. Kobrin, "Foreign Enterprise and Forced Divestment in the LDCs," *International Organization* 34 (Winter 1980), table 1.

NOTE: Kobrin defines an act as "the forced divestment of any number of firms in a single industry in a single country in a given year" (ibid., 72). Except for petroleum, industries are defined at the 3-digit SIC level.

in particular, no longer saw expropriation as necessarily a threat to all investors. (That is why they seek *customized* political risk analysis. One size does not fit all.) Likewise, capital-exporting states no longer saw expropriations solely as elements of radical political and economic change or as a broader threat to international commerce. Nor did they necessarily signal a realignment in the U.S.-Soviet rivalry. Expropriations in the mid-1970s in Saudi Arabia and Venezuela made that clear. This shift in the meaning of expropriation went hand in hand with the development of adaptive corporate strategies. They were designed to maintain profitable relationships abroad even though some types of equity investment were unacceptable or too risky. Fourth, the number of expropriations and other forced divestments increased markedly after the mid-1960s. In some industries, most notably petroleum, these changes of ownership entailed far-reaching changes in the relationship between the companies and host countries and, indeed, transformed the very nature of the companies. In almost all industries, they increased the risks of investing abroad.

The expropriations of the 1970s are striking for at least two reasons. First, they came at a time when many countries were also encouraging foreign investments, abandoning import-substitution and other more nationalist policies, and actively seeking more exports and better integration into the world economy. Second, the takeovers continued to grow despite sophisticated countermeasures by investors. It is well known, for instance, that wholly owned foreign investments are generally the most vulnerable. Some three-quarters of all takeovers have involved wholly owned subsidiaries. Foreign investors have been minority owners in only 4 percent of the cases.[34] Recognizing this, firms have changed their ownership and financing when possible, and many simply do not make vulnerable investments.* Given this corporate adaptation, the figures showing increased expropriations actually understate the impact of host-country economic policies on both investment security and corporate structure.

Obviously, foreign investments were most secure in the 1940s and 1950s. The only important expropriations in the 1940s were those in East Europe and China, paralleling the bipolar military division. In the 1950s, there were several more—in Iran, Bolivia, Guatemala, Egypt, Argentina, Brazil, and Cuba—but still far fewer than anticipated in the U.N. speeches of the day. Some of these expropriations were quite minor, such as the expropriations of power companies by municipal governments in Argentina and Brazil, and still others were overturned by successor governments.

In most cases, the United States concentrated on adequate compensation for the former owners. Ever since the Mexican expropri-

---

*Most multinational firms began by establishing wholly owned foreign subsidiaries. In recent years, however, they have been more sensitive to nationalist concerns about foreign ownership. They have adapted their ownership policies accordingly. In some cases, this has meant joint ventures with state-owned enterprises; at other times, it has involved local private partners, usually those with special marketing expertise or political influence.

While the trend toward joint ownership is clear enough, there are still significant differences among firms. Companies with a few crucial proprietary processes, for instance, are more reluctant to take on partners than are firms with large numbers of proprietary products and processes. That is intuitively plausible. Partnerships threaten loss of control over production secrets, a danger that is critical if the company depends on only one or two. Coca-Cola executives who intend to remain employed do not gossip about Coke's formula at cocktail parties. Indeed, only a handful know the formula, and they would rather pull the company out of India than disclose it. And they did.

Even if one holds constant these differences in organizational tasks, structures, and processes, it still appears that American corporations are more likely to favor high equity positions and Japanese firms low equity ones. For a strategic approach to these ownership issues, see Thomas N. Gladwin and Ingo Walter, *Multinationals Under Fire: Lessons in the Management of Conflict* (New York: John Wiley, 1980), chap. 8. For a statistical argument that the differences in equity ownership are ultimately founded on cultural differences (without, incredibly, specifying the nature of these cultural differences), see A. G. Puxty, "Some Evidence Concerning Cultural Differentials in Ownership Policies of Overseas Subsidiaries," *Management International Review* 19 (1979), 39–47.

ations, the State Department had acknowledged a state's right to expropriate foreign property if it did so for a public purpose and paid sufficient compensation. At the same time, the United States maintained a narrow, ideologically bounded interpretation of "public purpose," at least until the late 1960s. It tried, without always succeeding, to stick to the traditional concepts of private property and eminent domain.

Grudgingly, the United States accepted foreign state ownership of infrastructure, like its own TVA electric system. It even acknowledged Egypt's nationalization of the Suez Canal. Robert Bowie, an international lawyer and a State Department official at the time, observes that "it was hard to fault the nationalization as such, especially since fair compensation seemed to be tendered."[35]

In contrast, the United States strenuously objected to state ownership of manufacturing and raw materials. Legally, its argument was based on a limited notion of public purpose; ideologically, it concentrated on the expanding economic role of the state and the threat of socialism. This latter concern was a diffuse one, confused even further by the imprecise image of infrastructure. Thus, even when the State Department acknowledged a foreign government's right to nationalize an electric company, there was still some underlying tension and frequently outright objections from conservatives in the United States. Nevertheless, the ideological focus was clearest, and the opposition to socialism most relevant, when nationalizations involved sectors that led the local process of capital accumulation.

In Bolivia, for example, the expropriation of three major tin companies turned into a prolonged dispute. Proper compensation was the most important and complex issue, largely because the Bolivian government made its compensation offer contingent upon the payment of back taxes. Of all major disputes in the 1950s, this appears to be the only one in which force was neither threatened or used. The major reason was that the U.S. government had concluded that Bolivia's leaders were nationalists, not Marxists. The Bolivian government had indicated its stance by immediately calling for new foreign investments and by beginning indemnification well before a final settlement was reached.[36]

The expropriations in Guatemala followed a bloodier course. The most striking events were the nationalization of vast tracts of United Fruit land, followed by a right-wing coup restoring the company's land.

Yet U.S. concern about Guatemalan social reforms had begun well before the expropriations. Indeed, it began even before Jacobo Arbenz (who seized the United Fruit land) was elected president. His predecessor, Juan Arevalo, had allowed local communists into the state bureaucracy and worked to alleviate his country's dependence on United Fruit. The company responded by cutting its banana exports over 80 percent between 1948 and 1952. The blow to the local economy was reinforced by W. R. Grace and Pan American Airlines, both of which stopped promoting tourism to Guatemala. Meanwhile, the World Bank began withholding loans, and the United States cut off military assistance. All these sanctions began *before* Arbenz even took office. The dispute climaxed, of course, when Arbenz expropriated over 200,000 acres of uncultivated United Fruit property and offered to pay less than $3 per acre over twenty-five years.

The affair deeply disturbed United States policymakers. Not only did compensation fall far short of traditional standards, the events seemed to have a larger meaning. Officials in the White House, the State Department, and the CIA interpreted the whole episode as conclusive evidence that Arbenz was a communist, or very nearly one. The threat, then, was not only to United Fruit, but to the United States' broader economic and security interests, as well.

As the State Department moved to isolate Guatemala diplomatically, the CIA was busy helping Colonel Castillo Armas overthrow Arbenz's government. Not one to forget a favor, Castillo Armas promptly reversed the earlier reforms, returned United Fruit's land, abolished new taxes on foreign investors, and became a staunch U.S. ally.[37]

The Guatemalan expropriations and those in Iran and Egypt were still relatively isolated events, rooted in the peculiar circumstances of those countries. Nevertheless, they anticipated broader changes in international political and economic relations. Each expropriation was sustained, at least temporarily, by popular nationalism. And, in each case, that nationalism was defined primarily in anti-imperial terms. Equally important, all the expropriations demonstrated the conjuncture between nationalism and the changing economic role of the state. In every case, the state was trying to play an active managerial role in the process of capital accumulation. Thus, the expropriations in Guatemala, Iran, and Egypt alluded to a much more widespread aspiration to turn foreign, private assets into national, public ones.

The United States rejected this twofold transformation in both principle and practice—with extraordinary success until the late 1960s. The United States defined the effective limits of expropriation and the corresponding obligations of expropriating states. Except for communist countries, very few foreign investments were seized without adequate compensation during this period. Almost all major violations were overturned. The small number of expropriations and their ultimate settlements indicate that, in spite of U.N. Resolutions on Permanent Sovereignty, the international regime for foreign investments was still tight and secure in practice until the late 1960s.

The main sources of that security were the threat of coherent economic sanctions and the U.S. capacity for local military intervention, either overt or covert. Economic sanctions were a serious deterrent (or, if need be, a punishment) for several reasons. The United States dominated the world economy (outside the communist bloc) and all of the related major issue-areas and institutions until Europe and Japan had fully rebuilt their economies. American-based multinational companies were frequently the chief sources of foreign capital and technology.

The Proliferation of Multinational Firms and Its Impact on Investment Security

Even the largest European and Japanese firms did not develop substantial worldwide investments until the late 1960s. In raw materials, for instance, Japanese firms did not go abroad in substantial numbers until the late 1960s, and the real spurt of growth did not come until the early 1970s. Japanese oil and mineral investments doubled between 1968 and 1972 and continued to accelerate after the oil crisis.[38] Overall, Japan's foreign investment is now divided evenly between advanced and less developed countries and has been growing at a rapid, and increasing, pace (see table 9).

European multinationals had some head start on the Japanese, but they, too, were well behind the Americans. American firms had a long history of establishing foreign subsidiaries and were well positioned to extend those networks after World War II. European firms, delayed by the damage of war and the burdens of reconstruction, did not match the postwar American pace until the mid-1960s. (The Japanese, with an ample supply of cheap labor and substantial export

TABLE 9

JAPANESE FOREIGN DIRECT INVESTMENTS IN
LESS DEVELOPED COUNTRIES, 1951–1980
(MILLIONS OF DOLLARS)

| | Annual Averages | | | |
	1951–1966	1967–1977	1978–1980	Cumulative
Asia	13.5	555.6	1167.3	9830
Latin America	21.0	338.3	803.7	6268
Middle East	13.8	114.5	260.0	2259
Africa	0.9	81.6	177.3	1445
TOTAL	49.2	1090.0	2408.3	19802

SOURCE: U.N. Centre on Transnational Corporations, *Transnational Corporations in World Development* (3d survey; New York: U.N., 1983), Annex Table II.11. Their data are from the Economic Planning Agency of Japan.

markets, did not begin establishing foreign subsidiaries until even later. See table 10.)

In the cases of both Japan and Germany, the growth of foreign investments in the late 1960s and early 1970s was spurred by their substantial balance-of-payments surpluses. The appreciation of their currencies (after the breakdown of Bretton Woods' pegged exchange rates) facilitated the purchase of foreign assets.[39]

TABLE 10

NUMBER OF FOREIGN MANUFACTURING SUBSIDIARIES ESTABLISHED
BY MULTINATIONAL CORPORATIONS BASED IN U.S., GREAT BRITAIN,
CONTINENTAL EUROPE, AND JAPAN, 1946–1970

| | Nationality and Number of Large Multinational Parent Firms | | | |
Period	U.S. (187 firms)	U.K. (49 firms)	Continental Europe (94 firms)	Japan (66 firms)
1946–1952	386	202	129	2
1953–1955	283	55	117	5
1956–1958	439	94	131	14
1959–1961	901	333	232	93
1962–1964	959	319	229	160
1965–1967	889	459	532	235
1968–1970	N.A.	729	1,030	532

SOURCE: Yoshi Tsurumi, *The Japanese Are Coming: A Multinational Interaction of Firms and Politics* (Cambridge, Mass.: Ballinger Publishing Company, 1976), table 1–1, p. 2.

TABLE 11

OUTWARD DIRECT INVESTMENT FLOWS
PERCENTAGE DISTRIBUTION AMONG 13 INDUSTRIAL COUNTRIES

	1961–1967	1968–1973	1974–1979
United States	61.1	45.8	29.3
United Kingdom	8.7	9.1	9.2
Germany	7.2	12.5	17.0
France	6.9	5.2	7.8
Netherlands	4.4	6.8	9.6
Canada	2.3	4.5	6.2
Japan	2.4	6.7	13.0
Others[a]	7.0	9.4	7.9

SOURCE: IMF-OECD Common Reporting System on Balance of Payments Statistics, as reported in OECD, *International Investment and Multinational Enterprises: Recent International Direct Investment Trends* (Paris: OECD, 1981), table 3, p. 40.

[a] "Others" are Australia, Belgium, Italy, Sweden, Spain, and Norway.

Through the mid-1960s, then, U.S. foreign investments were more important than all others combined. But this dominance was effectively challenged in the late 1960s as firms from other countries caught up in many areas of technology and began searching abroad for investment opportunities. The U.S. share of new international direct investment dropped off markedly as a result (see table 11). This increased participation by multinational firms from all advanced countries meant increased competition among them. And that gave host countries powerful new advantages in their bargaining with multinational firms.

The Brazilian figures are illustrative. As late as 1969, U.S. investments constituted nearly half of all foreign investments. That percentage dropped markedly over the next five years and continued to decline thereafter. Between 1969 and 1974, the stock of American investments in Brazil actually increased by 250 percent. But other investors set an even swifter pace. West German investments quadrupled and French investments expanded even faster. Japanese holdings increased tenfold during this five-year period (see table 12).

This pace continued throughout the 1970s and into the 1980s. In 1970, for example, Japan was investing some $20 million annually in Brazil. That figure rose to $250 million in 1974 and $409 million

TABLE 12

DIRECT FOREIGN INVESTMENT IN BRAZIL, 1969–1982

(MILLIONS OF DOLLARS)

Investor Country	1969		1974		1982	
	Total	Percent of total	Total	Percent of total	Total	Percent of total
United States	816	47.7%	2022	33.5%	6601	31.2%
West Germany	177	10.4	710	11.8	2932	13.8
Japan	55	3.2	598	9.9	1948	9.2
Switzerland	105	6.1	560	9.3	1993	9.4
Canada	168	9.8	401	6.7	977	4.7
United Kingdom	109	6.4	401	6.7	1087	5.1
France	35	2.1	242	4.0	726	3.4
Other	251	14.7	1093	18.1	4912	23.2
TOTAL	1710	100.0	6027	100.0	21176	100.0

SOURCES: 1982 figures are from Banco Central do Brasil, *Boletin Mensal* 19 (March 1983), tables on pp. 252–257; earlier figures from Stefan H. Robock, *Brazil: A Study in Development Progress* (Lexington, Mass.: D. C. Heath, 1975), 67. Reprinted by permission of the publisher. Robock's data are from the Banco Central do Brasil.

in 1979.[40] Germany's net investments were some $35 million in 1970, $165 million in 1974, and $229 million in 1976.[41]

The pattern is clear. Even though U.S. investments in Brazil remained larger than any other country's (in terms of both stock and flow), their *relative* importance had declined. Even more important than these average investment figures is the increasing competition at the margin—the availability of alternative sources of long-term capital. Other investors had cut deeply into a former U.S. preserve and had become significant competitors.

This change, together with greater international competition in many industries, has given host countries such as Brazil more leverage over the terms on which foreign capital can be invested.

Until these developments took hold in the late 1960s and early 1970s, American companies were well protected against expropriations and unilateral contract revisions. As long as less developed countries were oriented to external markets and dependent upon foreign capital, they had few alternatives. Most industries were not highly competitive at the international level. Moreover, for most countries, U.S. direct foreign investments were virtually the only source of long-term private capital from abroad, and the primary source of all foreign capital. Portfolio equity investments were not widespread, as they had been in the nineteenth century, and private loans were generally for short or medium terms, usually in the form of trade financing. In 1940, 66 percent of all long-term U.S. investments were direct investments;[42] in 1970, that figure had risen to 74.4 percent.[43] Still, New York's dominance as a financial center gave the United States additional leverage in protecting foreign direct investments, as did the U.S. position as a key export market.*

National Commitments to Investment Protection

What forged coherent sanctions out of these diverse economic relationships during the 1940s, 1950s, and 1960s? Probably it was the shared norms and perceptions of foreign investors and the

---

*Too little attention has been paid to the complex relationship between direct investments and international lending. For many LDCs, however, they represent alternative sources of long-term financing, each with their own advantages and disadvantages.

As a rule, countries have more control over the initial use of funds borrowed from commercial banks. But once debt servicing becomes difficult, they find themselves highly constrained. Not only do they face a coherent set of lenders, but they also face debt repayment schedules that are unrelated to the state of their economy.

Except in the case of highly organized oligopolies, direct investors are seldom as well organized as commercial lenders. This gives host states greater bargaining leverage over existing direct investments than they have over existing loans. Until recently, however, most host countries had little control over the terms on which direct investors entered their countries (even if they had considerable regulatory control once the investments were in place). The development of investment screening procedures over the past fifteen years has given host states more detailed control over the initial terms of these investments. Moreover, profit repatriation, unlike debt service, is closely related to the state of the local economy.

During the 1970s, the largest and fastest growing LDCs turned to the Eurocurrency financial markets as a principal source of long-term capital. For countries such as Brazil and Mexico, these bank credits permitted the rapid expansion of state-owned enterprises. Between 1975 and 1978, for instance, flows of external commercial debt to LDC public enterprises increased by 350 percent, reaching over $12 billion in 1978. According to one study of public-enterprise finance, "The expanded flows of international debt capital to public enterprises has been a prime factor in the buildup of large and potentially troublesome stocks of external debt in such countries as Brazil, Peru, Zaire, and Zambia through 1979 and Indonesia from 1972 to 1976."

These debt troubles have choked off the growth of many state enterprises and have fostered more attractive terms for direct investments in LDCs. The *Economist* makes that general point in an article on the Association of South-East Asian Nations (ASEAN): "Rivalry among southeast Asian countries for foreign investment is intensifying as the rich countries get stingier on aid and bankers grow leery of lending to

prevailing conception of anticommunism. By associating both social reforms and nationalism with the overthrow of world capitalism, anticommunist ideology integrated potentially divergent economic and security interests. It fused together various private investors and suggested an identity between their interests and public economic welfare. Finally, it implied that economic interests were parallel to compelling, if broad, notions of military security.

At a time when expropriations were rare, they were firmly associated with a poor environment for all foreign capital and, quite often, with an anti-American political alignment as well. As a result, even a single expropriation was often wrapped in rich symbolic meaning. It could evoke a variety of U.S. economic sanctions—public and private, individual and collective—which were severe because the U.S. economy was preeminent. These sanctions were remarkably effective through the mid-1960s. The threat of invoking them belonged to the U.S. government and U.S. multinational firms, both of which played vital roles in protecting foreign investments in most regions. Self-interest was surely their primary interest, but the geographic spread of U.S. investments ensured the United States a stake in most regions and most expropriation disputes.

The most important exception to this generalization was (and is) sub-Saharan Africa. American investments there, although increasing, remain below those of former colonial powers.[44] France and Britain still have substantial investments in their former colonies, and each has played a significant diplomatic role since independence. Yet their policies, and the scope of their involvement, have been as different as their colonial experiences.[45]

While Britain has carefully limited its involvement—part of its more general retrenchment from empire—France has cultivated extensive economic and military ties to its former dependencies. The

---

the third world." Along the same lines, a Mexican economist, asked to explain the relaxation of his country's foreign-investment rules, said that "allowing more foreign investment is the only way Mexico can get hold of large amounts of money without getting on its knees and begging to the banks."

This new receptivity to foreign direct investments is based on more than serious debt problems. For many countries, including those in ASEAN, it is part of a larger strategy of export-oriented development.

Malcolm Gillis, Glenn P. Jenkins, and Donald R. Lessard, "Public-Enterprise Finance: Toward a Synthesis," in *Public Enterprise in Less-Developed Countries*, Leroy P. Jones, ed. (Cambridge: Cambridge University Press, 1982), 262–263; *Economist*, April 2, 1983, p. 76; "Mexico Eases Foreign Investment Rules, But Investors Still May Be Hard to Attract," *Wall Street Journal*, June 20, 1983, p. 21.

different patterns of postcolonial involvement are clear, as Colin Legum states:

> Unlike the United Kingdom, France has tried to use its political ties with its former colonies, as well as its aid programs, to maintain and expand its sphere of economic interest. French post-colonial policy has been decidedly more aggressive—and adventurous—than the other former colonial powers. The United Kingdom, for example, has not made the least attempt to use the Commonwealth of Nations as an economic instrument.[46]

France, meanwhile, has fashioned a number of economic and military instruments to maintain its links to former colonies. Through a network of bilateral defense treaties, it has acquired the right to station troops or advisers in some twenty-five countries.[47] Aside from any specific intervention (such as the 1983 fighting in Chad), France has almost 10,000 regular soldiers on duty in central Africa, plus bases on two Indian Ocean islands and strike aircraft in Senegal and Gabon.[48] In addition, some 22,000 French civil servants are working in African governments and local schools under various technical agreements.[49]

The centerpiece of France's relationship with its former colonies is its economic aid, particularly its financial support for the CFA franc, the currency used in most of francophone Africa. Djibouti, for instance, receives some $38 million in bilateral development assistance from all sources; over $31 million of that comes from France.[50] Figures for other former French colonies such as the Ivory Coast are similar.[51] As part of this large and visible commitment, France has proved willing to intervene—economically, diplomatically, even militarily—in a variety of "trouble cases," including those where its economic interests were at stake.

France's efforts to maintain a diplomatic and economic presence contrast sharply with Britain's retreat after colonial independence. Compare a country such as Sierra Leone, a former British colony, with its francophone neighbors. In 1981, Sierra Leone received $40 million in bilateral aid. Britain, which provided $7 million, was only the third largest national donor.[52] In general, Britain's economic and military assistance has been strictly limited, and its willingness (and ability) to intervene militarily virtually nonexistent. Waldemar Nielsen, writing in 1969, observed that Britain was "steadily less encouraging" to its African investors and had "not offered to intervene militarily in troubled situations even where major economic interests were at stake."[53] As a result, in Britain's former colonies (but not in France's), foreign investments have been secured only by host-country policies and by the implicit but diffuse threat that maltreatment of existing investments would retard the flow of new capital and technology.

The absence of strong, coherent sanctions is one reason why expropriations have proliferated in Africa, especially in former British colonies. Although the expropriations there have generally been smaller and less important than those in the Middle East and Latin America, they have been much more numerous. According to United Nations data, expropriations in Africa reached forty-five per year in the 1970s, a rate far ahead of any other region and fully half the global total.[54]

These numbers reflect indigenization programs in several African states.[55] Zambia, Uganda, and the Sudan—all former British colonies—expropriated more than thirty foreign enterprises each. In fact, nearly half of all expropriations in the region affected British investors. Other ex-colonials make up most of the remainder. The largest expropriation was Zaire's takeover of the Belgian copper firm, Union Minière du Haute Katanga, an investment worth over $500 million. But the British experience stands out because it recurs in so many former colonies and because it differs so markedly from that of the other major colonial power, the French. Of all expropriations in Africa south of the Sahara, only 5 percent affected French companies.* Worldwide, over half the countries that have expropriated thirty-one or more foreign investments were former British colonies; none were French.[56]

The same point comes through in Stephen Kobrin and Robert Hawkins's data on expropriation programs. Of the seventeen states with more than ten "acts" of forced divestment each, only Morocco and Algeria are former French colonies. Most of the others are former British and Portuguese colonies.[57]

A comprehensive explanation of this pattern would have to analyze colonization and decolonization procedures, investment patterns, and indigenous political developments. Still, the rapid withdrawal of British political and military involvement was an important contributing factor.

---

*U.S. investors were involved in 12 percent of the cases.

Despite the uneven protection given foreign investments in black-ruled Africa and other former colonial areas, it was not these new states that ultimately posed the greatest challenge to foreign capital. It was the old states of Latin America. And nowhere was U.S. economic power to deter expropriations more apparent. Access to foreign capital, technology, and organizational skills were largely limited to U.S. sources. Until the late 1960s, Latin Americans had relatively few opportunities to diversify their economic relations among industrial nations or even, in many cases, among competing U.S. companies.[58] Until 1955, new, non-U.S. foreign investments were negligible. Through the mid-1960s, they represented less than one-third of all new foreign capital.[59] The lack of diversity in Latin American economic relations, which is simply another index of U.S. dominance, ensured that anti-expropriation sanctions would be severe *because they were coherent.*

Industrial Structure and Private Sanctions

One source of coherent sanctions was the oligopoly structure of multinational industries. Strong oligopolies could ensure that individual firms would not pursue their most immediate and narrow goals in ways that undermined collective corporate interests. Certainly one overriding collective interest has always been a politically secure environment for foreign capital.

The most conspicuous example of oligopoly sanctions comes not from Latin America, but from the Middle East. In May 1951, after months of fruitless negotiations, Iranian Premier Mossadegh and his National Front government nationalized the Anglo-Iranian Oil Company (AIOC). The British government responded swiftly and decisively. They blocked Iran's bank accounts in London (plus ça change) while the Royal Air Force compelled at least one Panamanian ship to surrender its Iranian oil at Aden.[60] Still, as Dankwart Rustow has observed, the oil companies' most effective weapon in this showdown "was not the colonial courts, or warplanes buzzing overhead, or financial retaliation in London, but their network of Middle Eastern concessions."[61] The seven major oil companies, who stood together in their opposition to nationalization, controlled 98 percent of world oil trade and could easily meet their needs from reserves in Saudi Arabia, Kuwait, and Iraq.[62]

Their boycott of Iran was total, and it was devastatingly effective. Iran did not have the technicians to operate the nationalized facilities, the refineries to crack the crude oil, the tankers to ship it, or the marketing facilities to dispose of it.[63] In 1952 and 1953, Iran barely managed to sell 3 percent of what it had produced before national-ization.[64]

The major U.S. oil companies—Exxon, Mobil, Gulf, Texaco, and Standard of California—stood firm alongside the British. They were eager to share in Iran's oil reserves, but they (and the U.S. govern-ment) were unwilling to break the boycott to win their goals. They were, in fact, able to gain an important foothold in Iran after the CIA and the British had overthrown Mossadegh and installed Shah Mo-hammed Pahlavi.*

---

*The coup against Mossadegh was coordinated by Kermit Roosevelt of the CIA. "I owe my throne to God, my people, my army—and to you!" the Shah told him with good reason (but not necessarily in the proper order).

The installation of the Shah on the Peacock throne did not, however, return the Anglo-Iranian Oil Company to its former preeminence. The Americans had played too big a role to forgo the spoils entirely. True, AIOC was compensated for its troubles, and its owners were given the majority position in the new concession arrangement. But the big American producing firms also came in.

The whole episode—nationalization, boycott, coup, and new concession agree-ment—set in motion some important changes in the production and distribution of Middle Eastern oil. First, the new consortium included a few independent U.S. oil companies in a minor role alongside the big firms. The independents thus got their first taste of cheap and highly profitable Middle Eastern crude. The major firms privately considered the inclusion of independents mere window dressing—a sop to U.S. an-titrust laws and the sentiments behind them—but it had significant long-term effects. Seeing firsthand the extraordinary profitability of Persian Gulf production, they began exploring for more and so weakened the majors' once-exclusive hold on international oil production and distribution.

Second, the consortium won complete control over the foreign sales of Iranian oil— a remarkable rollback of Iran's hopes for a national oil company. However, Iran did achieve 50–50 profit sharing, giving it parity with other Persian Gulf states and con-firming the trend that Venezuela had begun in 1948. Equally important in the long run, the concession agreement provided for the firms' eventual relinquishment of some producing territories. This technique, begun in Saudi Arabia and extended in 1955 and 1961 by Libya, was to prove crucial. It meant that key producing countries could later invite bidding by U.S. independent firms and European state companies, eager to find rich fields abroad. That, together with the tightening of global supplies and the rise of industrial demand, was to tip the scales toward the producing countries in the early 1970s.

L. P. Elwell-Sutton, *Persian Oil: A Study in Power Politics* (London: Lawrence and Wishart, 1955), 321–327; Henry Cattan, *The Evolution of Oil Concessions in the Middle East and North Africa* (Dobbs Ferry, N.Y.: Oceana Publications, 1967), 11–13; Robert Stobaugh and Daniel Yergin, eds., *Energy Future* (3d ed.; New York: Vintage Books, 1983), 25; Frank C. Waddams, *The Libyan Oil Industry* (Baltimore: Johns Hopkins Press, 1980), 32–33, 66; Kermit Roosevelt, *Countercoup: The Struggle for Control of Iran* (New York: McGraw-Hill, 1979), 199, 201.

What is crucial here is that the major oil companies—the Seven Sisters—were able to act collectively even though their most immediate and narrow interests were not identical. The companies' ability to enforce private, collective sanctions was directly related to their small numbers. Had there been many more multinational firms wanting more crude oil (as there were in the 1960s and 1970s), the pressures to break ranks would have been overwhelming.

This logic is demonstrated in the renegotiation of oil concessions. As more and more companies searched for oil supplies, the bargaining position of producing countries naturally improved. To compete with the established international oil companies, U.S. "independents" and European state-owned firms had to offer better terms, including wider participation for host governments. This process foreshadowed the more important expropriations and forced renegotiations that came a decade later. Most significantly, it was the proliferation of multinational oil firms that gave producer states continued access to international markets, *even after expropriation*. According to the *Petroleum Economist*,

> Attempts at nationalization over the years were generally not successful unless and until agreement was reached with the concessionary companies to bring the state's activities within the framework of the existing world system. This was due not only to the oil companies' control of world markets but also to the lack of technical and managerial expertise in the exporting countries. Without such agreement, the state-operated industries invariably declined.[65]

The rising position of independent companies was a critical transitional stage in the transformation of the world oil industry. It undermined the security of the majors' investments and facilitated the transfer of control to producing countries' national oil companies. As Peter Cowhey observes:

> Numerous new entrants—large and small domestic firms from the United States, state-supported firms from Europe and Japan—made the skills of the majors more dispensable, while national oil companies (NOCs) of oil-exporting nations grew in technical competence and could reasonably hope to direct subcontractors on projects. . . . Thus the newcomers gave the OPEC nations more latitude in selecting commercial partners for selling their oil.[66]

They used this new latitude to develop their embryonic national oil companies into major producers, revising earlier contracts with concessionaires and buying out their local holdings. (The former concessionaires often stayed on as managers and as oil purchasers.) True, the national companies were still not integrated producers and marketers like the majors and larger independents. But Kuwait has already taken important steps in that direction and others are likely to follow. Until now, most national companies have been content to diversify their sales and remain at home. But this alone represents a remarkable and profound change in world oil relationships.

The scale of this transformation can be shown by looking at the ownership and production of crude oil. In the 1950s, as I have already noted, the Seven Sisters controlled virtually all oil produced outside North America and the communist block. By the early 1970s, their percentage of ownership had declined to three-fifths, with independents controlling the rest. Producing countries still owned no crude, but they were now in a better bargaining position and had increased their share of the revenues.

By 1979, these relationships had changed dramatically, the result of massive nationalizations throughout OPEC. Within a decade, the majors' share of crude ownership had dropped from 61 percent to 25 percent. The independents' share had slipped from 33 percent to 20 percent. Whose share rose? OPEC state oil companies. By the end of the 1970s, they owned over half of all international crude supplies, which they marketed through the old multinationals or through new government-to-government deals.[67]

The private companies, and especially the majors, were transfigured. From World War I until the late 1960s, they were fully integrated multinationals. In the mid-1970s they were privileged buyers of OPEC crude, taking large quantities at a slight discount. By the end of the decade, they saw themselves as suppliers of exploration services and production technology, management consulting, transportation, refining, and marketing. All are profitable, but the change in the structure of these giant organizations is striking.[68] So was its rapidity. As late as the mid-1970s, Japan was buying fully half its oil from the major companies. By 1980, it was getting less than 10 percent from them.[69]

Given the scale of oil investments and the prominence of the companies, this transformation has had a broad impact on international property relationships more generally.* To begin with, it showed that host countries could achieve effective control over their concessions, contracts, and foreign investments, regardless of prior arrangements. Not much was left of international minimum standards. Second, it showed that demands for national control over resources and foreign capital were not limited to leftist regimes but rather included all sorts of governments, ranging from narrowly based monarchies to populist democracies. Third, it demonstrated that international firms were willing to adapt to the new circumstances—usually by taking non-equity or minority positions—and could often do so profitably. Finally, it marked a dramatic change in the character of expropriation disputes. The nationalization programs in Venezuela and Saudi Arabia were even larger than the one Mossadegh had attempted in Iran.[70] The terms offered were not much different either. But they went smoothly. Coherent resistance would surely have been impossible, the firms were willing and able to adapt, and the countries held out the olive branch of continuing commercial relationships.

Since the vast changes in world oil stemmed, in no small part, from the international expansion of independent firms, it is important to understand why they went abroad in such numbers. Some of the reasons are historically contingent: the shift from coal to petroleum as the basic industrial fuel, the difficulty of finding new reserves in the United States, a steady increase in demand for oil throughout the industrial world, and the relative security for foreign operations provided by the United States.

Equally important were changes at the organizational level. Communications and transportation costs were decreasing; the difficulties of sustaining international operations were declining. Moreover, as the oil industry matured, it followed a familiar path of increasing

---

*Oil investments have long been the most prominent form of foreign direct investments. Before the nationalization programs of the early 1970s, petroleum accounted for about one-third of both the stock and flow of foreign direct investment in LDCs. Well into the late 1970s, the potential profitability of new discoveries kept exploration rates high despite the uncertainty of future ownership.

In recent years, manufacturing investments have outpaced those in natural resources. They now exceed petroleum investments in both LDCs and advanced countries.

It should be noted, however, that petroleum investments were long the most prominent and that manufacturing investments cover a bewildering variety of industries, none individually as significant as oil.

World Bank, *Private Direct Foreign Investment in Developing Countries,* Staff Working Paper no. 348, prepared by K. Billerbeck and Y. Yasugi (Washington, D.C.: World Bank, 1979), table SI.8, p. 73; Ned G. Howenstine, "Growth of U.S. Multinational

competition. According to Raymond Vernon, as industries grow older, their products, processes, and marketing arrangements become more familiar, less mystifying. Unless brand loyalty is high or capital costs excessive, new companies will begin competing with older ones.[71]

This broad pattern clearly fits the oil industry. Once, only a few "international majors" had the capacity to operate globally. Their large scale, long experience, and geographical diversification remain important advantages, but smaller independents are now able to compete. They have learned how to find oil in remote deserts and Arctic oceans, to produce and transport it in quantity, and to market the finished products.

The routinization of knowledge and the spread of competition are continuing processes that erode tight oligopolies. Oil is hardly unique. Although many factors obstruct new competitors—increasing capital requirements in some industries, for example—most basic industries have grown more competitive. This is especially true at the international level now that large European and Japanese firms have developed global strategies.

This change in industrial structure can be measured in several ways, but all measures focus on the *number* of firms in an industry and their relative *market shares*. Vernon, for example, has shown steadily increasing international competition in the production of eight basic commodities. Using the Herfindahl index of market concentration,* he found declining ratios of concentration in each industry he studied (see figure 1).

This trend toward weaker oligopolies in basic industries directly affects investment security. In the absence of strong institutional arrangements (which are quite unusual), more competition weakens

---

Companies, 1966–77," *Survey of Current Business* 62 (April 1982), table 5, p. 39. The Commerce Department's more recent data on U.S. petroleum investment is not included in its public tables ("Suppressed to avoid disclosure of data of individual companies"). See Obie G. Whichard, "U.S. Direct Investment Abroad in 1981," *Survey of Current Business* 62 (August 1982), 11–29.

*The Herfindahl index measures industry concentration by adding the squares of each firm's market shares.

$$H = \Sigma S_i^2, \text{ where } S_i \text{ is the market share}$$
$$\text{of the } i^{th} \text{ firm.}$$

For example, if one company controlled 75 percent of the market and another firm the remaining 25 percent, the index would be $(.75)^2 + (.25)^2 = .625$. If four companies each controlled 25 percent of the market, the Herfindahl index would be .25.

the possibilities of collusion and so undermines private sanctions.*
With investors unable to coordinate their response, host governments
can expropriate equity or renegotiate contracts without facing a unified boycott (or even a boycott by investors in the affected industry).
In contrast, when a few companies control global production in a
particular sector, they can usually deter expropriation by threatening
collective sanctions. Or, as the Seven Sisters did in Iran, they can
punish a transgression. Such self-reliant strategies can effectively
complement home-states' diplomacy and coercion.

To summarize, the threat of coherent, private economic sanctions
can help preserve a tight global regime for foreign investment. Weaker
oligopoly structures, which lack the capacity for private sanctions,
can speed the dissolution of universal anti-expropriation rules by
encouraging individual acts of short-run aggrandizement.

Maintaining the Regime:
The Array of Sanctions

Taken together, the policies of the U.S. government,
U.S.-based multinationals, and (to a lesser extent) the World Bank
assured that potential expropriations faced overpowering opposition
until the late 1960s. To expropriate under these circumstances was
to risk all, since it implied an isolation from international commercial
and financial markets and self-reliance for new industrial capital and
technology. The threat of coherent, severe sanctions was a major
reason why, despite widespread and pronounced declarations about
Permanent Sovereignty over Natural Resources, there were so few
expropriations until the late 1960s. Likewise, two major elements in

---

*American antitrust laws further inhibit the development of collective action. The
issue has come up most often with respect to Middle Eastern oil consortia. Indeed,
the Justice Department filed antitrust suits against Exxon, Standard of California,
Texaco, Mobil, and Gulf in 1952. These cases were sharply limited by Presidents
Truman and Eisenhower on national security grounds, most notably the ongoing
conflict with Mossadegh in Iran.

The only sector with a well-institutionalized (and legal) capacity to coordinate in
"trouble cases" is international banking. The sources of this unusual capacity are
discussed in chapter 5.

In the oil case, the antitrust issues are most thoroughly treated in Burton I. Kaufman,
The Oil Cartel Case: A Documentary Study of Antitrust Activity in the Cold War Era (Westport,
Conn.: Greenwood Press, 1978); and Kaufman, *Trade and Aid: Eisenhower's Foreign
Economic Policy, 1953–1961* (Baltimore: Johns Hopkins Press, 1982), chap. 5.

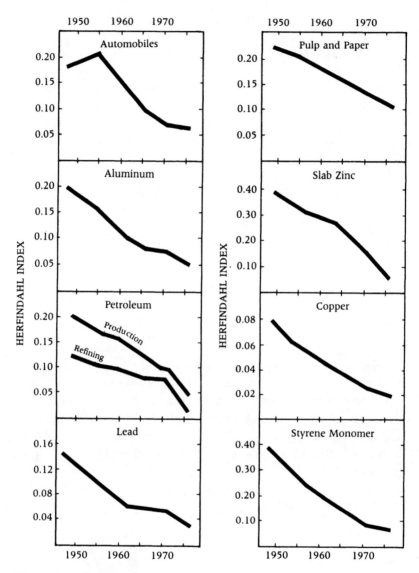

Figure 1. Herfindahl Index of Concentration of World Production in Eight Commodities, 1950–1975

SOURCE: Raymond Vernon, *Storm over Multinationals: The Real Issues* (Cambridge, Mass.: Harvard University Press, 1977), 81.

recent expropriations and contract renegotiations have been the slow diffusion of national control over international markets and the slackening of international oligopolies in a number of sectors critical to industrialization.

These arguments certainly do not imply that force has had no role in protecting investments since World War II. The interventions in Guatemala, Iran, and elsewhere suggest otherwise. Yet the coup against Mossadegh also suggests that the character of interventionary force has changed considerably since the days when Britain enforced the rules.

Through the first quarter of the twentieth century, it was sea power that furnished military protection for most foreign investments in underdeveloped countries. Direct investments were generally located in coastal enclaves or port cities—or, like railroads, they depended on a coastal terminus. These sites were well covered by British (and sometimes French) naval forces. Loan portfolios posed only slightly more complex issues of military protection. They were secured by collateral that could be seized if necessary. Moreover, local customs-houses, which were vital sources of government revenues, were always potential hostages to interventionary force.

Even if one (mistakenly) assumes that advanced capitalist states are still willing to use their navies and marines so freely, neither is as well suited to protecting foreign investments as it once was. Besides the obvious rise of indigenous opposition, there is the changing character of the investments themselves. Geographic and economic enclaves have declined since the days of the nitrate producers. There are still export platforms—indeed, they have become more important recently—but most investments are imbedded in the host economy. That includes most exporters.

One indication of this trend is the steady rise in foreign manufacturing and service investments throughout the Third World, with much of the production destined for local or regional markets. In 1950, the United States had less than $850 million in LDC manufacturing facilities. By 1981, it had over $19 billion, more than any other type of investment and growing at more than 10 percent annually.[72] Nor is this growth limited to U.S. companies. European and Japanese companies have increased their manufacturing investments substantially,[73] as have the new multinationals based in less developed countries.[74]

As foreign investments such as these are integrated into the local economy, their security comes to depend not only on civil order but also on the character of government regulation and control. This regulation ranges from restrictions on ownership, profit remittances, and local acquisitions to demand for local managers and local production.

These regulations, like the changing character of expropriation itself, reveal the increasing role of less developed states in managing their own foreign and domestic economic activity. Customary international law and nineteenth-century enforcement were never designed to handle this issue. It was presumed that investors' rights would be preserved by the normal processes of local laissez-faire governments. Expropriations were assumed to be aberrations, attributable to local disorder or isolated executive decrees. According to Burns Weston, these were well-grounded assumptions:

> While not rare during the approximately one hundred year period preceding World War I, neither were foreign-wealth deprivations then common. . . . The reason is clear. This was a century of relative harmony in which the principal powers enjoyed a virtual universal adherence to *laissez-faire* notions of common justice and fair dealing, to a credo of individualistic capitalism that was transmuted into broad patterns of acceptable behavior beyond the confines of their own economies to far-flung empires and commonwealths. . . . Indeed, these notions . . . could be established and maintained even in the new nations of Latin America, embodied as these notions were in their own fundamental, Western European derived laws. Far from representing a primal assault upon fundamental beliefs, the wealth deprivations imposed in Latin America and elsewhere during these years were the result largely of unpremeditated, though chronic, internal disorder and instability.[75]

The failure of these assumptions after World War I is nicely summarized by a parallel semantic development: "expropriations" came to be called "nationalizations." This terminology suggests that even single acts of expropriation, such as the IPC (Exxon) case in Peru, are rooted in broad conceptions of the social character of property rights. To prevent expropriations under these circumstances is to empower a government with a different ideology.

Since economic nationalism is now the issue, the United States has found it not only cheaper but also more effective to use covert (rather than overt) force, if force is to be used at all. When truly covert, it even permits the newly empowered governments to consolidate mass support through nationalist appeals.

Yet as a means of preserving foreign investors' privileges, even this strategy is sharply limited by the strength and character of economic nationalism. A wide variety of governments—of all ideological hues and with differing bases of domestic social support—now pursue state-led industrialization strategies. They have demanded, and gotten, ownership of their own natural resources regardless of the prior status of foreign firms.

This point is most vividly illustrated by OPEC's leadership in the 1970s. It was then that OPEC established its control over world oil markets, and its members took control of their own reserves and production facilities. The leadership, it will be recalled, came from Saudi Arabia and the Shah's Iran. Both were staunch anticommunists with narrow class bases, but neither hesitated to control petroleum prices or to seize foreign oil facilities.

In the process they transformed the issue of expropriation. What was once a symbolic, highly charged issue—marked by uncompromising appeals to sovereign rights and legal obligations—became rather a matter of dividing and preserving economic gains. Most current expropriations (and most other restrictions directed at foreign firms) are *not* part of a broader effort to radically reorient domestic society. Their rationale is more narrowly economic, giving the host state a bigger share of locally generated profits and more control over investment decisions and operating strategies. Instead of a generalized assault on foreign capital, they have become a way of transferring ownership and control in selected cases.

The changed meaning of expropriation is reflected in the *form* it now takes. Mass expropriations, covering whole industries and accompanied by powerful nationalist appeals, have given way to more selective takings.* Between 1946 and 1966, three-fifths of all expropriations involved entire industries dominated by foreign firms. That percentage falls off rapidly during the late 1960s. By 1972–1973 it had dropped to around one-fourth of all expropriations. During the same period the proportion of *selective* expropriations rose. (This category covers the takeover of specific foreign firms, either in one industry or in several, while leaving other foreign firms untouched.) Between 1946 and 1966, such selective takeovers accounted for less than one-third of all expropriations. Since then, however, more than half of all expropriations have covered only selected firms.[76]

These figures indicate that expropriations are becoming more se-

---

*Stephen J. Kobrin, "Foreign Enterprise and Forced Divestment in the LDCs," *International Organization* 34 (Winter 1980), 86.

While expropriations have become more selective, they are still blunt instruments, too clumsy for many purposes and not always the best means of guaranteeing future revenues. They are being replaced, especially in the manufacturing and service sectors, as LDCs develop more effective regulatory institutions and more complex policy instruments (such as investment screening).

lective and complex. Most are *not* attempts to rid a country of all foreign firms, or even the largest ones. More often they are a way of changing the terms on which international business is conducted. Expropriated companies are frequently asked to remain in some capacity, providing management advice or marketing connections. Although these arrangements are generally less profitable than secure ownership, they are still valuable opportunities. And, given the choice between exit or adaptation, nearly all expropriated companies are choosing to adapt.

Thus expropriations are no longer the stark events they once were. They no longer attack all foreign companies, or even all those in a particular industry. In most cases, especially the major expropriations of oil producers, they are not accompanied by sharp nationalist rhetoric or invectives against foreign exploitation. Nor are they generally a part of a strategy of radical social change. In broad terms, they are part of a state-led push toward industrialization, combining national planning, state-owned enterprises, local capital, and foreign investment.* In this context, expropriations take on a tactical meaning— they are a way of controlling investments in critical sectors and directing surpluses to chosen targets. Moreover, the expropriations are typically part of a continuum of state economic activity, ranging from regulation to joint ownership to outright management of some projects. The shadings of difference are sometimes fine, offering multiple opportunities—and pitfalls—to multinational firms.

As the character of expropriation changes, so does its diplomatic handling. It slips out of the realm of bilateral confrontation, economic warfare, and military intervention. If the transfer of ownership is accompanied by some counteroffer—perhaps a new marketing agreement plus partial compensation—then most investors would prefer to avoid diplomatic intervention. A strong statement from the ambassador might evoke a strong nationalist response, escalating the dispute and undermining future business opportunities. While it might lead to more compensation, it is also a risky course, one that most companies shun until all else fails. Unless the expropriation is con-

---

*This strategy did, however, involve an important shift in the composition of capital inflows—from direct foreign investments to loans (which might be called "indirect investments"). As long as major LDCs such as Brazil and Mexico could borrow freely, they favored the importation of nonequity capital and its use in parastatal enterprises. See Jeff Frieden, "Third World Indebted Industrialization: International Finance and State Capitalism in Mexico, Brazil, Algeria, and South Korea," *International Organization* 35 (Summer 1981), 407–431.

sidered part of a generalized attack on foreign capital, most investors would prefer quiet business negotiations, sometimes accompanied by low-key commercial diplomacy. As the clashing symbols recede, so do the calls for the marines. Indeed, as multinational firms take a more self-reliant approach to political risk, they rarely try to raise investment disputes to the intergovernmental level.

Nationalist Challenges, Corporate Responses

The assertion of national economic power, frequently including the expropriation of some foreign investments and the extensive regulation of others, now appeals to even the most retrograde governments. This developmental role is a common theme among otherwise diverse governments. It goes well beyond the provision of economic infrastructure, investment incentives, and entrepreneurial guidance. The state is typically a comprehensive regulator and developmental planner, and may well act as banker and entrepreneur as well.[77]

It is a self-consciously interventionist role, although one that often relies on private capital (both foreign and domestic) as the chief engine of growth.* James Petras has called this *state capitalism* because

---

*In his studies of Brazil, Peter Evans has argued that state entrepreneurship can effectively complement foreign direct investment and local private capital. The state can provide cheap industrial inputs, for instance, and stabilize the investment climate through joint ventures with foreign firms. These ideas are crystalized in his concept of a Triple Alliance between the state, local capitalists, and foreign firms.

Evans's argument is a significant contribution to understanding state intervention in LDC economies and a useful corrective to the idea that such intervention is necessarily opposed to the interests of foreign investors.

Even so, the argument is not fully developed or properly circumscribed. Two important points have either been omitted or unnecessarily depreciated. First, state-owned enterprises can substitute for privately owned companies, not just complement them. Indeed, most expropriated foreign properties have been transferred to state firms. Moreover, as I have argued, the increased capacities of state-owned firms to handle both production and distribution have inevitably weakened the bargaining position of foreign firms. They have undoubtedly contributed to forced divestments. A more complex argument would seek to differentiate instances of substitution and complementarity between state-owned firms and MNCs.

Second, although Evans is himself attentive to historical developments, his basic argument is curiously ahistorical. It implies what is most problematic: that there is a stable arrangement among the partners in the Triple Alliance. One could cite many potential sources of instability. The rapid rise of state-owned firms in the 1970s, for example, depended on the availability of external financing. Brazil, like other newly industrializing countries, had no difficulty raising the needed capital in international financial markets. With the spread of debt crises in the 1980s, that has changed

it relies on an expansive state apparatus to foster industrial market relations. Although a few Third World states tried *dirigiste* policies in the past—Turkey did in the 1930s, as I noted in a previous chapter—they are now a much more widespread phenomenon:

> What is . . . different today from the earlier period is the extent to which state capitalism has become an increasingly commonplace form of rule. . . . What in an earlier period (in Turkey, Mexico, and Bolivia) appeared as specific socio-political formations reflecting national peculiarities and revolutionary impulses [have] recently become the dominant modes of nationalist capitalist development in the Third World.[78]

It is not my purpose here to analyze the countless ways in which state capitalism and economic nationalism can affect the multinational corporation, or the many distinct expressions of economic nationalism among less developed states. It should be clear, however, that nationalizations and state regulations are not usually intended to exclude foreign capital. Rather, the demand for management expertise, technical skills, and access to foreign markets frequently translates into a demand for corporate services.

The key is agreement on compensation and on future ties between the host state and foreign firms. To keep its links to foreign capital and technical resources, the expropriating country must not appear arbitrary or careless about foreign property rights.

This suggests a residual role for international law. As attenuated as it is, it still reinforces the values of due process and mutually approved compensation. If compensation standards have shifted markedly, they still have not vanished entirely. Not even the U.N. Resolutions on Permanent Sovereignty have completely abandoned them.

What does compensation mean in practice? At one time it meant restitution or full compensation. Now, after widespread expropriations, it generally means good faith negotiations followed by mutually

dramatically. I am *not* arguing here that the Triple Alliance is fragile or unstable, merely that its durability is an open question not adequately analyzed. What is missing is a historically situated and dynamic account of the triangular relationship between local capital, foreign investors, and peripheral states.

See Peter Evans, *Dependent Development: The Alliance of Multinational, State, and Local Capital in Brazil* (Princeton, N.J.: Princeton University Press, 1979); John R. Freeman, "State Entrepreneurship and Dependent Development," *American Journal of Political Science* 26 (February 1982), esp. 95.

approved payments. If foreign firms are asked to stay on in some profitable capacity—managing exploration, for instance, and sharing production at preferential rates—then the compensation offered may be quite low, even nominal. What is essential to future relations is often not the amount of compensation but mutual agreement on its acceptability.

Such agreements seldom vanquish the fears of foreign companies, but they can reduce them considerably. Even if compensation falls below book value (as it usually does now), many companies want to continue local operations, or even expand them.

The expropriated companies, like French ex-colonials, often keep close ties to their old properties. They might sign long-term contracts to transport and market the newly nationalized production. Or they might stay on to manage their old facilities, or to help modernize them. Arrangements such as these can be quite lucrative, and they are now commonplace. They have proliferated, especially in the Middle East.[79]

In Latin America, the most prominent examples followed Venezuela's large-scale oil nationalizations of the mid-1970s. "The companies," according to George Philip, "were willing to be nationalized and simply sought satisfactory terms."[80] The relevant terms involved not only payments for expropriated assets but also continued involvement in Venezuelan oil production.*

Crude supplies were tight at the time, and the multinationals still wanted access to Venezuelan reserves. By the same token, Venezuela

*There is often a tight relationship between the terms of nationalization and the companies' later involvement in the host country. George Philip's discussion of Venezuelan oil offers direct evidence on this point. Speaking of the Venezuelan national oil company, Petrovén, he says:

Petrovén's various investment plans implied a need, in the short-term at least, to rely more heavily upon foreign expertise than had earlier been anticipated. As part of the original nationalization agreement, the foreign oil companies contracted to supply technical services to the various operating companies which took over from them in return for a per barrel fee plus the actual cost of supplying the technical specialists. The per barrel fee—around $0.16 for Shell and $0.19 for Jersey Standard [Exxon]—was criticized within Venezuela for being too high and it was widely believed that a somewhat inflated technical services fee was a *quid pro quo* for company acceptance of nationalization terms which provided compensation only at book value. Nevertheless, the technical experts provided by the companies were undoubtedly needed and demand for these proved to be greater than expected.

George Philip, *Oil and Politics in Latin America: Nationalist Movements and State Companies* (Cambridge: Cambridge University Press, 1982), 474–475.

needed secure access to foreign markets and a reliable cash flow. Thus, in March 1975, when Venezuela drafted its nationalization law, Article V enabled the government (with congressional approval) to contract with private companies to provide various oil services.[81] The article was controversial among radical nationalists but, as one leader of the ruling Acción Democrática party observed, "Our greatest political problem is management capacity."[82] Recognizing this crucial limitation, Venezuela's oil minister offered this telling defense of his country's nationalization policies: "I consider that it is much better for the country not to have [nationalized] 'heroically' because that would not have allowed the oil industry, when nationalized, to continue to bring in the income which the country requires for its development plans."[83]

The multinationals wanted the continued flow of crude; Venezuela needed to produce and sell it. The result was a marriage of convenience. The expropriated firms continued to transport and market Venezuelan oil and to provide management and technical services to the state-owned companies.

Just how close these postnationalization ties were is revealed in one remarkable statistic. During the first three months of 1976, Venezuela produced 1.7 million barrels of petroleum per day and sold 1.6 million to the expropriated companies.[84] This dominance was not to last, however, as Venezuela slowly found new markets and a wider range of customers. Sales to nontraditional customers have risen steadily: from 26 percent in 1977 to 42 percent in 1979 to around 60 percent in 1983.[85]

The fact that foreign companies now maintain economic ties to the host country after their investments have been nationalized is a genuinely novel feature of forced divestments in the 1970s and 1980s. It contrasts sharply with the bitter nationalization struggles of the past, which always signaled a clear break between the host country and the expropriated firm (and often a break with *all* foreign firms).

The novelty and importance of these continuing ties, however, has obscured another trend: the slow erosion of the foreign firms' subsequent position. Venezuela's cultivation of new customers is a common pattern. Saudi Arabia, for instance, relied on the four Aramco partners (Exxon, Texaco, Standard of California, and Mobil) to market virtually all its oil even after the Saudis took over Aramco's producing operations in 1976. The firms continued to influence Saudi production levels in their role as buyers. By 1983, however, the Saudi state firm, Petromin, was selling over 2 million barrels per day directly to foreign governments—about the same amount Aramco was dividing among its four member companies.[86] There were also telltale signs that the Saudis had entered the spot oil market for the first time, bypassing the Aramco partners.[87] The Kuwaitis, meanwhile, are developing an integrated international oil company that completely sidesteps the private companies.

Despite the companies' shifting position after nationalization, there are still profits to be made. To make them, multinational firms have had to adapt their ownership strategies to a new environment, one in which long-term direct investments are very risky in many sectors. This adaptation is much more important than the detailed data on how many companies have been expropriated and how much they are paid. What is crucial is that

- international standards regarding the treatment of foreign property have largely given way to idiosyncratic national policies; and
- multinational companies have transformed their international operations to cope with these diverse environments and increased political risk.

A number of options are available to individual companies. Several are complementary, and many are currently being tried.

One perverse (and now rarely used) strategy is actually to *increase* foreign equity, expand production, and modernize facilities. Such expansion is almost always a response to the host country's insistent demands. To avoid nationalization, some companies may accede to it. Among larger LDCs, such as Mexico or Brazil, it is common to require expanded production in exchange for access to their larger consumer markets.

While many companies have complied, the strategy is obviously dangerous. By modernizing local facilities, a company risks still more of its capital. Depending on its partnership arrangements, it may even compromise some technical secrets. Instead of placating host-country demands, the new investments may simply become larger hostages for further demands. They may even prove more attractive targets for nationalization, as Anaconda discovered in Chile in the early 1970s.[88]

A compromise approach involves partnerships with either local investors or the host government.[89] The joint-ownership strategy has obvious advantages. The right local partners can help in many ways—in knowing local markets, in securing government contracts, in deflecting political demands.

For some companies, however, the joint-venture strategy poses special problems. Companies that spend huge sums for research and development are naturally jealous of the results. Even if they maintain control over their innovations, compensation for new products and advanced technology may be hard to arrange. According to Louis Wells and John Stopford, companies that specialize in a narrow line of high-technology products are strongly averse to joint ventures. IBM, for one, has been unwilling to dilute its control over foreign subsidiaries. But other research-intensive firms—those that sell a wider variety of products—are often willing to set up joint ventures.[90]

Now that wholly owned investments are politically vulnerable, the joint-venture strategy has special appeal. For some firms, especially those headquartered in Europe, joint ventures are nothing new. Even before World War II, more than 60 percent of European manufacturing subsidiaries in less developed countries were jointly owned. These figures hold steady for the postwar era. Most significantly, these are *not* partnerships with other foreign investors. The overwhelming majority involves local investors or host states.[91] The percentages run even higher for Japanese firms. Before 1950, only 16 percent of Japanese affiliates abroad were minority owned. By the late 1960s, some 74 percent were minority owned.[92] A survey of the ten leading Japanese trading companies shows that less than 6 percent of their subsidiaries are wholly owned. In over 80 percent of the investments, they are minority partners.[93]

American and German firms are significantly less involved in minority partnerships,* although they, too, have been willing to accept local partners when necessary. Before 1951, almost 60 percent of all U.S. manufacturing affiliates were wholly owned, a proportion that had declined to 44 percent by the mid-1970s. Extractive and service firms have been much more flexible, and there is a clear trend away from majority-owned affiliates in all sectors.[94] The Organisation for Economic Co-operation and Development, surveying these trends, has observed that

*These cross-national differences in ownership policies have not yet been explained adequately.

international direct investment through wholly-owned subsidiaries can no longer be thought of as the typical way of engaging in international business. Rather, the emerging trend seems to be a tendency toward flexible and pragmatic forms of ownership, management and control inside increasingly complex arrangements, often involving several forms of control, cross-control or joint activities.[95]

Multinationals often have little choice about ownership arrangements. Many countries now regulate the extent of foreign ownership, some prohibit wholly owned investments in key sectors, especially natural resources. Significantly, this regulation of ownership can occur alongside policies designed to stimulate new foreign investment. Brazil, for instance, strongly encourages new investments and permits unrestricted foreign ownership in most industries. At the same time, it requires joint ventures in minerals and petrochemicals, among others.

While some firms have tried partnership arrangements, others have de-emphasized all types of direct investment. They rely primarily on management contracts and nonequity participation, sometimes buttressed by control over other critical aspects of global production and sales. Japanese raw-material ventures have been especially successful in minimizing direct investments. "[They] stand out by their very limited capital involvement," says Robert Swansbrough. "The Tokyo government provides technical assistance and capital for the infrastructure development . . . while private firms contribute management expertise and foreign markets."[96]

But even minimizing direct investments carries some risks. Long-term contracts may be a phantom. Contracts can be renegotiated, just as direct investments can be expropriated.[97] Oil, once again, is a good example. Now that producing countries have taken control of their own fields, they find it even easier to sell surplus crude to Japanese, European, and medium-sized American companies. Among producers generally, there is a dual interest in developing more diverse markets and controlling downstream operations.*

*Often, however, there is a price to be paid. Producing states pay it when they lack the funds, expertise, or marketing resources to operate their nationalized production efficiently.

Michael Shafer has pointed out another potential cost, one that Zaire and Zambia had to pay after they nationalized copper production. They became independent, marginal producers rather than elements of a vertically integrated corporate oligopoly. As such, they were fully exposed to the wide price swings of commodities such as copper. Shafer, "Capturing the Mineral Multinationals: Advantage or Disadvantage?" *International Organization* 37 (Winter 1983), 93–119.

Unlike direct investments, long-term contracts and management agreements have not yet achieved symbolic status. They are not yet charged with nationalist meaning. But who can say if, or when, they will be? Even now, contracts and direct investments are best protected in the same way—mutual profitability.

As long as nationalism threatens multinational firms, their investments and contracts will depend heavily on their ability to generate an unending stream of commodities or services desired by the host government and not available cheaper from someone else.

This complex, but critical, quality is usually associated with technological sophistication, managerial innovation, and marketing skills. IBM, for one, provides a constantly improving array of hardware and software. Other companies provide unique access to export markets in the United States, Europe, and Japan. Still others, such as Coca-Cola, hold the copyrights to famous brand names and have the marketing know-how to keep them popular. These last examples, though varied, share two features well adapted to avoiding expropriation. Each involves complicated ongoing activities, and the activities are impossible to seize and expensive to duplicate. They are the products of organizational learning.

Even though corporations have begun adapting to the threat of expropriation, the threat remains significant. It is aggravated by important changes in industrial structure. First, in many sectors crucial to industrial development, production is no longer controlled by a small group of multinational firms. Several contrasting trends are at work here. On the one hand, more and more of the world's production is concentrated in a couple of hundred worldwide companies. That trend is reinforced in some industries by the increasing scale of efficient production. Large scale, as in aluminum smelters, requires more than vast sums of capital. It demands organizational sophistication, a steady supply of material resources, and the ability to sell the final product in several national markets. On the other hand, the increasing share of global production attributable to multinational corporations does not necessarily mean tighter control within specific industries, although the two are sometimes associated. For one thing, more companies are becoming multinational. In individual industries, such as automobiles or consumer electronics, that means more competition. This competition is especially vigorous in older, more mature industries—precisely those that have long been essential elements of economic development. As Raymond Vernon, Theodore Moran, and

Raymond Mikesell all point out, the slackening of once-tight oligopolies in those industries erodes the bargaining position of individual firms. When firms lose their near-monopoly over technical knowledge and production methods, their chances of being expropriated multiply. After all, the ability to sustain production is a necessary (if not sufficient) condition of rational expropriation.

A second major change in industrial structure has been the disaggregation of direct investment. At one time, almost all foreign direct investment comprised a unified "package" made up of capital, technology, management, and sales. Now that package has been broken open in many mature industries and its components provided separately. Japanese companies have led the way, signing long-term management contracts and purchase agreements while minimizing direct investments. Although these arrangements can be profitable for individual firms, they tend to weaken the investment security of all firms. They provide attractive alternatives to existing direct investment and thus increase its vulnerability.

Ironically, one reason for this change has been the firms' own individually rational responses to the risks of forced divestment. As the risks grew, many firms minimized their exposed equity and required higher returns on investments. In general, they invested as little initial capital as possible and expanded cautiously through retained earnings and local borrowing. Superfluous funds were transferred out of the country.*

Although this strategy diminished the capital exposed to expropriation, it entailed other risks. Borrowing locally creates local enemies, as well as friends, since it drains capital away from domestic entrepreneurs. More significantly, by providing organizational services without the infusion of capital, multinational firms invite still more criticism of their contribution to development. To many governments, direct investment by multinational firms seems a costly way to procure technical and management skills, especially if those skills are closely held within the firm. As a result, numerous firms have been told to train more local managers and technicians and to give them operational responsibilities.

---

*The international transfer of surplus funds was not simply (or even primarily) to avoid risk. It was intended mainly to avoid taxes, to maximize the corporation's net profit worldwide. Because multinational firms prefer to adopt global profit strategies, they find national restrictions on remitted earnings an onerous burden. Many consider them a subtle form of confiscation. They are, in any case, a blow to the financial integration of the multinational firm.

These demands pose dilemmas for the companies. To avoid confrontation—and possibly adverse consequences— it may be essential to meet the host country's demands: hire more nationals, for instance, and speed the diffusion of technology.* But to do so will probably hasten the day that local entrepreneurs, engineers, and state officials can run the business themselves.

Even if they cannot, they can turn to others who can. It is now possible to buy major capital goods, even entire industrial complexes, on a ready-to-operate basis from international contractors such as Fluor or Bechtel.[98] Likewise, essential management and technical services are increasingly available by contract, either for a fee or on a production-sharing basis. Many of these services are offered by companies that once limited themselves to wholly owned investments. This development can be attributed to the maturation of industrial processes, the spread of new European and American multinationals, and the special willingness of Japanese firms to provide such services.

Conclusion

While these evolutionary corporate strategies may well be profitable, they also signal the marked weakening of once-traditional international property rules.

Recall the postwar rules. Expropriation was limited to infrastructure. Adequate compensation (book value or more) was demanded and generally paid. What the capital-exporting states considered clear rule violations were punished, either by economic sanctions or by interventionary force, depending upon the United States' evaluation of the foreign government's social policies and political alignment.

LDCs accepted these guidelines in practice, although sometimes reluctantly. They did not mount a serious, sustained challenge to their normative properties until the U.N. resolutions of the early 1960s.

---

*Some of the more strident demands on multinational firms have receded in the mid-1980s, the product of widespread LDC capital shortages plus greater attention to export growth. But this more receptive climate for foreign investment, while important in its own right, should not be mistaken for a reversal of other long-term trends. In particular, it does not overturn the increasingly idiosyncratic national treatment accorded foreign capital or the erosion of international minimum standards. Corporate investors are well aware of these limitations on the improved climate for foreign investment. That is why they are so attentive to political-risk analysis and so willing to accept minority ownership and nonequity positions abroad.

The investments themselves remained relatively secure until the late 1960s and early 1970s.

Today, however, these expectations about how foreign property will be treated—and should be treated—have evolved considerably. Forced divestments have substantially altered the character of natural-resource industries and other major sources of capital accumulation. Scores of countries have nationalized at least some foreign investments—some sixty countries have undertaken between one and ten acts of forced divestment, and over a dozen have embarked on more extensive programs[99]—a compelling fact that has slowly altered the symbolic meaning of expropriation and the security of foreign property. Compensation standards have also changed significantly. Expropriating governments almost always agree to pay something but usually less than the book value of the investments and far less than their market worth.*

Through this combination of successful nationalizations and their vigorous rhetorical defense, LDCs have managed to redefine the rules affecting international investments and so alter the context of bargaining between individual firms and host countries. If the governments negotiate some mutually agreed compensation, they can usually retain their access to global markets and modern technology, although the perception of higher risks may slow the flow of new investments. Public and private economic sanctions have lost much of their coherence and severity, although they may still be important when there is a perceived shift toward communism or a flat refusal to negotiate adequate compensation.

At the same time, advanced capitalist states find it much more difficult to intervene successfully in LDCs. The change is critical because interventionary force has played a many-sided role in sustaining property rules. It punishes violators by helping their local opponents remove them from office. It deters others from trying the same thing. It helps install governments that seem likely to preserve and defend

---

*Book value is usually less than market value, and sometimes a good deal less. There are many reasons, including taxation advantages and standard accounting practices. For extractive industries, however, there is an additional, and much more significant, reason. Book value does not include the cost of exploring for raw materials, while market value does.

The most thorough exploration of these valuation issues is in Richard B. Lillich, ed., *The Valuation of Nationalized Property in International Law*, 3 vols. (Charlottesville: University Press of Virginia, 1972, 1973, and 1975) and Lillich and Burns H. Weston, eds., *International Claims: Contemporary European Practice* (Charlottesville: University Press of Virginia, 1982).

the rights of foreign investors. Yet its use is now inhibited by widespread opposition: reluctance at home, forcible resistance abroad, and diplomatic hostility from interested third parties (either on grounds of sovereignty abused or energies misspent).

The effectiveness of interventionary force as a rule-sustaining instrument has been impaired in another, more complex way. Not only do advanced states now find it extremely costly to remove governments by force, they also recognize that they cannot freely pick and choose the successor government's policies. True, when conservative or reactionary leaders replace radical ones, they are usually eager to entice foreign investments and will often provide attractive incentives. But, even so, they may be unwilling or unable to overturn their predecessor's popular nationalizations. Nor can they guarantee a secure future for new foreign investments. The reasons are straightforward. Their government may not survive and, even if it does, it may later adopt its own policies of state-led industrialization and economic nationalism.

In the first two decades after World War II, right-wing coups meant friendship with the United States and a quick vindication of foreign property rights. Guatemala and Iran are good examples. Today, as well, such coups entail closer ties to the United States and better treatment for foreign capital: agreement to compensate previously seized companies, for instance, and the reentry of foreign investors to manage their properties with a much freer hand. But there are also important limits now that did not exist earlier.

One way to understand them is to look at an extreme case: the Chilean junta. After overthrowing Allende in September 1973 and establishing martial rule, the junta eagerly invited foreign investors back to Chile. They returned to local owners the enterprises that had been taken by quasi-legal means and sold many others that had been formally nationalized. They settled the long-festering compensation disputes with Anaconda, Kennecott, and Cerro over their mines and reestablished Chile's good standing among multinational investors. Since then, a number of foreign firms, including Exxon and Goodyear Tire, have made substantial new investments there.[100]

So it is all the more striking that this right-wing junta, with its powerful ideology of limited state intervention in the economy, decided to retain control of Chile's four major copper mines: Chuquicamata, El Salvador, El Teniente, and Andina.[101] They did so because national support for these expropriations was (and is) virtually unanimous, encompassing most of the military as well.[102] Chilean state ownership of the major copper mines had become, irreversibly, an issue of national sovereignty. The nationalizations, after all, had begun before Allende took office, were supported by both Allende's Popular Unity coalition and the Christian Democrats during the 1970 elections, and were enacted as constitutional amendments with near-universal support.[103] The Pinochet government has also accepted them. That the junta would retain ownership of Chile's most important mineral resources is an indication of how the old assumptions governing foreign investment have faded.

Neither the social composition of conservative governments nor their anticommunist fervor binds them to the old anti-expropriation rules. They are generally more willing than populist governments to pay adequate compensation and to retain strong ties to foreign companies, but that does not prevent them from nationalizing major foreign investments or managing them as state enterprises. Forced divestments, in other words, are no longer exclusively associated with leftist governments and with dreary prospects for all multinational firms.

Today, rightist governments, such as those that line the Persian Gulf, have expropriated some of the world's largest foreign investments, paid partial compensation, and then invited the former owners to stay on as partners and managers. By the late 1970s, multinationals were lined up to enter joint ventures like so many tankers waiting to be filled. The governments' quest for technical expertise, skilled management, and global markets ensures a profitable role for many of these firms. And yet, as Aramco's owners know, that quest is not inconsistent with selective nationalizations.

To summarize, the spread of economic nationalism has undermined the effectiveness of force as a tool to sustain foreign investors' rights. The costs are much higher now, the results less certain. Forcibly replacing leftist governments can still renew military alliances and assist multinational firms in their drive for global operations and global profits. But it can no longer prevent major expropriations or roll back the growth of state enterprises. The point is *not* that covert force and economic sanctions are trivial—even in this context. It is rather that such instruments can no longer sustain an international regime in which foreign investments are politically secure.

The simultaneous dilution of economic and military sanctions has seriously weakened the regime for foreign investments. Actually, the regime has been bifurcated, with portfolio loans remaining secure against renunciation while expropriations have multiplied and spread. So far, in spite of serious economic difficulties in servicing international loans, nearly all have either been repaid on time or rescheduled on mutually agreed terms. Outright debt repudiation or a unilateral moratorium on repayments, the closest equivalents to expropriation, have been extremely rare. In recent years, only Cuba, North Korea, and the newer communist states of Southeast Asia have renounced their bank debts and severed their ties to Western finance. What is remarkable is not the infrequent repudiations but the extraordinary economic contraction that most debtors have undertaken rather than risk default.

In contrast to the deterrents against expropriation, the deterrents to debt repudiation are impressive. In crises, the lenders are reasonably well equipped to work together and the IMF steps in to provide further coordination. Major public creditors typically meet in Paris to reschedule the official debt and set new lending conditions. Private creditors hold similar sessions in New York or London. The IMF becomes involved by providing new credits, for which it requires changes in the debtor's economic policies. This coordination and institutionalization through the IMF has no equivalent for direct investments.

Foreign loans are also protected by the legal remedies available to banks in Europe and the United States. Debtors can hardly afford a radical break with Western banks, which they must rely on to conduct international trade. Whether they are exporting or importing, LDCs require bank deposits, short-term trade credits, financial transfers, and other bank services. If foreign debts were simply renounced, lending institutions would move quickly to block these operations and legally attach the country's foreign financial assets. The effects would reach far beyond the loans in question; they would impair the full range of the debtor's international transactions. Both lenders and debtors have understood the point well. As David Beim of the United States' Export-Import Bank states:

> Short of a total break with the West, debt renunciation is not likely to be a workable solution for the over-extended government of [an] . . . LDC. Most governments depend quite totally on the international banking system to handle their flow of trade. . . . The LDCs cannot afford to flout the banks. Indeed, the tendency in real life is for the banks and the troubled LDC to draw closer together.[104]

The same less developed countries have considerably more flexibility in cases of expropriation. They do not confront a highly coordinated, tightly linked system as they do in international finance. Nor do they face the same legal hurdles in selling their products. Although direct investors have tried to enforce legal claims, they have generally found it difficult to prove ownership of the commodities or illegalities by the expropriating state.[105]

With less developed states anxious to increase their economic control, and without effective economic or military deterrents to expropriation, seizures of direct investments have multiplied since the late 1960s. They now encompass major sources of capital accumulation, especially in oil, mining, and other natural-resource industries. Yet they are not limited to a few highly visible industries—raw materials, public utilities, and agriculture—as they once were. There has been a notable increase, for example, in expropriations of low-profile manufacturing investments. That is especially true when those investments are in mature industries producing for local markets. According to Hawkins, Mintz, and Provissiero, whose data cover the expropriation of individual firms, *no* U.S. manufacturing investments outside of communist countries were expropriated between 1946 and 1960. By the early 1970s, however, they accounted for 40 percent of all U.S. expropriations.[106] Stephen Kobrin's data, which are coded differently, show that manufacturing firms now account for 27 percent of all forced divestments, compared with 41 percent for extractive industries.[107]

One old guideline remains important, however, if only in weakened form. Except for the most radical, most governments still prefer to reach some compensation agreement after they expropriate. A prolonged dispute could imperil the government's credit, frighten other multinational firms, and tie up nationalized exports in complicated suits.[108] Even so, the compensation agreements seldom approach book value.

The spread of expropriations and the decline in compensation standards clearly indicates that the United States can no longer protect foreign investments by itself. The next step is obvious: seek help. But help has always been hard to find, difficult to organize, and nearly impossible to sustain. As I have already observed, multilateral investment codes have been beyond reach and collective enforcement beyond mention in the years since World War II. The debate over these issues is an old one, stretching back to Lenin's attack on Kautsky.

Lenin still seems to be winning: coordination in these matters is difficult at best.[109]

Nevertheless, some have suggested that two new conditions make condominium feasible for the first time. First, they point out that national firms have been supplanted by multinational ones. Will that lessen conflict among advanced capitalist states—at least with respect to investment protection? Probably not. Corporate ownership and top management are still defined nationally. Moreover, it is U.S. companies—not European or Japanese firms—that have been hardest hit by expropriations. Except for West Germany, few advanced states have joined U.S. efforts to form a new and tighter regime.

Actually, the *image* of multinationality may be more important than the location of stockholders or corporate headquarters. In a world of bristling nationalisms, it is risky to be overly identified with a foreign power, especially if that state cannot effectively protect foreign investors from host-country demands. The most common response is to adapt, to appear stateless if possible.

Yet the prospects for condominium probably depend less on the rise of "stateless" capital than on the development of international institutions managed jointly by advanced capitalist states.

The World Bank has already made some tentative moves in this direction. The Bank, as I have already noted, has supported traditional anti-expropriation rules since its inception. And it has been willing to use its aid disbursements as leverage. After Chile expropriated its major copper mines without compensation, Bank officials told Chile that it would not extend new aid. While the United States strongly supported this posture, it also had deep roots in the Bank's own Articles of Agreement and its Blue Book of standard operating procedures. The Bank's policy, in its own words, has always been to "inform governments who are involved in [expropriation] disputes that the Bank . . . will not assist them unless and until they make appropriate efforts to reach a fair and equitable settlement."[110]

Beyond these aid policies, some have proposed tying the Bank's project loans directly to foreign investment. In May 1976, for instance, Secretary of State Henry Kissinger proposed a new multibillion dollar bank for international resources, to be managed by the World Bank. It would have raised some funds from World Bank members and the rest in international financial markets. Future production from the projects it financed would be pledged as collateral. Multinational firms would then contract to build and manage the investments, and host states would promise not to expropriate them. One U.S. official, quoted in *Business Week,* summarizes the hoped-for result: "For all practical purposes, the investing company or consortium would be in the position of making a direct investment, except that the bank would assume the political risk."[111]

Had this proposal been adopted, it would have made expropriations extremely costly while insulating multinational firms from any residual risks. Multinational mineral investments would be enmeshed in a complex network of international finance and multilateral institutions. As long as a host government desired Western trade and technology, or sought subsidized loans from the Bank, it would find expropriation prohibitively expensive. For all these reasons, UNCTAD vigorously rejected it. Nor did it find much support at the World Bank, which would have been inserted directly into the most politically contentious investment issues.

The same problems have slowed the development of alternative proposals. Perhaps the most likely is some form of multilateral investment insurance, providing guarantees against certain forms of political risk. Such a program has been discussed since the early 1960s, but is still not in place two decades later.

Although the quest for new institutions and better rule enforcement has not succeeded, the search for alternatives will inevitably go on. At the state level that means finding institutional alternatives to unilateral enforcement. At the corporate level, it means adapting to profit from new circumstances. Meanwhile, new bargains are replacing old rules.

CHAPTER FIVE

The Sources of International Property Rules

W hy has the character of expropriation changed so dramatically? What efforts have been made to prevent it? What roles have multinational corporations and advanced capitalist states played in this transformation?

These questions are central to understanding the changing treatment of foreign capital. To analyze them systematically, I have concentrated less on individual disputes (with all their contingent elements) and more on the basic rules and norms regarding foreign investment. Besides examining their institutional setting, I have focused on

- expectations about the proper treatment of foreign capital (the normative issues of sovereign rights and international minimum standards); on

- expectations about future interactions (the assessment of political risks and strategic adaptation by firms and states); as well as on

- standard practices and observed regularities (the size, scale, and sectoral distribution of successful nationalizations, and the types of governments that have undertaken them).

Taken together, these three elements provide the context for day-to-day bargaining between individual companies and host states. (They are, in turn, reproduced and transformed by this bargaining.) All three are central to understanding the shifting treatment of foreign capital and the debates surrounding it.

My analysis, then, is not limited to behavioral regularities—as important as they are—or to the impact of past practices on current negotiations. I am also concerned with the character of disputes, with the sanctions that are applied, and with the values invoked. As previous chapters indicate, the values that justify or delegitimate investment rules are expressed in several forms: international law; public statements and diplomatic representations by both capital exporters and host states; and the resolutions of international organizations.

Although the debate over all these issues continues, my analysis of expropriation regimes reveals two significant trends, one concerning the rules and another their justification. A strict set of de facto rules was accorded legal status in the nineteenth century and was strictly observed until World War I. These rules were challenged during the interwar period by several major expropriations and were restored in modified form after World War II. This reconstituted regime remained strong until the late 1960s. Over the past decade the regime has been bifurcated. Portfolio loans have remained relatively secure while direct investments have been expropriated in increasing numbers without negative sanctions (see figure 2, column 1: regime characterization).

The ideological contest over foreign investment has followed a different pattern (figure 2, column 2: normative issues). Although the privileges of foreign investors were sometimes attacked during the nineteenth century, the legitimacy of international property rules was not significantly questioned until the interwar period. In their own separate ways, both the Soviet and Mexican constitutions challenged the prevailing ideology of private property rights, as did the state mobilization of capital in Turkey. At the same time, the issue of foreign investors' rights was brought up in the League of Nations conferences and, unlike the debates in prewar forums, was fought to a stalemate.

This attack accelerated after World War II, encumbered but not stopped by the tremendous economic and military power of the United States. In the 1960s, the LDCs began pressing these issues repeatedly at the United Nations, where they were increasingly well organized (through the Group of 77) and where they now had substantial voting majorities. Their main goal was to justify contemplated national economic policies and to deny the validity—or even the permissibility—

Figure 2. International Regimes Governing the Expropriation of Foreign Investments

Regime Characterization	Normative Issues	Enforcement
19th Century to World War I:		
Strong regime:		
Rules embodied in customary international law, requiring prompt, full compensation in convertible currency; eminent domain implicitly limited to exceptional public purpose; simple bond default not usually a rule violation, but occasionally ambiguous	Few disputes; Latin American countries contest the right to use naval force on behalf of bondholders; no other substantive challenges	British navy, with some assistance from other European navies; British bondholders; Various colonial powers in their colonies; U.S. in Western Hemisphere after 1900
		Primary means: naval force and bondholder sanctions
World War I to World War II:		
Relatively strong regime:		
Same substantive standards, but major expropriations in Soviet Union and Mexico; minor ones in Bolivia and East Europe; settlements negotiated, but generally delayed and for partial value	Several important challenges to older norms; Soviet, Mexican, and Turkish acts challenge earlier limits to eminent domain; Mexico disputes concept of international minimum standards; League of Nations conferences end in stalemate over rights of foreign investors	United States in Western Hemisphere; Collective enforcement against Soviets; No enforcement in East Europe; Colonial powers in their colonies and contiguous areas
		Generally less use of force, except against Soviets and in Caribbean

World War II to Late 1960s:			
Strong regime (but limited to noncommunist countries): International standards requiring negotiated compensation at book value or above; allowed expropriation of infrastructure (RR, telephones, etc.) but not raw materials or manufacturing; expropriation generally limited to infrastructure	Progressive success in challenging moral authority of existing rules; use of U.N. to assert permanent sovereignty over natural resources; some success in attacking international minimum standards of compensation	U.S. government	U.S. multinationals also: World Bank; IMF; ex-colonial powers in their former colonies
		Primary means: U.S. local interventionary force, overt and covert; collective sanctions by corporations and economic sanctions by U.S. government	
Late 1960s to Present:			
Portfolio loans: *Strong regime* Direct investments: *Weak regime* (excluding communist countries) All foreign property subject to expropriation, but most frequent seizures of raw materials producers; compensation usually paid, at book value or less; increasing government regulation of investments; meaning of expropriation blurred by forced sales and extensive regulation	Old legal norms rejected implicitly by expropriation, explicitly by U.N. resolutions; General Assembly votes permanent sovereignty over natural resources plus local standards of compensation; progressive challenge to general concept of diplomatic protection for foreign investors	Same as above, except role of ex-colonial powers diminished, especially in case of Britain	For portfolio loans, primary means: IMF, ad hoc creditor conferences

of counterclaims by foreign firms and their home states. The U.N. Resolutions on Permanent Sovereignty over Natural Resources, which had previously balanced these national claims against aliens' traditional legal rights, began to stress sovereign prerogatives as the preeminent value. In the 1970s, the Group of 77 managed to pass resolutions certifying the unlimited right to nationalize raw materials and denying the legitimacy of international standards of compensation. The meaning of these resolutions, according to international lawyer Richard Lillich, goes well beyond the issue of expropriation. They undermine the more profound principle of diplomatic protection for nationals abroad.[1]

Two patterns emerge then. Traditional investor rights, embodied in international property law, have lost their approval slowly—in an almost linear fashion. The actual treatment of foreign capital, however, has not always paralleled this change in values. Most significantly, the rules were effectively reconsolidated after World War II. In spite of this cyclical variation, however, the long-term trend is unmistakable. Investment security, enforceable if need be, has given way to varied national treatment.

If the two patterns are distinct, they are not wholly independent. The gradual withdrawal of legitimacy reduced investment security, but its impact was neither immediate nor direct. In fact, investment security increased during the late 1940s and 1950s, just as the U.N. General Assembly began passing Resolutions on Permanent Sovereignty over Natural Resources. Still, the shifting battle to justify investors' claims has had serious repercussions in the long run. It made enforcement more difficult and costly. When sanctions were used, they entailed more troublesome international consequences. Their public defense, awkward as it usually was, impinged on other diplomatic initiatives. Perhaps more important, the withdrawal of legitimacy implied that investment security rested more heavily on external sanctions and less on internalized standards. Ultimately this shift placed an unbearable burden on those sanctions—that is, on interventionary force and economic coercion. It made them almost impossible to organize on a multilateral basis, for example. The withdrawal of legitimacy thus contributed to the transformation of property rules.

Rule enforcement has already been discussed extensively (for a summary see figure 2, column 3). In the nineteenth century the British Navy and Foreign Office played vital roles; in the twentieth century, it has been up to the State Department, the Marines, and the CIA. Yet, as we have seen, enforcement has never been limited to state agencies. It has always included private investors. When most long-term investments were loans, British bondholders actively sustained international property rules. Later, U.S. multinational corporations played the same role. Their control over world markets and modern technology proved formidable instruments of order.

The three previous chapters suggest an intimate connection between these sanctions and the international regime governing the treatment of foreign investment. This chapter will formulate that relationship systematically.

A simple model of regime change should include *restraints* on the varied national treatment of foreign capital, as well as the *impetus* for such treatment.*

I posit three basic external constraints on the national treatment of foreign capital (including expropriation):

1. the capacity to employ local interventionary force;
2. the capacity to invoke coherent, severe economic sanctions; and
3. the capacity to manipulate relevant international organizations.

---

*According to standard usage, the entity being modeled is the *reference system*, which is simply some object, system, structure, or process of particular interest to the modeler. In this case, the reference system is the regime governing the treatment of foreign investment.

The essence of all models, regardless of their purpose or mode of expression, is that they represent selected features of the reference system and their assumed interrelationships. Thus, a model serves as a "simplified representation of the interrelationships among elements of a given reference system," according to Martin Greenberger, Matthew Crenson, and Brian Crissey.

Of course, social scientists are primarily interested in formal models, usually descriptive or deductive models that display expected behavior of the reference system under specified initial conditions. Assuming this statement of parameter conditions, a model is really (in Thomas Schelling's phrase) "a precise and economical statement of a set of relationships that are sufficient to produce the phenomenon in question."

Although such statements are often embodied in multiple equations or symbolic terms (since they are particularly well suited to precision and manipulation), they need not be so expressed. In fact, formal models can be stated in a variety of languages, including natural ones.

For a clear, useful discussion of modeling, see Greenberger, Crenson, and Crissey, *Models in the Policy Process* (New York: Russell Sage Foundation, 1976), chap. 3 (the quote is from p. 49). Schelling's comment is in *Micromotives and Macrobehavior* (New York: W. W. Norton, 1978), 87. For a sophisticated statement of modeling problems in international relations (with particular attention to levels-of-analysis issues and parametric conditions), see Morton Kaplan, *Towards Professionalism in International Theory: Macrosystem Analysis* (New York: Free Press, 1979), chaps. 1–3.

I assume that each capacity is greatest when pertinent resources are most highly centralized. Conversely, when resources and capabilities are diffused, I assume that sanctions will be more difficult to organize and constraints on host countries less compelling. Although capital-exporting states and multinational firms may share a basic interest in investment security—and could, hypothetically, organize sanctions among a large group—their immediate interests in specific investment disputes are often divergent. These divergent (if narrow) interests and the absence of institutional coordination make it difficult to organize a unified response. This task, if it is to be performed at all, is likely to fall on one or two key states and on tightly organized industrial oligopolies. So concentration of resources is important.

Set against these restraints is the historically expanding role of the state in less developed countries. That role includes an impressive increase in administrative staffs, a wider scope for public policy, an ideology of state-led industrialization, and an interpenetration of public and private decision making, especially in development policy.

This secular trend, profound and widespread though it is, should not obscure vast differences among less developed states. I am *not* assuming isomorphic social or political structures. Rather, I am highlighting certain common features—the growth of state capabilities, increased state intervention in the economy, the rise of economic nationalism—which together form the immediate domestic context of expropriation.

I will return to these issues later. My purpose now is to clarify the model of regime change to test its adequacy.

The first step is to show how the distribution of economic and military capabilities and the ability to manipulate international organizations are related to investment protection. I will briefly recapitulate historical changes in these capabilities and indicate their causal links to investment protection.

Of course, any model that relies *solely* on international sanctions cannot adequately represent regime change. Such a model assumes that, in the absence of coherent restraints, host states would expropriate foreign capital. Should such an assumption be made? The issue here is *not* whether it is empirically accurate, even in gross terms. It is not intended to be a realistic description but a theoretical simplification. It must be evaluated primarily in terms of its predictive value and explanatory usefulness.

In these terms, however, it is inadequate. A narrow "restraint model" would predict strong regimes only when sanctions are coherent and severe. When they are not, the regime should weaken. Therefore, the restraint model would incorrectly predict a weak regime during the interwar period, when sanctioning capacity was substantially weaker and less coherent than in the nineteenth century. In Eastern Europe, for example, international restraints were extremely weak. Certainly no major state exercised hegemonial control in the region. Yet aside from some minor agricultural reforms, no major expropriations took place. In this case, then, the security of foreign capital must be located domestically, in local social structure and political organization.

Thus, an empirically accurate and causally sound model of regime change must include both international restraints and domestic sources of expropriation.

Military Force and Investment Protection

Military force is the best-known obstacle to expropriation—and not without reason. Interventionary force has been used repeatedly to protect foreign capital, either as a goal in itself or as part of a more comprehensive foreign policy.

Yet interventionary force has taken on a new and different meaning as the nature of foreign investment has changed and as new expropriation threats have arisen. In the nineteenth century, for instance, interventionary force meant naval force. Underdeveloped states, weak and isolated as they were, could do little to prevent the successful use of force by Great Britain and other European powers. Port cities could be shelled or occupied without threat of recrimination. Then, too, foreign investments were located where naval force could easily protect them. Direct investments were either situated along the coast or, like railroads, dependent upon access to the sea. Long-term portfolio loans were secured by collateral in port cities, sometimes including the most vital source of local government revenues, the customs house. Local interventionary force is still important today, but its substance has changed considerably. It now means either covert force (such as CIA-assisted coups in Iran or Guatemala) or the capacity to mobilize swiftly for direct military intervention.

For simplicity and generality, this model conflates these historical forms of interventionary force. It posits the capacity to employ such force as a principal restraint on the varied national treatment of foreign capital. My assumption is that military restraints are greatest when interventionary capacity is most centralized.

Although it is difficult to specify the exact distribution of interventionary capacity, the overall pattern is well defined. The concentration of resources was especially high in the nineteenth century and after World War II. In the nineteenth century the British navy was easily the most prominent interventionary force. Until the prewar dreadnought race with Germany, its supremacy was hardly tested. Even then, the British admiralty was without parallel as an instrument of forceful intervention over long distances.* Similarly, in the first two decades after World War II, the United States held a near monopoly on the capacity to intervene in noncontiguous areas. Whatever measure is used—firepower, mobile forces, or covert capabilities—the concentration of resources in these two periods is striking.

During the interwar period, by contrast, interventionary capacity was relatively decentralized. The U.S. fleet equaled the British. The Japanese were not far behind. This new pattern was codified in 1922 at the Washington Naval Conference. The Conference established tonnage ratios for capital ships: parity between the United States and Great Britain, 60 percent of parity for the Japanese. Whatever the treaty's limitations, the new ratios clearly indicate the diffusion of naval power.[2] Since other kinds of interventionary force were not yet well developed, this shift in naval power represents a significant decentralization of interventionary capacity.

Turning to the most recent period (from the late 1960s onward), we again find some redistribution of interventionary capacity. The Soviet navy has grown impressively, and so has that country's capacity to airlift troops and supplies over long distances. According to Robert Legvold:

---

*Nevertheless, as I noted in chapter 2, the British strictly limited their use of force to protect foreign investments. Until the late nineteenth century, most long-term foreign capital was invested in bonds. The biggest threat was default, and default was not outright confiscation unless it resulted from fraud. Among other things, the British Foreign Office was reluctant to use military force to rescue bondholders from a situation that might well have been of their own making. As a result, the bondholders assumed a self-reliant posture. They protected their investments mainly by controlling new sources of credit.

If power is to be measured in terms of a country's ability to ferry material support great distances to friends fighting in settings like Angola in 1975, the Soviet Union is immeasurably stronger than it was 15 years earlier when Patrice Lumumba needed help. But if it is to be measured in terms of a country's ability to intervene over the same distances with its own military forces when it does not have friends or when we [the U.S.] move to prevent it, the Soviet Union is not strong enough.[3]

The implication is that, although the United States retains its leadership, interventionary capacity is less highly concentrated than in the 1950s or 1960s.

I have already indicated (in previous chapters) the causal links between investment security and concentrated interventionary capacity. In the nineteenth century, for example, naval force was well suited to protect foreign capital. With most investments along the coast, the Royal Navy could stand guard against riots, arbitrary seizures, or fraudulent misappropriation. At the same time, Britain's uncontested naval superiority seems to have encouraged joint action and prior consultation by other European powers. Weak independent states were hardly equipped to constrain this liberal use of naval power. Indeed, it was their very weakness that best protected them from persistent military coercion. Frequent intervention would threaten the basis of local government—a self-defeating course for Britain in Latin America.

By focusing on the distribution of interventionary capacity, our model simplifies the relationship between force and investment protection. That relationship is modeled in structural terms, dealing with the concentration and diffusion of specific coercive means. The diffusion of resources implies weaker international restraints on the treatment of foreign capital.

According to the model, British and American military strength contributed to the security of *all* foreign capital, not merely their own. (The same assumption is made about economic strength.) The connection between British gunboats and the security of French or German investments may seem remote at first, but it exists nonetheless. First, as Robert Gilpin notes, "The international political order created by dominant powers . . . has provided the favorable environment for economic interdependence and corporate expansionism."[4] There may be problems with Gilpin's hegemonial model, but he is surely correct on this crucial point: in both the British and American cases, centralized economic and military strength were used to create an open global economy. Even though French and German companies were rivals of their British and American counterparts, they were not excluded from the benefits of that open world order. Quite the contrary: the British in the nineteenth century and the Americans after World War II permitted the international spread of capital from all national sources. Second, the threat or use of military sanctions affected all foreign investments, often quite directly. The reason is that both British and American investments were widespread and were generally caught up in the most serious controversies affecting capital exporters. In protecting themselves, they protected others. Except for America's Caribbean interventions in the early twentieth century, neither power intervened primarily to protect another's foreign investments. Rather, in protecting their own endangered capital, they protected nearly all endangered capital—both directly and in terms of the expectations they established. One could cite the restoration of order in port cities by the British Navy during the nineteenth century—acts that aided all foreign investors. By the same token, the installation of the Shah by the United States reversed the nationalization of Anglo-Iranian Oil.

The one significant exception to this global military-economic protection has been in former colonial areas, where the Americans had been excluded or showed little interest. Until recently, when American investments began to rise, the United States had no direct stake in expropriation controversies in these former colonies. It is there that the former imperial powers, particularly the French, have acted aggressively to provide their own network of sanctions to protect their investments.

In general, the model's stress on interventionary force is most convincing for the nineteenth century, the interwar period, and the immediate postwar years. It is useful, but somewhat less apt, for the past two decades. As my brief examination of the Soviet Union indicates, interventionary force has been less concentrated in recent years. Although this diffusion of resources is important, the higher costs and diminished effectiveness of interventionary force are equally significant. The distinction here is between the international *structure* of force (the distribution of coercive means) and the *process* of achieving rule-sustaining outcomes (including cost and effectiveness). Because this model does not incorporate procedural developments, it probably overstates the current military restraints on expropriation.[5]

Why is it now more difficult to translate a hierarchy of military power into a stable international regime governing foreign investment? To begin with, the costs of using interventionary force have risen markedly for all advanced capitalist states. The underlying reasons for this change, at both the domestic and international levels, are beyond the scope of this work. But the impact of this change is significant. The high and rising costs of using force against less developed states seriously undermines its value as a threat and presents major barriers to its use.*

While the costs of using force have risen, its potential targets have multiplied. Decolonization has created scores of new states, expanding the tasks of investment protection considerably. Among ex-colonial powers, only the French maintained a serious capacity to intervene militarily in their former colonies and they, too, have given up the struggle recently. The British, despite their fascination with the Commonwealth, allowed their military capacity to deteriorate during the 1950s and 1960s.** In the end, the United States was left alone with the military responsibility for protecting foreign investments. With force so costly and with so many fetters on its use, the task was beyond accomplishment.

Finally, the status of interventionary force has been transformed by long-run changes in the character of both foreign investments and host states. The day-to-day security of foreign capital has always been borne locally. International force provides only indirect supervision; its effects are mediated through local political structures. The character

*Richard Bilder, writing specifically about raw materials, highlights this general decline in the use of overt force to protect foreign investments:

The fact that developed nations in recent years have rarely attempted to use military force to protect natural resource interests threatened by developing nations' actions—for example, in response to the wave of recent nationalizations of foreign oil, copper, and other concessions or to the 1973 oil embargo—suggests the extent to which overt coercion has been discarded even by powerful countries as a way of implementing natural resource objectives. Although developed nations have sometimes intervened in support of resource interests in Africa, in Chile, and elsewhere, their intervention has usually been indirect or covert rather than direct and overt.

These costs of using force were undoubtedly magnified after America's bloody fight in Vietnam, but the obstacles to using force—and using it effectively—have increased over the longer term as well.

Richard B. Bilder, "International Law and Natural Resource Policies," in *Resources and Development*, ed. Peter Dorner and Mahmoud A. El-Shafie (Madison: University of Wisconsin Press, 1980), 391–392.

**In fact, the real question is whether, given Britain's senescent economy, they maintained their forces for too long.

of these local structures defines the political tasks of capital exporters. During the nineteenth century, the basic task was to ensure that underdeveloped states did not occasionally overstep the bounds of laissez-faire practice or permit public order to disintegrate. In practice, this task was simplified even further because foreign investments were outposts, situated along the coast and linked primarily to the Europe-centered world economy. Today, capital exporters confront a substantially different array of host states. Less developed states are much more willing to direct their economies and manage substantial industrial projects. While some foreign investments are still export enclaves, economically and geographically, many more are enmeshed in local economies. All are subject to far-reaching state regulation.

These long-term changes cannot be rolled back by force. They can, at times, be contained. International force can be used to set permissible limits on state economic intervention. Indeed, setting those limits has been the fundamental goal of U.S. anti-expropriation policy since World War II.

When those limits are breached, the success of forcible international sanctions is defined by the capacity to empower new governments—governments willing to sustain various investor privileges. To sustain traditional anti-expropriation rules in the face of serious violations, the United States must install rule-abiding successors, a task that has become increasingly problematic.

So far, this analysis has concentrated on the higher costs of using force. But the benefits have also changed. Although it is risky to generalize about less developed countries, there does appear to have been a pervasive development of economic nationalism, even among socially conservative governments (or, perhaps, *especially* among those governments). It is closely linked to the whole task of state-building.

Neither expropriations nor extensive economic regulations are the exclusive preserve of leftist governments today. There are important ideological differences in the treatment of foreign investment, of course, but governments of all stripes have assumed direct control over some productive facilities and introduced a variety of performance targets affecting foreign investments.

The spread of economic nationalism implies that the United States can no longer sustain traditional investment rules merely by underwriting right-wing coups. Conservative governments may be a boon to foreign investors in many ways, and their definition of economic nationalism may bear the indelible marks of its domestic supporters, but even the most reactionary governments are now willing to nationalize some foreign investments. OPEC's leadership provides the most salient examples.

These developments are directly related to the effectiveness of force in protecting foreign capital. Since the nineteenth century, at least, the capacity to employ interventionary force has played a central role in restraining varied national treatment of foreign investments. When appropriate military resources have been highly concentrated, sanctioning capacity has generally been most severe, and most effective. When the capacity for intervention has been decentralized, the security of foreign capital has rested more on the character of local governments.

In recent years, however, this close relationship between investment protection and the distribution of force has been attenuated. The rise of economic nationalism, the entanglement of foreign investment in local economies, the higher costs of using force, and the proliferation of new states—each of these has muddied the connection between external force and investment security.

National and Transnational Economic Sanctions

In considering economic sanctions, I assume what I initially did about interventionary force: that the concentration of resources is a critical determinant of investment security. That is, when relevant economic resources are highly concentrated, foreign investments are most secure.

But economic sanctions, unlike military coercion, are not the sole property of nation-states. Transnational actors play an important role: sometimes reinforcing national sanctions, sometimes replacing them, occasionally undermining them. Thus, I posit two sets of actors and two fundamentally different types of economic sanctions. In the case of national sanctions, I am concerned principally with the denial of public funds and restricted access to advanced markets. In the case of transnational actors, I am concerned with the cessation of new foreign investment and impediments to the efficient operation of existing investments. When international commercial and financial markets are consolidated, when aid is confined to a few sources, then

diverse national treatment of foreign capital should be most constrained. Likewise, when multinational industries are highly oligop-
olistic, when private finance is limited to a few organized markets,
then international restraints should be most easily organized and most
severe. In each case, the concentration of relevant resources is assumed to be the basis of effective sanctions.

I have already shown, over the last three chapters, how both nation-states and transnational actors have used economic sanctions to
protect foreign investments. Actually, state sanctions are relatively
recent. During the nineteenth century, economic sanctions were primarily a private matter. The British, whose markets were critical to
independent states, did not favor public intervention in commerce or
finance. In this case, domestic institutional arrangements were an
independent curb on public investment protection.

Private investors amply compensated for the state's political in-
capacity. Their main weapon was the denial of credit, a policy enforced entirely by privately organized bondholders in London and
elsewhere. This policy succeeded for two reasons. First, lenders were
able to coordinate their claims through the Corporation of Foreign
Bondholders.[6] And, second, the City of London was the preeminent
center for loans to underdeveloped regions. Through this combination
of circumstance and effort, private lenders were largely able to exclude
defaulted debtors from international capital markets.* Private sanctions were effective, then, because transnational networks were highly
centralized.

After World War I, these networks were much less concentrated.
Until the Depression halted foreign lending, New York and London
were the dual seats of international finance. London's new status
scarcely resembled its nineteenth century preeminence. There was a
greater emphasis on domestic finance, a strong preference for loans

---

*A history of the London Stock Exchange describes these sanctions concisely.

Bondholders' committees were often formed when borrowers defaulted and, in
1868, more concerted action was taken with the formation of the Corporation of
Foreign Bondholders. . . . The Stock Exchange Committee also had helped by refusing a quotation to the loans of states that were in default, a practice which had
been followed since 1827. . . . Not many cases of this kind came before the Committee, but the rule was nevertheless a powerful sanction; governments and contractors alike knew that it was useless to apply for a quotation for a new loan while
an old one was in default, and a number of governments came to terms with their
creditors in order to gain re-admission to the market. (E. Victor Morgan and W. A.
Thomas, *The Stock Exchange* [2d ed.; London: Elek Books, 1969], 93.)

within the empire, and even an unofficial embargo at times on foreign loans. As London declined and the United States continued its vigorous industrial expansion, New York became the world's leading financial center. But until World War II consolidated international finance in American hands, Wall Street did not command the position the City of London once had.

The postwar reconsolidation was short-lived. By the mid-1960s, the Eurodollar market was thriving. Although based mainly in London, U.S. branch banks were among the leaders, joined by banks from Germany, Switzerland, Canada, Britain, and other major capital exporters. In national terms, the market for medium- and long-term loans was once more decentralized and highly competitive (although, as I have noted, the impact of this decentralization was tempered by the development of new international financial institutions).

Direct investments have followed a similar pattern over the past thirty years: American dominance and limited competition in the immediate postwar years followed by increasingly vigorous competition. Until the European and Japanese recoveries were complete, most multinational investors were American. And American investment was at first limited to the very largest corporations. In most industries, the concentration ratios declined markedly as the postwar period wore on. European and Japanese firms, together with medium-sized U.S. companies, went abroad in search of new consumer markets, additional raw materials, and cheaper labor. In the oil industry, for instance, more than 300 private companies and 50 state-owned firms entered the foreign oil industry between 1953 and 1972.[7] Over 400 firms now buy their oil directly from OPEC.[8] Advances in communications and transportation facilitated this international growth.

The United States provided the political context for this remarkable expansion.[9] Both directly and through the Bretton Woods institutions it had erected, the United States ensured a relatively open system of trade and investment.[10] By standing firm against a permanent political division of world markets, the United States allowed all corporations to compete on a global scale.[11]

As competitors proliferated, private (transnational) sanctions against expropriation declined. Confronting this genuine competition and LDC demands, many firms became less insistent on majority ownership and more willing to devise new arrangements for management, ownership, and technology transfer. Indeed, they were often willing to provide a full range of services for countries that had just nationalized other foreign firms, depending on their assessment of the climate for their particular company. A World Bank study attributes these new attitudes to the growth of corporate competition:

> New competitors, mainly European and Japanese or smaller and lesser known U.S. firms, are eager to capture markets and increasingly ready to negotiate arrangements which satisfy new host government policies, while still allowing sufficient control . . . to provide adequate returns on investment.[12]

This growing competition has been an integral feature of the world economy since World War II, fostered by American political preeminence and American policies. In a sense, then, the very success of the postwar economic order undermined the protection of foreign capital.*

There are good measures of this increased competition in several basic industries. A survey by the Harvard Multinational Enterprise Project of eight such industries found that most were two or three times more concentrated in 1950 than in 1975 (see figure 1, p. 118). One important element of this rising competition, as I have said, was the international growth of European and Japanese firms and the relative decline of those based in the United States. Lawrence G. Franko has charted the declining market share of U.S. industrial firms.

---

*This analysis suggests that the investment regime evolved in part because of its internal tensions. A secure investment climate fosters greater international competition which may, in turn, worsen the national treatment of foreign capital.

Such tensions—or, in stronger form, contradictions—may be a fundamental source of regime change. The best-known example is the collapse of Bretton Woods's pegged exchange rates. They depended upon an insupportable premise: that U.S. dollars could be used as an ever-expanding source of international reserves and that, at the same time, dollars would always remain convertible into gold at $35 per ounce. It was Robert Triffin who first understood the full implications of this contradiction and called attention to it in the late 1950s, more than a decade before the system collapsed.

Oran Young has suggested that such contradictions are but one of three ideal-typical forms of regime change. The other two are exogenous forces, such as technological change, and shifts in the underlying structure of power. In practice, as my analysis indicates, all three elements are interwoven and may even be difficult to distinguish. Changes in technology and communications costs, for instance, encouraged more corporations to go abroad—at once an exogenous change and a change in the competitive structure of industry.

Oran Young, "Regime Dynamics: The Rise and Fall of International Regimes," *International Organization* 36 (Spring 1982), 290–297; Robert Triffin, *Gold and the Dollar Crisis* (New Haven, Conn.: Yale University Press, 1960).

Of the top dozen pharmaceutical firms in 1959, for instance, U.S. companies accounted for 61 percent of all sales. In 1978, they accounted for only 34 percent. In chemicals, American companies' share fell from 66 percent to 37 percent. The fall-off was less dramatic in automobiles, electrical equipment, and food products, but it was still substantial.[13] Out of thirteen industries surveyed, the number of U.S. firms among the world's top twelve decreased in all but one. Japanese firms, by contrast, increased in eight industries and continental European firms in nine.[14]

These figures may actually *underestimate* the increase in international competition. As corporations have spread across national boundaries they have entered each other's markets with increasing regularity. While attempts to stifle such competition are not infrequent ("People of the same trade seldom meet together but the conversation ends in a conspiracy against the public, or in some diversion to raise prices," wrote Adam Smith), they are seldom durable. Despite the recent growth of state-run producer cartels (themselves hardly stable), private cartels have declined substantially since the interwar period, when market-sharing agreements covered chemicals, copper, tin, rubber, electrical appliances, and nitrates, among others.[15] Best known was the oil cartel, solidified by the Achnacarry Accord. Its history is instructive. In 1929, the leading firms—Jersey Standard (now Exxon), Royal Dutch Shell, and Anglo-Persian (now British Petroleum)—agreed to organize and manage world markets to minimize competition. Yet they were unable to control new discoveries worldwide and could not prevent the rise of new international firms.[16] Their orderly arrangements began to collapse piecemeal within three or four years, eroded by the same engine of competition that gave birth to them. They did not last more than a decade.

To summarize: the secular decrease in private cartels, together with the growing interpenetration of corporate markets, has fostered greater effective rivalry among multinational firms.*

As competition in basic industries increased, transnational sanctions weakened. These sanctions, whether by nineteenth-century bondholders or modern multinational firms, depend on the effective

---

*The size of multinational firms and their often-crucial role in smaller economies may obscure this trend toward more competition. But the trend itself is unambiguous in most basic industries and carries with it, I argue, significant opportunities for national controls by LDCs.

organization of private resources. That organization is usually easier in small groups. When oligopolies are tight, multinational corporations can effectively boycott governments that have nationalized one of their number. The boycott of Iranian oil by the major oil companies in the early 1950s is the most prominent example.

It is important to understand the essential logic of collective action among multinational firms. As a rule, it is far easier to act collectively in small groups (although it may well be possible in large groups without central organization if they are built up from the overlapping interactions of constituent small groups). In small groups, such as industrial oligopolies, the participants' continuing interaction fosters the knowledge essential for conventional behavior and provides opportunities for low-cost sanctions.[17] As most industries grow competitive, however, they find coordination difficult because they lack extensive networks of reciprocal interaction.

The most significant exception is commercial banking. There are extensive reciprocal ties among overlapping small groups of banks. They are joined together by cross-depositing, correspondent banking services, continuing participation in syndicate lending, and so forth. These extensive, long-term ties among banks, which are essential to their profitability, have aided significantly in coordinating their response to troubled debt. The largest banks are usually able to devise a common position among themselves regarding, say, Peru's debts, and then gain acceptance from hundreds of small lenders. Most simply sign on the dotted line, but the large banks have a variety of potential sanctions to bring recalcitrant creditors back to the common position. The most important is the credible threat to isolate individual small creditors from further participation in various banking networks.[18]

Multinational manufacturing and extractive firms, by contrast, have far fewer overlapping activities. For that reason, they have far fewer potential sanctions (positive or negative) *against each other* that could be used to facilitate common action, such as coordinated sanctions against an expropriating country. As industries become more competitive, they find collective action more and more difficult since they lack the extensive networks of reciprocal interaction that encourage coordination.

Firms in more competitive industries are pulled by opposing currents. They may hope to join with their competitors to punish an expropriator, but they also know that some of their legion may well break ranks. This threat of defection grows as the number of competitors increases. The likelihood of cheating makes it virtually impossible to forge stable, informal monopolies out of competitive industries.* (Nevertheless, nationalization can evoke diffuse, uncoordinated sanctions, even from competitive industries, because it discourages new investments by raising the associated risks.)

The problem, as far as each corporation is concerned, is that anti-expropriation sanctions carry substantial individual risks. That is especially true if the firm still has investments that have not yet been touched by the target country. But if the risks face each individual corporation, the benefits of investment protection are largely collective. That is why I have stressed the importance of concentrated economic structure, which facilitates the provision of public goods.**

Over the past decade, the balance of corporate risks and benefits has shifted, making collective sanctions less likely. More corporations in more industries have developed multinational investment capabilities. In basic industries especially, they have "uncoupled" the investment package, offering nonequity arrangements and joint ventures as well as fully owned investments. These changes make collective sanctions less likely for several reasons. First, since many companies can adapt profitably to new host-state restrictions and even to expropriation, they see fewer benefits in joining with others to oppose them. Second, if host states can find alternative investors, the costs and risks of opposing their restrictions increase. As competition grows within an industry, these alternatives become progressively easier to find. Finally, as the number of investors grows, the transaction costs of achieving agreement among them also grows. Free riders may become a problem, for instance, since some benefits of collective sanctions accrue to all investors, whether they participate or not. For all these reasons the proliferation of multinational investors has decreased the likelihood of collective sanctions.

Collective sanctions, in this case, means the cessation of a desired flow of corporate resources—perhaps technology, or capital investments, or export-marketing skills. While there are no detailed statistical studies concerning the effect of expropriation on capital flows,

---

*That is the lesson of the old "trusts": monopoly had to be formalized because there were too many participants for informal methods and too great incentives to cheat.

**The alternative, of course, is the provision of public goods through externally imposed coordination, either through the state or international institutions. I shall return to this point later in this chapter.

the general trend is obvious. As late as the mid-1960s, expropriations shut off a nation's access to foreign capital. They symbolized a broad attack on foreign corporations, and so dramatically raised the (perceived) risk of investing in that country. Furthermore, since corporations were committed exclusively to a strategy of direct equity investments, they could not profitably engage in *any* activities without exposing themselves to expropriation. Now, of course, many firms are willing to "unbundle" their activities, supplying some services under contract or through licensing agreements. Some companies may even make direct investments despite the expropriation of a fellow national, if they calculate that the expropriation was aimed narrowly at a specific firm or sector, as it often is today. As a result of these adaptive corporate strategies and a more selective pattern of foreign takeovers, expropriations no longer uniformly cut off the flow of corporate resources, although they may diminish it substantially in highly vulnerable sectors such as mineral extraction.*

In contrast to expropriations, debt default still has a serious impact on related resource flows: portfolio loans. Unlike most direct investments, portfolio lending involves a high degree of coordination and linkage among investors. The loans are generally syndicated and the

---

*The risks to extractive industries have unquestionably slowed investment in those sectors where projects typically require years of stable, profitable operation to recover the initial investment. The sums involved are huge. In copper, for example, major new projects now cost between $4,000 and $8,000 per ton of annual capacity—$300 to $500 million for large mines—to construct the mine itself and the concentration plant, smelter, refinery, necessary infrastructure, and auxiliary installations. With such large sums at stake and such a long pay-out required, the risks are enormous. They are associated, to some extent, with *all* less developed countries, since even the most receptive might be in exile before the first copper reaches the market.

One study of the copper industry, commissioned by the Economic and Social Council of the United Nations, pays appropriate homage to the goal of local control and then states that the "quantum jump in the risk of foreign investment in the mining sector of developing countries" has choked off new investment. "The drop has been especially severe in the case of exploration spending."

This perception of increased risks has slowed direct investments in extractive industries at a time when future supplies of raw materials are a serious concern to industrialized consumers. Out of this dilemma have grown various proposals for an "international presence," such as Kissinger's abortive International Resources Bank and a U.N.-proposed International Minerals Investment Trust. Both are designed to provide a steady flow of new capital while sharing the corporate risks in raw-materials extraction. Neither proposal has been spelled out in detail, however, perhaps because they failed to generate much initial support. Still, the U.N. study concludes:

If copper is to make its rightful contribution to the development process . . . and if the metal is to be produced at even approximately minimum cost, then a resumption of capital exports for copper investment must occur. But, this will require a reduction in and wider distribution of the risks of such investment. The latter, in turn, may require the use of supplemental financing arrangements.

lenders interlocked in numerous other ways. Because of this interlocking credit structure, a nation that unilaterally suspends debt repayment cannot simply turn to new lenders in the Euromarkets or elsewhere. Rather, to default deliberately (without creditor-approved rescheduling) is to exclude oneself from international capital markets. Access to international banking networks is instantly severed, and financial assets abroad are subject to blockage and seizure.

This powerful array of private, transnational sanctions does not rule out tough bargaining between impoverished debtors and their creditors. Such bargaining is commonplace since both parties have a strong interest in avoiding default. But significantly, it always takes place *before* default. (In the case of forced divestments, by contrast, the bargaining over terms, the future role of the firm, and other conditions often occur after the state takeover.) Debtors naturally fear the impending loss of credit, which is essential for financing trade as well as for capital imports. Creditors wish to avoid writing off bad loans. Since even coherent sanctions cannot extract hard currency from truly impoverished debtors, the creditors may prefer to refinance their outstanding loans and even provide some new credit. In any case, both debtors and creditors consider mutual agreement essential, and the creditors have succeeded in making IMF participation a condition for that agreement.*

This debt refinancing is a collective adaptation to investment insecurity and, as such, parallels the adaptation by multinational firms. There are, however, fundamental differences. In most cases, expropriation does *not* halt the flow of direct investment. Unilateral default, by contrast, always halts portfolio lending. This basic difference in sanctioning capacity derives from the different organization of portfolio and direct investment (a point already touched upon and one that will be subsequently explored). It directly affects the relative risks of the two types of investment and, coming full circle, encourages still further adaptation by multinational corporations, who cannot deter expropriation by private, self-reliant sanctions.

The same could be said for other natural resources. Wolfgang Gluschke, Joseph Shaw, and Bension Varon, *Copper: The Next Fifteen Years* (Dordrecht, The Netherlands: D. Reidel Publishing for the United Nations, 1979), 77–79, 115 (first quotation), 119 (second quotation). Gluschke, Shaw, and Varon work for the Center for Natural Resources, Energy and Transport, the United Nations Secretariat.

*The centerpiece of IMF participation is its negotiation of a national economic stabilization program and then its ongoing surveillance of that program's implementation.

Thus, as expropriation risks have increased over the past decade, most corporations have responded flexibly and individually, rather than punitively and collectively. The greater risks did not necessarily prevent new investments, but they did affect their form. Ad hoc responses proliferated. Political risks were considered more carefully during the investment decision process. When new investments were planned, their size and location, financing and prospective pay-out were all analyzed with reference to expropriation risks and were often modified as a result. As Theodore Moran has shown, some firms have arranged their expansions with a keen eye toward self-protection.[19] Still others adapted by relying less on risky direct investments and more on management contracts, long-term production agreements, and other aspects of vertically integrated production and distribution networks. Japanese firms have been especially innovative,[20] with American and European firms quickly following suit.

These newer investment strategies, as well as more careful attempts to assess political risks, can be understood as self-reliant efforts to reduce vulnerability. They expand corporate options within host states and, if successful, preserve the firm's larger transnational network. These sophisticated strategies both *reflect* the rise in expropriation risks and *contribute to it.* By giving host states a wider array of investment possibilities, they make wholly owned foreign investments less attractive. Thus, the individual firm's adaptation actually heightens the vulnerability of all firms.*

Although transnational corporations cannot act effectively by themselves, it is possible that unity might be forced upon them. There are currently two major obstacles, however. First, no single state has sufficient jurisdiction. European, Japanese, and American corporations are all involved. Only an international organization could coordinate them all. Such organizations exist in international finance, but they have no counterparts in direct investment. What about less comprehensive solutions then? The U.S. government could, hypothetically at least, impose some order on its own investors while seeking agreements with other capital-exporting states. Apart from the enormous diplomatic tasks involved, there are serious domestic difficulties. Of all advanced capitalist states, the United States is probably least able to formulate coherent public policies in the face of

---

*The irony could be termed ecological. That is, increased security at the level of the firm does *not* imply increased security for all firms—the international regime level.

competitive private interests. The state apparatus is relatively fragmented, its policy networks decentralized.[21] The result, as Stephen Krasner has observed, is that "it has been very difficult for American central decision makers to change the behavior of non-state domestic actors."[22]

That difficulty is exacerbated by the limited array of U.S. policy instruments. Compared with Japan, France, or West Germany, the United States has few means of manipulating specific firms or economic sectors.[23] In the case of anti-expropriation policy, for instance, it has almost no tools to curb transnational anomie. Its policies are largely confined to informal persuasion and the demonstration effects of its diplomacy. The U.S. government is ill equipped, then, to prevent ad hoc corporate adaptation to expropriation. Thus, the coherence of transnational sanctions—to the extent that it exists—is primarily a function of oligopoly structure.*

Although the U.S. government could not forge transnational sanctions, it could employ national ones. In fact, U.S. economic sanctions were an important source of investment security through the late 1960s. They included:

1. informal sanctions, such as the quiet termination of bilateral assistance; and
2. formal sanctions, including
   (a) termination of bilateral assistance as explicit retaliation for expropriation, for example, the Hickenlooper amendment;
   (b) restricted access to U.S. commercial and financial markets, for example, the Trading with the Enemy Act; and
   (c) legal restraints on the purchase of commodities or natural resources produced at expropriated facilities.

*This analysis illustrates the empirical plausibility of our theoretical assumption: private economic sanctions derive their coherence from industrial or financial structure. But note that the usefulness of this assumption for our model does not depend on its descriptive accuracy. See Kenneth Waltz, "Theory of International Relations," in *Handbook of Political Science*, vol. 8, *International Politics*, ed. Nelson W. Polsby and Fred I. Geenstein (Reading, Mass.: Addison-Wesley, 1975), 36.

My analysis also suggests that public policies could, under hypothetical conditions, forge unified transnational sanctions *in spite of the actors' divergent interests*. If so, then our model could be simplified by deleting reference to transnational actors. Economic sanctions could be analyzed exclusively in terms of nation-states and international organizations. This would set aside complex questions about market structure and unified private action since their effects would be contained by political institutions. In fact, as I have shown, neither Great Britain nor the United States actually imposed such unity on private actors. Hence, the structure of transnational networks is a prime determinant of private economic sanctions.

Most of these were postwar innovations or, like the restrictions on Export-Import Bank lending, only slightly older. The only significant exception is the Trading with the Enemy Act, which was passed during World War I.

Leaving U.S. policy at the World Bank and the IMF aside, there are several specifically American programs to consider. Both the Agency for International Development (AID) and the Export-Import Bank can channel funds to compliant states and sanction others by omission. And, unlike Victorian Britain, the United States has shown some willingness to manipulate imports and exports as policy instruments—a stance that dates back at least to the 1917 Trading with the Enemy Act. The Hickenlooper amendment (designed to cut off aid to expropriating countries, discussed in chapter 6) was reinforced by similar legislation on sugar quotas. These quotas could be denied if U.S. firms were expropriated without prompt, adequate, and effective compensation. The United States has also used the Export Control Act of 1949 and its successor, the Export Administration Act of 1969, to control the trade of U.S. companies and their foreign affiliates. It was used, for example, to embargo grain sales to the Soviet Union after the 1980 Afghanistan invasion and is far tougher than any European law. Still, as I noted earlier, attempts to control corporate trade and investment are relatively infrequent. Sanctions at the national level have been far more important.

According to the model, these sanctions derive their impact from the prominent position of the United States in the world economy. As major alternative markets developed, first in Europe and then in Japan, the capacity for coherent sanctions naturally declined. Consider the U.S. share of manufacturing output among ten major industrial countries. Between 1950 and 1955, the United States held about a 60 percent share; in the 1970s, it was about 43 percent.[24] U.S. merchandise imports—a crucial item for many countries—are now about one-fifth the total for all industrial market economies.[25] Or consider the declining status of America as an aid donor. In the early 1960s, America's net contribution far exceeded what all others gave. In 1960, for instance, the United States gave about one and a half times the amount given by all other OECD countries. By the late 1960s, however, the figures were roughly equal, and by 1982, other OECD countries were giving almost two and a half times as much as the United States.[26] The figures for trade with less developed countries, export credits, and other resource transfers may differ, but their trend is surely similar. Whatever measures are used, America has obviously lost much of its postwar preeminence in world markets. According to our model, this decentralization of national economic resources implies weaker international restraints against expropriation.

The restraints against expropriation obviously include both public and private sanctions, but it is difficult—perhaps impossible—to make reliable assessments about their distinctive effects. The basic analytic problem is that public sanctions, both economic and military, and private transnational sanctions have followed roughly similar patterns. This collinearity makes it virtually impossible to attach relative weights to each type of sanction. It does not, however, confuse the evaluation of these sanctions taken together.

Both interventionary force and transnational finance were highly concentrated from the mid-nineteenth century until World War I. According to our model, that concentration of resources implies severe restraints against expropriation. Those restraints were indeed effective. The international regime governing foreign investment was well articulated, and foreign capital was well protected. During the interwar period, when military and economic resources were more diffuse, the regime weakened. Our model of international restraints indicates such a weakening. But to focus exclusively on international restraints would be misleading in this case. Although restraints were weak during the interwar period, the international regime remained relatively strong. There were, of course, major expropriations in the Soviet Union and Mexico. But, on the whole, foreign capital was relatively secure. To model this result adequately, one must refer not only to international restraints but also to the policies and capabilities of host states.

Turning to the postwar period, our model of international restraints again indicates severe external limits on expropriation, followed by their progressive weakening. That accurately represents the regime *in general terms*. There are, however, some gaps that can only be illuminated by a more complete model. For example, the postwar regime included a wider scope for host-state action than in the nineteenth century. Once again, the model should include some reference to the changing policies and capabilities of host states. Second, the model, as developed so far, cannot adequately discriminate between direct investments and portfolio loans. In the most recent period, direct investments have been subject to a broad range of national treatment. Yet medium- and long-term loans have been relatively secure, despite widespread refinancing and fears of default. Most loans have been repaid or rescheduled. There have been almost no cases of unilateral debt renunciation. The differential security of loan portfolios and direct investments can be clarified by reference to their different organizational characteristics.

International Organizations and Investment Protection

No international institution has exclusive jurisdiction over the treatment of foreign capital. Nor is the issue divided systematically among several institutions, each handling a functionally distinct problem. Rather, several institutions have asserted partial jurisdiction, creating a series of overlapping domains and conflicting claims.

At least three types of international institutions have been drawn into foreign investment disputes. *General international forums* have facilitated debate over traditional anti-expropriation norms and have helped host countries advance their political claims. The United Nations has been especially prominent. Because of its broad membership and egalitarian voting rules, its resolutions grant politically significant approval (or disapproval) to national policies and international property rules. *International financial institutions,* such as the IMF and World Bank, have reiterated traditional values and punished violators by withholding loans. Because they furnish balance-of-payments credits, capital financing, and budgetary support, these institutions have obvious powers to sanction expropriation. So, in theory, do *regulatory agencies* such as the International Court of Justice, although in practice their authority has been curtailed severely.

Despite their differences, these institutions share one common feature. With only one exception, no existing institutions are devoted entirely to foreign investment issues. Only the World Bank's International Center for the Settlement of Investment Disputes (ICSID) concentrates exclusively on such issues. The rest deal with investment questions as important items on their already long agendas. (For a summary of these distinctions, see figure 3.)

Because expropriation is such a contentious issue, regime-specific

Organizational Domain

	Regime Specific	General
Capital transfer (economic sanctions)	Proposed International Resources Bank	IMF; World Bank Group: IBRD, IFC, & regional development banks
Regulation	ICSID	International Court of Justice OECD
Forum for debate		U.N. General Assembly and U.N. agencies, esp. UNCTAD

Organizational Function (vertical label at left)

Figure 3. International Organizations Affecting Investment Security

institutions have an extremely difficult time gaining support, or even getting started. The pervasive fear is that the organizations will fall into the wrong hands. As a result, the regulation of foreign investment has always been a many-sided contest involving international organizations, host states, home states, and multinational investors (with the last two usually, but not always, allied). Each can appeal to the normative authority of international law, and the respective states can take their claims to a variety of international institutions. But no international body has the authority to set investment rules, and none has broad regulatory powers. Indeed, the most recent proposal to create such a regulatory agency—a GATT for investment—failed badly.[27] Proposals to take up investment issues at the regular GATT trade negotiations have also failed.[28]

The limitations of existing regulatory agencies are exemplified by ICSID. Not only is ICSID limited to an arbiter's role, it lacks the power to enforce its own decisions. Its jurisdiction is confined to disputes submitted voluntarily by *both* parties, a requirement that excludes the most important and controversial cases.[29] Even so, Latin American states have refused to join ICSID, claiming that its jurisdiction inherently conflicts with national economic sovereignty.

The International Court of Justice (ICJ) is hampered by similar restrictions: all parties must submit the dispute voluntarily, and awards are not enforceable by the court. The ICJ is further limited because, unlike ICSID, its litigants must be national governments. The investor's home state must decide whether to sponsor the claim, while the host state must decide whether to submit to ICJ jurisdiction. The final award, in any case, must be executed by the parties themselves. Not surprisingly, few investment disputes have been resolved through these channels, and neither the ICJ nor ICSID has had much impact on the treatment of foreign investment.

International financial institutions have been much more aggressive, and certainly more successful, in restraining adverse national treatment of foreign capital. Both the IMF and World Bank group have extensive resources, which can be withheld as sanctions. Their financial power has been used to deter expropriations and ensure prompt settlements.

The World Bank has acted at times like the United States' junior partner in protecting foreign investments. This close connection is partly the result of direct U.S. influence at the Bank and partly the result of similar institutional interests. The Bank's charter mandates it to encourage international investments, the Bank's donors continue to support that policy, and its administrators have been more than willing to comply.*

This pro-investment policy is reinforced by two of the Bank's central features: its voting procedures and its sources of capital. Member states vote in proportion to their capital subscriptions. This arrangement ensures that donor states will control the Bank's basic policies, if not its details. Since the United States is the Bank's leading subscriber, it carries considerable weight at the International Bank for Reconstruction and Development, at the International Development Agency, and at the Inter-American Development Bank. Besides these voting rules, the Bank is dependent upon capitalist states (and now

---

*Edward Mason and Robert Asher, *The World Bank Since Bretton Woods* (Washington: Brookings Institution, 1973), 338. In addition, a clause in one internal World Bank document, policy memorandum 204, states explicitly that the Bank will not lend to countries that nationalize foreign property without adequate compensation. This clause was invoked after the Peruvian government expropriated the International Petroleum Company, an Exxon subsidiary, in 1968 and a few years later when Chile expropriated its major copper mines without offering significant compensation. See "Peru and the International Finance Agencies," *Andean Air Mail and Peruvian Times*, May 7, 1971, p. 9, and Paul E. Sigmund, *Multinationals in Latin America: The Politics of Nationalization* (Madison: University of Wisconsin Press for the Twentieth Century Fund, 1980), 153–154, 194, 207.

a few oil-rich states as well) for its capital resources. These financial relations inevitably reinforce the Bank's weighted voting. As Charles Frank, Jr., and Mary Baird observe:

> Voting power is only a reflection of a more fundamental relationship between power and source of finance. The African Development Bank lacks financial resources precisely because of the lack of developed country participation. Regardless of the distribution of voting power, the World Bank and the regional banks cannot follow policies grossly inconsistent with the desires of major donors. They cannot jeopardize their main sources of finance.[30]

Neither donor states nor private lenders have been willing to underwrite expropriations through their loans. The Bank's policy is framed in terms of its developmental mission and illustrates, in turn, the Bank's conception of development. According to a 1971 memorandum, the Bank will not lend to a country or appraise its projects if a country's "position . . . with respect to alien owners of expropriated property is substantially affecting its international credit standing."[31] The memorandum merely records the Bank's long-standing policy. The Bank's historians, Mason and Asher, conclude that ongoing expropriation disputes held up a number of loans during the 1960s and 1970s.[32]

None of this means that the United States and the World Bank follow absolutely identical policies. The Bank is the collective instrument of all advanced capitalist states, the United States foremost among them. Even the dominance of U.S. citizens in the Bank's top positions does not mean total agreement with U.S. policies. Clearly, the Bank's bureaucracy has independent procedures, its own organizational interests and perspectives, and some autonomous authority. Its discretionary authority expands when major donors disagree, as they sometimes do in expropriation cases. In sum, the Bank is bound to the United States, but not always tightly. Their anti-expropriation policies are similar and usually reinforcing, but not always coincident.

The Bank's policies toward defaulted debt are comparable.[33] These policies date back to the Bank's opening days, when it refused to lend to states with defaulted loans from the 1930s. Although the Bank applied this policy uniformly, its initial burden fell on the region with the most defaults—Latin America.[34] The Bank, eager to win support from a skeptical financial community, took a tough stand. With strong support from the IMF, the Bank forced the resolution of most Depression-era defaults. Most were settled by the mid-1950s,[35] but, in the case of Guatemala, the Bank persisted until the debts were settled in 1966. The Bank's tenacity is especially noteworthy since the Guatemalan bonds had been issued in 1829.[36]

The Bank's policies on expropriation and default are duplicated by its companion institution, the IMF. The two institutions have comparable voting and financial arrangements, and both are committed to an open international order for investment.[37] When they share a common interest in an issue, say a debt rescheduling in which the Bank is a major creditor, the two institutions work closely together. The Bank has also increased its "structural adjustment lending" for countries with fundamental balance-of-payments problems, setting conditions that are quite similar to the IMF's. It is the Fund, however, that still takes primary responsibility for debt rescheduling and for subsequent oversight of the debtor's economic stabilization program.

If the IMF and World Bank share their opposition to expropriation and debt renunciation, and if national and transnational resources are dispersed among many actors in both cases, why are loans substantially more secure? The question did not arise until recently, since portfolio loans and direct investments had long shared roughly similar treatment. They could be characterized jointly in a single regime governing all foreign capital. Their marked divergence dates to the late 1960s, when expropriations proliferated but debt renunciation (and default more generally) did not.

To account for this divergence one must look beyond national and transnational restraints, which are substantially less concentrated in both cases. *The fundamental difference is the better institutionalization of international finance.*

Despite numerous sources of short-, medium-, and long-term finance, international lenders are well coordinated when default is near. This political coherence in international finance has two basic sources. The first, discussed earlier, is the high degree of interconnectedness among private lenders. The second is the unique institutional capacity of the IMF to manage international debt crises.

When default draws near, the debtor generally approaches its creditors seeking new loans and the extension of old ones. Talks with the IMF begin, while private and official creditors organize themselves into separate conferences to begin their own negotiations. The IMF discussions are crucial to the other negotiations, and the outcomes are closely aligned. The IMF generally agrees to provide additional credit if certain conditions are met. The debtor promises to embark on an austerity program designed to restore balance to external accounts. The program typically includes devaluation, restrictions on domestic credit, and a cutback on government expenditures. Performance targets are set, and the IMF provides its credit in several phases as the borrower adapts to the agreed guidelines.

These stern conditions and the proven ability of the IMF to oversee them form the basis for the private debt talks. Both official and private lenders accept the IMF agreement as solid evidence that the debtor intends to clamp down on its external deficits. Relying on the conservative, highly professional standards of the IMF as well as on its unique access to confidential information, private lenders consider an IMF standby loan a condition for their own renegotiations. Richard Hill, former chairman of the Bank of Boston, offers a particularly incisive view of the IMF's role:

> Sophisticated borrowers and lenders increasingly look to the Fund to set standards for economic stabilization and adjustment. . . . Conditional credit from the Fund is increasingly viewed as an "international certificate of approval," which enhances the ability of a country to borrow in the private market place.[38]

In this manner, public and private creditors jointly negotiate limits on the debtor's economic policies, attempting to secure their investments in the process.*

*Even before the debt crises of the mid-1980s, debt reschedulings were not unusual. To cope with these loan arrearages and balance-of-payments problems, private lenders and international financial institutions developed a network of close (but complex) working relationships. A set of conventionalized expectations emerged from this process, serving to regularize debt rescheduling in the absence of centralized political oversight.

These arrangements were shaken, but not overturned, by the debt crisis of 1982–1983. High real interest rates, heavy debt loads, and a prolonged recession in major export markets combined to produce serious and widespread loan arrearages and dozens of reschedulings. On the South American mainland, for instance, all but one country had been forced to reschedule their debts by 1983.

In spite of the unprecedented scale of these reschedulings, many earlier practices were retained, particularly the insistence on mutual agreement and the implementation of tough economic stabilization programs under IMF supervision.

Still, there were some changes. The IMF's role grew, and it intervened more directly in creditor relationships. In doing so, the IMF was essentially acting to coordinate private refinancing. It did so by providing institutionalized leadership when other, self-reliant means of coordination seemed fragile and perhaps inadequate. The problem

The stakes are substantial, going well beyond one country's financial predicament. Rescheduling and refinancing exercises are designed not only to contain direct losses but also to maintain the integrity of international finance. They are self-conscious efforts to manage the international regime.*

These formal debt renegotiation conferences are well-established arrangements for maintaining order and resolving disputes. They have no counterparts for direct investment, even though the World Bank and IMF do play a role in sanctioning expropriations.

To understand the impact of these organizational arrangements, it is useful to follow Samuel Huntington's analysis of domestic institutionalization. Huntington distinguishes between the *level* of institutionalization and the *scope* of organizational support. Institutionalization, in this case, is defined as the "process by which organizations acquire value and stability. The level of institutionalization of any political system can be defined by the adaptability, complexity, autonomy, and coherence of its organizations and procedures."[39] None of these multilateral financial arrangements could be deemed autonomous, since they are closely monitored and controlled by creditors. Although the World Bank and IMF do have some organizational independence, it is limited. As Frank and Baird observe, "Donor countries have significant control over the basic directions of policy of multilateral institutions, although perhaps not over policy details."[40]

---

lay with smaller creditors, who had few ties to the debtor and were reluctant to postpone their loan collections and make new credits available. Many went along, but some regional banks were reluctant. By balking, they hoped that larger creditors would buy out their loans rather than risk an abortive rescheduling. The IMF stepped into this breach. In some large reschedulings, it authoritatively established the level of new credits to be provided by each private bank. The IMF then refused to sign an economic stabilization package until all banks agreed. The larger banks were grateful, but all private lenders worried about the shifting locus of institutional leadership in debt reschedulings.

*If the rescheduling exercise is traumatic for the debtor, it is also delicate and complicated for the creditors. Obviously they want to place the borrower under close supervision and strict limits. Their capital hangs in the balance. But if those limits are too harsh, they become self-defeating. The deflationary policies demanded by lenders may exceed the political capacity of the state. Or the repayment terms may go beyond the state's ability to pay. If, by contrast, the terms are lenient, creditors may have to put more capital at risk and postpone loan amortization. Such terms may make it harder to convince all creditors to agree to the rescheduling package. Moreover, if lenient terms are implemented, they would hold out an attractive possibility to other debtors. If rescheduling is done swiftly and painlessly for some debtors, then others will be reluctant to meet their more stringent obligations.

Nevertheless, both the IMF and the rescheduling conferences have demonstrated remarkable coherence, coordinating creditors and imposing discipline on borrowers. This coherence is a distinguishing feature of debt management, with few parallels in direct investment. Coherent responses to expropriation have been limited to periods when national or transnational resources were highly concentrated.

While the rescheduling procedures have remained relatively simple, they have proved highly adaptive. First, they have been modified organizationally in the wake of massive oil price increases and, so far at least, have forestalled widespread defaults despite escalating debt burdens. Ad hoc rescheduling procedures have been supplemented by new devices to avoid credit crises. Both the IMF and World Bank have raised their capital subscriptions, stepped up their lending, and set up new balance-of-payments facilities. While their ultimate success is still in doubt, the range of these adaptive responses is itself quite striking.

In terms of adaptability, complexity, and coherence, international lending is much more effectively institutionalized than direct investment. Equally significant, the coordinating organizations have broad support among creditors. Their scope is inclusive, covering the full range of debt crises and encompassing virtually all lenders and borrowers. Nearly all debt crises are dealt with by multilateral institutions.

Unilateral debt renunciation is extremely rare, as is the flat refusal to submit to IMF controls or other joint creditor arrangements.* North Korea provides one of the few modern examples of complete renunciation. Even socialist Chile, which confiscated numerous U.S. direct investments and suspended its debt service, nevertheless refused to repudiate its inherited debts. Instead, it asked—with only partial success—for a renegotiation of payments falling due between 1971 and 1973.[41]

---

*The debtor is not without bargaining power in the rescheduling exercise. Although creditors are naturally reluctant to provide still more credit, they may be even more hesitant about writing off their earlier loans by refusing. If they think the new loans will secure the older ones, their own interests may compel them to provide additional credit. The creditors' stake in saving their existing investments gives borrowers some leverage.

Many commentators, especially those writing for banking publications, emphasize this power of the debtor. They note that creditors seldom refuse to reschedule and that rescheduling inherently involves some concessions by creditors, either stretched-out repayments or new loans. This commentary, correct as far as it goes, is deceptively

By the same token, rescheduling has incorporated all major creditors. They have strong incentives to form a joint policy and few reasons to act alone. Private creditors, for example, want public funds and multilateral supervision. Moreover, no creditor would be able to forge bilateral arrangements unless the borrower considered them more attractive than the collective solution. But, if that were so, the arrangements would be *less* attractive to the lender. In any case, individual creditors could seldom provide enough new capital to secure their loans and would run substantial individual risks. The only individual creditor capable of striking favorable individual bargains would be a major national creditor, such as the United States. The United States, however, has generally acted as a regime leader, declining bilateral arrangements and joining with smaller creditors in multilateral rescheduling.[42]

These multilateral arrangements may provide better security for portfolio lending than for direct investment, but that does not explain *why* one type of foreign capital is effectively institutionalized and the other is not.

The answer lies in two basic differences between the network of international lending and that of equity investments. The first is that multinational corporations have largely independent interests in expropriation disputes; financial institutions have joint interests. For example, when Peru expropriated an Exxon subsidiary in 1968, other foreign investors there were not directly affected. True, their own investments might be less secure, but they could continue to operate them alongside the newly nationalized oil company. The surest way to endanger these investments would be to make common cause with Exxon and attempt to retaliate against Peru. This kind of disaggregation is unknown in international finance. The lenders are interconnected and mutually dependent, even if they are numerous.

incomplete. The debtor almost always makes substantial concessions to receive the loan, including oversight of its economy and guidelines for policy. Collectively, debtors may have the power to disrupt international finance, but individually they are vulnerable to creditor demands.

When new loans are provided, one of the most intriguing questions is who provides them. It need not be the original lenders. Indeed, those lenders have every incentive to shift the burden. In most debt crises, private banks attempt to shift that burden onto national or multilateral institutions. In effect, they want to receive risk premiums without accepting the risks. (Palmerston said exactly that to mid-nineteenth-century British lenders.) Underlying the recent public discussion of growing debt burdens among less developed countries, one can detect both a desire to maintain the financial system as a whole and the desire of private banks to shift the risk of refinancing onto their home governments and multilateral banks.

Rescheduling one loan inevitably affects the repayment of others. Moreover, many of the loans are underwritten jointly. This mutual dependence among financial institutions is significant because it is continually rewritten on an international scale. Major banks are linked in a multitude of ways—from correspondent relations and cross-deposits to lending consortia. Because they are reciprocally vulnerable, there are strong deterrents to beggar-thy-neighbor policies. Among direct investments, only the tightest oligopolies have that kind of reciprocal vulnerability.

Because the interests of direct investors are separable, their home governments have little incentive to become involved in one another's expropriation disputes. In fact, to do so might endanger their own nationals' foreign property. Even the leading foreign investor—Great Britain and then the United States—has no immediate stake in the property rights of French or German investors. They may assume that stake, and sometimes have, when they hold hegemonial power in a region and wish to play a larger role in organizing its property relations. But more often they have protected others' investments as a by-product of protecting their own. Obviously, such a protective relationship is not symmetrical. The most serious investment disputes in the past twenty-five years have involved American investors, and other capital-exporting states have refused to commit their diplomatic resources to them. For the same reason, they have been reluctant to establish multilateral institutions. Knowing that institutions to protect foreign investment would be opposed fiercely by less developed states and would deal mostly with the problems of U.S. firms, other capital-exporters have shied away from institution building.

International lending, by contrast, typically involves American, European, and Japanese banks in joint arrangements. Given the international reach of banking syndicates, even the smallest debtors have hundreds of creditors from all around the world. About 220 banks, for instance, were involved in restructuring Costa Rica's $3 billion debt.[43] A much larger debt such as Brazil's is owed to over 700 foreign banks.[44] Every capital-exporting country has banks involved in one Brazilian loan or another. This kind of coincident national involvement provides powerful incentives to coordinate action.

Of course, powerful incentives do not imply successful coordination, especially if there are many actors. Rather, the prospect of joint gains and joint losses merely implies that coordination could benefit many creditors *if it were provided institutionally.*

The IMF and, to a lesser extent, the World Bank are well situated to provide that coordination. As major creditors themselves, they often have a direct stake in debt questions. As potential suppliers of refinancing, they are capable (within limits) of setting its terms, which include fiscal and monetary policy directives and the repayment of other debts. Harold van B. Cleveland and W. H. Bruce Brittain, bankers familiar with debt-service problems, acknowledge the central position of the IMF:

> The IMF enters the picture when a country has trouble servicing its foreign debt and difficulty in borrowing privately. When the problem is traceable to the debtor country's own macroeconomic policies, the IMF may be able to persuade the government to adopt a stabilization program in return for standby credit and the IMF's seal of approval. This in turn helps create conditions in which the country's private creditors will be willing to reschedule their claims, in order to reduce its current service debt burden.[45]

Cleveland and Brittain allude to the central difference between debt renunciation and confiscatory expropriation. It is *not* the existence of multilateral sanctions, for they are present in both cases. Rather, it is that multilateral institutions are able to coordinate *all* sanctions in international finance, while in direct investment they cannot. Only in international finance do multilateral arrangements serve to organize a comprehensive network of restraints. In the case of direct investment, multilateral sanctions are important, but they do not extend beyond the institutions' own resources.

Both types of sanctions have their limits, of course. Debt rescheduling does not bar new loans. In fact, by improving the debtor's credit structure and imposing restraints on domestic economic policies, it actually encourages them. But the greatest weakness of all investment protection measures is the absence of broad international approval, covering both host states and debtors. At most, the sanctions are obscure, remote, and difficult to oppose effectively.

The legitimation issue is posed most sharply in the case of direct investment. The World Bank's voting procedures may make it simple to withhold credit from expropriating countries, but they still cannot effectively justify traditional anti-expropriation norms. That function has been taken over by other international organizations—those with large memberships (universal or regional) and nominal equality in voting procedures. Organizations such as the United Nations serve as forums for the political initiatives of weak states. And it is those states that have used them to reorder the international agenda and establish congenial norms for national policies.

In fact, the rights of foreign investors have long been debated in international arenas. As early as 1889, at the First Inter-American Conference, some Latin American states challenged the right of the United States to intervene to protect the lives and property of its nationals. During the interwar period, special League of Nations conferences were stalemated on the issue of investors' rights and host states' obligations. The same issues came to the same end at the International Trade Organization (ITO) conferences in the late 1940s. They later resurfaced at the United Nations, where less developed states now regularly pass resolutions asserting permanent sovereignty over natural resources.

Beneath this obvious continuity lies significant change. First, the number of independent, less developed states has expanded dramatically. At the League of Nations and ITO conferences, rich and poor nations were nearly equal numerically. At the United Nations, advanced capitalist states are far outnumbered. The Group of 77 is now only a symbolic title for the group of less developed states; they number well over a hundred.*

Equally important, these states now debate investment questions in *permanent* forums, most notably the U.N. General Assembly. Less developed states are brought into protracted contact in a congenial forum and, as a result, have a better chance to identify common concerns and policy preferences. Working out these joint programs is a complex, delicate process; permanent institutional arrangements can play a vital facilitating role. The same institutions also present an attractive platform to proclaim these joint concerns and common demands.

While the U.N. General Assembly is the most important of these permanent forums, it is not alone. UNCTAD has been a regular site for developing common positions and forcing their international consideration. The Economic Commission of Latin America (ECLA), especially under Raul Prebisch's leadership, articulated a distinctive strategy for economic development while training an impressive number of national administrators. Taken together, these U.N. agencies form a complex, permanent communications network for less developed states.

*The term was taken from the original membership of less developed states in UNCTAD.

The new numbers, the permanent forums, and the egalitarian voting procedures combine to furnish a setting well disposed to normative change. Less developed states have used that setting to reject international standards regarding the treatment of foreign investment. They have slowly delegitimated the traditional rules governing foreign investments. In their place they have put economic sovereignty.

The extent of this change can be seen in day-to-day expropriation questions. Negotiations are almost always limited to compensation. Unless the expropriations are extensive, the host state no longer needs to justify its takings internationally. Multinational firms and home states seldom challenge, in principle, the extension of state control.[46]

This normative change reinforces the bargaining position of host states and weakens that of multinational corporations and home states. It makes property rules more difficult and costly to enforce. The same process has eroded, but not obliterated, traditional legal standards. It is still important to avoid the appearance of arbitrary or capricious disregard for foreign property, and there is considerable incentive to agree on compensation.

These normative changes, like the multilateral economic sanctions discussed earlier, are the proximate result of majority coalitions in international organizations. In the United Nations, as in the IMF, organizational policies are determined by the ability to manipulate coalition formation. Coalition formation, in turn, is a function not only of the members' policy preferences but also of the institutions' internal arrangements: its membership, its voting procedures, its committee structure, its sources of finance. In the United Nations, these arrangements have facilitated a normative attack on traditional investor privileges, including the fundamental notion of international minimum standards of treatment. In international financial institutions, where most of the same states are members, the organizations' alternative arrangements (especially their weighted voting procedures) define a different universe of power and facilitate alternative coalitions and policies.

Economic Nationalism

The United Nations may have facilitated collaboration among less developed states, but that does not account for the substantive character of that collaboration. The U.N. Resolutions on Permanent Sovereignty can be comprehended only in the context of pervasive, if variously defined, economic nationalism.

Accompanying this nationalism has been a dramatic secular growth of state economic capabilities and a corresponding increase in the scope of public policy. More and more states have developed the administrative capacity to manage large-scale production, or regulate it with sophistication. In many countries, in many industries, it is now possible to nationalize production without technical confusion or economic disruption. The growth of these state capabilities and the parallel rise of economic nationalism form the immediate domestic context of expropriation. According to the model, this increasing propensity to expropriate, combined with diffused international restraints, has severely weakened the international regime governing foreign direct investment.

Without denying the wide variety of social structures and political institutions among less developed states, some common features are also evident. The growth of state administrative staffs and the expansion of their tasks is quite widespread. In diverse settings, for diverse reasons, less developed states have taken on a more substantial economic role. Most now attempt to plan the development process; they often play a major role as goal setter, fiscal agent, regulator, and, in some cases, allocator of capital and producer.* Likewise, across a broad range of countries, the sponsorship of economic development has become a prime source of state legitimacy.[47]

The result is seldom that less developed economies are more self-reliant, but rather that their transnational networks of trade and investment are more often subject to state manipulation. Again, some common elements appear: increased surveillance of corporate activity, attempts to increase commercial competition for local markets, efforts to secure alternative sources of foreign capital, pressure on multinational firms to structure their local activity to meet state goals (such as in exports, import substitution, reinvestment, hiring and promotion, local participation, and so forth).[48] By the same token,

---

*If this were an effort to understand the domestic context of expropriation in detail, I would need to formulate a more complicated model. That model would presumably offer some theoretical basis for disaggregating less developed states, permitting one to set expropriation in systematically differentiated national contexts.

My model is simpler: it does not subdivide less developed states, just as it does not assume distinctive regional structures of force. In both cases I have made simplifying assumptions—assumptions which are properly judged by their consequences. If the international regime were systematically differentiated by type of host state or by region, then additional complexity might be warranted.

most expropriations and forced sales are really state efforts to re-structure transnational networks and redistribute their economic benefits, not to shut them out entirely. They are usually designed to increase local participation (either through state ownership or indigenization) and to exercise direct control over the distribution of profits, direction of new investments, and operation of local facilities. Foreign capital is usually still welcome in other sectors. Indeed, the expropriated owners themselves are often invited to remain in a managerial capacity and given incentives to stay.

Generalizations about state economic capabilities must be carefully limited since policies and institutions differ not only by country but also by sector and even subsector. State management and detailed regulation are most effective in mature sectors, which are basic to future industrialization. Nationalization strategies have generally aimed at eliminating foreign predominance in those key areas and in economic infrastructure. Miguel Wionczek's observations about Mexico are applicable more broadly:

> Industrialization . . . was considered a purely nationalist undertaking that—it was expected and hoped—would change in the long run the political and economic power relationship between Mexico and the outside world. Such a strategy called for progressive elimination of foreign enclaves from agriculture, transport and communications, banking, oil, electric energy, and, finally, mining.[49]

In all but the least developed countries, state technocrats have been able to manage these sectors adequately, though sometimes they have exercised that control through private consultants and foreign management contracts.

The growth of state capabilities is especially clear-cut in mature industries such as oil production. National firms in oil-producing countries have taken over smoothly from multinational operators in recent years. By contrast, when Bolivia expropriated Standard Oil in 1937, it was unable to operate the facilities and ultimately had to import oil to replace its nationalized production.[50]

State intervention has been least successful, and frequently self-defeating, in sectors where technology and international markets change rapidly and continuously. Even advanced states have been unable to foster successful firms in these sectors, as John Zysman points out in his study of French economic policy.[51] The state's unique advantages—its ability to channel domestic capital flows, control local competition, and provide a stable, captured market—are only marginally important in these sectors. The critical advantage of multinational investors is their intimate knowledge of these changing markets and their ability to adapt swiftly and innovate continuously. Even if multinational companies were willing to sell their proprietary knowledge—and they vary on this touchy issue—national firms would still lack a steady flow of market-related innovations. In technologically advanced markets, relevant technology is not a discrete product or process. It is a continuing function of organizational intelligence.[52]

Because of these distinctive features, less developed states have been unable to expropriate or control technologically advanced and rapidly changing industries without simultaneously destroying their basis for international competition. Sophisticated national negotiators, the Mexicans, for example, have recognized this dilemma and have modified their demands accordingly. Rather than insisting on local control, which might be unattainable or self-defeating in some advanced industries, they have pushed instead for more exports and more local content.*

The difference between mature and technologically advanced industries is important, therefore, for investment security. I have already noted that international restraints are no longer capable of preventing diverse national treatment of foreign capital. Investment security thus hinges on domestic social and political structure, especially the (politically mediated) assessment of gains from alternative policies. If the state is concerned about national shares of transnational markets, it will avoid intrusive regulations in advanced industries. In mature industries, however, there are no such incentives (although individual firms may still be insulated from political risks because of their marketing techniques, export networks, etc.). In dealing with mature industries, then, the symbolic extension of sovereignty is reinforced by potential economic gains. Whatever policy is chosen, the security of foreign direct investment is currently determined by national-level political decisions, not by international restraints.

So far, I have indicated a general increase in state economic capabilities. Administrative staffs have grown, their oversight and operational responsibilities have widened, and their bargaining has

---

*Host-state demands on high-technology industries are also eased because such industries promise a positive net balance on merchandise trade and seldom confront indigenous competitors.

generally become more sophisticated. Closely linked to these changes is the rise of national economic development as a state responsibility. The economic tasks of the state have expanded in tandem with its capabilities. Although national policies vary considerably, there are important common foci: economic infrastructure, key inputs needed to accelerate industrialization, and major sources of economic surplus are the most frequent targets of nationalization or extensive regulation.

Related to this growth of state responsibilities is the wider domain and increasing sophistication of economic policy instruments. These include a variety of restrictions against multinational investors:[53]

local equity obligations	financing restrictions
remittance controls	restricted markets
forced sales	tax discrimination
local content requirements	export quotas
licensing restrictions	supervision of transfer prices
expropriation	prevention of local acquisitions

The proliferation of these policy tools permits the value of an investment to be manipulated in a number of ways. The distinctiveness of expropriation is lost, its meaning blurred.

These restrictions, plus the weakening of international restraints, tend to isolate investors and make coalitions difficult. Each firm faces a distinctive configuration of policies, not a shared threat. There is no clear fixing point to rally a common defense. Intermediate norms are difficult to specify and, in any event, lack the clarity and salience needed to spur a collective response.

From the perspective of the host state, the multiplication of regulatory tools permits discrimination among various types of investment and the pursuit of more complex policy goals. But, just as investors lack a rallying point, so does the state. National bargaining positions were buttressed by expropriation's symbolic character. Investment issues were endowed with a comprehensible mass character. Export quotas and transfer prices are simply less compelling.

One result is that quiet negotiations multiply, differing from country to country, from industry to industry. With no powerful overarching constraints on the national treatment of foreign direct investment, the political risks of individual investments vary widely. The risks depend on the particular attributes of each investment—its size, industry, location, market, and so forth—and on the political structure of the individual host state.* For all these reasons, the assessment of political risks has become a detailed and complex task, one that must be undertaken on a disaggregated basis.[54]

The political characteristics of host states are important in another way. The growth of administrative capabilities and economic tasks, while an essential feature of modern expropriation, does not necessarily imply a willingness to nationalize foreign capital. After all, advanced capitalist states also have far-reaching domestic economic responsibilities and even more extensive bureaucracies. Yet they have not seized foreign investments.** In the absence of communist or popular-front governments, foreign capital has remained reasonably secure in all OECD countries.† That it has been insecure in less de-

---

*The actions of host states, according to one experienced international-business consultant, are now

> specific not only to an industry, but to a particular industry sector or subsector and, most importantly, are implemented discriminatingly against specific corporations. . . . The new level of sophistication on the side of host governments must be met with more sophisticated management.

Warnock Davies of Business International Corporation says that corporate vulnerability is related less to its general behavior than to its behavior in specific products and processes.

> For example, for a particular corporation, the degree and form of local participation, its profits repatriation—reinvestment ratio, the countries to which it exports directly, whether it provides import substitution or domestic displacement and the compatability of the product with the cultural values of the host country may be the critical issues; whereas for another corporation, operating in the same country, the issues may be indigenization of non-technical administrative positions, local purchasing policy, the percentage of long term debt drawn from local sources, the sophistication of technology being transferred, the effect of the project on the physical environment, the operating subsidiary's relations with the authorities of the province in which it operates and the relations between the parent company's home and host governments.

All this implies much more complicated assessments of risks and corporate adaptation to them. W. Davies, "Beyond the Earthquake Allegory: Managing Political Risk Vulnerability," *Management International Review* 21 (March 1981), 5, 9, 7.

**I am excepting, as always, the seizure of enemy investments during wartime. In fact, political officials and legal scholars have carefully segregated the whole matter of wartime seizures, treating it as a distinctive legal issue.

†Only two advanced states have undertaken extensive nationalization programs in recent years. France, under Mitterrand, nationalized a number of banks and industrial enterprises. Canada, under Trudeau, screened foreign investments rigorously for a time and established special tax and incentive policies in the oil and gas industry that

veloped countries is a function not only of state expansion but also of the distinctive character of Third World economic nationalism.

Here, as elsewhere, there are dramatic differences between conservative and leftist governments. These differences make common traits and shared values all the more striking. Yet there *are* common dilemmas and even some common responses, as one group of economists has noted:

---

discriminated against foreign firms. Both programs had an impact on foreign companies but neither developed into a sustained, successful attack on foreign capital.

Mitterrand defeated Giscard d'Estaing in 1981, having campaigned on the promise to nationalize important sectors of the French economy—the first such attempt in thirty years. The first wave of nationalizations included some international banks, who vigorously disputed the compensation they were offered. While this debate was going on, France's Constitutional Council ruled that some key elements of the original legislation were discriminatory and unconstitutional, and the Socialist cabinet responded by tendering substantially better compensation. In 1982–1983, the Socialist government nationalized six big industrial groups, a move that was not aimed especially at foreigners. In any case, the companies were nearly broke during Giscard's last years and were already seeking government aid. "Perhaps that is why we have not seen a single case of shareholders contesting their compensation," one French banker told the *Economist* (July 16, 1983, p. 83).

If the French policies were aimed at structural economic changes, the Canadian oil and gas policies were targeted more directly at foreign dominance in a growing sector.

The early 1980s was a boom time in the energy business, and exploration in western Canada was vigorous. It was then that Ottawa established a new national energy plan with a goal of reducing foreign ownership in the oil industry from around 70 percent to approximately 50 percent by 1990. Americans asserted that the special tax and subsidy benefits funneled to Canadian-owned companies would reduce the value of their own holdings and could force them to sell to Canadians at bargain prices.

Within two years, the sting was gone from these policies. Douglas Martin of the *New York Times* notes the change:

The atmosphere [for foreign investment] has improved markedly. The reason, in essence, is that Canada has retreated on many of its earlier initiatives, partly in response to American pressures and partly due to inexorable forces at work in the world economy. (July 18, 1983, p. 17)

American pressure consisted of the threat to disrupt reciprocal exchange. Congress threatened to block Canadian investments in the United States and obstruct various trading arrangements. The global softening of the energy market and Canada's serious balance-of-payments problems also worked to make foreign investments more attractive. At the same time, U.S. companies quit complaining about the new rules since they had managed to adapt successfully to them. By restructuring their drilling arrangements, for example, they became eligible for Canadian government subsidies. Imperial Oil, which is 70 percent owned by Exxon, takes Canadian partners into its various drilling groups and is eligible for the maximum federal subsidy. Similarly, Gulf Canada Ltd. (60 percent owned by Gulf Oil Corporation) has acquired potentially lucrative exploration and development leases on over 20 million acres in Arctic and offshore areas controlled by the Canadian government. Its capital spending, some $450 million in 1980, nearly doubled within two years—at a time when most exploration budgets were sagging. As Martin put it, "American oil executives these days are complaining less about Canada's nationalistic energy policy, having gradually learned how to take advantage of some of its features" (*New York Times*, July 18, 1983, p. 20). See also, *Business Week*, October 4, 1982, pp. 114–121 and June 8, 1981, pp. 70–71; *Chicago Tribune*, July 26, 1981, Sec. 5, pp. 1–2.

> Despite unevenness of growth performance in different countries, there have been uniform tendencies, particularly as regards external trade and finance, which present common difficulties to most third world governments. These common problems provide a basis for the present community of interest between them on demands for change in the international trading and financial system.[55]

At the broadest level, these demands are based on fears of economic vulnerability and dependence, fears that transnational networks are beyond their control (individually and perhaps collectively) and are eroding state authority, and desires for national economic gain (although with markedly different distributional concerns).[56]

The UNCTAD group has been able to move beyond these general concerns and formulate specific proposals. Despite internal differences, they have developed common positions on commodity stabilization, trade preferences, technology acquisition, debt relief for the "most seriously affected" countries, and a number of additional development issues. The UNCTAD position on multinational investment was best stated in the Charter of Economic Rights and Duties of States, approved by the U.N. General Assembly in 1975. Article Two declared that "every state has . . . full permanent sovereignty, including possession, use and disposal, over all its wealth, natural resources and economic activities." The question of compensation was to be "settled under the domestic law of the nationalizing State."[57] The effect, as Tony Smith has pointed out, is to warn multinational corporations that they operate at the discretion of sovereign host states.[58]

Between these proposals and their achievement lies a chasm unlikely to be bridged soon. So far at least, North-South economic conferences have produced minor agreements and major quarrels. In the case of direct investments, for example, there has been no agreement over compensation criteria, capital transfers, or procedures for settling investment disputes.[59]

Yet the UNCTAD proposals are important even if they are rejected. By raising the salience of national control over multinational firms, they strengthen individual states' ability to bargain with those firms. Their broad acceptance *within* nations makes it even more costly and difficult to translate interventionary force into effective investment protection. By clearly asserting the unlimited right of national sovereignty over foreign investments, they affirm a common denominator among nationalist ideologies. This assertion of economic sovereignty cuts across Latin America, Asia, and Africa, across economic, social, and political structures.[60]

This common value, together with the growth of state administrative capabilities and the prospect of economic gain, suggests why such diverse states have been willing to expropriate foreign investment. Older rules, stating international minimum standards, are no longer internalized. Some internal restraints remain, of course, but they differ according to national political and economic structures and institutions, development strategy, and industrial sector. They are, at most, an uneven, erratic basis for investment security.

This broad shift in domestic capabilities and values places the burden of protecting foreign investments squarely on international restraints, precisely when those restraints are weakest.

Conclusions

Let me summarize the model's representation of the regime governing foreign investment and compare it with the historical record.

In the nineteenth century

1. international restraints—economic and military—were concentrated and coherent; and
2. host states (outside Europe) generally had rudimentary administrative structures and no ideology of state-directed development.

The inference, then, is that foreign investments should be subject to uniform treatment. The regime governing foreign investment ought to be strong and the investments secure against expropriation. Likewise, foreign debts should be secure against fraud or renunciation.

That inference accurately represents, in general terms, the treatment of foreign capital. At the same time, the model illuminates the central features of investment protection. The concentration of private, long-term finance and interventionary force *did* imply coherent international restraints, as our model assumes.

The model also suggests the principal challenge to investment security: lapses of internal order. Day-to-day security of foreign capital was the province of laissez-faire host states, which lacked administrative capacity and a supporting ideology of state-directed development. The chief risks, besides bankrupt ventures and impoverished debtors, were breakdowns in local order and aberrant seizures by local officials, usually in their own behalf. These were not sustained public acts against foreign capital. International norms regarding proper treatment of foreign capital were largely internalized, despite limited objections from Latin American jurists.

When rule violations did occur, the British navy and privately organized bondholders were well placed to sanction them. Through the Corporation of Foreign Bondholders and the Stock Exchange Listing Committee, London creditors could effectively prohibit access to capital markets until accounts were settled. The British navy, sometimes joined by smaller European fleets, could threaten, bombard, or land sailors when foreign capital was threatened. Its limitations were largely self-imposed. The Foreign Office was cautious about military interventions because such acts tended to undermine local governments, introduce new sources of political instability, and entail long-term commitments. The British government was also unwilling, as a rule, to bail out bondholders after simple defaults. It considered commercial default the consequence of imprudent investment, not an appropriate object of military intervention or diplomatic protest. Fraud or the misappropriation of funds, however, were subject to full military sanctions.

This tightly ordered system was shaken in the aftermath of World War I:

1. international restraints (economic and military, national and transnational) were less concentrated than before the war; and
2. while most states still lacked ideologies of state-directed development and appropriate political structures, at least two states had generated such structures.

According to the model, the international regime should thus be characterized by greater national diversity and less security for foreign capital. Because international restraints are less concentrated, and therefore less stringent, the security of foreign capital is more dependent on domestic political organization. There is the potential, at least, for varied national treatment. When laissez-faire norms are rejected and administrative capabilities are sufficient, foreign investments may be subject to state seizure. Alternatively, host states may forgo expropriation either out of administrative weakness or policy choice. The central point is that, in the absence of concentrated international resources, foreign investment is subject to potentially diverse national treatment.

Because international restraints were generally passive during the interwar period, a detailed analysis of investment security would compare *domestic* political and economic structures and processes. The model simplifies by incorporating an empirical assumption: state capabilities and economic tasks are assumed to have grown substantially over the long term, with most of that growth occurring after World War II. During the interwar period, state capabilities were still modest and state-directed development still rare. The result, according to the model, is that the investment regime remained relatively strong, despite weaker international restraints.

That result generally conforms to empirical observation. In the absence of elaborate administrative structures and state-directed development strategies, nearly all foreign investments were secure. The only major departures from prewar property rules were the nationalization programs in the Soviet Union and Mexico, and perhaps the state purchase of foreign property in Turkey. The model not only illuminates their exceptional character but also their common features: the strident rejection of traditional property norms, the elaboration of alternative development policies under state leadership, and the creation of appropriate administrative structures.

These features were more prevalent after World War II. But, except for the new communist governments, expropriations were still rare. From the end of the war until the late 1960s

1. international restraints were again concentrated and coherent; and
2. state capabilities and economic tasks continued to expand, justified by nationalist claims of economic sovereignty.

Any projections would be indeterminate unless concentrated international restraints were given more weight than countervailing host-state capabilities. With this clarification, our model describes a tight international regime. As long as restraints were coherent and severe, state expansion and economic nationalism seldom led to expropriations.* The most prominent exceptions, Iran and Guatemala, were

*Likewise, coherent restraints in portfolio lending have prevented debt renunciation, despite borrowers' persistent calls for relief.

reversed and the strong international regime maintained. At the same time, the appropriate limits of eminent domain were extended to include economic infrastructure. This grudging accommodation of enlarged state responsibilities differentiates the postwar regime from its nineteenth-century counterpart.*

Beginning in the late 1960s

1. international restraints were decentralized, except for portfolio lending, where multilateral financial institutions played a significant coordinating role; and
2. host-state capabilities and economic tasks continued to increase; state-directed economic development was accepted, in different forms, by a wide variety of governments.

The projection is that the regime for portfolio loans should remain strong and debt renunciation rare. For direct investments, however, the regime should weaken considerably, with investments subject to much more diversified national treatment.

This diversity is limited mainly by *decentralized* sanctions: the cumulative effect of discreet, uncoordinated investment decisions. Investment risks and capital flows are inevitably affected by the specific character of state economic intervention. This anticipated effect has probably limited the size and scope of expropriations. It has certainly imposed some minimal order on the process of nationalization and the subsequent bargaining over payment. Host states have considerable incentive to avoid the appearance of arbitrary seizures or capricious disregard for property rights. And, although they rarely pay market value (or even book value), host states do typically agree to some compensation for the expropriated company.

---

*John Gerard Ruggie emphasizes the same point when he distinguishes between laissez-faire liberalism, with its limited role for state intervention and its priority on external adjustment, and "embedded liberalism," which characterizes the post–World War II international economic order. Embedded liberalism, in Ruggie's view, is really a compromise between the economic nationalism of the 1930s and the orthodox liberalism of the nineteenth century. The goal has been to secure domestic stability without triggering trade wars or competitive devaluations. "This was the essence of the embedded liberalism compromise: unlike the economic nationalism of the thirties, it would be multilateral in character; unlike the liberalism of the gold standard and free trade, its multilateralism would be predicated upon domestic interventionism."

In investment issues, the United States was slow to acknowledge this expanding scope of state authority. Yet the changing character of state intervention, together with LDC economic nationalism, was eventually to undermine some crucial assumptions underlying traditional property rules.

John Gerard Ruggie, "International Regimes, Transactions, and Change: Embedded Liberalism in the Postwar Economic Order," *International Organization* 36 (Spring 1982), 393.

Except for these broad limits, the current regime is characterized mainly by its fragmentation, as the model suggests. The security of foreign capital varies by host state and industrial sector. It often differs according to the investment's particular history, its methods of finance and operation, its place in the nation's development program, and its home state.

For multinational investors this fragmentation of the regime has far-reaching consequences. Each corporation confronts a distinctive array of political risks. Unless those risks are associated with radical social change, there is little chance of collective action or effective diplomatic resistance. At the same time, widespread economic nationalism raises the salience of foreign direct investment and undermines its legitimacy. The effect is to buttress the bargaining position of host states and force investors to justify their activities individually in terms of national economic objectives. These changes put a premium on individualized risk forecasting and corporate adaptation.

In most cases, multinational firms have developed impressive capacities for managing these new relationships. They have created new, more sophisticated modes of investment. They have accommodated themselves profitably to a larger state role and have generally been able to settle expropriation disputes peacefully. Their demands for diplomatic assistance have also moderated (a change I shall examine in Part II). Their attitude echoes that of nineteenth-century British traders, who believed that persistent interference by Her Majesty's government "endangered their property and persons and broke their carefully constructed contracts with local traders, officials, and politicians."[61]

While the model does not depict the current regime in such detail, it does accurately forecast its fragmentation and reveals the international context of corporate adaptation and investment bargaining. Indeed, the model closely reproduces the general characteristics of investment security from the nineteenth century onward.

It is possible, naturally, to construct alternative models—models that represent other features of investment protection. A simple model, for instance, would rely exclusively on the presence or absence of a single regime leader: Great Britain in the nineteenth century, the United States since World War II.*

*Charles Kindleberger, Robert Gilpin, and Stephen Krasner all use this model, but their emphases differ. Kindleberger, for example, stresses the burdens of international leadership and the special costs borne by the hegemon for the benefit of all nations. His influential treatment downplays the role of negative sanctions, including coercion,

A hegemonic model, like the one suggested by Robert Gilpin or Stephen Krasner, assumes that systematic order is a public good and that its provision is solely a function of national leadership in the world economy. Such a model underscores the role of interventionary force and national economic sanctions. To maintain parsimony, it omits international organizations and the changing role of less developed states. Similarly, it either ignores transnational economic sanctions or lumps them together with public ones. It is a state-centric model and requires only modest information to forecast investment regimes.[62]

In fact, despite these powerful simplifications, the hegemonic model illuminates several important features of regime change. It predicts strong regimes in the nineteenth century and after World War II, weaker regimes between the wars and more recently. It strongly suggests parallels among various economic issues—investment security, open trade, a well-ordered monetary system—all managed by a single power.

The model's omissions, however, create at least two predictive problems. First, it cannot differentiate the interwar regime from the current one. The interwar regime was relatively strong, despite the absence of a hegemonic leader. Today, expropriations are much more common, and foreign direct investment is subject to much more diverse treatment. Our model locates that change not in the international constraints on expropriation, which are relatively diffuse in both periods, but in the changing capabilities and ideologies of host states. Second, the simpler model cannot distinguish between portfolio loans and direct investments, even though the two have been treated quite differently in the most recent period. The model presented here, which refers to international financial institutions, permits that distinction.

These predictive discrepancies are linked to the analytic shortcomings of the hegemonic model. By omitting transnational economic sanctions, it obscures the economic processes that are crucial to investment protection. By omitting the (changing) economic role of less developed states, it misrepresents the consequences of hegemonic

in forging international order and depreciates the hegemon's unique capacity to select international policies and institutional arrangements. The carrot is prominently displayed; the stick is hidden. See Charles P. Kindleberger, "Systems of International Economic Organization," in *Money and the Coming World Order*, ed. David P. Calleo (New York: New York University Press for the Lehrman Institute, 1976), 32–34; Kindleberger, *The World in Depression 1929–1939* (Berkeley, Los Angeles: University of California Press, 1973), esp. chap. 14.

decline. In terms of investment security, the interwar period was far different from the 1970s. Nor were all issues affected uniformly in the interwar period. The absence of a hegemonic leader had a more profound impact on trade and monetary relations than on investment security. Thus, the hegemonic model is, at best, a gross depiction of environmental restraints on expropriation.*

My earlier analysis suggests that regime change cannot be understood or predicted by focusing exclusively on environmental restraints, even if those restraints are broadened to include transnational and multilateral sanctions. For that reason our model refers to economic nationalism and host-state capabilities.**

*Hegemonic models, especially those that emphasize the provision of public goods, have other analytic shortcomings as well. First, true international public goods are rare. Nations that fail to undertake reciprocal obligations can usually be excluded from participation in relevant international arrangements. Contracting parties to the GATT, for instance, undertake trade obligations only to one another. Article I says that any tax exemption given to the products of one contracting party must be given unconditionally to the products of every other signatory. Nations that fail to sign the GATT, however, need not receive such treatment. The fact that most international arrangements, such as the GATT, permit exclusion is not some arcane quibble. It is directly related to the incentives that each state has for contributing to the costs of sustaining international institutions. Second, the whole treatment of international public goods has been marked by confusion about exactly what is being provided. Quite often, the term *public good* is used when the relevant process is really one of international cooperation, perhaps involving a leader who provides side-payments, external sanctions, and salient choices around which others converge.

I am indebted to Duncan Snidal for his discussions on these points. See his "International Political Regimes and International Cooperation: Different Regimes for Different Problems," unpublished paper, National Science Foundation Conference, Spring Hills, Minnesota, 1982.

**It might be objected that both economic nationalism and vast state capabilities are present in advanced countries but have rarely produced seizures of foreign property.

There have, of course, been nationalist objections to both inward and outward foreign investment in Europe and North America. The French were particularly anxious about the American Challenge of the late 1960s. Canada has shown persistent concerns about foreign ownership of its natural resources. In the United States, labor unions have fought against "runaway" plants since the early 1970s, most conspicuously with the unsuccessful Burke-Hartke amendment.

These objections to foreign investment must be taken seriously since most advanced states are well equipped to channel capital flows. As Morton Kaplan and Nicholas Katzenbach observe in their discussion of economic relations within the Atlantic alliance, "The increase in governmental sectors of the economy in industrialized nations has greatly complicated the task of restoring a favorable climate for private trade and investment."

Similar issues have arisen in North-South commerce, but the differences are profound. Symbolically, foreign capital is a much more salient issue for LDCs since it is an emblem of dependence and since resistance can serve as both a national rallying point and a vehicle for state building. Even more important, the demands of LDCs are seldom tempered by a compelling interest in reciprocity—the right to invest freely abroad.

This interest in reciprocal exchange (and a more positive evaluation of economic openness in general) characterize the OECD's 1976 Declaration on International Investment and Multinational Enterprises. A purely voluntary code, without real com-

More complex models could be constructed, of course, but none seems to contribute significantly to forecasting regime change or to understanding its essential dynamics. Our model, for instance, maintains simplicity by treating international restraints and host-state capabilities on a global scale. One could add complexity by disaggregating, examining the structure of environmental restraints and host-state capabilities at the regional or subregional level. A regional model would simply extend our assumptions about resource concentration. In some cases it might produce more accurate forecasts. During the late nineteenth century, when Britain and the United States were uneasy duopolists in the Caribbean, the investment regime weakened locally. According to Burns Weston, those expropriations were "largely the result of the coincidence of newly won Latin American political independence on the one hand, and of geographically proximate and increasingly expansive United States commercial interests on the other."[63] A regional model could also clarify some aspects of the postwar regime by specifying its bipolar limits.

These predictive refinements are the products of the regional model's complexity. It is built on the empirical assessment that investment security differs significantly by regions. Incorporating that assumption complicates our earlier global model and adds to its informational requirements. Such a model is confusing analytically and its predictive improvements are modest. Except for the bipolar limits of the postwar regime, the regionalist assumption merely obscures the impressive geographic uniformity of investment security.

This does not imply that our model is without its own analytic limitations. Although its projections generally conform to historical regime changes, the model deliberately omits the foreign policy aspects of investment protection. It analyzes restraints on expropriation solely in terms of international structure: the distribution of national and transnational capacities. It abstracts from the process by which concentrated resources are translated into effective anti-expropriation policies. Thus, it is not particularly helpful in analyzing the sources of the regime leader's policies.

---

pliance mechanisms, the declaration underscores the importance of international standards. Its "national treatment instrument" contains the basic idea that foreign investors are entitled to treatment "consistent with international law and no less favorable than that accorded in like situations to domestic enterprises."

OECD, *International Investment and Multinational Enterprises: Mid-Term Report on the 1976 Declaration and Decisions* (Paris: OECD, 1982), 18; OECD, *National Treatment for Foreign Controlled Enterprises Established in OECD Countries* (Paris: OECD, 1978); Kaplan and Katzenbach, *The Political Foundations of International Law* (New York: John Wiley, 1961), 77.

A closely related issue concerns the model's representation of transnational sanctions. Those sanctions are treated independently of political organization and social structure in capital-exporting states. This assumption is a theoretical one and should be judged by its predictive results. In practice, however, the relative independence of transnational actors depends on the historical development of individual capital-exporting states, the character of their policy networks, and their political coalitions. In both the United States and Great Britain, the state lacked the political and organizational capacity to impose unity on its transnational actors. If there were many actors with cross-cutting interests, transnational sanctions were likely to be diffuse. Neither regime leader was willing or able to offset this incoherence by managing its transnational relations. In fact, in the U.S. case, the incoherence of private interests limited *state* sanctions.

Our model of international restraints and host-state capabilities does not address these issues, which are central to anti-expropriation policy. These issues will be the subject of Part II.

PART II

Domestic Sources
of
U.S. Anti-Expropriation Policy

So far the issue of investment security has been treated primarily at the international level. British and American policies have been discussed from time to time, but my central goal has been to understand the international dynamics of investment protection, not its domestic politics. I have asked what kinds of international rules characterize the treatment of foreign capital, why these rules have changed, and why some types of investments have been more secure than others.

Although I did consider nineteenth-century British policy and its role in universalizing international property rules, I have not asked why more recent investment-protection policies have been adopted. Indeed, my model of the international regime abstracts from even the most basic foreign policy considerations. It is based on the international distribution of economic, military, and organizational capacities and on the long-term trend toward greater state involvement in less developed economies. It merely assumes, for example, that the capacity to invoke coherent economic sanctions will be translated into appropriate investment-protection policies. It says nothing about the domestic sources of these policies, nothing about the form these policies might take, nothing about their phenomenological dimensions.

Part II will try to fill this gap. It considers the formulation of United States anti-expropriation policy, concentrating on the decisive role played by multinational corporations and their shifting policy objectives. I deal, then, with the same actors that figured in the study of regime change, but now in a different context and with different purposes. My aim is to interpret the regime's changing meaning for key actors, their stakes in the rules, and their strategies for adapting to new circumstances.

This exercise, with its emphasis on the formulation and substance of foreign economic policy, complements my earlier emphasis on international rule making. It is complementary in two senses. First, as Morton Kaplan observes in his critique of Kenneth Waltz, "It is impossible to interpret a concrete system without some reference to the characteristics, as well as the interrelationships, of the parts."* Second, it can illuminate the changing policy goals adopted by private investors as international rules have changed. Faced with serious challenges to the stability of contracts and the permanence of foreign property relations—issues analyzed in Part I—foreign investors ultimately faced fundamental choices about the kind of public policies they would push for. Their most basic choice was between policies of genuine resistance—tough economic sanctions and diplomatic denunciation—and policies of quiet disagreement, deflecting foreign challenges if possible and, if not, then adjusting to new circumstances. These choices are critical to the design of public policies toward foreign investment.

The next two chapters analyze the formation and evolution of two major policies designed to deter expropriation or cope with its consequences. The policies examined, foreign aid sanctions and investment guaranty insurance, are easily the most important U.S. policies dealing specifically with expropriations. In addition to their prominence, they are attractive analytically because of their longevity and divergent histories. Each stretches through several presidencies, and each has been debated time and again. Over that time, one has been progressively expanded and endowed with its own bureaucracy, the other effectively repealed. Taken together, they offer a unique purchase on the changing national problems of investment protection and the changing patterns of corporate-state interaction in this area.

The focus, then, is on the regime leader's policies, particularly the policies fashioned to deal with investment disputes. To explain their evolution, chapters 6 and 7 develop and test a radical hypothesis, as

---

*Kaplan's point is made in reference to Waltz's treatment of reductionism. Morton A. Kaplan, *Towards Professionalism in International Theory: Macrosystem Analysis* (New York: Free Press, 1979), 8.

well as several more conventional alternatives. The radical hypothesis is notable because it predicts investment-protection policy on the basis of dominant corporate preferences. The underlying notion is that as corporations have themselves moved toward more adaptive investment strategies, they have urged similar policies at the national level, producing a long-term shift away from public policies that vigorously resist forced divestment.

As a research strategy, there are important reasons to begin with this hypothesis. First, it is simple, requiring little information about the domestic sources of investment protection yet purporting to explain a wide array of legislative and diplomatic outcomes. Second, even if it is rejected, it sets a useful agenda for inquiry. It highlights four central issues in investment protection:

1. the protective strategies of private investors;
2. the interaction of private strategies and public policies;
3. the content of the regime leader's policies; and
4. the process of formulating and administering them.

These are the basic issues taken up in Part II.

CHAPTER SIX

Foreign Aid Sanctions and Investment Protection

The relationship between corporate preferences and American public policy is frequently debated but too little researched. Nevertheless, radical analysts of American foreign policy have always considered it crucial, both theoretically and historically. They posit a causal relationship between the expansion of international trade and investment and the efforts of advanced capitalist states to protect and extend those economic networks. Often termed the "Open Door Policy" in its American version, this focus informs radical scholarship as diverse as that of Harry Magdoff and William Appleman Williams. It also differentiates radical criticism from its more conventional counterpart, which tends to emphasize the "confusion and uncertainty over the ends and means of [U.S.] foreign policy,"[1] rather than its self-interested coherence.

Unfortunately, the theoretical power of radical analysis has for many political scientists been obscured by its presentation. Radical arguments have frequently relied upon a number of implicit yet controversial assumptions. Too often the conclusions have lacked the precision required to test specific propositions empirically. As a result, skeptical readers have tended to dismiss radical analysis quickly, often contemptuously, turning a potential debate into a standoff between mutually insulated polemics. In this chapter I hope to avoid that confusion and to demonstrate the value of a radical critique by recasting some fundamental concepts in the form of explicit and testable propositions.

Radical analysts assume that basic U.S. government policies to protect direct foreign investments generally conform to the predominant preferences of the most vitally affected large corporations. One can define that subset of corporations as multinational firms large enough to be listed as one of *Fortune*'s "500 largest industrial firms" or "50 largest commercial banks." Using that definition, the radical assumption can be treated as a hypothesis to be tested.

A corollary is that changes in government investment-protection policies reflect changes by the affected corporations in the strategy they predominantly prefer. Another corollary hypothesis holds that substantial disunity among large multinational firms results in government policies that are either ambiguous, contradictory, or modest in scope.

Although the term *predominant strategy* requires further specification in some cases, these hypotheses clearly posit structural political-economic relationships in a specific issue-area. They are clear, falsifiable inferences, based on radical analyses, that can be evaluated empirically.

These hypotheses will be tested in a specific policy area: those aspects of foreign aid policy that deal explicitly with investment protection. While that limitation closes the universe of data, it also qualifies our ability to generalize inferences based on that data.* In particular, one would expect the influence of large corporations to be more limited when issues are more salient and competing political groups more active and numerous.

While one cannot simply generalize from foreign aid to foreign policy, aid does constitute an important policy area. It has long been a central feature of U.S. relations with less developed countries and has attracted substantial domestic attention, engaging a varied array of governmental and nongovernmental actors.

Over the past two decades, Congress has modified aid legislation in several explicit, but contradictory, attempts to protect U.S.-based multinational corporations from confiscation and contract nullification. The modifications in question are the Hickenlooper amendment (passed in 1962, expanded in 1963 and 1964), the Gonzalez amendments (1972), and the effective repeal of the Hickenlooper amendment in 1973.

---

*This limitation is a vital one. Though the hypotheses are developed from concepts fundamental to radical analysis, they treat only one of its aspects. Certainly few radical analysts would argue that U.S. military interventions, for example, are explicable in terms of such hypotheses.

The Hickenlooper amendment is especially important because of its strong language, its clear strategy, and its recurrent role in investment disputes with less developed countries.* The law created a statutory link between disbursement of aid and repayment for expropriations. Unless a foreign government promptly compensated an expropriated U.S. company, or initiated "appropriate steps" to do so, the amendment *required automatic suspension* of bilateral aid. Furthermore, it defined expropriation quite broadly. The 1962 law, for example, specifically mentioned "discriminatory treatment" as well as confiscation.[2] In the following year, restrictive operating conditions and discriminatory taxes were also included. At the same time, the amendment's sanctions were extended to incorporate bilateral aid other than the Foreign Assistance Act, such as food shipments made under Public Law 480.[3]

These sanctions were not only tough, they were legally mandatory. Bilateral aid had to be suspended to any country that expropriated U.S. citizens' property without prompt, full, convertible compensation—the traditional standards of international law. The mandatory aspect was weakened somewhat because the president was permitted to determine whether an expropriation had occurred, according to the amendment's definition. By the same token, the amendment's definition of expropriation was an expansive one, leaving little room for presidential discretion. Moreover, once the determination had been made, the president had no choice but to suspend aid until the U.S. company was fully compensated. Subsequent debate, both in Congress and in business forums, concentrated on the usefulness of this automatic deterrent provision. This same provision was later used as a model for the Gonzalez amendments, which prohibited U.S. approval of multilateral loans (such as those from the World Bank) to states where U.S. investors had been expropriated without full compensation.[4]

Since both the Hickenlooper and the Gonzalez amendments depended upon their inflexibility, a revision permitting a presidential waiver of their sanctions would effectively repeal them. In fact, the 1973 effort to delete the Hickenlooper amendment was finally transformed into a successful attempt to add such a waiver. Though

---

*Its importance is disproportionate to its formal usage, which occurred only once, in Ceylon (1963). But frequently its sanctions have been contemplated or have become an important policy issue, for instance in Brazil (1962), Honduras (1962), Argentina (1964), and in Peru, Ecuador, and Bolivia in the late 1960s.

the Gonzalez amendments were not formally affected, it was widely understood that the new discretionary policy contradicted and superseded the "automatic sanctions" policy embodied in the multilateral amendments. Tough, mandatory sanctions had become obsolete.

In practice, however, even the earlier policy had not been automatic. Most notably, President Nixon did not formally invoke the Hickenlooper amendment when Peru confiscated an Exxon subsidiary. Other, less prominent examples can be cited for Presidents Kennedy and Johnson.

Two primary patterns emerge from this overview. One is that presidential nonapplication of the Hickenlooper amendment contradicted the congressionally approved policy of "automatic sanctions." The other is that legislative policy itself changed sequentially, first ordering mandatory action and then allowing a presidential waiver.

My hypothesis is that these varied investment-protection policies, including the patterns of legislative change and executive implementation, have conformed to predominant corporate preferences. That proposition could be falsified if one found that large multinational firms predominantly opposed (1) the passage of the Hickenlooper amendment, (2) the passage of the Gonzalez amendments, (3) the effective repeal of the Hickenlooper amendment, or (4) the specific cases of application and nonapplication of the Hickenlooper amendment by the executive. After the history of the policy has been analyzed and the radical hypothesis tested, the hypothesis can be compared with the most salient alternatives: propositions derived from bureaucratic and pluralist models.

The Background of the Hickenlooper Amendment

The stringent text of the original Hickenlooper amendment was written in early 1962, a time of widespread corporate support for tough anti-expropriation measures. That attitude arose fundamentally as a reaction to Cuban communism and the indirect challenges it posed to United States investments in Latin America. The loss of corporate investments as well as a cold-war ally had a multifaceted effect on the environment in which the Hickenlooper amendment was passed. It heightened the importance of the expropriation issue for international businessmen and most congressmen. Throughout the 1950s both groups had generally assumed that foreign investments were politically safe.[5] The confiscations in Cuba undermined that assumption and helped to shape a new framework for the perception of investment challenges. Many investors and congressmen began to fear that eminent domain seizures might escalate drastically, as they had in Cuba.[6] There was general agreement that failure to insist on full compensation would encourage a domino effect. Viewed in these terms, even minor expropriations might ultimately sabotage a principal objective of U.S. aid: the encouragement of development through direct foreign investment.[7]

Because expropriations were identified as an integral aspect of global communism, they also appeared to threaten the policymakers' strategic objectives. The Cuban expropriations thus reinforced the conventional cold-war view that political alliance was linked to trade and investment security. In this respect their context was quite different from that of the Mexican oil seizures twenty-five years earlier. Those confiscations had been linked only indirectly to the fascist military threat. In fact, that threat posed a basic choice between vigorous action to protect particular U.S. investments in Mexico and the more serious need to conserve resources and build regional military alliances.

The Cuban expropriations naturally underscored the linkage between economic and security issues. It also focused attention on what some considered the State Department's reluctance to pursue controversial economic issues. The expropriations simply reinforced traditional corporate mistrust of American diplomacy. According to many business leaders, the State Department was too tepid in their defense, too solicitous of other countries' problems, and insufficiently concerned with economic issues. Although mistrust was especially pronounced under the Kennedy administration, it had been quite widespread under Eisenhower as well.[8]

Congressmen immediately expressed their outrage over nascent Cuban communism. After debates in which the recent expropriations there figured prominently,[9] an amendment that can be considered a forerunner of the Hickenlooper amendment was attached to the Mutual Security Act of 1959. Named after Senators Olin Johnson and Styles Bridges, it provided for the immediate suspension of aid to any country that expropriated the property of U.S. citizens and then "failed within six months . . . to take steps determined by the president to be appropriate to discharge its obligations under international law."[10] The Johnson-Bridges debates centered on presidential discretion, and not on the wisdom of imposing formal economic sanctions. The Senate refused to pass the bill unless the president was permitted to waive its provisions "in the national interest." Even though the final Johnson-Bridges amendment did not carry Hickenlooper's mandatory language, it indicated that Congress meant to deter expropriations by threatening to suspend foreign aid.

Certainly the boldest new use of aid during this period was the Alliance for Progress. Despite the defensive character of the early Alliance, its scope and novel strategy worried the heads of many U.S.-based multinational businesses. They had not been explicitly included in its planning and were dissatisfied with the Punta del Este charter. Concerned primarily with investment safety, they saw only vague, inconsequential support in that document.[11] Neither the charter nor the conference discussions had addressed their central concerns: stopping expropriation, abolishing restrictions on profit remittances, and expanding the coverage of investment guaranty insurance. Admittedly, the new administration's plan depended on a substantial influx of U.S. capital; but, according to many corporate executives, it ignored the reality of net disinvestment, caused mainly by unacceptable political risks to foreign investments. Jerome Levinson and Juan de Onís have concluded that "what [business leaders] wanted most at the time was security for foreign investments, and the charter offered no specific guarantees against expropriation."*

---

*Levinson and de Onís, *The Alliance That Lost Its Way* (Chicago: Quadrangle Books, 1970), 72. Corporate dissatisfaction with the early Alliance suggests that corporate preferences are not related "mechanically" to the U.S. government's investment protection policy. Rather, we argue that the two are generally consistent. If one found repeated or long-term inconsistencies for policy instruments which were directly related to investment protection issues, this aspect of a radical argument would be falsified.

It might be argued that, in spite of its brevity, early Alliance policy demonstrated such an inconsistency. Clearly, multinational corporate interests were to some extent contradictory during that period. While there was unanimous support for the objective of insulating communism, there was also widespread corporate agreement that the common objective should be secured by a strategy that unambiguously preserved property rights. Thus, even though the Alliance's aspirations were compatible with the extension of investment and trade, there was substantial corporate opposition to a strategy that relied heavily on social reform. After all, a strategy that entailed redistribution was a risky one: it could undermine the ideological foundations of private property, as well as redefine the "legitimate" scope of state economic power.

Passing the Amendment

The Hickenlooper amendment, enacted in 1962, spoke directly to the problem of investment security. Corporate opinion affected its passage in several direct ways:

1. the timing of the amendment;
2. the specific language involved;
3. the scope and central issues of the debate; and
4. the legislative outcome.

Corporate interest in a new amendment was rekindled by two expropriation controversies that climaxed in 1962.* In Brazil, where the central government's dispute with one company, American and Foreign Power, remained unresolved, a federal state seized ITT's phone company. Hoping to defuse the controversy before there was any congressional reaction, the Kennedy administration unsuccessfully attempted to secure compensation for both companies.[12] At about the same time, the government of Ceylon (now Sri Lanka) ordered Texaco, Esso Standard Eastern, Standard Oil of California, and Shell to begin handling lower-priced Soviet products. When the companies unanimously refused, their gas stations were nationalized.[13]

Though the investments in Ceylon were trivial, the issues were not. The Soviet Union's role was especially significant, since it had recently become the world's second largest oil producer and was an increasingly important crude-oil exporter. The low prices and barter

---

It is particularly important to note that the Kennedy administration could not continue to ignore investment protection issues when formulating Alliance policy. Multinational firms could act collectively, employing multiple channels to affect government policy. The Hickenlooper amendment, for example, was a clear message about the priority of investment protection. Directed at Latin American governments, it was a stick; at the Kennedy administration, a pointer. Probably even more important was the cumulative effect of individual corporate decisions not to invest (or reinvest) in Latin America. Since the Alliance was admittedly dependent upon an influx of U.S. capital, continued capital flight effectively attracted the attention of decision makers.

*Concern over the political security of foreign investments was not new and, indeed, had already been debated with reference to foreign aid. The 1959 Johnson-Bridges amendment, although it was not mandatory, did underscore congressional interest in the issue and showed a willingness to use aid as an appropriate sanction.

Since the 1959 amendment had been passed, however, the United States had substantially revamped its basic foreign-aid legislation. The Foreign Assistance Act of 1961 had replaced the old Mutual Security Act. In the process, a variety of supplementary legislation, including the Johnson-Bridges amendment, had been allowed to lapse. As a result, congressional and corporate concerns about investment security had no expression in the new foreign-aid statutes until the Hickenlooper amendment.

arrangements of the USSR particularly frightened the major international oil companies, whose main source of profits was their oligopoly control of crude-oil sales.[14] Soviet oil exports and transfers of technology left the companies' enormous equity exposed to nationalist threats. The companies clearly recognized the dual Soviet-nationalist challenge to their industry's oligopoly structure.[15]

With these broad concerns in mind, the companies were willing to stand firm against Ceylon's actions. The sums involved were insignificant. The American companies figured their 108 gas stations were worth about $3.5 million. The Government of Ceylon figured they were worth about one-third that. The difference was hardly more than $2 million. Yet nothing was resolved for months and, in the summer of 1962, the U.S. Embassy quietly told Ceylon that its foreign aid was in jeopardy. Even so, compensation talks were put off until late January, and the companies were not optimistic. Before the talks resumed, the Hickenlooper amendment, with its mandatory aid cut-off, had become law. Some of the oil companies had been directly involved in its passage, and they were now ready to see it wielded as a threat. The State Department, however, still hoped for a lump-sum agreement and delayed its decision about future aid. The companies were irritated, and privately they said so. Secretary of State Dean Rusk told President Kennedy (in a now-declassified memo):

> It was made clear by Esso and Caltex executives and lawyers when we decided on February 1 to delay suspension [of foreign aid] that the oil companies were unhappy with our decision and would have preferred to see an example made of Ceylon at that time. The crucial February 6 meeting failed to produce the evidence of "appropriate steps" being taken [toward compensation] which we need to forestall the suspension of aid. . . . Before we actually carried out the suspension, we spoke to the Presidents of the two companies and they said they saw no objection to our action.[16]

As usual, Rusk understates. The companies and other multinational businesses applauded the U.S. action, which cut off Ceylon's subsidized loans and nearly one-fourth of its food imports. The oil companies' tough line is especially interesting because most of their investments on the island had not been touched. The State Department calculated that only about 20 percent of their property had been taken.[17]

The companies, of course, saw larger issues at stake and had from the beginning. They had a world full of refineries and gas stations, so precedent mattered. And in Ceylon they saw several bad ones. Besides inadequate compensation—offered at less than book value instead of full market price—they objected to Ceylon's agreement to distribute cheaper Soviet oil supplies. These were serious challenges with global scope. Simple, successful expropriations in one less developed country would embolden others, or so the companies feared. They would encourage the Soviets to continue their assault, selling or bartering oil as a political weapon. The companies' fears were multiplied by the memory of Cuba's massive expropriations, which began soon after U.S. oil companies there refused to process Soviet oil.

Behind the 108 gas stations in Ceylon stood a worldwide network of oil fields, refineries, and sales facilities, all needing protection from nationalist challenges and Soviet encroachment. The way to do it, the companies agreed, was to retaliate. As in Ceylon, that meant tough policies, a willingness to bear short-term costs, and some help from the U.S. government.[18]

The major international oil companies agreed, then, with most other large multinational firms that easy confiscations anywhere would only encourage nationalists everywhere. This nationalist challenge confronted a variety of industries, particularly those with large investments in raw materials, agriculture, and telecommunications. Possibly because these sectors were considered basic for future industrialization, foreign predominance raised sensitive issues of national sovereignty. In addition, many firms in these sectors continued to operate under long-standing and highly advantageous arrangements even though the firms themselves no longer possessed distinctive advantages or unusual capabilities. In many cases (for instance, oil in Ceylon, Cuba, Peru, and Argentina; telephone and electricity in Brazil), neither scale nor technological complexity presented insurmountable barriers to local private or state ownership. Under these circumstances, foreign firms often found themselves clinging to old bargains that were now economically obsolete.[19]

In response to the threat of nationalization, corporations could pursue a variety of strategies. As Theodore Moran has shown, these included minimizing the equity exposed to nationalization, expanding the number of political allies (by creating economic interests congruent with those of the firm), and attempting to convince politically influential actors that the corporation confers unique, continuing benefits.[20]

A complementary strategy was to raise the potential cost of nationalization by threatening recourse to official U.S. sanctions. That strategy implied the denial of the tangible resources and symbolic support of American aid.

A corporate campaign to legislate foreign aid sanctions began in 1962 with widespread backing. The most active lobbyists were companies whose large fixed investments were politically sensitive and whose production techniques were no longer mystifying to host-country governments. Several interviewees have cited initiatives in 1962 and 1963 by ITT, Texaco, Standard Oil (N.J.), United Fruit, and several copper companies.[21] Manufacturing firms were not actively involved.

The importance of the legislation was further underscored by the personal involvement of Harold Geneen, the head of ITT, and several high-level oil executives. Key business organizations, including the American Petroleum Institute, the National Foreign Trade Council, and the U.S. Chamber of Commerce, were also prominent advocates. Respondents in many confidential interviews mentioned the amendment's extensive corporate support. No corporations or business organizations appear to have opposed the Hickenlooper amendment, actively or tacitly, in 1962 or 1963.

Senator Bourke Hickenlooper of Iowa was the obvious choice to sponsor legislation to protect multinational investments. An effective legislator, he was the ranking Republican on the Foreign Relations Committee and one of a small nucleus of active workers. Hickenlooper was not doctrinally opposed to foreign assistance but was sensitive to corporate preferences about its proper uses. In particular, he shared corporate concern about expropriations and capital flight from Latin America.[22]

Hickenlooper's efforts were widely approved by his colleagues, including such liberal Senate leaders as Hubert Humphrey and Mike Mansfield.[23] The *New York Times* aptly described the mood of most legislators when it stated that "congressional leaders probably have not been so concerned about the treatment of United States private property abroad since . . . the Nineteen Thirties."[24]

Though the president and the State Department shared these concerns, they opposed mandatory legislation because it limited their foreign policy discretion and bureaucratic flexibility. In their attempts to prevent these restrictions, they relied on sympathetic members of the Foreign Relations Committee, especially Senators Fulbright and

Sparkman, to effect some compromises. Aid would be allowed to continue if the president determined that a government had taken "appropriate steps to discharge its obligations as required by international law" within six months. Limits were established on the bill's retroactivity, and the president retained authority to appraise the value of expropriated property. Nevertheless, Senator Hickenlooper passed a tough bill. He and his supporters agreed that mandatory language was essential if the amendment was to be taken seriously, in the administration and abroad. They demanded and got that language. The overall result conformed to corporate preferences.[25]

Did the executive branch strongly oppose these preferences? We know that concern about the amendment reached the presidential level. In response to a press conference inquiry, Kennedy went on record as opposing mandatory sanctions.[26] His office files reveal moderate attention to the subject, including at least fifteen references in various summaries of pending legislation.[27] But prominent State Department officials have privately acknowledged that the executive branch did not actively intervene to prevent the Hickenlooper amendment's passage. Said one well-informed official, "Our position was clear and we carried through, but we didn't really apply pressure. We more or less had to live with it."

The Kennedy administration's weak opposition belied its verbal support for structural economic reforms in underdeveloped countries. The message of Punta del Este had been that the United States would support such reforms financially and politically. Yet, when faced with a measure that would undermine redistributive reforms by demanding full compensation, the administration offered only modest opposition.[28]

The U.S. attitude toward structural reforms was tested soon after the passage of the Hickenlooper amendment. In 1962, Honduras passed an important land reform measure allowing redistribution of uncultivated United Fruit property. At first the U.S. Embassy was noncommittal. The company, however, responded vigorously, moving unilaterally to curtail Honduras' major export by ceasing to plant a disease-resistant banana strain. At the same time, it activated local organizations that were apprehensive about economic reforms, principally the Agricultural Cattlemen's Association, the Honduran Chamber of Commerce, and the Association of Industrialists.[29] Still, the company wanted diplomatic assistance, including the threat to stop foreign aid if the Hondurans proceeded. The Hickenlooper amendment's provisions were explicit, no corporations or legislators opposed their promulgation, and several senators offered active support.[30] Under these pressures, the embassy informed Honduras of the amendment and its serious implications. Because these actions by United Fruit and the U.S. government were simultaneous and mutually reinforcing, it is exceedingly difficult to distinguish their causal effects. It is more important to observe that the threat of Hickenlooper amendment sanctions could complement autonomous corporate efforts to protect foreign investments. The product of these complementary efforts was a causally overdetermined one: Honduran President Morales reversed his previous stand and agreed to substantially amend the agrarian reform law. Later he wrote to United Fruit President Thomas Sunderland that the company could safely expand production and need not fear expropriation or confiscatory taxes, a promise kept by subsequent Honduran governments as well.

The events in Honduras demonstrated not only the policy significance of the Hickenlooper amendment but also its inconsistency with widely publicized Alliance goals such as land reform. Even so, when efforts were made to strengthen the amendment in 1963, the administration offered less opposition than it had the year before.

The amendment's supporters wanted to extend its sanctions and broaden its definition of expropriation. The latter change was instigated by several major oil firms whose contracts in Argentina were disputed by the new president, Arturo Illía.[31] When the companies broached the matter of diplomatic support, State Department officials indicated that the problem was not covered by the Hickenlooper amendment, as company officials believed. Such counsel reinforced the companies' mistrust of the executive and substantiated their anxieties about investment security, the dual concerns that had animated their earlier legislative efforts. Some of the companies contacted Senator Hickenlooper, who was equally distressed. Results were swift. Only ten days after Illía's inaugural speech, the Foreign Relations Committee redefined "expropriation" to include contract nullification.[32]

Opposition from the administration was feeble and ineffective. During the Senate hearings, Secretary of State Rusk made a major, probably tactical, concession: "Our experience thus far has meant that [the Hickenlooper] amendment has been a good thing."[33] The best evidence of the administration's weak efforts is a memorandum from AID Administrator David Bell to the president:

> We do not expect to fight this amendment on the floor, and are working
> with Hickenlooper to try to find the best solution. . . . We have acquiesced
> in the Hickenlooper amendment. . . . We hope we can draw the line
> against further restrictive amendments offered from the floor.[34]

Not only were the administration's efforts weak, their context was
remarkably narrow. The State Department acknowledged support for
Hickenlooper's policy principles and ratified them as traditional U.S.
goals:

> The United States has never accepted any principle other than fair com-
> pensation for expropriated property. We continue to adhere firmly to this
> view, not only because of its moral propriety . . . but because we recognize
> the necessity of encouraging private capital to invest in the developing
> countries.[35]

Only in its forceful instructions to the executive did the Hickenlooper
amendment represent a variation from traditional U.S. investment
protection policies.

The real novelty, then, was not in the amendment, but in the
proposed Alliance reforms. The amendment simply attached formal,
unilateral sanctions to the traditional United States assertion that
international law requires prompt, full, convertible compensation for
expropriated foreign investment. Yet the State Department never faced
the tension between that policy and the much-heralded Alliance strategy of social reform. While reform does not necessarily imply forced
divestment, the U.S. effort to restate and enforce anti-expropriation
norms seriously limited the scope of "legitimate" reform. For example, in most less developed countries, far-reaching agrarian reform
would be impossible if full compensation were required. Moreover,
even if such compensation were feasible, it would tend to offset any
broader policy of redistributing wealth. Because there were relatively
few major U.S. landowners in Latin America (outside Central America
and the Caribbean), the Hickenlooper amendment's standards of
compensation seldom affected agrarian reform directly. However, the
amendment did reinforce the general principle of full compensation
by insisting on its ethical validity and by subordinating economic
reform to its requirements.

In opposing the Hickenlooper amendment, the State Department
emphasized its support for that principle. Its primary argument was
that existing diplomatic channels could best ensure such compensation, improve investment security, and prevent future expropria-

tions. In one sense, the amendment's supporters agreed on the importance of existing channels. Their central objectives were the content and priorities of diplomatic policy. But, for reasons I have already discussed, multinational companies could not accept administration assurances that their interests would be protected vigorously. Such assurances were undermined still further by the State Department's other argument against the amendment—that diplomatic flexibility best served the "national interest" by allowing the "balancing of many factors."[36] Though deliberately ambiguous, the statement seemed to imply that other policy goals might intrude upon efforts to deter expropriation. Still, the department's most prominent argument was that it could protect corporate interests most effectively if it were not forced to support every intransigent company or every minor claim.

The policy debate was thus a tactical one, bounded by the consensus that the protection of corporate investments was a fundamental and long-standing goal of U.S. foreign policy. The administration's basic agreement with corporate objectives, as well as its tactical disagreement, is evident in the previously cited Bell memorandum to President Kennedy:

> We seek the same objectives Hickenlooper does. But formal amendments of this type may arouse nationalistic feelings and exacerbate rather than ease the problems at issue (this is plainly happening now in Argentina). Working quietly but forcefully behind the scenes is a far better way to bring about the results we are after.[37]

Within a decade, many firms would adopt this position themselves. But this was the early 1960s, and they had not adopted it yet. They wanted public policies that stated clearly and unequivocally, "Expropriation is not acceptable."

Applying the Hickenlooper Amendment[38]

Because the amendment posed such a stern threat to less developed countries, it figured prominently in several investment disputes. Like its legislative history, its diplomatic history raises important questions about the relationship between corporate preferences and public policy. The radical hypothesis advanced earlier suggests that the amendment's use would conform to predominant corporate preferences. To evaluate that hypothesis, I shall examine those major investment disputes in which the employment of the Hickenlooper amendment was an issue. If the radical hypothesis is not to be rejected, then it must accurately predict the amendment's use without requiring the introduction of other policy considerations.

As I have already stated, investment disputes in Brazil, Honduras, Ceylon, and Argentina were important factors in the amendment's passage and subsequent modification. In Honduras, the only interested U.S. corporation was United Fruit. Though the State Department was reluctant, it finally did inform the Honduran government of the amendment and its significance. As I have noted, United Fruit's objectives had been achieved before the date when formal sanctions were required. The more important disputes in Brazil and Argentina were also resolved (or were the subjects of substantive negotiations) before the amendment's sanctions had to be applied. Both the president and Attorney General Robert Kennedy gave personal attention to the Brazilian conflict, helping to settle ITT's claim, and starting talks about American and Foreign Power's losses. According to David Bell's 1963 testimony, "In the Brazil case, thus far appropriate steps, satisfactory to the private firms concerned, have been taken."[39] The Johnson administration's decision not to invoke sanctions in Argentina did not contravene the oil companies' preferences there. Rather than pressing for sanctions, the companies wanted and got high-level attention to the conflict, which was slowly resolved to their satisfaction. In fact, formal sanctions were applied only once, in Ceylon, where the oil dispute had continued to fester. Was that action approved by most corporations? The best evidence is a quite striking memorandum from Secretary Rusk to President Kennedy, which has since been declassified: "American businessmen and Congressmen have widely applauded our action [in Ceylon]; failure to suspend under the circumstances would have had adverse repercussions on the Hill and elsewhere."[40]

Except for the Ceylon dispute, most investment quarrels and their ad hoc solutions appear to have concerned only those few corporations that had been expropriated. For the others, issues of investment protection lacked both urgency and focus in the mid-sixties. The calm was broken in 1968 and early 1969, when Peru expropriated the International Petroleum Company (IPC), a subsidiary of Standard Oil of New Jersey (now Exxon). The prospect of formal sanctions quickly became the most important aspect of the dispute, which touched all phases of U.S.-Peruvian relations.[41] The United States quietly suspended aid without formally invoking the Hickenlooper amendment, despite the absence of fruitful negotiations between the company and Peru.

Did the Nixon administration's refusal to apply the amendment in this important dispute run counter to corporate preferences, as is sometimes suggested? First, one must note that the issue separated Standard Oil from most other U.S. firms in Peru. Led by Marcona Corporation, almost all U.S. businesses feared that their investments were endangered by an escalating intergovernmental dispute. They forcefully opposed sanctions.* In contrast, Standard Oil initially urged the State Department to apply the Hickenlooper amendment, arguing that only a tough policy could deter future expropriations or ensure compensation. The company, however, was internally divided on the policy issue. Some officials had concluded that formal sanctions would only strengthen nationalist hostility to foreign investment throughout Latin America. As a result, they expected that compensation would become politically impossible in Peru, and confrontations elsewhere would become more likely. For reasons not yet clear, Standard Oil's position changed before the date for applying sanctions. According to a government official close to the negotiations, "Originally Standard was straightforward. They wanted Hickenlooper. But later on they neither urged it nor opposed it." Standard's final neutrality represented a substantial policy shift, and U.S. officials recognized it as such.[42] My conclusion is that Washington's refusal to employ the Hickenlooper amendment conformed to the preferences of most corporations and did not conflict with those of Standard Oil.[43]

Other expropriation disputes in the late 1960s followed a similar pattern. According to State Department officials, Gulf did not seek application in Bolivia after the leftist government there seized some property.[44] In Ecuador, the government seized ITT's phone company and numerous tuna boats, while simultaneously inviting U.S. companies to exploit its offshore oil. The oil firms, joined by most other U.S. investors there, successfully opposed the aggrieved companies' appeals for formal sanctions.

*In Peru, as in Honduras, the intergovernmental dispute precipitated a transnational coalition. U.S. corporations opposing use of the Hickenlooper amendment worked closely with allies in Peruvian banking and legal circles. For example, the meeting between U.S. Special Envoy John Irwin and President Velasco—the legal pretext for not applying the Hickenlooper amendment—was arranged jointly by a Peruvian lawyer and a U.S. businessman. See "Editor's Note" in *U.S. Foreign Policy and Peru*, ed. Daniel A. Sharp (Austin: University of Texas Press, 1972), 285–287.

Confusion, Ferment, and More Sanctions

Separately, these solutions satisfied interested corporations. Cumulatively, they created doubts about basic U.S. policy. After the Peruvian episode, many corporations reconsidered the problem of protecting their investments and decided that formal, mandatory sanctions were self-defeating. Their use would pointedly raise issues of sovereignty, thereby reinforcing nationalism in the affected country and possibly elsewhere.[45] The potential leverage of foreign aid had been eroded by reduced appropriations, and the problematical application of formal sanctions was more likely to confuse corporate negotiators than to threaten foreign officials.

The best evidence that corporate attitudes were changing is a survey taken in August 1970 by the Council of the Americas, whose members account for 90 percent of U.S. investment in Latin America. Most companies considered expropriation a remote threat at that time, and 76 percent thought that the Hickenlooper amendment had "outlived its usefulness."[46] Only extractive industries, whose large investments were immobile and especially sensitive politically, were equally divided about the amendment's usefulness.

If corporate opinion generally opposed the amendment in 1970, why was its substance retained and actually extended to multilateral aid two years later? This legislative behavior seems to cast doubt on the radical hypothesis and deserves serious examination.

Basically, corporate opposition to the Hickenlooper amendment arose because the amendment appeared to endanger investments rather than protect them. Revisions were in order then. It was unclear what form these revisions should take, but it was implicitly assumed that both their content and timing should enhance investment security. When Salvadore Allende was elected president of Chile a few months after the council's survey, that assumption became critical. Under the new circumstances, any revision would appear to weaken America's anti-expropriation posture at a time when foreign investments were under attack. Not surprisingly, active support for revision collapsed completely, and the initiative shifted to the amendment's remaining supporters. Their success in passing the Gonzalez amendments is attributable to the neutralization of their corporate opponents and to their own special ability to affect multilateral aid policy.

Multilateral aid is administered by the Treasury, the department that has most energetically supported a strong deterrent policy to protect investments. Particularly under Secretaries Connally and Shultz, Treasury wanted the government to state clearly that confiscations were intolerable and would be opposed by stringent sanctions. This posture was shared by members of the Banking and Currency Committee, which handles multilateral authorizations in the House. The relevant subcommittee, chaired by Henry Gonzalez of Texas, had to draft new aid authorizations at the height of the Chilean expropriations; he demanded a tough policy.

The administration's internal debate began in June 1971, when the National Security Council asked for an "urgent study on U.S. policy toward expropriation without compensation."[47] Treasury, of course, took a hard line. The other central actor, the State Department, defended the existing policy of "situational response" and opposed any public statement of policy. In the complex maneuvers that followed, Treasury's position was greatly enhanced by the Gonzalez subcommittee, which threatened to pass mandatory legislation if the president did not make a strong public statement. By October, the Treasury Department had won a compromise victory: when "significant" expropriations occurred, there would be the "presumption" of sanctions unless "reasonable steps were taken to provide adequate compensation."[48] It was a firm, clear, publicly stated policy, but not an automatic one. Though the State Department could not modify the decision, it did manage to delay its issuance. The postponement succeeded only in angering the Treasury and the subcommittee, which voted to add mandatory language to the multilateral authorizations. The presidential statement was finally made in January 1972, just two weeks before floor action. Its poor timing probably assisted passage of the mandatory amendments, instead of relieving pressure for them.

What role did corporate preferences play in the passage of the amendments? I have already noted that business opinion was divided about their utility. Even corporations which shared relatively similar expropriation dilemmas disagreed. Some, such as Gulf, American Smelting, Standard Oil of California, Marcona, and Occidental, had concluded that mandatory sanctions were no longer useful. Manufacturing, financial, and service industries generally concurred. But ITT, Texaco, Grace, and others continued to favor virtually automatic sanctions, articulated in advance. According to the *Mexican-American*

Review, published by the American Chamber of Commerce in Mexico, about two-thirds of the trustees of the Council of the Americas responding to a survey opposed the continuation of Hickenlooper-type sanctions.[49] Nevertheless, in August 1971, when Peter Peterson asked for the council's views on the Hickenlooper amendment, its president could state only that the membership was internally divided on that question.[50] The time was inappropriate and the divisions were deep enough to prevent the council's support of revision.[51] In contrast, interviewees stressed the diligent efforts of hard-line corporations, especially some in extractive industries. Their exact role in initiating and lobbying for a strong anti-expropriation policy is unclear. But it is known that these companies were vocal, well-connected advocates of a tough, preannounced policy.

Repealing the Hickenlooper Amendment

Within a year the furor about Chile had declined (in direct proportion to the "destabilization"of the Allende government), and corporate opposition to mandatory sanctions surfaced and grew. Members of the House Foreign Affairs Committee returned from a Latin American trip convinced that "even those who allegedly benefit from these types of amendments favor their repeal."[52] Led by Representatives Culver and Whalen, they deleted the decade-old Hickenlooper amendment from the committee's 1973 bilateral aid bill. Aware that their move was potentially divisive, neither the committee nor interested corporations lobbied in the House. When the bill reached the floor, Culver and his allies were surprised and defeated by Representative Gonzalez, who substituted mandatory language consistent with his multilateral amendments.[53]

The Gonzalez substitute was unacceptable to State, AID, and the Council of the Americas. For the first time, the council's trustees decided to work actively against the mandatory sanctions. They supported only the addition of a presidential waiver, since they believed that more extensive revisions would appear to soften U.S. policy. A proposal to that effect was advanced by Senator Jacob Javits, Republican of New York, a senior figure on the Foreign Relations Committee. The committee, and later the full Senate, accepted his proposal, which then went to conference committee. Throughout this period, the Council of the Americas had been quite active. Its trustees had met with President Nixon, Secretaries Shultz and Dent, and Presidential Assistant Peter Flanigan. Describing these meetings, the council's newsletter noted, "There was agreement with the Council that in cases under dispute there should be flexibility in U.S. response."[54] Extensive liaison work was done with both congressmen and committee staff.

State and AID moved forcefully as well. They confronted Treasury by asking for an "executive branch position" on the legislation, and won. The decision, made by the President but not for attribution, supported a waiver provision.[55] Armed with that statement of administration policy, House conferees could rationalize a vote for revision, which they had long supported individually. Without debate, the conferees voted overwhelmingly to accept the waiver. Their report was accepted by both houses.[56] After more than a decade, bilateral aid sanctions against expropriations were no longer mandatory.

The new waiver provision created a bizarre inconsistency. Multilateral policy was now more stringent legally than was bilateral policy. Of course, proponents of bilateral revision preferred similar multilateral laws, but they were unable to act. Both the Council of the Americas and AID concluded that an effort simultaneously to reform multilateral laws would severely compromise their work on the Hickenlooper amendment. Furthermore, any effort would implicitly challenge the jurisdiction of the Banking and Currency Committee over multilateral aid. Perhaps the most important difficulty was demonstrated the following year. The 1974 International Development Association bill was in such deep trouble that no one who supported its general concept dared to burden it with controversial modifications.[57] Still the radical hypothesis suggests that generalized corporate opposition will prevent Treasury from pursuing a policy of automatic sanctions. And, indeed, they have not pursued such a policy.

Conclusions

My initial hypothesis was that government policies to protect foreign investment, including the passage of laws and their enforcement, conform to the predominant preferences of the largest U.S. multinational corporations. To evaluate that hypothesis, I analyzed several debates concerning investment protection legislation and its application, ranging over fifteen years, and with quite varied outcomes. Throughout these debates corporate preferences were actively and directly expressed. The legislative politics of the Gonzalez amendments, however, suggest a necessary refinement of the original hypothesis. Relevant preferences were those held with sufficient intensity and prospect of individual gain to evoke active expression by the largest multinational firms. Because that body of corporate opinion was congruent with political outcomes in this issue-area, our refined hypothesis cannot be rejected.*

The most prominent alternatives to that hypothesis are those derived from the pluralist and bureaucratic models. An exemplary use of the pluralist model can be found in *American Business and Public Policy,* by Raymond A. Bauer, Ithiel de Sola Pool, and Lewis Anthony Dexter, still one of the most important works by political scientists on that topic. Limiting their study to U.S. trade policy, they conclude that divisions within the business community, impediments to communication, and countervailing pressures vitiated the overall importance of corporate opinion in that issue-area.[58]

These findings cannot be generalized to the politics of investment protection, however. We found no constituencies that opposed multinational investors. Uncontested, and seldom weakened by internal dissension, corporate preferences effectively modified several aid bills. The Hickenlooper amendment was passed and expanded with unanimous and active business support. Disagreements about multilateral policy were primarily latent in 1972. The next year, the Council of the Americas clearly and successfully expressed the predominant multinational corporate view.

Though the conclusions arrived at by Bauer, Pool, and Dexter are inapplicable here, the pluralist model can yield reasonably accurate and economical predictions about the use of foreign aid to protect investments from expropriation. A pluralist hypothesis, like the radical one advanced earlier, would predict the predominance of large multinational corporations in this issue-area. A pluralist would expect large, intense, well-organized actors to predominate in the absence of a strong opposition. Not only does the pluralist model predict well but it also captures important aspects of the policy process. Unlike

---

*Congressional debates about investment protection have frequently considered corporate interests and preferences quite explicitly. However, such considerations were not preeminent for many legislators. Many invoked Palmerstonian imagery, conceptualizing corporations as citizens entitled to the full protection of their government. Senator Hickenlooper appealed to this notion, among others, in 1962 and 1963. Such imagery raises important questions about the social determination of a seemingly "neutral" ideology.

the bureaucratic model, it conceptualizes policymaking broadly, explaining outcomes in terms of the articulated interests and concerted efforts of nongovernmental actors.

Despite the important virtues of the pluralist model, there are serious difficulties in using it to explain U.S. anti-expropriation politics.[59] The most significant is the pluralist conception of the legislator, who is hypothesized as a broker responding solely to the direct influence of shifting environmental forces. With respect to investment-protection legislation, the pluralist model focuses attention on direct corporate action, such as that which initiated the Hickenlooper amendment. Yet the congressional debates also revealed strong, independent legislative interest in anti-expropriation policies. There was also broad, fundamental consensus about the international norms that should govern foreign direct investment. Although foreign governments' rights of eminent domain were not challenged directly, there was general agreement that it was improper (and usually imprudent) to transfer productive assets from private to state control. Most congressmen, administration officials, and executives of large multinational firms agreed that rigorous repayment principles should be maintained. Disagreements arose chiefly over which policies could most effectively achieve these objectives. Thus, government decision makers and corporate executives were bound by mutual sympathy, responding in broadly similar ways to changes in the global environment for foreign investment. For example, the Johnson-Bridges amendment was basically an independent congressional response to the Cuban expropriations. Representative Gonzalez's efforts in 1973 had some corporate support, but there was almost no lobbying before the House vote. His success in that vote, which overturned another committee's recommendation, reflected many legislators' stubborn, hard-line opposition to expropriation, the ideological remnant of a policy once supported by most multinational firms. Still, the debates over Representative Gonzalez's amendments in 1972 and 1973, like the earlier ones over the Hickenlooper amendment, demonstrated the government's underlying consensus about anti-expropriation norms and U.S. policy objectives. Within that consensus there were significant strategic and tactical differences, which were resolved in favor of the predominant preferences of large multinational corporations, as is predicted by the radical hypothesis.*

---

*More recent pluralist analysis comes closer to the radical propositions offered here, but in doing so it seems to abandon some fundamental bases of pluralist theory. From the very beginning, pluralists have emphasized the pulling and hauling of diverse

Bureaucratic analysts would explain these outcomes quite differently, referring almost exclusively to intragovernmental actors as the key elements in policy determination. For example, Jessica Pernitz Einhorn's careful study, *Expropriation Politics*, examines this topic solely in organizational terms. She emphasizes bureaucratic interests, formal and informal procedures, bargaining rules, and the formation of intragovernmental alliances.[60]

One cannot directly compare the predictions of the radical hypothesis with those of the bureaucratic model, which specifies some features of the policy process but does *not* predict outcomes. By contrast, our study empirically confirms predictions derived from the revised radical hypothesis about the outcomes of policy debates and the pattern of the Hickenlooper amendment's implementation. The predictive value of the radical hypothesis in this issue-area, as well as its parsimony, can be compared with that of the bureaucratic model, which is more complicated but adds no predictive power. Unlike the radical hypothesis, it offers no explanation for the long-term trend in anti-expropriation policy. Nevertheless, as a disaggregative, purposive account of intragovernmental action, the bureaucratic model can usefully complement a radical focus on domestic social structure.

According to Robert Art, the distinctiveness of the bureaucratic model must depend upon its assertion of three fundamental propositions:

1. organizational position determines policy preferences;
2. policy decisions and actions are the unintended consequences of intragovernmental bargaining; and
3. organizational routines and interests affect policy implementation more than they do policy formulation.[61]

---

social groups, each with its own agenda and each capable of winning on key issues by mobilizing significant resources. Yet, according to John Manley, the most recent work of both Robert Dahl and Charles E. Lindblom shifts away from that position and depicts a political arena in which major corporations play a structurally privileged role, including a hegemonic role in the establishment of political norms and public agendas.

Lindblom, in particular, acknowledges the inconsistency between these two perspectives and states that his recent arguments about "the privileged position of business . . . [are] antagonistic to pluralism" and are *not* simply amendments to resuscitate it (p. 384). See John F. Manley, "Neo-Pluralism: A Class Analysis of Pluralism I and Pluralism II," *American Political Science Review* 77 (June 1983), 368–383, and replies by Charles E. Lindblom (ibid., 384–386) and Robert A. Dahl (ibid., 386–389). Lindblom and Dahl's earlier position is set forth in *Politics, Economics, and Welfare* (New York: Harper, 1953). Their more recent positions are in C. E. Lindblom, *Politics and Markets* (New York: Basic Books, 1977) and R. A. Dahl, *Dilemmas of a Pluralist Democracy* (New Haven, Conn.: Yale University Press, 1982).

Throughout this study one finds evidence illustrating these assertions. As the disputes between State and Treasury indicate, policy calculations were not uniform and preferences were often a simple function of organizational interests. In addition, the bureaucratic division between bilateral and multilateral aid probably makes it easier to add automatic sanctions to the former and delete them from the latter. Responsibility for policy implementation in these cases seems to increase an organization's ability to formulate policy. Finally, as Art's second proposition indicates, decision making at the national level is an institutionally diffused, and frequently contested, process. The president, two White House councils, several departments, both houses of Congress, and several congressional committees have all played important roles in formulating investment-protection policy.

Despite these suggestions which supplement and enrich the analysis of anti-expropriation politics, the bureaucratic model is seriously flawed. The function that links organizational position and policy preference is currently quite ambiguous. Often one cannot deduce preferences about specific policy issues from vague conceptions of organizational essence. In any event, most bureaucratic analysts tend to qualify, and thus confound, that idea by recognizing both the pervasiveness of shared social images and the persistence of individual experience. Because it is fundamentally equivocal about the president's power, the model's elaboration of decision rules must remain tentative as well.[62]

The most serious inadequacy of the bureaucratic model is its ascription of a neutral, asocial character to government policymaking. The model presumes but does not analyze the domestic context that legitimates policy objectives, circumscribes the arguments of opposing bureaucracies, and, ultimately, limits policy outcomes. By failing to understand the logic by which certain options are excluded, the model must sometimes fail to illuminate the logic by which others are chosen. As a result, the bureaucratic model can best augment an analysis if its purposive account of intragovernmental decision making is located in a domestic context that makes policy goals and shared assumptions comprehensible.[63]

In investment-protection politics, multinational corporations were a vital aspect of that domestic context. Because those firms played such an important role in the United States' international economic relationships, the threat of expropriation inevitably raised serious foreign policy issues. Throughout the period we have studied, these issues were considered in an ideological context that stressed the positive contributions of foreign investments to domestic welfare. That implicit link between corporate well-being and domestic well-being had a complex effect on policymaking. Most significantly, it provided a convincing rationale for government efforts to protect foreign direct investments. It also suggested that there was a national stake in the outcome of expropriation disputes that was, to some extent, independent of corporate preferences. That independence was reinforced by the idea that investment-protection policies embodied implicit standards of justice. Though more sophisticated multinational businessmen and government officials understood that hard-line policies were self-defeating, others continued to believe not only that uncompromising anti-expropriation sanctions were effective deterrents, but that they were just retribution. Though that belief was declining in importance, its persistence was amply revealed in the difficult fight to repeal the Hickenlooper amendment in 1973.

But policy disputes should not obscure the fundamental consensus about the objective of investment protection. Offering U.S. corporations protection when they were confronted by nationalist demands was a shared goal of all relevant bureaucracies. None of the debates challenged the appropriateness of that basic policy objective, or even its rank-order prominence. Some have termed these intra-administration debates "expropriation politics"; they could more accurately be called "anti-expropriation politics." Even the State Department de-emphasized the potential conflict between investment protection and the pursuit of other policy goals. The central theme of the losers' arguments—those of the president (1962), the State Department (1962, 1963, 1972), and the Treasury Department (1973)—like that of the winners', was their strategy's superior ability to protect investments. That theme is even more noteworthy because the arguments were conducted within governmental forums that differed widely in membership. The narrow limits to policy debate, as well as the active participation of multinational corporations in the policy process, strongly suggest that the radical hypothesis is not confounded by problems of spurious causation.

Even though the predictions of the refined radical hypothesis have been empirically affirmed, two interesting questions about foreign aid sanctions have not been answered. Why was legislation needed to embody corporate preferences in public policy? Though the Kennedy administration's opposition was weak and narrow, interested corporations still considered the executive's initial response unsatisfactory. They had to work with Congress to prod the administration and induce more satisfactory policies. Second, why are the Gonzalez amendments still statutory law? The answer lies in the linkage between those sanctions and legislative support for multilateral aid. Opponents of the amendments generally support such aid and are unwilling to imperil the entire program by introducing controversial revisions. Nevertheless, the radical hypothesis correctly predicts that overt, mandatory sanctions are no longer official policy. Given current corporate preferences, the corollary hypothesis predicts that the Gonzalez amendments will not be formally invoked.

As the decline of the Hickenlooper amendment demonstrates, most multinational companies now think that inflexible threats to suspend foreign aid are either ineffective deterrents or self-defeating retribution. Their use would undoubtedly frustrate the solution of most investment disputes and, equally important, would undercut new corporate relationships with economic nationalists. Faced with extensive demands for shared ownership and control, their performance closely monitored, most multinational firms have adopted flexible, self-reliant responses to economic nationalism, including forced divestment. They have been forced to consider, and often adopt, formulas that give them only partial ownership and control, or management contracts without equity participation. They expect to protect profits by relying on their other advantages, including global networks for manufacturing, transporting, and marketing finished products. This new attitude is best summarized by the president of Exxon Services in Caracas. After Venezuela nationalized billions of dollars in foreign oil concessions, including Exxon's, he told *Business Week:*

> The government has gained control of the oil industry without risk, and we have found an attractive income for technology that we would have to develop anyway. . . . This is the way the world is going and it is, in itself, a profitable business.[64]

It is this kind of corporate accommodation to economic nationalism that best explains the decline of tough public sanctions against expropriation.

But self-reliance is not autarky. Corporate advantages can be—and certainly have been—complemented by diplomatic support in selected cases. The current problem for multinational firms is that bilateral diplomacy has been unable to protect their equity investments in a broad array of recent conflicts, especially those with economically powerful nationalists. Neither the companies nor the U.S. government has yet developed a coherent, effective response to this complex challenge. But most large multinational corporations now agree that the automatic application of sanctions would only automatically sever their future profits. Under the circumstances, self-reliance and accommodation is more prudent—and more profitable.

The Development of Expropriation Insurance: The Role of Corporate Preferences and State Initiatives

It is difficult to compare all the means of protecting foreign investments, but state-sponsored guaranty insurance is surely one of the most important. It is the most coherent and specific U.S. government plan, and one of the oldest. The basic idea is simple enough: the easiest way to both stimulate and protect foreign investments is to ensure them against significant risks such as confiscation, war, or the ability to convert local profits into dollars.

The United States developed such a program in the late 1940s, originally as part of the Marshall Plan. For more than a decade, however, it remained small and legally confined. It began to grow in the 1960s once the political risks to foreign investment had become more pressing and the program's own legal strictures had been loosened.

Throughout this period, the insurance program was administered as part of the larger foreign-aid program. This practice was consistent with U.S. aid policy, which had always sought to stimulate private capital flows alongside public ones. As the insurance sales multiplied, however, it became more difficult for the aid agency to handle them efficiently. Supporters of the program began pushing for new administrative arrangements so clients could be serviced in a more single-minded way and their applications processed quickly. The result was a 1969 reorganization that shifted the insurance program to a newly created government corporation: the Overseas Private

Investment Corporation (OPIC). OPIC's charter has been modified at each statutory renewal (in 1974, 1978, and 1981), but the agency still stands as the program's administrator, selling American companies coverage against expropriation, war, currency inconvertibility, and civil strife in less developed countries.

My aim here is to consider the program's evolution, its connection to larger foreign policy goals, and its support in Congress, the executive branch, and the business community. We are particularly interested in foreign investors' attitudes. What kinds of policies and administration did they want? How did their attitudes change over the years, and why? What kinds of divisions existed among foreign investors on these questions?

It may seem obvious that investors would strongly back a government-run insurance program and would seek its enlargement. In fact, their response has been more convoluted and more interesting. Many investors were wary of the program at first, uncertain of its implications for foreign economic policy and, indeed, for their own autonomous decision making. As the program developed an administrative history, most of these concerns were laid to rest. Still, it is surprising that a public offer to insure risky private investments had any corporate opposition at all, much less a divided business constituency.

My basic concern, then, is with the guaranty program's evolving character and its changing sources of support and opposition. I will evaluate alternative hypotheses that might account for its long-term growth and development. One proposition emphasizes growing corporate support for investment insurance. Another stresses the vital role of administration backing.

Each will be considered in detail at four crucial stages in the program's history:

1. the passage and initial elaboration of the investment guaranty law (1948–1951);
2. a major expansion of the guaranty law and insurance program (1961);
3. the reorganization of the program under the Overseas Private Investment Corporation (1969); and
4. the 1974 debate over OPIC, which fundamentally challenged its continuation.

These turning points, stretching over a quarter of a century, define the guaranty program and cover most of its major legislative and administrative changes.* They permit an unbiased consideration of the sources of that change.

One explanation is that these changes reflected the predominant preferences of the most vitally affected large corporations.** If these firms generally opposed the program's inception or if it grew rapidly without their approval, one could reject this hypothesis. A corollary holds that if there is substantial disagreement among large multinational firms, then the guaranty program should be either ambiguous, contradictory, or modest in scope. This corollary could be rejected

---

*Since then, the program has been modified twice. OPIC was renewed in 1978 despite the Carter administration's ambivalence and strenuous opposition from organized labor, which claimed the insurance coverage was costing Americans jobs. The floor fight was tough and the bill itself restrictive. OPIC had to increase its emphasis on small business (below the *Fortune* 1,000), human rights, and investments in the very poorest countries. Its activities were restricted in countries with per capita incomes above $1,000. By the same token, the bill did lift an earlier directive requiring OPIC to transfer some coverage to private insurance companies.

Most of these restrictions were rolled back and the program significantly expanded in 1981. *Business Week* describes the process:

> The Reagan Administration, in response to pleas from U.S. multinationals, is moving to expand an obscure federal agency that insures U.S. business activity abroad. . . . Leading the drive for a revamped OPIC is the Emergency Committee for American Trade, a Washington-based lobby representing 63 of the 100 largest U.S. multinational companies. "The expansion of OPIC makes a hell of a lot of sense," explains ECAT lobbyist Robert L. McNeill. He points out that OPIC offers 20-year coverage to U.S. companies abroad, compared to three-year policies typically available from private insurers.

The new law allowed OPIC to cover "civil strife" (alongside its existing coverage for war, expropriation, and currency inconvertibility) and removed some restrictions on types of eligible projects. For the first time, OPIC could insure letters of credit, which contractors often have to post (as a kind of performance bond) and which are commonly used in the Middle East. Most important, by tripling the per capita income limit, the new legislation permitted OPIC to operate freely in newly industrializing countries such as Brazil and Taiwan.

92 Stat. 213 (1978); 95 Stat. 1021 (1981); *Business Week*, August 3, 1981, p. 39; Theodor Meron, "OPIC Investment is Alive and Well," *American Journal of International Law* 73 (January 1979), 104–111; Gary H. Sampliner, "The 1981 OPIC Amendments and Reagan's 'Newer Directions' in Third World Development Policy," *Law and Policy in International Business* 14 (1982), 181–213.

**According to this hypothesis, the increased size, scope, and institutionalization of the investment guaranty program is causally dependent on increased support from large multinational firms. These firms are operationally defined, as they were in our earlier discussion of foreign-aid sanctions, as companies large enough to be listed as one of *Fortune* magazine's 500 largest industrial firms or 50 largest commercial banks. Comparable investment banks are also included. Relevant preferences are those actively expressed by these corporations.

if the program had a clear rationale and grew rapidly in spite of corporate disunity.

An alternative approach stresses the decisive role of *public* actors, primarily foreign policy officials in the executive branch. Investment insurance could be useful to them in several ways. First, it could lessen the impact of investment conflicts on diplomatic relations and larger policy goals. If an insured corporation was entangled in an investment dispute, the State Department could simply pay off its claims. By eliminating the company's financial stake in the conflict, it could insulate American diplomacy from specialized corporate demands. Second, by promoting new investment, the guaranty program could actually contribute to larger foreign policy goals. It nicely complements the foreign aid program and, for over two decades, was closely associated with it. Both, after all, try to promote capitalist development and open economic growth receptive to international trade and investment. This fundamental connection to major foreign policy goals has given the guaranty program a broad constituency in the executive branch. According to the state-initiatives hypothesis, the program is causally dependent on the support of this constituency.[1]

The two hypotheses—one focusing on state initiatives, the other on corporate preferences—have markedly different emphases, but they are not mutually exclusive. In fact, foreign-policy bureaucracies and multinational firms often share common interests, or at least complementary ones. Moreover, the two sets of actors are linked through extended policy networks, permitting reciprocal influence. While such connections facilitate a corporate role in policymaking, they also allow the state to manipulate institutional support for various programs. The executive's fine hand is especially evident in the selection of public review panels, appointed to suggest new policy initiatives or to justify old ones. The results are not always successful, as far as the administration is concerned, but the effort does suggest the interdependence of state initiatives and corporate preferences.

Besides examining these linkages and evaluating both hypotheses, I will once again consider changing corporate attitudes about investment protection. This time, however, the issue is not sanctions or retaliation but state guaranties against certain types of foreign loss. What role do investors think the state should play in this area? How, and why, have these attitudes changed since the 1940s? The debates over guaranty insurance highlight these questions because the program involves a very close association between multinational companies and the state.

Yet the very tightness of this association, and its visibility at home and abroad, poses certain risks to both partners. At first, some companies feared that foreign governments might misread the program's intent and actually use it as an excuse to expropriate. A more serious danger, at least for some of the program's early opponents, was that the U.S. government would itself pervert the program, twisting the right to insure foreign investments into the right to oversee corporate operations abroad.*

The government faced a different problem. It was offering a novel form of insurance, one not offered privately because the risks were unpredictable and often unique.[2] With no accounting principles on which to base its premiums, it turned to political criteria. The program's mission was to encourage and protect foreign investment. That militated for low fees. But low fees also posed dangers. If insurance claims outran fees, only taxes could make up the difference. That would vividly expose an unusually close relationship between the

---

*To understand these corporate fears, it is important to understand the general problem of "moral hazard" and the rationale it offers for close surveillance of insured corporations.

Investment guaranties, like many other forms of insurance, cover risks such as expropriation that depend partly on voluntary actions taken by insured firms. A corporation could thus increase the likelihood of collecting on its insurance by its own fraud, tax evasion, inattentiveness to host-country concerns, strident opposition to local laws, or other sins of omission or commission.

Consider, for instance, ITT's efforts to block Salvadore Allende's election as president of Chile. When newspaper columnist Jack Anderson broke the story, the Allende government broke off negotiations to compensate ITT for the nationalization of its Chilean subsidiary. OPIC delayed payment on ITT's insurance claim, stating that ITT had failed in its contractual duty to negotiate with Chile, a claim that arbitrators eventually rejected.

In general, if self-protection is costly, and if there is no way to make insurance premiums contingent on levels of self-protection, then there will be moral hazards that the insuror must guard against. To minimize them, the insuror may wish to inspect ongoing corporate activities, or, at the very least, to review relevant activities when claims are presented.

Given the problems of moral hazard, the insuror's concerns are understandable. But for multinational firms, eager to avoid surveillance by the U.S. government, such precautions would be unacceptable intrusions. These fears, all grounded in the problem of moral hazard, were key issues in the early stages of the guaranty program.

"International Telephone and Telegraph, Sud America-Overseas Private Investment Corporation: Arbitration of Dispute Involving U.S. Investment Guaranty Program," *International Legal Materials* 13 (1974), 1307–1375; Kenneth J. Arrow, *The Limits of Organization* (New York: W. W. Norton, 1974), 35–36; Isaac Ehrlich and Gary Becker, "Market Insurance, Self-Insurance and Self-Protection," *Journal of Political Economy* 80 (July-August 1972), 623–648; Mark V. Pauly, "The Economics of Moral Hazard," *American Economic Review* 68 (June 1968), 531–537.

state and multinational capital, a relationship unacceptable to many citizens. How would they react when they discovered that their taxes had been paid directly to expropriated corporations? If claims outran fees and general revenues had to be tapped, the public at large would be asked, in effect, to reimburse corporations that should have known the risks, still chose to invest abroad rather than at home, and now, having suffered the consequences, wanted somebody else to pay the price.*

These issues can be summarized as:

1. Policy signaling—How will other governments perceive the insurance program? How will it change their relations with foreign investors, if at all?
2. Corporate autonomy—Will the state's exposure to potential losses as an insuror lead it to supervise corporate operations more closely? Will the program intrude on corporate independence and self-governance?
3. State legitimacy—Will the program appear to aid large corporations unfairly at the expense of the broad public?

These issues are not unique to investment guaranty insurance. Rather, they are the central and perennial issues of all investment-protection policies. Yet they are rarely confronted openly. The debates over guaranty insurance are valuable in part because they raise them with unusual clarity.

The Origins of the Guaranty Program

The guaranty program began with the troubles of Europe and fit snugly into America's plan to solve them. Conceived as one aspect of European reconstruction, guaranties were intended to

---

*These legitimacy issues are far from hypothetical. They have been raised by OPIC's opponents, especially in 1974, when potential expropriation losses loomed large and the AFL-CIO was trying hard to block the program's renewal.

The same issues surface in many other debates over foreign economic policy. One of the most dramatic recent examples was the 1983 appropriation bill for the International Monetary Fund. Left-liberal and conservative opponents joined together in an unlikely coalition, encompassing both Ralph Nader and Jesse Helms. Their common theme: the proposed $8.4 billion contribution, coming on top of a current U.S. contribution of $14.6 billion, amounted to nothing less than a "bail-out for the big banks," who had overlent to LDCs and now wanted the U.S. Treasury and the IMF to rescue them.

supplement the Marshall Plan and reinforce its aim of unifying the North Atlantic economies.

The insurance concept originated in the President's Committee for Financing Foreign Trade, a specially appointed group of major industrialists and financiers. Chaired by Winthrop Aldrich of the Chase National Bank, the committee worked closely with the Treasury Department on the full range of international economic issues. By late 1947, with foreign investments still running at a trickle, they began to consider policies to stimulate them. The idea of guaranty insurance was first mentioned in December 1947 by Edward Hopkinson, a member of the Aldrich committee and president of the Investment Bankers Association. "Private financing," said Hopkinson, "is likely to continue to be practically non-existent until confidence is established in the ability of Europe to achieve political and economic stability and to maintain a sustained trend in this direction."[3] He recommended that the government step in and provide "transfer risk guarantees . . . [to] facilitate the private financing of capital equipment and the employment of private American technical and managerial services."[4] His suggestion was immediately endorsed by fellow committee member L. M. Giannini, founder of the Bank of America.

Led by these men, the Aldrich committee swiftly agreed on a bill to insure new investments against currency inconvertibility. Their proposal was carefully framed: insurance applications were to be screened carefully and the program administered conservatively.[5] The Aldrich committee thus played a key role in initiating guaranties and limiting their scope.

The guaranty proposal, cautious though it was, raised serious and divisive questions. Would guaranties lead to greater state supervision and regulation of foreign investments? Would they signal, inadvertently or not, a new permissiveness about investment security? Would the U.S. government use the insurance to pay off injured investors instead of deterring losses? Each question involved a forecast of state behavior, and, beyond that, each touched on the proper relationship between the state and multinational firms.

Anxious corporations raised these questions throughout the public debates of the 1940s and 1950s. Opponents of guaranties, such as the National Association of Manufacturers (NAM), were apprehensive about nearly all state regulation. Pessimistic about their ability to shape public policy, they feared the misuse of guaranties.

Proponents were varied but generally more sanguine. Some, such as the Committee for Economic Development (CED) and the National Planning Association, wanted more regulation of aggregate demand and more state monitoring of the economy. Their views on guaranties derived from their larger views on state planning. Others, such as the U.S. Chamber of Commerce, made a more limited calculation. They believed guaranties were a carefully defined and useful program that posed few dangers. Yet even this limited calculation has wider implications. It suggests that proponents had greater confidence in the state's handling of economic issues. And it suggests that they favored a wider range of state economic activity. *These fundamental differences over the future of the American economy and the state's proper role in steering it underlay the early debates over guaranty insurance.*[6]

Alongside these differences were important areas of shared corporate interest. All firms valued their autonomy, their ability to make investment and production decisions without state intrusion. To protect that independence, it was universally agreed that insurance should *not* be provided against "ordinary business or commercial risks," as they were called. Moreover, all foreign investors agreed that capital exports needed political backing, and uniformly assumed that the U.S. government should provide it. The real question was whether guaranties were an appropriate *means*.

These broad areas of intercorporate agreement are significant because they defined the scope and limits of public debate. Congress and the administration framed policy issues in the same terms used by the CED and NAM. There was no quarrel about the need to remove obstacles to foreign investment or the duty to protect it. No public officials suggested that guaranties should be used to liquidate investment disputes in order to pursue other policy goals. Discussion centered on the specific costs and benefits of guaranties, not on their purpose.

These policy debates divided large multinational investors, although not along systematic lines. Specific characteristics of individual firms do not seem to predict policy preferences, and industrial groupings were internally split. There is one notable exception. Commercial and investment banks lined up as key guaranty supporters. Their policy preferences were based on their interest in stimulating new investments and their excellent overview of the continuing obstacles. Their stance was reinforced by more immediate and tangible interests. Guaranty insurance provided fine collateral for foreign loans and could only stimulate new international lending.

Among other investors, policy divisions were less clear-cut. Opposition was led by the National Foreign Trade Council (NFTC), which included most large foreign investors, and the NAM. Institutional support for the program came from a variety of sources: the CED, the Detroit Board of Trade, the American Bar Association, the U.S. Chamber of Commerce, the U.S. Council of the International Chamber, and the Aldrich committee. Although advocates sometimes differed among themselves, they all wanted a more expansive program. They wanted to ensure against the most serious political risks, expropriation and inconvertibility, and perhaps war and revolution. They wanted to broaden the program's geographic scope and hoped to cover reinvested profits as well as new investments. The NFTC and NAM opposed them at each step. Neither side could claim predominant support among major foreign investors.

The resulting legislation was quite modest, conforming to the prediction of the corporate-preferences hypothesis. Initially, only new investments in Europe were covered, and then only for currency inconvertibility. The program was expanded in small increments over the next few years. Reinvested profits were made eligible in 1949. Expropriation coverage was soon added, and the program was made worldwide, at least in principle, after the Point IV technical assistance program was begun.* Despite these additions, the program was still sharply restricted. Insurance could only be offered after investment treaties had been signed.** Most less developed countries, especially those in Latin America, objected vigorously to the treaty provisions, claiming they infringed on sovereign rights. As a result, the insurance was available in only a few areas.

There were other important limitations as well. Inconvertibility and expropriation were covered, but war and revolution were not. The insurance policies lasted only ten to twelve years, sometimes less, until the law was revised in 1953. And all applications had to meet strict standards of U.S. ownership and incorporation.[7]

These limitations, along with corporate reticence about the pro-

---

*Until OPIC was passed in 1969, the guaranty program was administered by various foreign-aid agencies. As the focus of aid shifted from Europe to less developed countries, the focus of guaranty insurance also changed. By 1959, it was limited to LDCs.

**The treaties had a simple purpose. If the U.S. government paid an insurance claim, then it received the company's title to the impounded currency or expropriated investment just as a regular insurance company would. The treaty was designed to clarify the U.S. government's legal right to hold that title and to negotiate compensation for its holdings.

gram, severely curtailed sales. The aid agency was authorized to sell only $10 million worth of insurance each year, but it never reached even that tiny goal. In summary, the early guaranty program was innovative and suggestive rather than comprehensive. Basic authorizing legislation had been passed, but an effective global program was not yet in place.

This outcome empirically affirms the predictions of the corporate-preferences hypothesis. According to its corollary, if there is substantial disunity among large multinational firms, then state policies to protect direct foreign investments will be either ambiguous, contradictory, or *modest in scope.*

This analysis also indicates that corporate preferences played a decisive role in achieving that outcome. Besides the Aldrich committee, a number of corporate representatives were actively involved. Their testimony is public record, and so, curiously enough, is some behind-the-scenes work. In 1954, the Foreign Operations Administration (FOA, the foreign aid agency at the time) submitted a revealing statement on the origin of expropriation insurance. "Its essential features," said the FOA, "reflect the best judgment and 7 months' consideration . . . by an advisory committee of men prominent in the fields of banking, insurance, law, accounting, and manufacturing (chaired by Mr. Thomas McKittrick of the Chase National Bank)."[8] Thus, expropriation coverage began like the program as a whole— with a recommendation from a business advisory panel.

Yet the McKittrick committee, like the Aldrich committee before it, did not speak for all multinational investors. Others continued to oppose the entire program. This intercorporate debate circumscribed public discussion and raised the most salient issues in the debate. As long as this intercorporate discord lasted, as long as guaranties did not have predominant corporate support, the program remained small. These causal inferences do not appear spurious, then, and the corollary hypothesis cannot be rejected.

The state-initiatives hypothesis cannot be rejected either. The Truman administration endorsed the guaranty proposals and worked with Congress to enact them. Because the program fit into the administration's larger policies, it won support from the State, Treasury, and Commerce Departments, as well as from the White House. Furthermore, it was these larger policies that determined the program's timing and its public justification. Guaranties began as part of the Marshall Plan and were expanded worldwide as part of Point IV foreign aid program. Closely tied to these major initiatives, guaranties were well insulated from potential charges of corporate venality. Instead, they crept along unnoticed, shielded from serious questions about their legitimacy.*

The Expansion of Guaranties

The first major reconsideration of the guaranty program came in 1961, when the Kennedy administration proposed substantial changes. By that time, investor opinion had shifted markedly. Opposition had receded, support solidified. Evidence of this change comes from several sources: public recommendations by major business associations, congressional testimony by business leaders, and policy advice from special government commissions.

One significant indicator appears in the annual reports of the National Foreign Trade Council. Long the most prominent opponent of guaranty insurance, the NFTC finally stopped issuing their yearly condemnations in the late 1950s.[9] At the same time, proponents began to drop their reservations. For example, the U.S. Chamber of Commerce, which once expressed concern about corporate autonomy, now focused exclusively on the program's "healthy effect on the investment climate."[10]

The same shift is evident in reports by blue-ribbon presidential commissions. Nearly a dozen such panels reviewed foreign aid and economic policy in the 1950s.[11] Dominated by major multinational executives, and invariably chaired by one, these panels are another useful indicator of corporate attitudes. Their reports show a clear trend. From cautious approval they moved to open endorsement. For instance, the Gray report, written in 1950, simply called it a "worthwhile experiment."[12] The 1952 Paley report on raw-materials policy said the guaranty program was "too new for its effectiveness to be judged."[13] Two more reports, issued in 1954, recommended the program's limited expansion. The Randall Commission wanted it continued on a trial basis, with coverage extended to risks of war,

---

*Some small predictive discrepancies can be cited, however. The Truman administration tried and failed to transfer the insurance program from the Economic Cooperation Administration to the Export-Import Bank. In addition, the law covering reinvested profits was passed over the objections of the ECA. But these errors are minor. They are hardly sufficient to reject the state-initiatives hypothesis.

revolution, and insurrection. Peter Grace incorporated those findings in his report on Latin America and urged more aggressive and stream-lined administration. His advice was endorsed by still another panel, the International Development Advisory Board.[14] Even though these reports indicate some shift in corporate preferences, deep divisions still remained. As the Randall report pointedly observed, guaranties were still the most controversial government program to stimulate private foreign investment.[15]

By the end of the decade, corporate support for guaranties had crystallized. The Eisenhower administration commissioned several more reports during its final years, and each supported the program's permanent enlargement. The Straus report, prepared in 1959, rec-ommended several modifications to "maintain the confidence of the business community."[16] It sought to double the program's issuing authority (to $1 billion) and urged new coverage for revolution and civil strife. The President's Commission on National Goals also favored "broader guarantees" but omitted detailed suggestions. A supple-mentary chapter, written by John J. McCloy, chairman of the Chase Manhattan Bank, favored the "imaginative application and expansion of guarantee programs."[17]

Even stronger evidence of changing corporate attitudes comes from the Boeschenstein Committee. In 1958, President Eisenhower asked Harold Boeschenstein, the longtime head of Owens-Corning, to "ex-plore new ways in which the Government and the private sector of our economy could effectively join together to combat the Sino-Soviet economic offensive and promote free world economic growth."[18] The committee included board chairmen from J. P. Morgan, National Cash Register, Bechtel, Standard Oil of California, and Standard Oil of New Jersey, plus top officials from General Electric and CBS. If any group could accredit guaranties among large multinational firms, this was it. They roundly endorsed the program. They wanted new guaranties to cover revolution, insurrection, and other civil disorders and in-structed the State Department to continue its efforts to secure bilateral treaties. To speed these efforts, they suggested "reducing some of the requirements and conditions currently being imposed which are found objectionable by the foreign countries."[19]

These new corporate attitudes can be traced to two developments. First, the guaranty program had a track record of conservative ad-ministration, alleviating general fears about corporate autonomy and policy signaling. Neither issue turns up among the hundreds of cor-

TABLE 13

INVESTMENT GUARANTY INSURANCE,
ISSUED AND PENDING, 1948–1963
(MILLIONS OF DOLLARS)

	Insurance Issued		Applications Pending	
	Under-developed countries	Total	Under-developed countries	Total
1948	—	2.0	—	5.4
1949	—	3.9	2.3	34.3
1950	—	19.6	12.9	49.1
1951	—	8.5	10.3	38.2
1952	2.8	5.8	17.2	53.2
1953	—	2.6	46.1	87.3
1954	—	6.1	34.0	132.0
1955	8.3	46.0	160.0	273.0
1956	7.8	29.0	327.7	510.1
1957	18.6	64.0	476.7	631.6
1958	113.3	212.0	611.0	1,040.0
1959	29.8	97.5	1,072.5	1,072.5
1960	63.6	63.8	1,440.1	1,440.1
1961	71.1	71.1	3,173.6	3,173.6
1962	440.8	440.8	3,173.2	3,173.2
1963	362.4	362.4	5,756.1	5,756.1

SOURCE: Selections from tables 4 and 5 in Marina von Neumann Whitman, *Government Risk-Sharing in Foreign Investment* © copyright 1965 by Princeton University Press. Reprinted by permission of Princeton University Press. Pp. 94–95.

porate responses to a 1958 Department of Commerce questionnaire.* Furthermore, many corporations were now interested in buying political risk insurance. Sales picked up in the mid-1950s and expanded rapidly after Egypt's nationalization of the Suez Canal. They rose to a flood tide after the massive Cuban expropriations (see table 13).

*U.S. Department of Commerce, Office of the Assistant Secretary for International Affairs, *Reportorial Review, Responses to Business Questionnaire Regarding Private Investments Abroad* (1959), 15–16. The point here is not that businessmen were less concerned with the general issues of corporate autonomy and state intervention, but rather that they were satisfied their concerns no longer applied to the guaranty program.

Congressional hearings held in 1961 show extensive corporate support for guaranties. The Kennedy administration proposed a major extension of the program and got widespread corporate approval for it. Representative Ross Adair of the House Foreign Affairs Committee observed that "a number of businessmen testified as to the value of these provisions in the law. Businessman after businessman came in and said that without this they could not have conducted the affairs of their business and expansion abroad as they would have wished."[20] Only one executive testified against the program and he, appropriately enough, had recently retired. All others backed a strong insurance program, one that covered more countries and more risks.*

The Kennedy administration had its own reasons for proposing new guaranty legislation. It saw guaranties as a convenient way to balance the foreign aid bill, which was top-heavy with public funding for Latin America. It also wanted to stimulate foreign investment in the region, fulfilling a pledge made in the Alliance for Progress charter. Because investors feared political upheaval and economic reform, new investments were running far below expectations. The administration's hope was that guaranties could offset investors' fears without affecting other aspects of the Alliance.

The administration's attitude is best shown in a 1962 memorandum on which President Kennedy commented. Writing to presidential aide Kenneth O'Donnell, Don Daughter commented:

> We must remember the "Alliance for Progress" was conceived not only as a vastly stepped up flow of public funds to Latin America during this decade of progress, but was also contingent upon an increased flow from private sources at least equal to an average level achieved in the 1950s. . . . The chilling drop in the flow of private capital this year [1962] to the entire region indicates clearly investor doubts and fears. The barrage of Castroite propaganda beamed from Cuba to all of Latin America, his intensified guerilla and subversion campaigns in rural areas, in labor unions, etc., has no doubt contributed to the heavy outflow of private capital to safe havens outside the continent. While the U.S. then has substantially increased its contributions from public funds, the flow from private sources is on a sharply declining curve.[21]

---

*Their support still had clear limits. They wanted a program that helped manage political risks, not a substitute for diplomatic protection. As such, their demands for better guaranty insurance were consistent with their demands for stronger State Department action to deter expropriation.

President Kennedy checked off the last two sentences mentioning the heavy outflow of private capital and then wrote "guarantees" directly below it.

The administration's legislative proposals came from its Task Force on Foreign Economic Assistance. After examining the increased risks to foreign investment, especially in Latin America, the task force proposed a major expansion of the guaranty program. Its main recommendations were:

1. expanded coverage to include risks of insurrection, revolution, and accompanying civil strife;
2. wider eligibility requirements, permitting coverage of foreign-chartered, but U.S.-owned corporations;
3. new provisions making bilateral treaties easier to negotiate;
4. arbitration procedures to settle investor claims;
5. experimental use of guaranties to cover all risks, including ordinary business risks, in selected, high-priority cases.[22]

Most of the proposals had been anticipated by earlier presidential commissions. They had overwhelming backing among large multinational investors. What the Kennedy administration did was erase the difference between predominant corporate preferences and existing law.

With some minor exceptions, the ideas of the task force were enacted. As in the past, the outcome hinged on compromises between the aggressive House Foreign Affairs Committee and its more reluctant Senate counterpart. But all five major recommendations were passed.[23] The result was a major expansion of the guaranty program, giving it a clear legislative mandate and covering a wide range of political risks.

This outcome is consistent with both corporate preferences and state initiatives. Focusing on state actors does provide a slightly better account of the timing. The program changed little during the Eisenhower years, when the administration remained silent, but expanded after the Kennedy task force asked for major modifications. By the same token, the policy debate was shaped and bounded by specific corporate concerns, expressed in congressional testimony and in repeated recommendations by advisory panels. In a deeper sense, however, both corporate interests and state policies converged on the basic goal of stemming net disinvestment in Latin America after the Cuban revolution. A stronger insurance program was an obvious vehicle.

In summary, both hypotheses accurately predict the expansion of guaranty insurance, leaving no empirical basis to reject either. The program's enlargement, like its inception, is theoretically overdetermined.

The Founding of OPIC

The enormous success of the 1961 law led to unforeseen problems and eventually set the stage for reorganization. Insurance sales rose sharply during the 1960s. A high point was reached in 1968, when 93 percent of eligible new investments were covered. Outstanding coverage jumped twentyfold, from $500 million in 1960 to $9.8 billion at the end of the decade. AID was overtaxed and ill-equipped. The result was a yearlong backlog of applications and growing investor complaints about bureaucratic inertia.[24] Out of these grumblings came proposals for an Overseas Private Investment Corporation.

For nearly a decade there had been speculation about reorganizing the guaranty program. That talk grew louder in the late 1960s, when New York Congressman Leonard Farbstein began examining specific proposals. Senator Jacob Javits sponsored a related amendment calling for a reappraisal of the entire aid program. He asked for special consideration of proposals for a federally chartered corporation "designed to mobilize and facilitate the use of U.S. private capital and skills in less developed friendly countries and areas.".[25]

The idea was obvious and, to many, persuasive. The corporate form had been used since 1948 to manage government programs that involved a large number of business transactions, generated substantial revenues, and were potentially profit-making. The guaranty program, it was widely agreed, met all these criteria. Moreover, there were special advantages in using the corporate form. It was exempt from Civil Service hiring requirements and had greater administrative and financial flexibility. It could also sue and be sued—a reassuring possibility to corporations purchasing substantial amounts of insurance. If they had claims and were not adequately reimbursed, they could readily appeal to the courts.

These points were noted with approval by the government commission studying possible reorganization. That group was the International Private Investment Advisory Council (IPIAC), a permanent AID advisory board consisting of six representatives from major business and banking associations. They appointed a "select working panel of business and banking experts," each one an executive from a large multinational firm. The working panel met for three months to evaluate AID's investment incentive programs. Their report was entitled *The Case for a U.S. Overseas Private Enterprise Development Corporation.*

OPIC originated with this report. The advice was detailed, and the Nixon administration adopted almost all of it. IPIAC wanted most of the new corporation's directors to come from the "private sector" and stressed the need to develop "a professional staff of experienced, business-oriented career personnel [and] a more entrepreneurial-minded management." They hoped reorganization would achieve "greater administrative and financial flexibility . . . , more business-like methods . . . , [and the] widening of present insurance and guaranty programs."[26]

Not only did the 1969 law accomplish these general goals, it authorized most of IPIAC's specific recommendations. The House Foreign Affairs Committee held hearings on the proposal and enthusiastically backed it. The Senate committee decided not to hold hearings and, on a tie vote, elected not to report the OPIC authorization. Their objections, however, were not substantive. They simply wanted to wait for the Peterson commission's advice on the entire aid program before accepting any House initiatives.[27] But Senator Javits would not be put off. In 1948, as a member of the House Foreign Affairs Committee, he had helped draft the original guaranty bill. Now, as a member of the Senate Foreign Relations Committee, he was equally committed to founding OPIC. He took the issue to the Senate floor and won handily.

What Javits won was the transfer of existing AID investment programs to a streamlined corporate organization. Although some features of the program were enlarged, these changes were less important than the reorganization itself. The core was still political-risk insurance, which hardly changed at all.[28] There was a general instruction that OPIC should pay more attention to risk management than AID had, but OPIC was left with ample discretion. That was the main point, after all. OPIC could set its own fees. It could settle insurance claims directly or, with the consent of the insured party, seek arbitration. It could insure U.S. investors in joint ventures, licensing agreements, and management contracts, as well as in wholly owned subsidiaries. It could guarantee institutional loans to U.S. companies in less developed countries and could even make its own loans. And everything it did was backed by the full faith and credit of the United States government.[29]

Most large multinational corporations supported the new law and many played a direct role in enacting it. Congressional hearings and floor debates reveal both corporate preferences and the role they played in shaping OPIC. Charles S. Dennison, vice president of International Minerals and Chemical Corporation and a member of the IPIAC working panel, candidly described the process.

> An intercommunity business group [i.e., the IPIAC working panel] was pulled together, working with IPIAC, the advisory committee to the administrator of AID, to cooperate in drafting this legislation.
> This intercommunity group represented the NAM . . . , also the U.S. Chamber of Commerce, the U.S. Council of the International Chambers . . . the CED, National Foreign Trade Council, et cetera.
> We thought it was appropriate that these groups which have separate constituencies in the United States should cooperate on a matter that involves foreign economic policy.[30]

Javits, too, called OPIC a "creation of the eminent members of [the] International Private Investment Advisory Council."[31] He added that the concept was endorsed in the Rockefeller Report on Latin America and in the Pearson commission's report to the World Bank. The Perkins commission on foreign aid, appointed during the last year of the Johnson administration, also gave OPIC some early support.[32]

The list of corporate backers is more than impressive, it is extraordinary. Javits gave the Senate a partial list:

> the U.S. Chamber of Commerce, the U.S. [sic] Association of Manufacturers, the U.S. Council of International Chambers of Commerce, the National Industrial Conference Board, the Committee for Economic Development, the Agri-Business Council, and the Council for Latin America.[33]

August Maffry, senior consultant to the Bank of America and another member of the IPIAC working panel, added major banks to that roster: "We, and I speak now for the Bank of America and I think for the banking community, strongly support the proposed Overseas Private Investment Corporation."[34] The whole issue was wrapped up by another member of the working panel: "The leading American business associations were indeed, if not fathers, at least midwives to the concept. I don't believe there is any reputable business organization that has opposed it."[35]

The corporate-preferences hypothesis clearly predicts OPIC's passage. It not only had overwhelming corporate support, it was literally the brainchild of several major business associations. Their detailed proposals won wide and effective support from major multinational firms and from legislators who had supported the AID guaranty program. Thus our causal inferences appear sound, as well as predictively accurate.

Likewise, since the legislation had administration backing, the state-initiatives hypothesis predicts its passage. Despite this predictive accuracy, the hypothesis's causal inferences appear strained. The impetus for OPIC came from multinational investors and business associations. The IPIAC report was issued even before Nixon took office. The new administration simply lent its imprimatur to that report. In fact, Nixon's position was probably less important than that of Jacob Javits. It was Javits who played the key role in mobilizing legislative support.

The state-initiatives hypothesis does draw attention to a less obvious ideological point. OPIC, like previous guaranty legislation, involves a state effort to manipulate corporate behavior. Even if the program itself is small, it reflects an administration's willingness to intervene in the economy. It is noteworthy, then, that OPIC was proposed by a *new* Republican administration, one that did not share Eisenhower's reluctance to steer the economy. Even so, the causal inference of the hypothesis appears weak in this case.

The Tribulations of OPIC

If OPIC's birth was easy, its early years were not. Two years were needed to set up the new organization, which first had to establish risk-management procedures and then take responsibility for all previously issued insurance coverage. When it finally opened for business, it faced an immediate crisis: massive expropriations in

Chile. Most U.S. copper companies there had purchased expropriation insurance from AID in the mid-1960s. They now stood to collect
over $360 million—money that OPIC did not have.* With this fi-
nancial crisis as a backdrop, and with time running out on its initial
five-year authorization, OPIC returned to Congress in 1974 to renew
its mandate.

It faced a tough congressional battle and only barely survived.
OPIC's opponents, led by Senator Frank Church, wanted to transfer
the program gradually to private insurance companies. They proposed
mandatory deadlines to phase out the government's role. By January
1978, for instance, private insurance companies would have to underwrite at least half the new policies for expropriation and inconvertibility. Had OPIC failed to meet the projected targets, it would
have been terminated automatically. OPIC's supporters considered
the plan unworkable—a death warrant in disguise—and, under Javits's leadership, they fought hard to stop it.

The debate centered on two issues: OPIC's solvency and its now-
uncertain connection to other foreign policy goals. OPIC's main financial problem, aside from the Chilean claims, was its unbalanced
and risky portfolio. In fact, OPIC's portfolio may have been a little
less risky than AID's, at least in the short run, but it was even more
concentrated geographically. Fully 80 percent of OPIC insurance went
to just eight countries; half of that was concentrated in Brazil, Indonesia, and Korea. Not only was the portfolio undiversified but some
individual cases were also quite worrisome. In Jamaica, for instance,
AID and OPIC had together issued over $525 million in expropriation
insurance to five aluminum companies. Counting coverage for war
and other risks, OPIC's outstanding insurance in Jamaica amounted

---

*According to a GAO audit, claims against OPIC totaled $369.5 million as of April
10, 1973. OPIC took many of these claims to arbitration. It eventually lost most of
them, but not until its charter had been renewed.

Even with these losses, OPIC managed to protect its operating balances through a
variety of credit arrangements. Its main tactic was to negotiate compensation agreements with the Chilean junta. The junta agreed to pay most expropriated investors
and issued long-term bonds to do so. OPIC then guaranteed payment of those bonds.
The insured corporation was given the guaranteed bonds, which could be discounted
for cash, plus a cash payment from OPIC. This arrangement saved OPIC's current
reserves, but left it with long-term liabilities owed by foreign governments.

As of April 1977, OPIC had paid or guaranteed more than $246 million to investors
in over sixty claims. Some $96 million was paid in cash; the rest was in guaranteed
bonds. As disputes were settled and bonds repaid, about one-third of that money was
recovered. But, as of April 1977, OPIC was still liable for $111 million in foreign
government bonds. Its reserves amounted to $210 million. See OPIC, *Topics* 6 (March-
April 1977), 1–2.

to over $1.1 billion. The financial risks were substantial and the U.S. government was fully liable.[36]

In addition to these financial problems, OPIC faced serious questions about its basic purpose. Until 1974, the program had a straightforward mandate: it was supposed to encourage new foreign investment in less developed countries while remaining self-sufficient. It was effectively shielded from any larger discussion of foreign policy goals. The 1974 hearings revealed considerable dissatisfaction with that insularity. The AFL-CIO, in particular, was worried that guaranty insurance might encourage companies to transfer production abroad. Some congressmen were also concerned about its effect on foreign economic development. They wanted guaranties to encourage investments in extremely poor nations, not just Brazil and Korea.

OPIC's basic response was conciliatory. It promised to stimulate economic development, assist small businesses, and protect the U.S. balance of payments. Most significantly, it agreed to preserve American jobs whenever possible and to monitor its effects on domestic employment. These latter concessions had an important impact: they removed organized labor from the larger debate over OPIC's future.[37]

OPIC also made several administrative changes to dampen criticism and broaden its political appeal. Even before the 1974 law, it rejected applications from runaway plants. It brought private insurance companies into the program and raised premiums slightly. All in all, OPIC made a stronger effort to manage its insurance risks and show higher operating profits.

These changes paved the way for OPIC's renewal—but at a price. They subtly twisted OPIC's objectives, away from the primary goal of stimulating new investment.[38]

OPIC's renewal is accurately predicted by both the state-initiatives and corporate-preferences hypotheses. Yet in both cases the causal inferences are questionable. Although the Nixon administration certainly favored OPIC's continuation, the president was fully absorbed in his own losing fight for survival. On OPIC's renewal, as on so many other issues, the embattled White House provided no leadership. The rest of the executive branch was preoccupied with maintaining the ordinary processes of government. In the end, Javits led the fight for OPIC with little help from the administration.

Similarly, the preferences of multinational investors were unmistakable, but their import is uncertain. Several major business associations endorsed OPIC, and a number of firms testified in its favor.

In addition, two polls of foreign investors showed strong, broad support for the program. A 1971 survey by Business International, a private consulting firm, covered nearly 400 firms, mostly in the *Fortune* 500. Some 45.8 percent called the program "necessary," and another 47.6 percent called it "desirable." These results vary little by industry or by region.[39] The Council of the Americas, which represents virtually all U.S. companies in Latin America, got similar results from a 1974 membership survey.[40] These surveys, together with public testimony, reveal overwhelming corporate support for OPIC, a fact repeatedly cited by legislative proponents. Likewise, interviews with OPIC's opponents indicate that their position was undermined by the absence of corporate backing. But, in general, multinational companies played only an indirect role. They underlined the program's success in promoting foreign investment and argued convincingly that private insurance companies could not replace OPIC. In effect, they ratified OPIC as a productive state activity, one that still could not be performed privately. But despite this support for OPIC, multinational firms were much less active than they had been in 1969. It is difficult then to link corporate preferences to the policy process.

The corporate-preferences hypothesis is limited in another way. Even though it correctly predicts OPIC's renewal, it overlooks the new legislative and administrative restrictions placed on the agency. Although they were not severe, they did slow the process of issuing insurance and limited its availability. As a result, they made OPIC less valuable to investors.

In spite of these changes, OPIC survived with its fundamental purpose intact. The corporate-preferences hypothesis predicts that outcome, even though it fails to predict the new restraints on OPIC.

Reconsidering the Hypotheses

My method thus far has been to specify discrete turning points in the guaranty program, ascertain the preferences of key actors at each point, and then compare policy outcomes with those preferences. Using this method, one finds that corporate preferences and state initiatives yield strikingly similar predictions. The four stages of the guaranty program do not pose a crucial test because corporate preferences do not differ markedly from administration proposals.

Both yield generally accurate predictions, and neither hypothesis can be rejected on that basis. The result is theoretical overdetermination.

Yet my analysis should not stop with these static predictions. We also need to reexamine the causal inferences in historical perspective, linking discrete policy preferences to the evolving concerns of each actor. Seen in this light, the two hypotheses offer different projections of the program's longer-term growth and development.

Any focus on independent state initiatives must begin with the idea that guaranty insurance is a subordinate element of foreign policy and is valuable (or not) in relation to larger policy goals.* We have already noted that guaranty insurance promotes several important objectives. It assists U.S. foreign investors, encourages economic growth, solidifies an open world economy, and complements the aid program. Because it contributes to these overall objectives, the guaranty program has won broad support within the executive branch.

Moreover, several major foreign policy bureaucracies have found their own specialized reasons to favor the program. The Treasury and Commerce Departments, for instance, support guaranties because they encourage foreign investment without the direct outlay of tax dollars. The State Department is more concerned about its diplomatic mission. They recognize that guaranty insurance could be used to diffuse investment disputes. By settling an insurance claim, the United States could simply sidestep an investment conflict. The insurance program also helps to limit conflicts to compensation issues. The circumscribed dispute is more likely to be resolved and less likely to affect other aspects of bilateral diplomacy. Thus, from the State Department's perspective, the guaranty program not only advances broader policy goals, it contributes to the policy process as well.

The state-initiatives hypothesis suggests several plausible reasons why the guaranty program might have grown. One is that the state has supported it all along, providing an insurance program that could grow as corporate demand for its services grew. Demand, in turn, grew because investing in Latin America in the 1960s was simply riskier than investing in Europe in the 1940s. The state, in this view,

---

*Because of bureaucratic in-fighting and multiple decision channels, the assumption of rational policy hierarchies does not hold in some policy areas. However, it *does* hold for guaranty insurance, which has had consistent and undivided support within the executive branch. Hence, more complicated forms of bureaucratic analysis can be discarded in this case in favor of the parsimonious state-initiatives hypothesis.

is consistent but largely passive. An alternative explanation is that the state actively fostered the program because it promoted central foreign policy goals and helped ensure state autonomy. Certainly every major expansion of the program had clear, strong support from the White House and State Department, and frequently from the Treasury and Commerce Departments as well.* A final explanation stresses the political principles of specific administrations. This approach underscores the program's slow growth under Eisenhower, who sought to limit the state's economic role, and its more rapid growth under Kennedy and Nixon.

The core of the state-initiatives hypothesis is its emphasis on public actors seeking to promote central foreign policy goals. In one sense, that accounts well for what happened. Guaranties do reinforce larger state objectives and contribute to their implementation, particularly in expropriation cases. There is little evidence to sustain the Church committee's charge that OPIC pulls the United States into additional disputes. Instead, it seems to limit the scope and character of that intervention, focusing discussion on manageable financial issues. So far, *no* OPIC negotiations have escalated into full-scale diplomatic controversies.

At a deeper level, however, a focus on state initiatives cannot account for the program's long-term evolution. None of the rationales for state action can predict the program's sequence of growth, and none makes it comprehensible.

If, for example, the guaranty program were simply instrumental to broader foreign policy purposes, then it should have grown rapidly during the 1950s and early 1960s, the most expansive period of American foreign policy. Yet guaranties remained small until the very end of this period. The program operated under tight legal restraints, such as the requirement for investment treaties, which sharply curtailed sales. Nor did the program's administrators do much to overcome these obstacles (a point noted by the Grace report in 1954). Thus, the sluggish demand for guaranty insurance was partly a function of its indifferent supply. But why was the supply so indifferent and the program so modest? The answer cannot lie in larger policy commitments, for this was precisely the moment when the United

---

*Here, as elsewhere in this chapter, I am limiting the discussion to the four selected cases. The Carter administration was equivocal about OPIC's renewal in 1978. Reagan strongly backed the program's expansion in 1981.

States had assumed global responsibilities to contain communism and to promote liberal trade and investment.

In contrast, state policies toward guaranty insurance might have been shaped by a much more limited goal: the desire to insulate bilateral diplomacy from investment conflicts. By this view, the program's appeal to foreign policy officials was not its capacity to promote new investments but its usefulness in settling old quarrels.

This approach also fails. It cannot account for the program's beginnings and its first two decades. Although the early program was small, it was clearly initiated to foster new investments, not to resolve outstanding conflicts. When it became a worldwide program in the 1950s, expropriation and other investment risks were considered telling signs of the host country's political allegiance. Under the circumstances, no one was interested in settling investment disputes discreetly so that friendly political relations might continue. Certainly no public official ever suggested it as a reason to support the program. These concerns may have played a larger role during the past decade—it is difficult to tell—but it should also be noted that the program has not actually been used that way.

A third approach (under the state-initiatives rubric) attributes changes in the program not to fundamental national policies or to particular bureaucratic interests but to the policy goals of specific administrations. The legislative mandate of the program hardly changed at all under Eisenhower but grew significantly under both Kennedy and Nixon, who were more willing to intervene in the economy. But what about Truman, who conceived so many expansive policies but who kept the guaranty program small? Moreover, the Johnson administration was at least as willing as Nixon's to steer the economy and foster corporate activity abroad. Yet Johnson left the program untouched while Nixon undertook its last major expansion.* The program's changes do not neatly conform to presidential changes.

Each interpretation of the state-initiatives hypothesis fails to predict the program's uneven pattern of growth. Expansive national policies, presidential principles, the aspiration to free diplomacy from invest-

---

*The focus on presidential principles fairs better under the last two presidents. Carter pushed human rights onto the program's agenda and focused OPIC's attention on poorer countries. Reagan stripped OPIC of many such encumbrances and refocused its attention on investment promotion.

ment conflicts—each may have been important at various stages, but none can predict the overall pattern or make it comprehensible.*

These predictive discrepancies point to serious limitations in the state-initiatives approach. They do not, however, warrant its complete rejection. Not only did the executive branch play an active role in shaping guaranty policy, its initiatives had some independent logic— a logic of larger policy goals and bureaucratic missions. The executive branch offered consistent support for guaranties and played an important role in organizing support on Capitol Hill. By appointing blue-ribbon study commissions, the president may even have catalyzed corporate opinion on the program. In addition, the various administrations played a crucial role in determining statutory details and legislative timing.

This analysis suggests that the executive's position was founded on shifting concerns. From Truman to Nixon, each administration found its own rationale for the program. Likewise, the State Department's stake in guaranties has evolved. Its support was initially tied to larger policies: the Marshall Plan, Point IV, and the Alliance for Progress. More recently it has favored the program because it provides additional flexibility in expropriation disputes. *These shifting sources of support cannot predict the program's long-term growth, but they do provide an appropriate context for understanding executive branch positions.*

The corporate-preferences hypothesis offers a substantially different (but complementary) account, one that is both simple and predictively accurate. According to the corporate-preferences hypothesis, OPIC's survival is causally dependent on continued corporate support.

The program's legislative history repeatedly affirms the central role of corporate preferences. In at least three of the four cases we have examined, multinational firms played a direct, active, and crucial part. The program originated in the President's Committee for Financing Foreign Trade, with strong backing from the CED, American Bar

---

*It is possible, of course, to combine the various interpretations of state initiatives. Introducing such complexity enriches our study of executive policymaking but adds little predictive rigor. In the late 1940s, for instance, one would *still* wrongly predict a substantial guaranty program (based on an expansive foreign policy and Truman's willingness to intervene in the economy). By focusing exclusively on intragovernmental factors, one would *not* predict Nixon's inheritance of a much larger program or the program's expansion in 1969. True, there was increasing concern about state autonomy in investment disputes, but that was offset by Nixon's less expansive foreign economic policy.

Association, and others. Its expansion in 1961 was recommended by several more official commissions, once again dominated by representatives from major multinational firms. Eight years later another advisory panel (IPIAC) suggested a federally chartered corporation. That proposal was endorsed by most other investors and enacted in 1969. Renewed in 1974, it still stands as OPIC's basic mandate.

As this survey indicates, corporate attitudes changed dramatically during the 1950s. The original debates centered on two questions:

Would guaranty insurance encourage expropriations?

Would it jeopardize the independence of foreign investors?

These questions were never resolved in principle but were resolved in practice by the program's cautious administration. When it became clear that guaranties neither invited expropriation nor corrupted the autonomy of foreign investors, the program won solid corporate support.

Although this analysis leads to largely accurate predictions, some problems remain. The hypothesis cannot predict the details of guaranty policy, and it provides only a rough estimate of legislative timing. Yet the greatest weakness of the hypothesis is its inadequate account of OPIC's recent difficulties. It came perilously close to sinking in 1974 and 1978 and survived only with modifications. Except for predicting the program's renewal, the corporate-preferences hypothesis has little to say about these events.

This predictive weakness is analytically useful, since it suggests the limitations and implicit assumptions of the hypothesis. Until 1974, the guaranty program operated beyond public scrutiny, snug in its isolation. The corporate-preferences hypothesis is based on that premise. Its simple causal inference, from corporate preferences to guaranty policy, is predictively accurate because the program's legitimacy was not seriously challenged.

Faced with such challenges, the program's goals have shifted in subtle ways. The task of private capital accumulation is still preeminent, but no longer exclusive. It is unclear, therefore, whether corporate preferences alone can control OPIC's future. That future depends, at least in part, on the salience of other issues: public concern about corporate improprieties, the perceived conflict between OPIC and other policy goals, and the perception that foreign economic policy is biased in favor of large corporations.

Even if the corporate-preferences hypothesis does not deal adequately with these conceptual problems, it does offer a parsimonious, predictively rich, and distinctive approach. Its distinctiveness may not be immediately obvious, since it clearly shares some epistemological concerns with pluralist analysis. Each seeks the origins of public policy in the articulated preferences of private actors. Yet the differences are striking.

First, the corporate-preferences hypothesis assumes a durable hierarchy of power in this issue area, and then tests that assumption. Pluralists, from their earliest studies of community power, have resisted all notions of hierarchy and permanency. They assume transient coalitions, assembling around specific issues and then dissolving, without any a priori rankings or enduring power. They emphasize, in Polsby's words, the "time-bounded nature of coalitions" and search for a variety of actors playing temporary leadership roles.

Second, pluralist analysis begins with various actors' preferences, without inquiring into their structural basis or historical continuity. They are interested in the momentary interaction of conflict groups formed around specific issues. My analysis examines structured patterns of preference. It focuses on the origins of (corporate) preferences and their evolution in response to changing circumstances. Specific policy preferences are understood in terms of far-reaching problems faced by foreign investors. Thus, preferences are consistently linked to political and economic interests, even if those underlying interests are sometimes ambiguous or contradictory.

Third, pluralist analysis is essentially cross-sectional. It is designed to explain specific decisions, taken at discrete points. Although such analysis typically follows an issue through several stages, its chief concern is to discover points of public involvement in official decision making. It does not ask, as this analysis does, whether preferences occur in lasting clusters or whether outcomes follow historical patterns. In sum, pluralist analysis lacks a historical dimension.

My own research concentrates on the historical interaction between multinational corporations and the state. Like pluralists, I use articulated preferences to examine policy processes and predict outcomes. But my concern with those preferences, and my analysis of them, is different. I focus on long-term shifts in corporate preferences, their structural origins, and their relationship to larger political dilemmas of capital accumulation.

These concerns are reflected in the issues studied and the hypotheses tested. Guaranty insurance provides an extraordinary record of intercorporate debate and changing policy preferences. My findings must, of course, be treated carefully. It is impossible to generalize them to issues where large firms are less involved or where their preferences are more diverse. Nevertheless, guaranty insurance raises several questions of wider significance. Why, for example, were so many foreign investors reluctant to accept certain kinds of state aid in the late 1940s? Why have corporate attitudes changed? How are policy demands related to specific problems confronting investors? The debates over guaranty insurance provide a closed, manageable universe of data on such questions. The same debates raise fundamental questions about corporate autonomy, policy signaling, state autonomy, and legitimacy.

Until now, I have examined these questions by distinguishing sharply between the state and multinational corporations. The corporate-preferences hypothesis, for instance, formally ignores the position of the White House and various foreign policy bureaucracies. It assumes their actions are dependent on the autonomous stance of multinational firms. The predictive accuracy of this hypothesis, and the shortcomings of the state-initiatives hypothesis, suggest that the state's role was largely derivative and dependent. In fact, no autonomous conception of state initiatives (and we have examined several) can predict the program's long-term growth.

This interpretation of the state's role follows our simplified hypothesis and is necessarily incomplete. First of all, state initiatives sometimes diverged from corporate preferences. In the 1940s large multinational corporations were divided over guaranties; the Truman administration sided with one faction. In the late 1950s, the administration did nothing although most investors favored the program's expansion. Perhaps more important, the state frequently helped catalyze corporate opinion. Corporate preferences about guaranties were developed in the context of larger national policies—the Marshall Plan, Point IV, the Alliance. Moreover, corporate attitudes were often articulated through specially created state forums: presidential commissions and advisory councils. Some state actors (AID, OPIC, the House Foreign Affairs Committee, Senator Javits) also played entrepreneurial roles, rounding up corporate support for guaranties and introducing it into the legislative arena. The state's role, then, was not wholly dependent. It intervened to set the larger policy agenda, coordinate corporate support, time new legislation, and ensure its legitimacy. Thus, even in the narrow issue of investment guaranties, the relationship between multinational corporations and the state appears complex.

Yet complexity should not be confused with symmetrical influence. While the state played *both* a dependent and intervening role, its initiatives were continually shaped by corporate preferences. Those preferences were ultimately dominant because of the structural relationship between multinational firms and foreign economic policy. That relationship hinges on numerous private decisions to trade and invest. The success of much foreign economic policy—the success of much foreign policy in general—depends on those private decisions. New capital flows, for instance, were vital to the Alliance for Progress, both as an end in themselves and as a way to buttress reform governments in Latin America. When private investment slowed to a trickle, both goals were imperiled. Similarly, the absence of foreign investment in postwar Europe was a serious obstacle to capitalist reconstruction and trans-Atlantic economic integration. The question, in both cases, was how to restore capital flows. Investors and policymakers recognized that the fundamental, long-term answer lay in the restoration of a stable political and economic environment. But, in the short term, policymakers wanted to stimulate foreign investments precisely to help achieve that environment. To do so, they had to depend on certain policy instruments, such as guaranties, that directly affected investment decisions.

Why, then, did Truman and Kennedy propose such different guaranty programs? Once again, the answer lies in the connections between economic structure, policy goals, and corporate preferences. Guaranties, like other economic policies, are constrained by the very structure they seek to rationalize and direct. Because guaranties directly affect investment decision making, they directly threaten corporate autonomy. Such intrusions can dampen business confidence and actually discourage the behavior they seek to stimulate.[41] Early debates over guaranties focus on exactly this issue. Investors examined the young program in light of long-standing fears about corporate autonomy, as well as their specific problems. Although their conclusions differed, they shared a common concern about the program's potential for abuse. Under these circumstances, any proposal for a large-scale guaranty program would have been self-defeating. It would surely have reinforced investor fears and failed to stimulate new investments. Truman's modest proposals did not challenge these constraints. The Kennedy administration faced quite different corporate preferences and proposed a much larger program to stimulate investments in a volatile region.

Both the Truman and Kennedy proposals underline the policy significance of private investment decisions. *It is those critical, decentralized choices and the ensuing constraints on state action that give corporate preferences their extraordinary weight in guaranty policy. Those preferences are crucial because they seem to forecast investment behavior, the main subject of guaranties and of all investment-protection policy.*

The goal of that policy, challenged but still preeminent, is private capital accumulation. That basic goal, shared by private investors and the state, helps explain the most striking feature of guaranty policy: the basic identity between corporate preferences, state initiatives, and policy outcomes.

CHAPTER EIGHT

Conclusion: Rule Making and Policymaking

Over the past decade both international property rules and U.S. investment protection policies have changed dramatically. Expropriations were rare as recently as the mid-1960s, and reasonable compensation was expected. J. Paul Getty's observation still applied: the meek shall inherit the earth—but not the mineral rights. Now this same regime is fragmented, and the strictures against expropriation much weaker. Direct investments, in their many forms, are now subject to equally varied national treatment.

Two other changes have accompanied this transformation. Multinational corporations, aware of the changing property rules, have modified their investment strategies. Whenever possible, they have shifted from vulnerable, wholly owned facilities to more secure joint ventures, licensing agreements, and management contracts. Whatever measures have been chosen, their aim has been to assure the firms' continued profitability by avoiding excessive reliance on risky direct investments. At the same time, the U.S. government has modified its own policies—from resistant and sometimes punitive responses to adaptive ones. Gone are the overt sanctions and highly charged language of the Hickenlooper amendment. In their place stand quiet policies of government risk-sharing such as guaranty insurance.

The last two chapters indicate a causal link between these moderate investment protection policies and the adaptive strategies of

258

multinational corporations. The basic hypothesis, which predicted well and was not rejected, attributes these policy changes to altered policy preferences among large multinational investors. Clearly their policy preferences, which stress corporate self-reliance and low-key diplomacy, conform to their new investment strategies.

The origin of these investment strategies can be found in the metamorphosis of international property rules. As the regime changed, so did corporate behavior. And, as corporations modified their investment strategies and sought to make their presence abroad less visible and less salient politically, they naturally sought U.S. public policies that did not undercut their efforts. Thus, multinational corporations helped translate changes in the international regime into adaptive American policies. In turn, the accommodative policies of both multinational firms and the U.S. government ratified and reinforced the transformation of property rules.

To conclude this study of investment protection, I will explore these and other complex links between foreign policy and international rules. It is useful to begin by reviewing long-term changes in the foreign investment regime.

A Synopsis

Throughout Part I, my special concern was with international property rules—their normative properties and their implications for investment security. These are central, but sometimes divergent, elements of a more general concept: the international regime governing the treatment of foreign capital. My findings regarding historical regime changes are summarized in figure 2 (pages 142–143). Two patterns emerge.

While the norms dealing with foreign investment have never commanded universal agreement, one can still detect a gradual but significant shift in the terms of debate. Before World War I, expropriations were almost never considered acceptable and were, in fact, quite unusual. Large-scale nationalizations were unknown. Eminent domain, although not ruled out entirely, was narrowly construed in legal theory and in practice. Such acts were considered rarities, to be undertaken only for exceptional public purposes. When they did occur, compensation was supposed to be swift and complete (a point, like the limitations on eminent domain, that was not disputed). Contested cases were to be arbitrated before international tribunals, which in turn applied exacting guidelines.*

These values, and the strict enforcement that accompanied them, defined a remarkably open system of investment in underdeveloped, noncolonial regions. They assumed, with ample warrant in Latin America, that all property rights, foreign and domestic, would be safeguarded by local governments. In parts of Africa, Asia, and the Middle East, which lacked indigenous systems of modern property rights, the Europeans (and particularly the British), established these rights alongside the extension of foreign capital. Local standards of possession, exchange, and dispute resolution were either overturned or confined to native sectors. In either case, this thoroughgoing transformation of law and economy undermined the sinews of local authority and so accelerated the spread of colonialism.

Throughout this period, the state's limited intervention in the economy was simply assumed. This metalegal assumption began to crumble during the interwar period. The most important and dramatic event was the Russian Revolution, which challenged the basic relationship between the state and private property. But one can cite other important assaults on Europe-centered international property norms: the Mexican Constitution of 1917, the growing idea of state-administered agrarian reform, Turkey's active policies of state-led industrialization, and the League of Nations' conferences on investors' rights, which, unlike the prewar meetings, ended in stalemate.

The trend begun in those League conferences—away from investors' rights and toward investor responsibilities and sovereign rights—has accelerated since World War II. Today, the whole idea of international minimum standards is in dispute and in decline. The challenge has been building for decades in international forums, especially those (such as the United Nations General Assembly and UNCTAD) with broad memberships and equal voting rules. As a complement to sovereign rights, less developed states have advanced the idea of "national treatment" for foreign capital. In case of expropriation, that means compensation should be determined by local courts using local standards.** International law still plays a residual role, encouraging

---

*The right to international jurisdiction over investment disputes was, of course, contested—at least as a legal principle. That was the main point of the Calvo Doctrine.

**Advanced states do not entirely reject the concept of national treatment. But they do *not* consider it an acceptable alternative to international legal obligations, as they

due process and mutually approved compensation. But the trend has been one of slow, steady weakening of older international legal norms.

The pattern of investment security, and investors' expectations about the treatment they would receive, has followed a different course. Property rules were reconsolidated after World War II under American leadership in spite of growing challenges to their justification. These postwar arrangements were, in some ways, reminiscent of the strong nineteenth-century regime led by the British, just as the recent erosion of the American-led regime is reminiscent of the interwar period. But, in spite of the similarities, the pattern is not truly cyclical. First, modern injunctions against expropriation, even at their most effective, differed in content from those in the nineteenth century.[1] The postwar rules acknowledge, however grudgingly, the irreversible growth of state involvement in the economy, including direct control over productive capacity. Even in the 1950s, America recognized the rights of host governments to take control of their infrastructure, subject of course to fair compensation.[2] Eminent domain had a much more restricted meaning in the nineteenth century. *The overall pattern, then, combines some cyclical variation in regime strength with a long-term shift in the rules' substance and, more recently, a marked decline in their effectiveness.*

In the most recent period, there has also been a notable difference in the security of portfolio and direct investments. The regime, in other words, has been bifurcated. While expropriations have increased, debt renunciations have remained extremely rare. Arrearages and reschedulings are common enough, often involving billions of dollars, but they arise from genuine economic difficulties in the debtor country and not from purposive state action to seize foreign capital. Similarly, the defaults of the 1930s cannot be likened to expropriation. Their roots lay in the collapse of export markets and in the resulting scarcity of hard currencies needed to pay off debts. They indicate some weakening of the regime, perhaps, but no great differences from direct investments, which were relatively secure.

---

understand them. The OECD's voluntary code says that member states should treat MNCs in ways "consistent with international law and no less favorable than those accorded in like situations to domestic enterprises." Their confidence in national treatment is bolstered, no doubt, by their confidence in the fairness and independence of one another's judicial procedures. OECD, *International Investment and Multinational Enterprises* (Paris: OECD, 1982), 18; OECD, *National Treatment for Foreign-Controlled Enterprises Established in OECD Countries* (Paris: OECD, 1978); John Robinson, *Multinationals and Political Control* (New York: St. Martin's, 1983).

My model of these changes includes both the *impetus* for diverse national treatment of foreign capital and the *restraints* on such treatment. The impetus is the historically expanding role of the state in directing less developed economies. As the scope for public policy has grown, so have the requisite administrative capabilities. As a result, many states can now undertake extensive surveillance of local markets and regulate foreign actors within them. Unless restricted by internalized standards or international restraints, this growth of state capabilities translates into potentially diverse national treatment of foreign investment, including expropriation. Under these conditions, the specific treatment accorded investors hinges on the host state's domestic politics and on the bargaining resources of the actors involved.

As an integral part of this state-building project, less developed countries have vigorously asserted their rhetorical claim to exclusive jurisdiction over foreign enterprises. They have rejected (with increasing success) the counterclaim that international minimum standards apply. "National treatment" is thus ascendant as an *international* norm.

As for international restraints, I posit three basic sources:

1. the capacity to employ local interventionary force;
2. the capacity to invoke coherent, severe economic sanctions; and
3. the capacity to manipulate relevant international organizations.

I further assume that each capacity is greatest when pertinent resources are most highly centralized.* Concentrated international resources are thus a network of potential sanctioning power—a deterrent that constrains and guides host-state policy.

The predictions derived from this model generally conform to empirical observations of investment security. In the nineteenth century,

---

*This is really a rough-and-ready proxy for the ability to act collectively. Coordination and collective action may also be possible in large groups under special circumstances. Russell Hardin has shown that conventions and tacit contracts can encompass large groups if they are built up from the overlapping interactions of smaller groups. These smaller groups are critical because they foster the communication required for conventional behavior and because they permit low-cost sanctions (such as exclusion) to be imposed on those who do not cooperate. Indeed, we made exactly this point in discussing coordination among large numbers of international banks (pp. 158, 174–175). Hardin, *Collective Action* (Baltimore: Johns Hopkins Press for Resources for the Future, 1982), chaps. 3 and 11.

for instance, international restraints were concentrated and host states' administrative structures rudimentary. My inference is that the regime should be strong and foreign investments secure, and that was largely the case. Similar predictions can be made for subsequent periods. Chapter 5, on the sources of international property rules, makes such predictions and assesses them in detail. That evaluation suggests that the model is a useful simplification. On the whole, it accurately represents the changing pattern of investment security.

There are, of course, discrepancies. Perhaps the most interesting is the tendency to skim over the shift in property norms. That shift, as I have shown, is largely the result of two closely related factors: a widespread (and quite varied) economic nationalism among less developed countries and the increased role of broad-based international institutions in legitimating new standards.

My evaluation of the model also suggests that economic sanctions and interventionary force have changed a great deal over the years. When Britain was the principal underwriter of international property rules, interventionary force meant naval force. Later, it came to mean the capacity for either overt or covert intervention. Economic sanctions have evolved similarly. As long as Britain was reluctant to regulate foreign commerce (and as long as most long-term investments were loans), economic sanctions were the business of private bondholders. Organized through the Stock Exchange Committee and the Corporation of Foreign Bondholders, they could deny new credit to states in default. By threatening to block such credits until all arrears were settled, they stood guard over existing assets abroad. Their strength lay in London's near monopoly over certain foreign loans, especially those to Latin America, and in their own organizational ties. Now, of course, the state plays a much larger role, and the coherence of economic sanctions is a much more complex affair. It involves the relative severity of public and private sanctions and the coordination between them.

The power of private sanctions, for instance, depends on the likelihood of unified action. Because such action could cut off the flow of foreign capital, it is a potentially powerful weapon. The sources of that unity, and its likelihood, differ for portfolio and direct investments. Modern bank lenders, for example, are as well organized as Victorian bondholders, and far better coordinated than modern multinational enterprises. Unlike most direct investors, the banks are deeply bound together through their ordinary operations and are mutually vulnerable to beggar-thy-neighbor action. Despite sharp competition in offshore capital markets, the banks have no incentives to cut each other's throats in dealing with troubled debtors. Because lending syndicates are highly structured, with a few designated banks acting as managers, they can typically act on that coincident interest. They can refinance shaky debts, generally in cooperation with the IMF, which supervises the package. As a result of the banks' interdependence and their capacity to act jointly, they hold the powerful deterrent threat of cutting off future access to international capital markets and trade financing.[3]

Multinational corporations are not nearly so well placed. Their unity hinges on the symbolic meaning of expropriation and the oligopoly structure of the affected industry. Does an expropriation scare away other investors? Do a few firms so dominate an industry that they can effectively boycott an expropriating country? The answers depend partly on the special characteristics of each expropriation: the industry involved, the host country, and the political circumstances surrounding the expropriation.

There are, however, some significant trends. The symbolic meaning of expropriation has shifted over the past few years as the phenomenon has spread from leftist governments to those of almost every stripe. Corporations may still consider it immoral and illegal, but their moralism is tempered now that expropriation is less closely associated with anticapitalist upheaval. Few countries wish to break their ties to foreign firms after nationalizations, and now they do not have to. The firms themselves are unwilling to break off relations individually and have no collective means to do so.

These changes do not mean that individual companies are helpless to combat expropriation or to lessen the risks they face. They can employ a variety of self-reliant, defensive strategies based on a combination of global risk assessment and corporate strategic planning.[4] Most firms have assumed a low profile abroad and have paid careful attention to risk premiums when calculating their prospective returns on investment. They tend, naturally, to avoid projects with heavy initial investments or slow repayment schedules.*

---

*The most vulnerable investments are those that are highly visible, highly profitable, involve large fixed costs, and can be operated successfully by local citizens. Frequently, such investments are associated with a notorious history of foreign exploitation, such as the big Chilean copper mines or Exxon's La Brea y Pariñas oil fields in Peru. The least vulnerable investments are those that depend on the corporation's unique expertise, its ongoing activities, and its outside connections. Diversified corporations,

Many firms try to minimize direct investments as a general policy, or find that host states require them to do so. One approach is to subcontract production with local entrepreneurs (a common technique in East Asia) or to license proprietary products or processes. Alternatively, a multinational firm may contract to build ready-to-operate plants and then stay on (with a management and service contract) to run them while training local managers to take over.

Some firms that do invest directly also plan from the very beginning to phase out their stake. The riskiest projects (particularly those in raw materials) are the best candidates for such self-liquidation, which became popular during the Allende period.[5]

A much more common way to lessen the firm's exposure is to rely on local sources of financing. Both local borrowing and equity participation have the additional advantage of creating potential political allies, capable of deflecting the host state's demands on the firm.[6]

Political risk insurance, such as that sold by OPIC or West Germany's Hermes, can supplement all these techniques. So can currency-swap arrangements that insure against inconvertibility. For a fee, the multinational firm can contract with the LDC central bank to guarantee its foreign currency investment will be convertible later at some fixed rate. The MNC then lends its subsidiary funds that are covered by the swap agreement.* This arrangement is further protected if a commercial bank serves as an intermediary.[7]

Besides these financial techniques, an adroit firm can formulate its long-term strategy and arrange its global organization to minimize risk. Not only is its production likely to be scattered widely, rather than concentrated in a few countries, but also few of the subsidiaries may be able to stand alone. They will be situated, instead, in a tightly integrated worldwide network of production, distribution, and marketing. Each subsidiary then depends upon others to provide its crucial production materials, subsequent processing, or final sales. The archetypal example is research and development, which is usually

---

such as ITT, have found it prudent to shift their investments from vulnerable sectors (such as telephone systems) to safer ones (such as tourist hotels, which earn foreign exchange, depend on international marketing, and may be locally owned but operated under management contract by ITT-Sheraton). W. R. Grace, which owned agricultural properties in Latin America, has done an even more impressive job of diversifying out of vulnerable sectors and risky locales.

*There is a subtle but deadly trap in using this technique. The insured firm must be certain that the central bank has not signed more currency guaranties than it can honor.

kept centralized in the home country.* Along the same lines, many firms avoid local brands and rely instead on international trademarks and other protected proprietary resources—resources beyond the reach of the host country.**

In a more positive vein, companies try to enhance and publicize the unique or valuable services they provide. The underlying theme is that these services could be lost through nationalization or excessive taxes and regulations. Many multinationals, for instance, have stressed their special ability to earn foreign exchange.†

All these devices can affect transnational bargaining over the terms of foreign investment. They strengthen the firm's position, weaken the host state's, and generally add to investment security. As strategic adaptations to a new environment for foreign capital, they represent considerable corporate learning.

But if these strategies often succeed in protecting individual investments, they still cannot protect foreign investments as a whole.

---

*Like many other techniques to minimize risk, this one also carries the seeds of real friction between multinational firms and host states. The dominant effect, however, seems to be one of increasing the firm's bargaining leverage and its ability to locate its sources of profits where they are least vulnerable and least taxed. As Gary Gereffi points out in his study of the steroid hormone industry in Mexico:

> The production and control of knowledge in the pharmaceutical industry are jealously guarded by the MNCs as close to the center of their operations as possible. This contributes to a global situation of asymmetrical control in which industry profits are concentrated by multinationals in their home countries or in tax havens. . . . Mexico's bargaining power . . . is constrained because technology is controlled and there are alternative sources of supply. The MNC threat that "they can go elsewhere" is plausible.

Gereffi, "Drug Firms and Dependency in Mexico: The Case of the Steroid Hormone Industry," *International Organization* 32 (Winter 1978), 258, 285.

**Multinational firms have global reach; nation-states do not, no matter how great their localized authority. One of Raymond Vernon's most compelling insights in *Sovereignty at Bay*, and there are a number, is his elaboration of this simple but fundamental asymmetry and its consequences for bargaining between MNCs and host states.

†This may be a dangerous ploy, however. The multinational firm may be asked to meet unrealistic targets and, in any case, it cannot contribute to *every* country's foreign-exchange position. It can only hope to contribute where the issue is most important and where the benefits will be most appreciated. Furthermore, the meaning of a "benefit" is seldom as clear as earning foreign exchange. A company can use the latest technology in its foreign plants, for instance, only to be praised by some and damned by others. One person's sophisticated technology is another person's unemployment.

Corporate managers and business analysts are beginning to codify their experience in such matters. See David Bradley, "Managing Against Expropriation," *Harvard Business Review* 55 (July-August 1977), 75–83; Nathaniel H. Leff, "Multinationals in a Hostile World," *The Wharton Magazine* 2 (Spring 1978), 21–29; and Pravin Banker, "You're the Best Judge of Foreign Risks," *Harvard Business Review* 61 (March-April 1983), esp. 158–160.

Indeed, they signify the dilution of private sanctions and, as a rule, have weakened the strictures against expropriation and other types of forced divestments.

This process is accelerated by the decline of *public* economic sanctions.[8] Bilateral aid programs are less important now and come from more donor countries. For most less developed countries they are less significant than trade concessions, particularly open access for basic manufactures.[9]

This shift from aid to trade imposes some limits on advanced capitalist states. Tariffs and quotas are powerful instruments, but they are not adequate substitutes for foreign aid sanctions. They are harder to modify quickly on a nation-by-nation basis and are generally cumbersome to use as instruments of bilateral diplomacy. The General Agreement on Tariffs and Trade restricts their discriminatory use, and the availability of alternative markets reduces their potential leverage. Finally, trade sanctions are difficult to use because, unlike aid, they directly affect home-state producers and consumers. These domestic actors can argue, quite plausibly, that they are suffering as much as the target country, which can usually turn to alternative markets or suppliers.

As the character of economic sanctions has changed and their effectiveness decreased, the willingness to use them has also diminished. The legally mandated retribution of the Hickenlooper amendment has been replaced by presidential discretion. The Gonzalez amendments, although still on the books, are no longer active policy. Overt sanctions are in disfavor.

These changes add up to a marked shift in U.S. anti-expropriation policy, a transformation both in overall policy and in the tactics of specific disputes. Unless the expropriations are the result of major leftist reforms (a point that is no longer considered axiomatic), the United States has avoided stiff, public opposition. Its policy, like that of most corporations, has been adaptive. Outside of Chile and perhaps Jamaica (during the Manley years), it is hard to find recent examples of strenuous opposition to expropriation.

A major conclusion of Part II is that the coincidence of public and private policies is no coincidence at all. Rather, it results from the state's structure, its role in assisting private capital accumulation, and the decisive intervention of large multinational corporations (when the broad goal of promoting international capital flows is an insufficient guide by itself).

My hypothesis regarding foreign aid sanctions and investment guaranties was based on corporate preferences. But I did not argue, as a pluralist might, that the government is a tabula rasa on which corporate opinions are printed and erased. I noted that many policies are based on shared perceptions of the international environment, sometimes colored by specific bureaucratic functions. These shared perceptions and attitudes are reinforced by common symbols and ideology. The symbolic content of expropriation raised its importance for many policymakers, even those with no constituent interests in the issue. Anticommunist ideology went even further, implying that opposition to expropriations promoted the largest security objectives of American foreign policy.

This hypothesis is useful in predicting the passage of the Hickenlooper amendment, its extension through the Gonzalez amendments, and its effective repeal in 1973. It is also accurate in predicting the implementation of the Hickenlooper amendment in diplomatic disputes.

The same hypothesis predicted the expansion of investment guaranty insurance and its ultimate reorganization as OPIC. The corollary predicted initial restraints on the guaranty program, based on divisions among multinational firms about its wisdom. In each instance, the predictions were empirically affirmed.

Neither case forced us to reject the hypothesis or its corollary. Quite the contrary: they provided a credible account of longer-term changes in both programs.

Structural and Instrumental Aspects of Anti-Expropriation Policy

Although the hypothesis highlights corporate involvement in the policy process, it is not purely instrumental. That is, it does not depend solely on the concerted, direct efforts of business leaders, as a pluralist or interest-group approach would. Instead, our inquiry has concentrated on the broader setting of corporate initiatives and the systemic basis of the economic policy agenda. The idea of guaranties, for example, was first raised as an adjunct to the Marshall Plan. It was proposed as a task for a state already engaged in reforming the regime that protected foreign investments. Clearly, it was that context which nurtured public and private support for investment insurance. Likewise, the Hickenlooper amendment was proposed as a response to an embryonic, but potentially serious, threat to foreign investments. The immediate occasion for the amendment was small enough—minor expropriations in Ceylon and Brazil—but they only served to underscore the vulnerability of all foreign investments and the pervasive threat stemming from the Cuban revolution.

The question was how to respond to this more general threat to foreign capital, and it was at that level that our hypothesis predicted policy. Moreover, the whole issue of investment protection was forced on the Kennedy administration not so much by the howls of business executives as by the cumulative effects of their decisions not to invest in Latin America. Direct efforts to influence anti-expropriation policy were conducted within that favorable context.

Another structural aspect of this explanation is its focus on the boundaries of public debate. The White House, various executive agencies and departments, and the Congress all had strong, independent interests in anti-expropriation policies. These independent, but roughly parallel, interests were derived from common ideology, common symbolic referents, and a shared understanding of certain state functions. Together, they produced a broad area of agreement about anti-expropriation policy. Policymakers agreed on the international norms that should govern foreign direct investment, even though they often disagreed about how best to promote those norms. The legal right of eminent domain was not challenged directly, but it was defined narrowly. The transfer of productive private assets to public control was universally opposed, both within the U.S. government and among multinational corporations. Rigorous repayment principles were universally admired.

Despite these areas of agreement, various state institutions have semiautonomous (and varied) bureaucratic interests, which help shape their positions on policy issues. Differences between the Treasury and State Department on anti-expropriation policy were obvious and persistent. They were grounded largely in those departments' different functions, and, to a lesser extent, in their different clienteles.

These bureaucratic differences have legislative repercussions because well-established policy networks link specific agencies with corresponding congressional committees. There are, in other words, distinct decision channels with their own inherent biases. It is clear, for example, that the Gonzalez amendments were facilitated by the close cooperation between the Treasury and the House Banking and Currency Committee.

Guaranty insurance was even more deeply affected by bureaucratic autonomy, unresponsiveness, and inefficiency. The idea that government is cumbersome and restrictive was at the heart of the first debates over guaranties. The same critique, in a different context, led to OPIC's formation. OPIC was proposed precisely because AID's bureaucracy was overwhelmed by the program's expansion. The inefficiency and backlog were intolerable. "Bureaucratic structure," as Claus Offe has noted, "seems inadequate as the basis for the productive type of state activity."[10] OPIC was based on that supposition; it was supposed to introduce quasi-market criteria. The hope was that reorganization would aid private capital accumulation where bureaucratic organization had hindered it. But, in fact, the more OPIC resembles privately held liability insurers, the *less* it stimulates new investment. To meet true market standards, it would have to raise its rates across the board, drastically shorten the length of its insurance contracts, and impose much higher rates on very risky projects. Right now, it is unwilling or unable to do that. Its rates and terms are far more favorable than those of any private insurer. At the same time, it has limited its own exposure by rationing insurance to some high-risk projects.

In spite of these examples, the state's autonomy in expropriation issues is remarkably restricted. When policy issues were serious and intragovernmental disagreement important, corporate leaders intervened directly. In the case of both foreign aid sanctions and guaranty insurance, tactical and strategic differences within the government were ultimately resolved in favor of the predominant preferences of large corporations. When corporate opinions were deeply divided, policy was either erratic or indecisive.

This decentralized, society-centered policy network comes with an ironic price tag. When state leadership is most needed, it is least possible. The state's autonomy—its capacity for independent, decisive action—would be most useful when corporations are split over proper policy or when their individual, self-centered actions might become a source of collective misfortune. The U.S. government has been unable to perform this coordinating and disciplining function for two reasons. First, the rise of European and Japanese multinational corporations means that a significant portion of market competition is outside the U.S. government's domain. My model of regime change refers directly to this issue, positing weaker restraints against expropriation when economic resources are decentralized. Second, and equally important, the U.S. government lacks sufficient capacity for independent action. It is seldom willing or able to coordinate the responses of U.S. corporations to expropriation, contract nullification, or forced sales. Put differently, the United States is intrinsically limited in performing its role as regime leader because of its state structure, its social structure, and the character of relevant policy networks. The hypothesis about the importance of corporate preferences concentrates on this very point, stressing the U.S. government's limitations in organizing and leading private actors.

Policymaking and Regime Maintenance

This whole analysis suggests that policymaking is closely tied to regime maintenance. The implicit argument of Parts I and II is that the United States not only makes policy, it makes rules—or at least it tries to. As the most powerful capitalist state, and the one with the biggest stake in foreign investment, its anti-expropriation policies inevitably take on larger meaning. In protecting U.S. corporations abroad, it acts as the principal guarantor of international property rules. Its forced acceptance of widespread expropriations and partial compensation since the late 1960s signals the regime's deterioration.

The argument here is that the Americans, like the British before them, deliberately tried to sustain a particular kind of global order and foster common expectations regarding acceptable treatment for foreign capital. Evidence for the late 1940s is clear, and hardly surprising. The task of restoring international trade, payments, and capital movements all called for a broad, long-range view. The economic collapse of the 1930s was remembered with a bitter clarity. To avoid any repetition, the State Department drew up plans for an integrated system of world commerce and investment. Fundamental programs were proposed: first the Bretton Woods system and the International Trade Organization and later the Marshall Plan and Point IV. Programs of this scale could not be constructed, as so much American policy always is, by small increments, by "continually building out from the current situation, step-by-step and by small degrees," as Lindblom put it.[11]

Instead, both government and private planners adopted a comprehensive perspective. Their strategies for investment protection were worked out by considering the basic obstacles and then contraposing various programs. The State Department's 1949 publication, *Point Four*, says exactly that. It is concerned with basic policies and their relationship to international order:

> Many of the obstacles which arise from extreme forms of nationalism, from the fear of world instability and from economic dislocations due to the imbalance in the world trade pattern, will be affected by the broad programs and policies which are now a part of the whole foreign policy of the United States. . . . These efforts to help create a sense of security, an expanding and balanced world trade pattern, and to alleviate economic dislocations arising from the war, will, as they achieve success, eliminate many of the basic causes for imposition by foreign governments of deterrents to mutually advantageous investment.[12]

Business associations were similarly concerned. Almost all of them— the National Foreign Trade Council, the National Association of Manufacturers, the U.S. Chamber of Commerce, the International Chamber, the National Planning Association, the Committee for Economic Development—debated these policies extensively and issued public position papers filled with their conclusions and recommendations.

Even small programs, such as investment guaranties, were affected by the broad concerns. They, too, were novel, and it was important to make sure they complemented larger programs and objectives. Furthermore, since their basic design was untested and sometimes controversial, public debate over them might uncover basic fears and disagreements about policy formation and implementation.

A central issue in the guaranty debate, for instance, was whether the proposed scheme fit into larger bilateral efforts to protect investment. Bilateral negotiations were critical to the investment regime since, as the International Chamber of Commerce noted, multilateral agreements were woefully inadequate:

> Neither the proposed ITO Charter nor the Bogotá Agreement, with its many reservations, will induce a flow of investment on the scale desired. These recent failures to obtain adequate assurances on a multilateral basis of fair treatment for private foreign investment suggest that, as a new approach, negotiations should be conducted bilaterally with one or a few countries.[13]

The idea was that bilateral negotiations and unilateral enforcement would define international property rules. Some business organizations such as the NAM even wrote pamphlets setting out the main features they would like to see in the reorganized regime.[14] To a considerable extent, they evaluated individual proposals, such as that concerning investment guaranties, on the basis of their likely contribution to the new order. A good part of the guaranty debate ultimately boiled down to whether the proposed insurance would add to or detract from other efforts to define the regime.

That is also why so much discussion centered on the messages, intended and unintended, that the new policies would send. As Robert Jervis has observed, "A desired image (the substance of which will depend on the actor's goals and his estimate of the international environment) can often be of greater use than a significant increment of military or economic power."[15] While image-shaping never stops, some moments are more important than others. The early postwar years were obviously crucial, a time of fundamental recasting and reconstruction. Nations and corporations alike were uncertain about the prospective world order and about one another's intentions. Naturally, they cast about for whatever evidence they could find. In this uncertain world, attentiveness to images and policy signals was much more pervasive than in a world of stable expectations.[16]

Not only were national images especially significant (and none more so than those of the United States), but they were also highly manipulable. In the few years since the war, it had not yet been possible to send clear, credible messages about a number of capabilities and intentions. In investment protection, for instance, the United States had not yet faced an obvious test case. No one could really be certain how it would react when it did, or what the consequences would be.

These signaling issues formed a critical aspect of the guaranty debate. They reveal an intimate and purposeful link between policymaking and regime maintenance in the early postwar years.

The uncertainties gradually died away as a track record was built. The willingness and ability of the United States to enforce property rules was not much in doubt by the late 1950s. The Cuban expropriations, however, opened up new questions. How could the old rules be sustained after this challenge? The Kennedy administration's answer to this, and to the pressing question of hemispheric security, was the Alliance for Progress. Designed to accommodate reformist demands in Latin America and as a counterweight to communism, the program first succeeded in raising serious doubts among U.S. investors in the region. They were principally concerned that Alliance reforms might inadvertently endanger their property. Their immediate problem was to communicate these concerns to the Kennedy administration and to reverse some of the administration's policy initiatives. The Hickenlooper amendment was bound up in this larger project.

The clash, then, was between two strategies of regime maintenance: the Kennedy administration's, which relied on social and political reforms tied to aggressive anticommunism, and the conservatives', which relied on the brittle reaffirmation of traditional verities. The counterreformation won, in part because the Kennedy administration put up such a tepid defense of its own policies.

This kind of deliberate discussion of regime maintenance, and basic disagreement over policy directions, has been rare in the 1970s and 1980s. There are at least two major reasons. First, most corporations have successfully adapted to the new environment. Those that could not or did not, such as American and Foreign Power, have gone the way of the East India Company. Whatever the long-range effects of expropriations, they no longer uniformly frighten multinational companies. Nor do they uniformly impede profitable operations. Many companies have implemented flexible investment strategies that allow them to work with nationalist governments of all sorts, ranging from bureaucratic-authoritarian to socialist-populist. While the host state's ideology is not irrelevant, it is often balanced by other considerations: stable markets, cheap labor, social stability, incentive arrangements, and so forth.[17]

Second, and equally important, is the lack of effective, regime-strengthening options. Despite the Treasury's bluster in the early 1970s, economic sanctions against LDCs simply will not work without careful and extensive coordination. Other industrial economies must participate alongside the United States, and they are rarely willing to do so.[18] The availability of alternative markets in Europe and Japan seriously undermines the threat-value of economic sanctions. It is, of course, possible to restrict access to some of these markets and to some suppliers. That does impose costs on the target state. But it is virtually impossible to shut off all access to international economic intercourse. That is the principal lesson of the U.N. boycotts of so-called pariah states and America's boycott of Khomeini's Iran. Johan Galtung adds an important complementary point: target states may be able to blunt the impact of sanctions via internal countermeasures.[19] The urgency of these internal measures is usually minimized, however, because alternative foreign suppliers and markets are available.

Moreover, if any economic sanctions are to be effective, the state that employs them must be able to control its own multinational firms. They, too, must join the boycott.* But the same porous state structure that permitted large U.S. corporations to frame public anti-expropriation policy cannot simultaneously furnish such vigorous and self-conscious leadership. The state's relative lack of structural autonomy in foreign investment issues means that it is seldom able to overcome corporate fractionalization and divergent self-interest.

The United States, then, is faced with a weak, fragmented regime for direct investments, and no likely escape. Except for mutually acceptable payments and due process, regime standards are not at issue in most expropriation disputes. What were once international clashes are now businesslike negotiations over the distribution of future economic gains. Under the circumstances, few have shown much enthusiasm for resurrecting the old standards.

It looks like a losing battle to try. There are no obvious strategies and plenty of well-known obstacles. Coordination with Europe and Japan is essential—but unlikely. Coordination among U.S. multinationals is equally important—and not very likely either.

In the meantime, the U.S. government and multinational firms have taken up adaptive strategies. There may be dangers in the long run,** but for now, at least, they think it safe. They know it is lucrative.

---

*Efforts to restrict flows of high-technology goods to the Soviet Union illustrate just how difficult it is to organize such boycotts. That is even more true when security issues are not so prominent (as they seldom are in investment disputes with LDCs).

**These long-run problems are most likely in sectors such as raw-materials extraction that are, at once, very risky and capital intensive.

Notes

Preface and Acknowledgments

1. Hymer's thesis, which circulated for years in manuscript, was finally published as *The International Operations of National Firms: A Study of Direct Foreign Investment* (Cambridge, Mass.: MIT Press, 1976).

2. Ibid., 23–27. This approach is still influential; see P. J. Buckley, "A Critical Review of Theories of the Multinational Enterprise," *Aussenwirtschaft* 36 (1981), 70–87.

3. Charles P. Kindleberger, ed., *The International Corporation* (Cambridge, Mass.: MIT Press, 1970).

4. Richard E. Caves, *Multinational Enterprise and Economic Analysis* (Cambridge: Cambridge University Press, 1983).

5. Raymond Vernon, *Sovereignty at Bay* (New York: Basic Books, 1971). Vernon's subsequent work and that of the Harvard Multinational Enterprise Project, which he directed, are summarized in Vernon's *Storm over the Multinationals: The Real Issues* (Cambridge, Mass.: Harvard University Press, 1977).

6. J. M. Stopford and L. T. Wells, Jr., *Managing the Multinational Enterprise* (New York: Basic Books, 1972). Also see S. P. Sethi and R. H. Holton, eds., *Management of Multinational Operations* (New York: Free Press, 1974). These more scholarly studies are now supplemented by standard textbook treatments for prospective international managers, such as William H. Davidson, *Global Strategic Management* (New York: John Wiley, 1982) and David K. Eiteman and Arthur I. Stonehill, *Multinational Business Finance* (3d edition; Reading, Mass.: Addison-Wesley, 1982).

7. Mira Wilkins, *The Emergence of Multinational Enterprise: Colonial Era to 1914* (Cambridge, Mass.: Harvard University Press, 1970); Wilkins, *The Maturing of the Multinational Enterprise, 1914–1970* (Cambridge, Mass.: Harvard University Press, 1974).

8. M. Y. Yoshino, *Japan's Multinational Enterprises* (Cambridge, Mass.: Harvard University Press, 1976); Yoshihiro Tsurumi, *The Japanese are Coming* (Cambridge, Mass.: Ballinger, 1976); Lawrence G. Franko, *The European Multinationals* (Stamford, Conn.: Greylock Publishers, 1976). Along the same lines, Tamir Agmon and Charles P. Kindleberger have produced an edited volume on *Multinationals from Small Countries* (Cambridge, Mass.: MIT Press, 1977), and Louis Wells, a study on *Third World Multinationals: The Rise of Foreign Investment from Developing Countries* (Cambridge, Mass.: MIT Press, 1983).

9. The most elegant statement of these organizational issues is Oliver E. Williamson's *Markets and Hierarchies: Analysis and Antitrust Implications* (New York: Free Press, 1975), and Williamson's "The Modern Corporation: Origins, Evolution, Attributes," *Journal of Economic Literature* 19 (December 1981), 1537–1568. The application of this approach to the study of MNCs can be found in Peter J. Buckley and Mark Casson, *The Future of the Multinational Enterprise* (London: Macmillan, 1976).

10. Theodore Moran, *Multinational Corporations and the Politics of Dependence: Copper in Chile* (Princeton, N.J.: Princeton University Press, 1974). Moran, of course, is not the only student of multinational corporations to have examined investments in less developed countries, but his work is one of the few to also contain sophisticated political analysis.

Three other national studies offer detailed and useful analyses of multinational activities in Third World states. They are Richard L. Sklar's *Corporate Power in an African State: The Political Impact of Multinational Mining Companies in Zambia* (Berkeley, Los Angeles, London: University of California Press, 1975); Charles T. Goodsell, *American Corporations and Peruvian Politics* (Cambridge, Mass.: Harvard University Press, 1974); and Paul E. Sigmund's comparative study, *Multinationals in Latin America: The Politics of Nationalization* (Madison, Wis.: University of Wisconsin Press for the Twentieth Century Fund, 1980). Other important work, such as that of Miguel Wionczek and Constantine Vaitsos, is focused more narrowly on the economic impact of multinational investment.

11. At least two writers, Peter Evans and Gary Gereffi, have made important steps to link the literature on dependency with that on multinational firms. See Evans, *Dependent Development: The Alliance of Multinational, State, and Local Capital in Brazil* (Princeton, N.J.: Princeton University Press, 1979); Gereffi, *The Pharmaceutical Industry and Dependency in the Third World* (Princeton, N.J.: Princeton University Press, 1983). Gereffi, "Drug Firms and Dependency in Mexico: The Case of the Steroid Hormone Industry," *International Organization* 32 (Winter 1978); and Gereffi and Evans, "Transnational Corporations, Dependent Development, and State Policy in the Semiperiphery: A Comparison of Brazil and Mexico," *Latin American Research Review* 16 (1981), 31–64.

12. The Latin American literature is voluminous, and so are the efforts by North Americans to quantify it. The most influential treatment is Fernando Henrique Cardoso and Enzo Faletto, *Dependency and Development in Latin America* (Berkeley, Los Angeles, London: University of California Press, 1979). For a collection of empirical assessments, see James A. Caporaso, ed., *Dependence and Dependency in the Global System*, a special edition of *International Organization* 32 (Winter 1978). Cardoso criticizes this type of empirical work in "The Consumption of Dependency Theory in the United States," *Latin American Research Review* 12 (1977), 7–24.

13. Hans Morgenthau, *Politics Among Nations* (1st ed.; New York: Alfred A. Knopf, 1948), chap. 7.

14. Gilpin extends and generalizes some of these arguments in *War and Change in World Politics* (Cambridge: Cambridge University Press, 1981).

15. Stephen Krasner, "State Power and the Structure of International Trade," *World Politics* 28 (April 1976), 317–347. Krasner applies his argument to a contemporary economic negotiation in "The Tokyo Round: Particularistic Interests and Prospects for Stability in the Global Trading System," *International Studies Quarterly* 23 (December 1979), 491–531.

16. Stephen D. Krasner, *Defending the National Interest: Raw Materials Investments and U.S. Foreign Policy* (Princeton, N.J.: Princeton University Press, 1978), esp. 331.

17. Robert O. Keohane and Joseph S. Nye, *Power and Interdependence: World Politics in Transition* (Boston: Little, Brown, 1977), chaps. 4–6.

18. The security of foreign loans is discussed in chapters 2, 4, and 5. For a more complete analysis of the recent period, see the author's "The International Organization of Third World Debt," *International Organization* 34 (Autumn 1981), 603–631; and the author's "The IMF, Commercial Banks, and Third World Debts," in *Debt and the Less Developed Countries*, ed. Jonathan David Aronson (Boulder, Colo.: Westview Press, 1979).

19. For studies of economic stabilization in the wake of debt problems, see John Williamson, ed., *IMF Conditionality* (Washington, D.C.: Institute for International Economics, 1983); Williamson, ed., *Prospects for Adjustment in Argentina, Brazil, and Mexico: Responding to the Debt Crisis* (Washington, D.C.: Institute for International Economics, 1983); William R. Cline and Sidney Weintraub, eds., *Economic Stabilization in Developing*

Countries (Washington, D.C.: Brookings Institution, 1981); and Tony Killick, ed., *Adjustment and Financing in the Developing World: The Role of the International Monetary Fund* (Washington, D.C.: IMF in association with the Overseas Development Institute, London, 1982).

20. Keohane and Nye, *Power and Interdependence.* Keohane elaborates his perspective on issue differentiation in "The Theory of Hegemonic Stability and Changes in International Economic Regimes, 1967–1977," in *Change in the International System,* ed. Ole Holsti, Randolph M. Sieverson, and Alexander L. George (Boulder, Colo.: Westview Press, 1980), 131–162.

Chapter One: An Unruly World?
Anarchy, Rules, and
International Capital Flows

1. Blaise Pascal, *Pensées,* trans. W. F. Trotter, in *The Provincial Letters; Pensées; Scientific Treatises* (Chicago: Encyclopaedia Britannica, 1952), Sec. V, § 295, p. 226.

2. J. J. Rousseau, "The Second Discourse" (Discourse on the Origin and Foundation of Inequality), in *The First and Second Discourses,* ed. Roger D. Masters; trans. Roger D. Masters and Judith R. Masters (New York: St. Martin's, 1964), 141.

3. Ian R. Macneil, *The New Social Contract: An Inquiry into Modern Contractual Relations* (New Haven: Yale University Press, 1980), 1–2.

4. Durkheim develops this point in his work on the noncontractual elements of contract. "A contract is not sufficient unto itself," he writes, "but is possible only thanks to a regulation of the contract which is originally social." Emile Durkheim, *The Division of Labor in Society,* trans. George Simpson (New York: Free Press, 1933), 214.

5. See Morton A. Kaplan and Nicholas deB. Katzenbach, *The Political Foundations of International Law* (New York: John Wiley, 1961), esp. v.

6. Lon Fuller's account of law stresses this idea of law as a stabilizer of expectations and a baseline for human interaction.

> To engage in effective social behavior, men need the support of intermeshing anticipations that will let them know what their opposite numbers will do, or that will at least enable them to gauge the general scope of the repertory from which responses to their actions will be drawn.

Fuller, "Law and Human Interaction," in *Social System and Legal Process,* ed. Harry M. Johnson (San Francisco: Jossey-Bass Publishers, 1978), 61.

7. The term is Sally Falk Moore's. Moore, *Law as Process: An Anthropological Approach* (London: Routledge & Kegan Paul, 1978), 4.

8. James C. Riley, *International Government Finance and the Amsterdam Capital Market 1740–1815* (Cambridge: Cambridge University Press, 1980); Violet Barbour, *Capitalism in Amsterdam in the 17th Century* (Ann Arbor, Mich: University of Michigan Press, 1963); Alice Clare Carter, *Getting, Spending and Investing in Early Modern Times* (Assen, The Netherlands: Van Gorcum, 1975).

9. Mira Wilkins, *The Emergence of Multinational Enterprise: American Business Abroad from the Colonial Era to 1914* (Cambridge, Mass.: Harvard University Press, 1970); Charles Wilson, "The Multinational in Historical Perspective," in *Strategy and Structure of Big Business,* ed. Keiishiro Nakagawa (Tokyo: University of Tokyo Press, 1974), 265–286; P. L. Cottrell, *British Overseas Investment in the Nineteenth Century* (London: Macmillan, 1975).

10. George Schwarzenberger, "The Protection of British Property Abroad," in *Current Legal Problems, 1952,* ed. G. W. Keeton and G. Schwarzenberger, vol. 5 (London: Stevens and Sons, 1952); Clyde Eagleton, *The Responsibility of States in International Law* (New York: New York University Press, 1928). As early as Vattel, legal scholars

defended the rights of states to protect their citizens abroad. Vattel wrote that "Whoever uses a citizen ill, indirectly offends the state, which is bound to protect this citizen; and the sovereign of the latter should avenge his wrongs, punish the aggressor, and, if possible, oblige him to make full reparation; since otherwise the citizen would not obtain the great end of the civil association, which is, safety." Emeric de Vattel, *The Law of Nations*, ed. Joseph Chitty, with additional notes and references by Edward D. Ingraham (Philadelphia: T. & J. W. Johnson, 1855; originally published, Leiden, 1758), bk. II, chap. VI, § 71. The rule that local remedies must be exhausted before appealing under international law is examined in detail in C. P. H. Law, *The Local Remedies Rule in International Law* (Geneva: E. Droz, 1961).

11. Secretary of State Cordell Hull expressed the U.S. anti-expropriation position in his correspondence to the Mexican ambassador (issued as Department of State press releases in 1938). The essential correspondence is reprinted in Louis Henkin, Richard Pugh, Oscar Schachter, and Hans Smit, *International Law: Cases and Materials* (St. Paul, Minn.: West Publishing, 1980), 687–689.

12. American Law Institute, *Restatement of the Law, Second: Foreign Relations Law of the United States* (St. Paul, Minn.: American Law Institute Publishers, 1965), §§ 165–166, 185–188.

13. Ibid., § 165, Comment.

14. H. Neufeld, *The International Protection of Private Creditors from the Treaties of Westphalia to the Congress of Vienna (1648–1815)* (Leiden: A. W. Sijthoff, 1971), 6–7. Denmark, Poland, the Swiss Federation and others also signed treaties guaranteeing the economic rights of foreigners.

15. Ibid., 98.

16. Ibid., 144–145. Some treaties, however, exempted confiscated enemy debts from any general restitution. The aim was to make sure the belligerent country paid its liabilities after the war. According to Neufield, however, "The creditors' own sovereign was liable to pay [his own nationals'] damage if in a peace treaty he agreed to, or sanctioned confiscations of their property thus becoming an accessory to the expropriation." Ibid., 145.

17. J. B. Condliffe, *The Commerce of Nations* (New York: W. W. Norton, 1950), 218.

18. Reciprocity as the basis of rules and conventions is examined carefully in Russell Hardin, *Collective Action* (Baltimore: The Johns Hopkins University Press for Resources for the Future, 1982), chaps. 9–13. Reciprocity, beginning with a generous first move toward potential adversaries, is also the basis of a collectively rational solution to an iterated Prisoner's Dilemma. See Robert Axelrod, "The Emergence of Cooperation among Egoists," *American Political Science Review*, 75 (June 1981), 306–318; and Axelrod and William D. Hamilton, "The Evolution of Cooperation," *Science* 211 (March 27, 1981), 1390–1396.

19. John Gerard Ruggie, "Continuity and Transformation in the World Polity: Toward a Neorealist Synthesis," *World Politics*, 35 (January 1983), 261–285.

20. Brian Barry, "Do Countries Have Moral Obligations? The Case of World Poverty," in *The Tanner Lectures on Human Values*, ed. Sterling McMurrin, vol. 2 (Salt Lake City: University of Utah Press, 1981), 30. Barry's use of the term anarchy obviously differs from its more limited meaning in international relations: the absence of an international sovereign.

21. Simon Roberts, *Order and Dispute: An Introduction to Legal Anthropology* (New York: St. Martin's, 1979), 34.

22. Georg Simmel, *On Individuality and Social Forms*, ed. and with an intro. by Donald N. Levine (Chicago: University of Chicago Press, 1971), 77, and Levine's introduction, lvii-lviii. Simmel's position directly contradicts Parsons' on this point. Parsons' argument, which stresses the normative integration of societies, holds little hope for the analysis of international relations (and no hope at all for international order).

23. Robert O. Keohane and Joseph S. Nye, *Power and Interdependence* (Boston: Little Brown, 1977), 5.

24. See the definition of international regimes given by Stephen Krasner in his

introduction to *International Regimes* and used by most other contributors. Krasner, "Structural Causes and Regime Consequences: Regimes as Intervening Variables," in *International Regimes*, ed. Stephen Krasner, special issue of *International Organization* 36 (Spring 1982), 186–189.

25. This notion that sanctions are implicit in reciprocal bargaining is a very general one. For example, Malinowski considers these sanctions a crucial source of order among the Trobriand Islanders. See Bronislaw Malinowski, *Crime and Custom in Savage Society* (London: Routledge and Kegan Paul, 1926), and Malinowski's introduction to H. Ian Hogbin, *Law and Order in Polynesia* (London: Christophers, 1934), xxxvi.

26. Halil Inalcik, "Imtiyāzāt," in *The Encyclopedia of Islam*, New Edition, vol. 3 (Leiden: E. J. Brill, and London: Luzac and Co., 1971), 1180.

27. Ibid., 1187.

28. P. J. Cain, *Economic Foundations of British Overseas Expansion, 1815–1914* (London: Macmillan, 1980). Trade, finance, and grand strategy were thus intertwined in Britain's policy in the Eastern Mediterranean. As Stratford Canning wrote in an official memorandum in 1832, "To Great Britain, the fate of [the Ottoman] Empire can never be indifferent. It would affect the interests of her Trade and East Indian Possessions, even if it were unconnected with the maintenance of her relative Power in Europe." The full text of this memorandum on the Turco-Egyptian Question is in F. E. Bailey, *British Policy and the Turkish Reform Movement* (Cambridge, Mass.: Harvard University Press, 1942), 237–246.

29. Eliot Grinnell Mears, "Levantine Concession-Hunting," in *Modern Turkey*, ed. E. G. Mears (New York: Macmillan, 1924), 354.

30. Z. Y. Hershlag, *Introduction to the Modern Economic History of the Middle East* (2d ed.; Leiden: E. J. Brill, 1980).

31. E. G. Mears, Commerce Reports, 22 May 1920, reprinted in *Modern Turkey*, ed. E. G. Mears, 432–433.

32. Ibid., 432.

33. G. Bie Ravndal, "Capitulations," in ibid., 430–447. Ravndal well understood these concession agreements and extraterritorial laws. He had served as American consul general in Constantinople and founded the American Chamber of Commerce for the Levant.

34. David Laitin challenges this conventional interpretation of British policy. The suppression of the slave trade in West Africa, he says, is an example of the ideological, even mercantilist, cast in British policy. Britain's support for nondiscriminatory trade is, of course, the expression of a particular world view. It is even mercantilist in the limited sense that the state reserves to itself the right to establish trading rules. It rejects, however, other, more important tenets of mercantilism: the strong desire for a surplus of merchandise trade; the aim of acquiring precious metals (and their confusion with national wealth); and the imposition of detailed state controls over commercial relations.

Laitin is also misleading when he sharply distinguishes British trade policy on the Continent from policy on the periphery. He argues that "the systemic pressure on the hegemon to create and preserve openness in trade, if in fact it does exist, concerns primarily trade among core states of the international economy. The *consequences* of hegemony in the periphery appear to be different" (p. 709, emphasis added). Laitin's language is confusing. When he discusses trade among core states, he is referring to policy principles, such as openness. When he discusses the periphery, he is not referring to rules or principles but to transaction flows: the direction of trade. Actually, Britain supported the same principles of "fair field and no favor" in Latin America, the Near East, the Far East—and the Continent. In Europe, these rules of nondiscrimination were embodied in the Anglo-French Commercial Treaty of 1860 (the Cobden-Chevalier Treaty) and other commercial arrangements.

Rather than calling Britain's policy mercantilist (when it is closer to Adam Smith than to Colbert), it would be more accurate to say that Britain extended nondiscriminatory natory trading rules around the world in the nineteenth century, and, not incidentally, its nationals reaped a lion's share of the profits.

David Laitin, "Capitalism and Hegemony: Yorubaland and the International Economy," *International Organization* 36 (Autumn 1982), 687–713; Robert S. Smith, *The Lagos Consulate, 1851–1961* (Berkeley, Los Angeles, London: University of California, 1979); A. A. Iliasu, "The Cobden-Chevalier Commercial Treaty of 1860," *Historical Journal* 14 (1971), 67–98; and, on the distinction between rules and transactions, Charles Lipson, "The Transformation of Trade: The Sources and Effects of Regime Change," *International Organization* 36 (Spring 1982), 417–455.

35. D. C. M. Platt, *Finance, Trade, and Politics in British Foreign Policy, 1815–1914* (Oxford: Clarendon Press, 1968), 262–265.

36. John King Fairbank, *Trade and Diplomacy on the China Coast* (Cambridge, Mass.: Harvard University Press, 1968), 262–265.

37. Ibid., chaps. 8, 10.

38. Ibid., 172.

39. Ian H. Nish, "Japan's Policies toward Britain," in *Japan's Foreign Policy, 1868–1941*, ed. James William Morley (New York: Columbia University Press, 1974), 186; Arthur E. Tiedemann, "Japan's Economic Foreign Policies, 1868–1893," in ibid.; W. G. Beasley, *Great Britain and the Opening of Japan, 1834–1858* (London: Luzac, 1951).

40. Antony G. Hopkins, "Property Rights and Empire Building: Britain's Annexation of Lagos, 1861," *Journal of Economic History* 40 (December 1980), 787.

41. Ibid., 782.

42. This point is crucial to Fairbank in his analysis of the Chinese treaty ports. The foreigner, he concludes, sought "in self-interest to maintain the shrunken prestige of the regime" (p. 465). Even so, the early treaty system broke down as trade grew larger and diplomatic relations grew worse. Fairbank, *Trade and Diplomacy on the China Coast,* 465–467.

43. Quoted in Hopkins, "Property Rights and Empire Building," 782.

44. H. S. Ferns, "Latin America and Industrial Capitalism: The First Phase," *Sociological Review*, Monograph 11 (February 1967), 12.

45. Hopkins, "Property Rights and Empire Building," 797. Elsewhere, Hopkins and J. P. Cain write that some Latin American states "deliberately created the political structures that helped to integrate them into the world economy by encouraging foreign investment and migration." Cain and Hopkins, "The Political Economy of British Expansion Overseas, 1750–1914," *Economic History Review*, 2d series, 33 (November 1980), 483.

46. Ferns, "Latin America and Industrial Capitalism" (see n. 44), 7; Fernando Henrique Cardoso and Enzo Faletto, *Dependency and Development in Latin America*, trans. Marjory Mattingly Urquidi (Berkeley, Los Angeles, London: University of California Press, 1979), 34–73. The reciprocal influences of foreign commercial penetration and domestic class structure is, of course, the central problem of dependency theory.

47. Frederick Sherwood Dunn, *The Protection of Nationals* (Baltimore: The Johns Hopkins Press, 1932), 54–55.

48. Winthrop R. Wright, *British-Owned Railways in Argentina: Their Effect on Economic Nationalism, 1854–1948* (Austin: University of Texas Press for the Institute of Latin American Studies, 1974); Richard Graham, *Britain and the Onset of Modernization in Brazil 1850–1914* (Cambridge: Cambridge University Press, 1972); D. C. M. Platt, ed., *Business Imperialism 1840–1930: An Inquiry Based on British Experience in Latin America* (Oxford: Oxford University Press, 1977); John H. Coatsworth, *Growth Against Development: The Economic Impact of Railroads in Porfirian Mexico* (Dekalb, Ill.: Northern Illinois University Press, 1981).

49. This resistance to outside protection for foreign investors (embodied in the Calvo Doctrine) continues to the present. See Jorge I. Domínguez, ed., *Economic Issues and Political Conflict: US-Latin American Relations* (London: Butterworth Scientific, 1982); Paul E. Sigmund, *Multinationals in Latin America: The Politics of Nationalization* (Madison: University of Wisconsin Press for the Twentieth Century Fund, 1980).

50. At the end of 1981, according to the Commerce Department, the United States had a direct investment position in Latin America of $38.8 billion (book value). It had

$14.5 billion in all other LDCs. These figures cover only U.S. direct investors' equity in these affiliates and their net loans to them. The figures for *total assets* abroad are larger since they include not only investors' equity but also the affiliates' total liabilities. The last comprehensive measure of total U.S. assets abroad was the Commerce Department's 1977 Benchmark Survey. It was reported in April 1981 and covers nonbank affiliates of nonbank U.S. parents. United States affiliates in Latin America had total assets of $75 billion, according to this survey. Their assets in all other LDCs were $40.8 billion. Obie G. Whichard, "U.S. Direct Investment Abroad in 1981," *Survey of Current Business* 62 (August 1982), 11, 21; "1977 Benchmark Survey of U.S. Direct Investment Abroad," *Survey of Current Business* 61 (April 1981), 31, 36.

51. The Calvo Doctrine, as stated by the Argentinian jurist, Carlos Calvo, asserts that as a matter of international law, no state may intervene, diplomatically or otherwise, to enforce its citizens' private claims in a foreign country. This general principle has subsequently been written into investment contracts and national constitutions. As a specific constitutional clause, however, its meaning has varied considerably. Mexico, for instance, excludes diplomatic protection under any circumstances. Bolivia, by constant, grants limited rights of diplomatic protection when justice has been denied. David E. Graham, "The Calvo Clause: Its Current Status as a Contractual Renunciation of Diplomatic Protection," *Texas International Law Forum* 6 (Winter 1971), 289–290; Manuel R. Garcia-Mora, "The Calvo Clause in Latin American Constitutions and International Law," *Marquette Law Review* 33 (Spring 1950), 205–219. Donald R. Shea, *The Calvo Clause: A Problem of Inter-American and International Law and Diplomacy* (Minneapolis: University of Minnesota Press, 1955).

52. Calvo himself wrote extensively on what he considered the international legal injunctions against foreign intervention, whether diplomatic or military. "Il est impossible de découvrir une seule raison sérieuse et légitime qui puisse justifier jusqu' à un certain point ces ingérences européenes dans les affaires intérieures de l'Amérique." And, of course, Calvo argues that local rules and judicial decisions regarding foreign investment were "affaires intérieures." Charles [Carlos] Calvo, *Le Droit International*, vol. 1 (5th ed.; Paris: Librarie Nouvelle de Droit et de Jurisprudence, 1896), 348. See also Edwin M. Borchard, *The Diplomatic Protection of Citizens Abroad* (New York: Banks Law Publishing, 1915), chap. 4; K. Lipstein, "The Place of the Calvo Clause in International Law," *British Year Book of International Law* 22 (1945), 130–145.

53. Friedrich Katz, *The Secret War in Mexico: Europe, the United States and the Mexican Revolution* (Chicago: University of Chicago Press, 1981), 318.

54. Ibid., 568–569.

55. Platt, *Finance, Trade, and Politics in British Foreign Policy, 1815–1914*, 70–71.

56. Katz, *The Secret War in Mexico*, 4.

57. "Reversal of Policy: Latin America Opens the Door to Foreign Investment Again," *Business Week* (August 9, 1976), 42.

58. [Charles Oman], "New North-South Investment Strategies," *The OECD Observer* 112 (September 1981), 13–15.

59. The management of political risks is now a standard textbook subject for multinational managers. See, for example, Derek F. Channon with Michael Jalland, *Multinational Strategic Planning* (New York: AMACOM, 1978), chap. 9 ("The Management of Political Risk"), or David K. Eiteman and Arthur I. Stonehill, *Multinational Business Finance* (3d ed.; Reading, Mass.: Addison-Wesley, 1982), chap. 8 ("Political Risk Management").

60. David G. Bradley, "Managing Against Expropriation," *Harvard Business Review* 55 (July-August 1977), esp. 82–83; Pravin Banker, "You're the Best Judge of Foreign Risks," *Harvard Business Review* 61 (March-April 1983), 158–160.

61. Raymond F. Mikesell, *Foreign Investment in Mining Projects* (Cambridge, Mass.: Oelgeschlager, Gunn and Hain, 1983), 280; idem, *New Patterns of World Mineral Development* ([London]: British-North American Committee, 1979); and interviews.

62. Detlev Vagts, "The Global Corporation and International Law," *Journal of International Law and Economics* 6 (January 1972), 254.

63. D. Vagts, "Coercion and Foreign Investment Rearrangements," *American Journal of International Law* 72 (January 1978), 17.

64. Ibid.

65. William A. Stoever, *Renegotiations in International Business Transactions* (Lexington, Mass.: D. C. Heath, 1981); Samuel K. B. Asante, "Restructuring Transnational Mineral Agreements," *American Journal of International Law* 73 (July 1979), 335–371; David N. Smith and Louis T. Wells, *Negotiating Third World Mineral Agreements: Promise as Prologue* (Cambridge, Mass.: Ballinger, 1975).

66. J. Frederick Truitt, *Expropriation of Private Foreign Investment* (Bloomington: Graduate School of Business, Indiana University, 1974), 9.

67. For an incisive and unconventional argument about the theoretical value of case studies, see Harry Eckstein, "Case Study and Theory in Political Science," *Handbook of Political Science,* vol. 7: *Strategies of Inquiry,* ed. Fred I. Greenstein and Nelson W. Polsby (Reading, Mass.: Addison-Wesley, 1975).
According to Eckstein's unusual definition, the chapters in this work are not technically case studies. He defines a case as "a phenomenon for which we report and interpret only a single measure on any pertinent variable." All my hypotheses, however, are tested with several measures on each pertinent variable. In examining investment guaranty insurance, for example, I record its initial passage, its expansion, its transformation into a new agency (OPIC), and finally OPIC's renewal, all as part of a single study. I show a correlation between the measures of my independent and dependent variables and argue that a causal relationship exists.

68. The classic treatment of trade politics stressing interest groups, is E. E. Schattschneider's *Politics, Pressures, and the Tariff* (New York: Prentice-Hall, 1935). A more recent treatment, focusing on intergovernmental relations and critical of Schattschneider, is Robert A. Pastor, *Congress and the Politics of U.S. Foreign Economic Policy 1929–1976* (Berkeley, Los Angeles, London: University of California Press, 1980), chaps. 3–6, and Pastor, "The Cry and Sign Syndrome: Congress and U.S. Trade Policy," in *Making Economic Policy in Congress,* ed. Allen Schick (Washington, D.C.: American Enterprise Institute for Public Policy Research, 1983).

69. It would seem obvious that multinational corporations would play a crucial role in the formation of anti-expropriation policy. Yet the only other book on the subject completely ignores the firms and concentrates exclusively on bureaucratic politics. See Jessica Pernitz Einhorn, *Expropriation Politics* (Lexington, Mass.: D. C. Heath, 1974).

70. Robert Gilpin, for instance, argues strongly that foreign capital contributes little to welfare in the home state, may sap its industrial potential, and has a highly uneven distributional impact. In contrast, Stephen Krasner finds a much more positive connection between foreign investment and national welfare. His aim is to show that the protection of American raw-material investments is ancillary to the pursuit of larger policy goals—goals that are genuinely national in scope. See Robert Gilpin, *U.S. Power and the Multinational Corporation* (New York: Basic Books, 1975), esp. chap. 7; and Stephen Krasner, *Defending the National Interest* (Princeton, N.J.: Princeton University Press, 1978).

71. In recent years, North-South discussions have been focused on the call for a New International Economic Order (NIEO). While the demands for a new order have been vague, and have differed among countries and over time, their keystone has been an integrated program of commodity price supports. Control over multinational firms and technology transfer has also been high on the agenda and has been debated frequently. The literature on these debates is seemingly endless, but is not especially edifying.

72. For recent data on the sectoral composition of forced divestments, see Stephen J. Kobrin, "Foreign Enterprise and Forced Divestment in LDCs," *International Organization* 34 (Winter 1980), 77–81; and Robert G. Hawkins, Norman Mintz, and Michael Provissiero, "Government Takeovers of U.S. Foreign Affiliates," *Journal of International Business Studies* 7 (Spring 1976), 9–10.

73. The regulation of technology transfers has been a central topic in North-South relations, and the subject of an extensive literature. The major issues are summarized in Robert G. Hawkins and A. J. Prasad, eds., *Research in International Business and Finance*, vol. 2: *Technology Transfer and Economic Development* (Greenwich, Conn.: JAI Press, 1981); and Miguel S. Wionczek, "Less Developed Countries and Transnational Corporations: Conflicts over Technology Transfer and Major Negotiable Issues," in *Some Key Issues for the World Periphery: Selected Essays*, ed. Miguel Wionczek (Oxford: Pergamon Press, 1982), 311–337.

74. Theodore H. Moran, "The Availability of Natural Resource Supplies in the 1980's: Political and Economic Considerations," *Korean Journal of International Studies* 13 (Winter 1981–1982), 37. The triangular relationship between raw-materials investment, industrial demand, and the extension of LDC state controls is taken up in Peter Dorner and Mahmoud A. El-Shafie, eds., *Resources and Development* (Madison: University of Wisconsin Press, 1980), and James H. Cobbe, *Governments and Mining Companies in Developing Countries* (Boulder, Colo.: Westview Press, 1979).

75. Reported in Lars Thunell, *Political Risks in International Business: Investment Behavior of Multinational Corporations* (New York: Praeger, 1977), 8.

76. Hickenlooper's speech is in the *Congressional Record*, 87th Cong., 2d sess., 1962, vol. 108, p. 9940; Humphrey's is in *Congressional Record*, 88th Cong., 1st sess., 1963, vol. 109, p. 2136.

77. Senator Frank Lausche, Democrat of Ohio, in *Congressional Record*, 88th Cong., 1st sess., 1963, vol. 109, p. 2136.

78. As Kai Erikson observes, "Deviance is not a property *inherent* in any particular kind of behavior; it is a property *conferred upon* that behavior." K. Erikson, *Wayward Puritans: A Study in the Sociology of Deviance* (New York: John Wiley, 1966), 6.

79. A. P. Cohen and J. L. Comaroff, "The Management of Meaning: On the Phenomenology of Political Transactions," in *Transaction and Meaning: Directions in the Anthropology of Exchange and Symbolic Behavior*, ed. Bruce Kapferer (Philadelphia: Institute for the Study of Human Issues, 1976), 102. This point, of course, echoes the general position of Habermas.

The idea that politics is fundamentally the management of meanings is strongly influenced by cultural and symbolic anthropology and, more recently, by semiotics. It is prominently featured in a number of nonpositivist approaches to social and political analysis. An extreme, and elegantly crafted, example is Clifford Geertz's *Negara: The Theatre State in Nineteenth Century Bali* (Princeton, N.J.: Princeton University Press, 1980). Also see the essays in *Interpretive Social Science: A Reader*, ed. Paul Rabinow and William M. Sullivan (Berkeley, Los Angeles, London: University of California Press, 1979).

80. John L. Comaroff and Simon Roberts, *Rules and Processes: The Cultural Logic of Dispute in an African Context* (Chicago: University of Chicago Press, 1981), 5; Sally Falk Moore, *Law as Process: An Anthropological Approach*, 3.

81. The same distinction between descriptive and prescriptive rules is made by Friedrich Kratochwil and by K. N. Llewellyn and E. Adamson Hoebel.

Llewellyn and Hoebel's path-breaking work in legal anthropology is important to us for other reasons as well. To understand primitive law among the Cheyenne Indians, they investigated what they called "trouble cases." These are instances of "hitch, dispute, grievance, trouble; and inquiry into what the trouble was and what was done about it" (p. 21). My own study of expropriation disputes and investment protection is similarly concerned with these italicized moments of conflict and with the broader social practices and expectations they highlight.

Friedrich A. Hayek, *Law, Legislation, and Liberty*, vol. 1: *Rules and Order* (Chicago: University of Chicago, 1973), 78–79; Friedrich V. Kratochwil, *International Order and Foreign Policy* (Boulder, Colo.: Westview Press, 1978), 26; K. N. Llewellyn and E. Adamson Hoebel, *The Cheyenne Way: Conflict and Case Law in Primitive Jurisprudence* (Norman: University of Oklahoma Press, 1941); E. Adamson Hoebel, *The Law of Primitive Man* (Cambridge, Mass.: Harvard University Press, 1954), 35.

Chapter Two: Expropriation and the Great Powers Before World War I

1. Georg Schwarzenberger, "The Protection of British Property Abroad," in *Current Legal Problems, 1952,* ed. George W. Keeton and Georg Schwarzenberger, vol. 5 (London: Stevens and Sons, 1952), 298.

2. Gillian White, *Nationalisation of Foreign Property* (New York: Praeger, 1961), 244.

3. William L. Griffin, "International Claims of Nationals of Both the Claimant and Respondent States—The Case History of a Myth," *International Lawyer* 1 (1967), 400. Griffin dates this practice to the 1794 treaty between the United States and Great Britain (the Jay Treaty).

4. Henry Steiner and Detlev Vagts, *Transnational Legal Problems: Materials and Text* (Mineola, N.Y.: The Foundation Press, 1968), 314. See also Loftus E. Becker, "Just Compensation in Expropriation Cases: Decline and Partial Recovery," *Proceedings of the American Society of International Law* (1959), 337; Jorge Castañeda, "The Underdeveloped Nations and the Development of International Law," *International Organization* 15 (Winter 1961), 39.

5. Frederick S. Dunn, *The Protection of Nationals: A Study in the Application of International Law* (Baltimore: Johns Hopkins Press, 1932), 1.

6. James R. Kurth, "Industrial Structure and Comparative Politics," unpublished paper, Swarthmore College, 1975, pp. 13–14. Also see Kurth, "The Political Consequences of the Product Cycle; Industrial History and Political Outcomes," *International Organization,* 33 (Winter 1979), 7–10.

7. D. C. M. Platt, *Finance, Trade, and Politics in British Foreign Policy, 1815–1914* (Oxford: Clarendon Press, 1968), 312–316; H. S. Ferns, *Argentina* (London: Ernest Benn, 1969), 45–55.

8. William Ashworth, "Review of D. C. M. Platt, *Finance, Trade, and Politics in British Foreign Policy, 1815–1914,*" *Economic History Review,* 2d series, 22 (April 1969), 143.

9. Schwarzenberger, "The Protection of British Property," 299.

10. D. C. M. Platt, "Further Objections to an 'Imperialism of Free Trade,' 1830–1860," *Economic History Review,* 2d series, 26 (April 1973), 88.

11. David McLean, "Commerce, Finance, and British Diplomatic Support in China, 1885–86," *Economic History Review,* 2d series, 26 (August 1973), 465. Platt makes a similar statement in *Finance, Trade, and Politics,* 351.

12. McLean (see n. 11), 464–476.

13. S. B. Saul, *Studies in British Overseas Trade, 1870–1914* (Liverpool: Liverpool University Press, 1960), 67. The accelerated investment of the 1860s and 1870s was cut short by the onset of the Great Depression of 1873–1894. The resurgence in the late 1880s was stopped by the Baring Crisis of 1890.

14. E. J. Hobsbawm, *Industry and Empire* (New York: Pantheon Books, 1968), 161 (emphasis in original). Gilpin's view, expressed in *U.S. Power and the Multinational Corporation,* is similar. Their position is challenged by Donald N. McCloskey and others in *Essays on a Mature Economy: Britain after 1840,* ed. D. N. McCloskey (London: Methuen, 1971).

15. Raymond Vernon, *Sovereignty at Bay* (New York: Basic Books, 1971), chap. 3; idem, "International Investment and International Trade in the Product Cycle," *Quarterly Journal of Economics,* 80 (May 1966), 190–207.

16. D. C. M. Platt, "The Imperialism of Free Trade: Some Reservations," *Economic History Review,* 2d series, 21 (August 1968), 306.

17. Platt, "Further Objections," 87.

18. Platt, "Economic Factors in British Policy During the 'New Imperialism'," *Past and Present* 39 (April 1968), 137.

19. John Gallagher and Ronald Robinson, "The Imperialism of Free Trade," *Economic History Review,* 2d series, 6 (1953); Robinson and Gallagher with Alice Denny, *Africa and the Victorians* (New York: St. Martin's, 1961), chap. 1.

20. McLean, 473.

21. Irving Stone, "British Direct and Portfolio Investment in Latin America Before 1914," *Journal of Economic History*, 37 (Sept. 1977), table 1, p. 694.

22. United Nations, Department of Economic and Social Affairs, Economic Commission for Latin America (ECLA), *External Financing in Latin America* (New York: U.N., 1965), 10. Also J. Fred Rippy, *British Investments in Latin America, 1822–1949* (Hamden, Conn.: Archon Books, 1959), 25.

23. S. M. Yassukovich, "The Growing Political Threat to International Lending," *Euromoney* (April 1976), 10.

24. Quoted in Rippy, *British Investments*, 199.

25. Herbert Spencer, "State Tamperings with Money and Banks," in *Essays: Scientific, Political, and Speculative*, vol. 3 (London: Williams and Norgate, 1891), 354.

26. Rippy, *British Investments*. Stone ("British Direct and Portfolio Investment"), who gives figures only for 1875 and 1885 (and not for 1880), seems to have somewhat higher loan figures. The proportion of government loans to total investments is similar to Rippy's calculations.

27. D. C. M. Platt, "British Bondholders in Nineteenth Century Latin America— Injury and Remedy," *Inter-American Economic Affairs* 14 (Winter 1960), 34. Platt's discussion of autonomous bondholder sanctions (pp. 30–35) is the basis for my own treatment.

28. Platt, "Economic Imperialism and the Businessman: Britain and Latin America before 1914," in *Studies in the Theory of Imperialism*, ed. R. Owens and B. Sutcliff (London: Longman Group, 1972), 137.

29. William Ashworth, *A Short History of the International Economy since 1850* (3d ed.; London: Longman Group, 1975), 211.

30. Rippy, *British Investments*, 38.

31. Interestingly, Venezuela initiated such a request in 1879 in order to secure a loan. A promise that the British would intervene in case of default would have effectively bolstered her credit. Salisbury refused the request. Platt, "British Bondholders," 36–37.

32. W. M. Mathew, "The Imperialism of Free Trade: Peru, 1820–70," *Economic History Review*, 2d series, 21 (December 1968), 568–574.

33. Ibid., 564–565.

34. The outbreak of civil war in Peru made both the British and the French reconsider their plans, even before the bond settlement. See Mathew, "Imperialism of Free Trade," 576–577.

35. Platt, *Finance, Trade, and Politics*, 337.

36. William H. Wynne, *State Insolvency and Foreign Bondholders*, vol. 2 (New Haven: Yale University Press, 1951), 149.

37. Calculated from Stone, "British Direct and Portfolio Investment," table 1, p. 694.

38. Rippy, *British Investments*, 32–35.

39. David Joslin, *A Century of Banking in Latin America* (London: Oxford University Press, 1963), 104; William Ashworth, *A Short History of the International Economy*, 207–209.

40. Although table 3 does not show British investments in public utilities immediately before World War I, the same ECLA study presents such figures elsewhere. They indicate that public utilities accounted for over 15 percent of all British investments in Latin America. Hence, utilities and railways together amounted to over 60 percent of British investment in 1914. The comparable figure for U.S. investment in Latin America is 30.9 percent. Calculated from ECLA, *External Financing*, 17.

41. Miguel S. Wionczek, "Mexican Nationalism, Foreign Private Investment, and Problems of Technology Transfer," in *Private Foreign Investment and the Developing World*, ed. Peter Ady (New York: Praeger, 1971), 191–192.

42. Peaceful means included diplomacy, arbitration, or reference to some international tribunal. A. J. Thomas, Jr., "Protection of Property of Citizens Abroad," *Pro-*

ceedings of the 1959 Institute on Private Investments Abroad, Southwestern Legal Foundation (New York: Mathew Bender, 1959), 421.

43. Luis M. Drago, *La Republic Argentina y el Caso de Venezuela* (Buenos Aires, 1903), 140–41, cited in Platt, "British Bondholders," 41.

44. Platt, *Finance, Trade, and Politics*, 319–320. Equity investment figures are nominal values, taken from Rippy, *British Investments*, 37.

45. Platt, *Finance, Trade, and Politics*, 335–336.

46. Mathew, "Imperialism of Free Trade," 578 (emphasis added).

47. Inis Claude, "Collective Legitimization as a Political Function of the United Nations," in *International Organization: Politics and Process*, ed. Leland M. Goodrich and David A. Kay (Madison: University of Wisconsin Press, 1973), 209; Murray Edelman, *The Symbolic Uses of Politics* (Urbana: University of Illinois Press, 1964); Karl Marx and Frederick Engels, *The German Ideology* (New York: International Publishers, 1939), 58–62.

Stable class structures, reinforced by ideological symbols with broad appeal, can transform the state's coercive social power into an invisible hand. *Yet the stability of that social structure can also presuppose the obscurity of force.*

Thus, the maintenance of class divisions sometimes depends on a legitimation process that imposes high costs and substantial risks upon the exercise of coercive power. George Orwell put the matter elegantly, as usual. English society, he said, was "ruled by the sword, no doubt, but a sword which must never be taken out of the scabbard."

48. White, *Nationalisation of Foreign Property*, 245.

49. J. Lloyd Mecham, *The United States and Inter-American Security* (Austin: University of Texas Press, 1961), 52–54; Norman A. Bailey, *Latin America in World Politics* (New York: Walker and Co., 1967), 48.

50. Walter LaFeber, *The New Empire* (paperback ed.; Ithaca, N.Y.: Cornell University Press, 1967), chap. 4; confirmed by A. E. Campbell, *Great Britain and the United States* (London: Longmans, Green and Co., 1960), 169. According to Campbell, "American business men came to be haunted in the 1890s by an industrial problem to which they saw no solution—that of overproduction." Campbell, however, thinks that China, not Latin America, was seen as the ultimate market solution.

51. Mira Wilkins has suggested that the advantages of local European production were significant enough to stimulate important manufacturing investments by American firms that had formerly exported to those markets. See Wilkins, *The Emergence of Multinational Enterprise: American Business Abroad from the Colonial Era to 1914* (Cambridge, Mass.: Harvard University Press, 1970), 65–66.

52. LaFeber, *The New Empire*. LaFeber observes that in 1895 American trade constituted only one-seventh of Latin America's total foreign commerce. Visions of the other six-sevenths aroused great expectations among American merchants and manufacturers. Enthusiasm ran highest in the cotton and woolen textile industries. Ibid., 186–189.

53. Figures compiled by Cleona Lewis in 1938 and cited in Wilkins, *The Emergence of Multinational Enterprise*, table V. 2, p. 110.

54. LaFeber, *The New Empire*, 91.

55. Burns H. Weston, "International Law and the Deprivation of Foreign Wealth: A Framework for Future Inquiry," in *The Future of the International Legal Order*, ed. Richard A. Falk and Cyril E. Black (Princeton, N.J.: Princeton University Press, 1970), 47.

56. Ibid., 47n.

57. ECLA, *External Financing*, 10, 14.

58. Ibid., 17.

59. Ibid.

60. The whole issue of British-United States conflict in Mexico is examined in Peter Calvert, *The Mexican Revolution, 1910–1914: The Diplomacy of Anglo-American Conflict* (Cambridge: Cambridge University Press, 1968). Perhaps the most important dispute between the two countries was the Venezuelan boundary dispute of the mid-1890s.

For a full account, see Campbell, *Great Britain and the United States*, 11–47, and LaFeber, *The New Empire*, 242–282. The settlement's repercussions linger to this day and threaten to explode now that Venezuela has discovered oil in territory claimed by Guyana.

61. LaFeber, *The New Empire*, 91.

62. J. Lloyd Mecham, *A Survey of United States-Latin American Relations* (Boston: Houghton Mifflin, 1965), 69; Samuel Flagg Bemis, *The Latin American Policy of the United States* (New York: Harcourt, Brace, and World, 1943), 151–152.

63. Dana Munro, *Intervention and Dollar Diplomacy in the Caribbean, 1900–1921* (Princeton, N.J.: Princeton University Press, 1964), 65.

64. Bemis, *Latin American Policy*, 153.

65. Mecham, *United States and Inter-American Security*, 66–67. Wilfrid H. Calcott, *The Caribbean Policy of the United States, 1890–1920* (Baltimore: Johns Hopkins Press, 1942; reprint ed., New York: Octagon Books, 1966), 135–136, 208.

Chapter Three: The Interwar Challenge to Traditional Rules

1. Friedrich Kratochwil, *International Order and Foreign Policy* (Boulder, Colo.: Westview Press, 1978), 4; Raymond Cohen, *International Politics: The Rules of the Game* (London: Longman, 1981), 8–9; and Bruce Andrews, "Social Rules and the State as a Social Actor," *World Politics* 27 (July 1975), 526–528.

2. Derek H. Aldcroft, *The Inter-War Economy: Britain, 1919–1939* (New York: Columbia University Press, 1970), 265.

3. Ibid., 264–266; Aldcroft and Harry W. Richardson, *The British Economy, 1870–1939* (London: Macmillan, 1969), 87.

4. Aldcroft, *The Inter-War Economy*, 264–266. According to Aldcroft, Britain's total foreign investment in 1929 was approximately £3.7–3.8 billion; the figure for the United States was about £3 billion.

5. Carl P. Parrini, *Heir to Empire: United States Economic Diplomacy, 1916–1923* (Pittsburgh: University of Pittsburgh Press, 1969), 152–171.

6. Ibid. Britain's relations with the new Soviet Republic are examined in detail in works by Richard Ullman and by Stephen White. Ullman, *Anglo-Soviet Relations, 1917–1921*, esp. vol. 3: *The Anglo-Soviet Accord* (Princeton, N.J.: Princeton University Press, 1972); and White, *Britain and the Bolshevik Revolution: A Study in the Politics of Diplomacy, 1920–1924* (New York: Holmes and Meier, 1979).

7. Joan Hoff Wilson, *Ideology and Economics: U.S. Relations with the Soviet Union, 1918–1933* (Columbia: University of Missouri Press, 1974), 165.

8. Mira Wilkins, *The Maturing of Multinational Enterprise* (Cambridge, Mass.: Harvard University Press, 1974), 87–88, 207, 233–234.

9. Samy Friedman, *Expropriation in International Law* (London: Stevens and Sons, 1953), 18–23.

10. White, *Nationalisation of Foreign Property*, 11.

11. Schwarzenberger, "The Protection of British Property Abroad," 298.

12. Friedman, *Expropriation in International Law*, 56.

13. Piotr S. Wandycz, *France and Her Eastern Allies, 1919–1925* (Minneapolis: University of Minnesota Press, 1962), 371–373, 387.

14. See the essays in *Political Modernization in Japan and Turkey*, ed. Robert E. War and Dankwart A. Rustow (Princeton, N.J.: Princeton University Press), 1964.

15. The phrase is Guillermo O'Donnell's. O'Donnell, "Comparative Historical Formations of the State Apparatus and Socio-Economic Change in the Third World," *International Social Science Journal* 32 (1980), 722.

16. Z. Y. Hershlag, *Introduction to the Modern Economic History of the Middle East*, 2d ed., 172–178.

17. Turkey's tariff levels were initially frozen by the Lausanne Treaty, but those provisions expired in 1929. Richard D. Robinson, *The First Turkish Republic* (Cambridge, Mass.: Harvard University Press, 1963), 106.

18. Hershlag, *Modern Economic History of the Middle East*, 179–190. The introductory paragraphs of the first Five-year Plan (drawn up in 1933 and begun the next year) read like a page from the modern dependency literature.

> This relation of dependence between the industrial countries of the West and the agricultural and primary producing countries created a state of affairs in which the industrial countries developed further and the primary producers gradually disintegrated. . . . The role of Turkey in the world commodity trade is to serve as an outlet for the industrial products of the West and, as an agricultural country, to provide raw materials to the same industry. . . . Despite the political and economic troubles and disagreements between them, the powerful industrial countries are basically in agreement in subjecting agricultural countries to a permanent status as primary producers and in dominating their internal markets.

Quoted in Korkut Boratav, "Kemalist Economic Policies and Étatism," in *Atatürk: Founder of a Modern State*, ed. Ali Kazancigil and Ergun Özbudun (Hamden, Conn.: Archon Books, 1981), 186.

19. Boratav, "Kemalist Economic Policies," 174; Max Weston Thornburg, Graham Spry, and George Soule, *Turkey: An Economic Appraisal* (New York: Twentieth Century Fund, 1949), 34.

20. Thornburg et al., *Turkey*, 34.

21. Ibid., 79.

22. James Brown Scott, ed., *The Hague Conventions and Declarations of 1899 and 1907* (2d ed.; New York: Oxford University Press, 1915), 89–95; James Brown Scott, *The Hague Peace Conferences of 1899 and 1907*, vol. 1 (Baltimore: Johns Hopkins Press, 1909), 392–422; Ian Brownlie, *International Law and the Use of Force by States* (London: Oxford University Press, 1963), 23–25; Gordon Connell-Smith, *The Inter-American System* (London: Oxford University Press, 1966); C. Neal Ronning, *Law and Politics in Inter-American Diplomacy* (New York: John Wiley and Sons, 1963), 47–52.

23. Konstantin Katzarov, *The Theory of Nationalisation* (The Hague: Martinus Nijhoff, 1964), 286.

24. Pitman Potter, "International Legislation on the Treatment of Foreigners," *American Journal of International Law* 24 (October 1930), 749; Arthur K. Kuhn, "The International Conference on the Treatment of Foreigners," *American Journal of International Law* 24 (July 1930), 571.

25. League of Nations, *Proceedings of the International Conference on Treatment of Foreigners*, 1st sess., Paris, November 5–December 5, 1929 (Geneva 1930), 268–274.

26. Green H. Hackworth, "Responsibility of States for Damages Caused in their Territory to the Person or Property of Foreigners: The Hague Conference for the Codification of International Law," *American Journal of International Law* 24 (July 1930), 500, 515; Edwin M. Borchard, "'Responsibility of States' at the Hague Codification Conference," *American Journal of International Law* 24 (July 1930), 538–539.

27. Bryce Wood, *The Making of the Good Neighbor Policy* (New York: Columbia University Press, 1961), chap. 7.

28. Howard F. Cline, *The United States and Mexico* (revised ed.; New York: Atheneum, 1971), 241.

29. Marvin D. Bernstein, *The Mexican Mining Industry, 1890–1950* (Albany: State University of New York, 1965), 181–186; Wood, *Good Neighbor Policy*, 223–233.

30. Bernstein, *The Mexican Mining Industry*, 186.

31. Ibid., 185.

32. Cline, *U.S. and Mexico*, 241; Wood, *Good Neighbor Policy*, 223–226. Bernstein (*The Mexican Mining Industry*) puts the percentage of U.S.-owned silver production in Mexico at 80 percent.

33. Platt, "Economic Imperialism and the Businessman: Britain and Latin America before 1914," 301.

34. Thomas, "Protection of Property of Citizens Abroad," 425–426.

35. Fereidun Fesharaki, *Development of the Iranian Oil Industry: International and Domestic Aspects* (New York: Praeger, 1976), 10.

Chapter Four: "The American Century": The Revival and Decline of International Property Rules

1. William Adams Brown, Jr., *The United States and the Restoration of World Trade* (Washington: Brookings Institution, 1950), 58, 97–104.

2. Clair Wilcox, *A Charter for World Trade* (New York: Macmillan, 1949), 146. See also William Diebold, Jr., *The End of the ITO* (Princeton, N.J.: Princeton University Essays in International Finance, no. 16, October 1952), 19.

3. Brown, *The U.S. and The Restoration of World Trade*, 153, 362, 366.

4. Charles G. Fenwick, "The Ninth International Conference of American States," *American Journal of International Law* 42 (July 1948), 561–562.

5. General Assembly Resolution 626 (VII), reprinted in *Yearbook of the United Nations, 1952* (New York: Columbia University Press in cooperation with the United Nations, 1953), 390.

6. Francisco Orrego Vicuña, "Some International Law Problems Posed by the Nationalization of the Copper Industry by Chile," *American Journal of International Law* 67 (1973), 721.

7. Stanley D. Metzger, "Private Foreign Investment and International Organizations," in *The Global Partnership*, ed. Richard N. Gardner and Max F. Millikan (New York: Praeger, 1968; originally published as *International Organization* 22 [Winter 1968]), 296.

8. General Assembly Resolution 3041/XXVII. According to one writer, this resolution was drafted by UNCTAD's Trade and Development Board. M. S. Rajan, "The United Nations and Sovereignty over Natural Resources," in *The Future of International Organization*, ed. Rüdiger Jütte and Annemarie Grosse-Jütte (New York: St. Martin's Press, 1981), 49fn.

9. Peter P. Gabriel, "The Multinational Corporation in the New International Economic Order," in *International Resource Flows*, ed. Gerald Garvey and Lou Ann Garvey (Lexington, Mass.: D. C. Heath, 1977), 65.

10. Richard Lillich, "The Diplomatic Protection of Nationals Abroad: An Elementary Principle of International Law Under Attack," *American Journal of International Law* 69 (April 1975), 359.

11. The idea that international law has several standard sources (which, of course, may not be internally consistent) is repeated in virtually all international legal texts and is included in the statutes of the International Court of Justice. See, for example, Michael Akehurst, *A Modern Introduction to International Law* (4th ed.; London: George Allen and Unwin, 1982), chap. 3; Ian Brownlie, *Principles of Public International Law* (2d ed.; Oxford: Clarendon Press, 1973), chap. 1; Statutes of the International Court of Justice, Article 38 (1). The legal status of U.N. resolutions is discussed in Hanna Bokor-Szego, *The Role of the United Nations in International Legislation* (Amsterdam: North-Holland Publishing Co., 1978).

12. John King Gamble, Jr. and Dana D. Fischer, *The International Court of Justice* (Lexington, Mass.: D. C. Heath, 1976), 51, 75.

13. Inis Claude, Jr., *The Changing United Nations* (New York: Random House, 1967), 88.

14. Claude, "Collective Legitimization as a Political Function of the United Nations," 212; Castañeda, "The Underdeveloped Nations and the Development of International Law," 43.

15. Stephen Zamora, "Voting in International Economic Organizations," *American Journal of International Law* 74 (July 1980), 566–608.

16. International Bank for Reconstruction and Development [the World Bank], *The World Bank, IDA, and IFC, Policies and Operations* (June 1969), 31, as quoted in Edward S. Mason and Robert E. Asher, *The World Bank Since Bretton Woods* (Washington: Brookings Institution, 1973), 338.

17. Mason and Asher, *The World Bank*, 338. For a contrasting view, see Truitt, *Expropriation of Private Foreign Investment*, 79–84.

18. International Monetary Fund, *1982 Annual Report*, Appendix IV, pp. 148–149.

19. "Mexico Issues Rules Affecting Foreign Firms," *Wall Street Journal*, October 13, 1982, p. 30; "Mexico Rattles the Multinationals," *Business Week*, October 4, 1982, p. 87.

20. "How Foreign Banks Still Get Rich in Brazil," *Business Week*, August 22, 1983, p. 102.

21. In the IMF's Articles of Agreement, article 1 defines the fund's purposes. These include the promotion of international monetary cooperation, the expansion of international trade, the maintenance of orderly exchange arrangements, and the correction of balance of payments problems "without resorting to measures destructive of national or international prosperity" (article 1[v]). One of the fund's basic purposes is "to assist in the establishment of a multilateral system of payments in respect of current transactions between members and in the elimination of foreign exchange restrictions which hamper the growth of world trade" (article 1 [iv]). For key documents on the fund, see J. Keith Horsefield, ed., *International Monetary Fund, 1945–1965*, vol. 3: *Documents* (Washington, D.C.: International Monetary Fund, 1969), esp. 187–209; and Margaret Garritsen de Vries, ed., *The International Monetary Fund, 1966–1971*, vol. 2: *Documents* (Washington, D.C.: International Monetary Fund, 1976).

22. When a country borrows heavily from the IMF, it must pledge to revise its economic policies in ways acceptable to the fund, a practice known as *conditionality.* These promises are set out in Letters of Intent, extremely sensitive documents that are never made public. Recently, however, an old agreement between the Italian Government and the IMF was published. The Italians specifically addressed the problem of capital restrictions in this 1974 document. For the time being, they said, they had to continue capital controls, including dual exchange-rate policies.

The adequacy of exchange controls to limit unauthorized capital outflows will be kept under review, but it is the firm intention of the Government not to introduce new restrictions on payments and transfers, or new multiple currency practices, for current international transactions, or new restrictions on imports. (Letter from Emilio Columbo, Italian Minister of the Treasury, to H. Johannes Witteveen, IMF Managing Director, reprinted in Luigi Spaventa, "Two Letters of Intent: External Crises and Stabilization Policy, Italy, 1973–1977," in *IMF Conditionality*, ed. John Williamson [Washington, D.C.: Institute for International Economics, 1983], 467.)

23. Harold van B. Cleveland and W. H. Bruce Brittain, "Are the LDCs In Over Their Heads?" *Foreign Affairs* 55 (July 1977), 749; Charles Lipson, "The IMF, Commercial Banks, and Third World Debts," in *Debt and the Less Developed Countries*, ed. Jonathan David Aronson (Boulder, Colo.: Westview Press, 1979), 317–333.

24. *Business Week*, August 22, 1977, p. 73.

25. "Faults in the Default System," *Economist*, August 27, 1983, p. 53.

26. Roger S. Leeds, "Co-Financing for Development: Why Not More?" Development Paper no. 29, Overseas Development Council, Washington, April 1980; Special Report on Co-Financing, *Asian Finance*, June 15, 1982, pp. 36ff; Don Babai, "Between

Hegemony and Poverty: The World Bank in the World Economy," manuscript, University of Maryland, 1983, pp. 204ff.

27. Quoted in Cheryl Payer, *The Debt Trap: The International Monetary Fund and the Third World* (New York: Monthly Review Press, 1974), 38.

28. For an elaboration of this point, see Ismaïl-Sabri Abdalla, "The Inadequacy and Loss of Legitimacy of the International Monetary Fund," *Development Dialogue* 2 (1980), 25–53.

29. Quoted in Seymour J. Rubin, *Private Foreign Investment* (Baltimore: Johns Hopkins Press, 1956), 75–76.

30. Herman Walker, Jr., "Modern Treaties of Friendship, Commerce and Navigation," *University of Minnesota Law Review* 42 (1958), 805–824; Walker, "Treaties for the Encouragement and Protection of Foreign Investment: Present United States Practice," *American Journal of Comparative Law* 5 (1956), 229–247; Kathleen Kunzer, "Developing a Model Bilateral Investment Treaty," *Law and Policy in International Business* 15 (1983), 276–277.

31. Kunzer, "Model Bilateral Investment Treaty," 281–282.

32. United Nations, General Assembly, Report of the Economic and Social Council, *Permanent Sovereignty Over Natural Resources* (A/9716) (New York: United Nations, September 1974), annex table 2.

33. Stephen J. Kobrin, "Foreign Enterprise and Forced Divestment in the LDCs," *International Organization* 34 (Winter 1980), 74.

34. Ibid., table 6, p. 82.

35. Robert R. Bowie, *Suez 1956: International Crisis and the Role of Law* (New York: Oxford University Press, 1974), 34.

36. George M. Ingram, *Expropriation of U.S. Property in South America* (New York: Praeger, 1974), 131–133.

37. Richard J. Barnet, *Intervention and Revolution* (revised ed., paperback; New York: New American Library, 1972), 269–276.

38. Yoshi Tsurumi, *The Japanese Are Coming: A Multinational Interaction of Firms and Politics* (Cambridge, Mass.: Ballinger Publishing Company, 1976), table 2–1, p. 38. Also see M. Y. Yoshino, *Japan's Multinational Enterprises* (Cambridge, Mass.: Harvard University Press, 1976), chap. 2.

39. Organisation for Economic Co-Operation and Development (OECD), *International Investment and Multinational Enterprises: Recent International Direct Investment Trends* (Paris: OECD, 1981), 9.

40. Data are from Japan's Ministry of Finance, International Financial Bureau, as cited in ibid., table 29, p. 80.

41. Data are from Bundesminister der Justiz, *Bundesanzeiger*, various issues, as cited in World Bank, *Private Direct Foreign Investment in Developing Countries*, Staff Working Paper no. 348, prepared by K. Billerbeck and Y. Yasugi (Washington, D.C.: World Bank, 1979), table SI.22, p. 87.

42. Mira Wilkins, *The Maturing of Multinational Enterprise: American Business Abroad from 1914 to 1970* (Cambridge, Mass.: Harvard University Press, 1974), 205.

43. Ibid., 408n.

44. Leslie L. Rood, "Foreign Investment in African Manufacturing," *Journal of Modern African Studies* 13 (March 1975), 24.

45. Ibid., 19–34; Waldemar A. Nielsen, *The Great Powers and Africa* (New York: Praeger, 1969), 25–127.

46. Colin Legum, "Foreign Intervention in Africa (I)" *Yearbook of World Affairs, 1980*, p. 87.

47. "France's Role in Africa: The Colonial Master Who Didn't Go Home," *Wall Street Journal*, July 22, 1981, p. 1.

48. "Former African Colonies Keep Strong French Ties," *New York Times*, national ed., April 18, 1983, p. 4.

49. *Wall Street Journal*, July 22, 1981, p. 1.

50. Organisation for Economic Co-operation and Development (OECD), *Geographical Distribution of Financial Flows to Developing Countries 1978/1981* (Paris: OECD, 1982), 72–73. Figures in text are for 1981.

51. Ibid., 118–119. The Ivory Coast's 1981 bilateral official development assistance was $106.6 million, of which France provided $77.5 million.

52. Ibid., 186–187.

53. Nielsen, *The Great Powers and Africa*, 44, 61.

54. U.N., *Permanent Sovereignty Over Natural Resources*, annex table 2.

55. Adebayo Adedeji, ed., *Indigenization of African Economies* (New York: Africana Publishing Co., 1981), especially Reginald Herbold Green, "Foreign Direct Investment and African Political Economy," 331–352.

56. U.N., *Permanent Sovereignty Over Natural Resources*, annex tables 1, 8.

57. Stephen J. Kobrin and Robert G. Hawkins, "An Analysis of Forced Divestments of Foreign Subsidiaries by Host Countries, 1960–1979," manuscript, New York University, table 1. As I noted earlier, Kobrin concentrates on "acts" of forced divestment as his basic unit of analysis. An "act" is defined as the forced divestment of *any* number of firms in a single industry (at the three-digit SIC level) in a single country in a single year.

58. Constantine V. Vaitsos, "The Changing Policies of Latin American Governments Toward Economic Development and Direct Foreign Investments," in *Latin American-U.S. Economic Interactions: Conflict, Accommodation, and Policies for the Future*, ed. Robert B. Williamson, William P. Glade, Jr., and Karl Schmitt (Washington: American Enterprise Institute for Public Policy Research, 1974), 95.

59. United Nations, Department of Economic and Social Affairs, Economic Commission for Latin America, *External Financing in Latin America* (New York: U.N., 1965), 148.

60. Dankwart A. Rustow, *Oil and Turmoil: America Faces OPEC and the Middle East* (New York: W. W. Norton, 1982), 78; Duane Chapman, *Energy Resources and Energy Corporations* (Ithaca, N.Y.: Cornell University Press, 1983), 84.

61. Rustow, *Oil and Turmoil*, 98.

62. Robert Stobaugh and Daniel Yergin, eds., *Energy Future* (3d ed.; New York: Vintage Books, 1983), 24.

63. Richard W. Cottam, *Nationalism in Iran* (Pittsburgh: University of Pittsburgh Press, 1964), 205.

64. Rustow, *Oil and Turmoil*, 98.

65. "End of an Era," *Petroleum Economist* 42 (January 1975), 22.

66. Peter F. Cowhey, "The Engineers and the Price System Revisited: The Future of the International Oil Corporations," in *Profit and the Pursuit of Energy: Markets and Regulation*, ed. Jonathan David Aronson and Peter F. Cowhey (Boulder, Colo.: Westview Press, 1983), 13.

67. Ibid., 9–52; Cowhey, *The Problems of Plenty: Energy Policy and International Politics* (Berkeley, Los Angeles, London: University of California Press, forthcoming); J. E. Hartshorn, "From Multinational to National Oil: The Structural Change," *Journal of Energy and Development* 5 (Spring 1980), 207–220. I am indebted to Peter Cowhey and Edward L. Morse for their discussions of the changing roles of international oil companies.

68. "Government oil firms gain spotlight," *International Petroleum Encyclopedia 1981* (Tulsa, Okla.: PennWell Publishing, 1981), 424–429; Peter Cowhey, "The Future of the International Oil Companies and the Probable Evolution of the World Energy System in the Eighties," in *World Hydrocarbon Markets*, ed. M. S. Wionczek (Oxford: Pergamon Press, 1983), 225–246; Edward L. Morse, "International Political Environment for Petroleum Investments," in Wionczek, *World Hydrocarbon Markets*, 251–252.

69. *International Petroleum Encyclopedia 1981*, 426.

70. Fadhil J. Al-Chalabi, *OPEC and the International Oil Industry: A Changing Structure* (Oxford: Oxford University Press on behalf of the Organization of Arab Petroleum

Exporting Countries, 1980), 7–31; Gustavo Coronel, *The Nationalization of the Vene-zuelan Oil Industry* (Lexington, Mass.: D. C. Heath, 1983).

71. Raymond Vernon, "International Investment and International Trade in the Product Life Cycle," *Quarterly Journal of Economics* 80 (1966), 190–207.

72. Obie G. Whichard, "Trends in the U.S. Direct Investment Position Abroad, 1950–1979," *Survey of Current Business* 61 (February 1981), table 1, p. 41; Whichard, "U.S. Direct Investment Abroad in 1981," *Survey of Current Business* 62 (August 1982), table 3, p. 13; Committee for Economic Development, *Transnational Corporations and Developing Countries: New Policies for a Changing World Economy* (New York: C.E.D., 1981), 80–83.

73. World Bank, *Private Direct Foreign Investment in Developing Countries*, table SI.6, p. 71.

74. Louis T. Wells, Jr., *Third World Multinationals: The Rise of Foreign Investment from Developing Countries* (Cambridge, Mass.: M.I.T. Press, 1983); Krishna Kumar and Maxwell G. McLeod, eds., *Multinationals from Developing Countries* (Lexington, Mass.: D. C. Heath, 1981).

. 75. Burns Weston, "International Law and the Deprivation of Foreign Wealth: A Framework for Future Inquiry," in *The Future of the International Legal Order*, ed. Richard A. Falk and Cyril E. Black (Princeton, N.J.: Princeton University Press, 1970), 47–49.

76. These calculations are made from figures in table 1, Robert G. Hawkins, Norman Mintz, and Michael Provissiero, "Government Takeovers of U.S. Foreign Affiliates," *Journal of International Business Studies* 7 (Spring 1976), 9.

77. John R. Freeman, "State Entrepreneurship and Dependent Development," *American Journal of Political Science* 24 (February 1982), 90–112; Douglas Bennett and Kenneth Sharpe, "The State as Banker and Entrepreneur: The Last Resort Character of the Mexican State's Economic Intervention, 1917–1970," in *Brazil and Mexico: Patterns in Late Development*, ed. Sylvia Ann Hewlett and Richard S. Weinert (Philadelphia: Institute for the Study of Human Issues, 1982), 169–211; Guillermo O'Donnell, "Comparative Historical Formations of the State Apparatus and Socio-Economic Change in the Third World," *International Social Science Journal* 32 (1980), 717–729.

These works revive, and significantly revise, the arguments developed in the late 1960s by Albert Hirschman. (Hirschman's work on "late, late industrialization" is itself a revision and extension of Alexander Gerschenkron's highly original work on economic development.)

The common thread through all these arguments is that the prior development of other national economies provides a crucial context for later developers—foreclosing some options, opening others, and significantly modifying the state's role in the industrialization process. Thus, all these works are sharply critical of development theories that ignore or belittle the international setting of national economies.

Hirschman, "The Political Economy of Import-Substituting Industrialization in Latin America," *Quarterly Journal of Economics* 82 (February 1968), 2–32; and Alexander Gerschenkron's essays reprinted in *Economic Backwardness in Historical Perspective* (Cambridge, Mass.: Harvard University Press, 1962) and *Continuity in History and Other Essays* (Cambridge, Mass.: Harvard University Press, 1968).

78. James F. Petras, "State Capitalism and the Third World," *Development and Change* 8 (1977), 5.

Norman Girvan, among others, makes a similar argument but uses class categories. Petras argues that traditional uses of class categories, such as Girvan's, are inadequate to comprehend the social character of many of these new states. Petras maintains that many important socioeconomic changes are primarily state projects and that in these cases the state's role cannot be understood "within classical class schemes." See Girvan, "Economic Nationalism," in *The Oil Crisis: In Perspective, Daedalus* 104 (Fall 1975), 151.

79. For examples of the arrangements concluded immediately after nationalization in the Middle East, see "New Roles for the Oil Giants," *Business Week*, May 28, 1975, pp. 52, 54; and three comprehensive articles in the *Petroleum Economist:* "From Conces-

sions to Contracts" (December 1974), 459–461; "End of an Era" (January 1975), 21–25; and "Implications of Nationalization" (April 1975), 122–123. Much of this discussion applies directly to raw-materials investments in Latin America.

These arrangements continue to evolve. In particular, producing countries have lessened their reliance on foreign firms for oil marketing, if not for exploration.

80. George Philip, *Oil and Politics in Latin America: Nationalist Movements and State Companies* (Cambridge: Cambridge University Press, 1982), 306.

81. Ibid., 307.

82. Pérez Guerrero, quoted in ibid., 306.

83. Valentín Hernández, quoted in ibid., 307–308.

84. *Dollars and Sense*, no. 18 (Summer 1976), 3.

85. Philip, *Oil and Politics*, 476; *Business Week*, February 28, 1983, pp. 61–62.

86. *Economist*, August 27, 1983, pp. 42–43; *Business Week*, September 12, 1983, pp. 56, 57, 60.

87. Ibid. The instrument for these spot sales is a Swiss company, Norbec, with mysterious ownership but an excellent source of supply: the Saudi oil ministry. In the summer of 1983, shortly after its founding, Norbec was selling some 200,000 to 300,000 barrels per day. These sales, according to *Business Week*, are "stirring fears among the four U.S. oil majors that make up Arabian American Oil Co. (Aramco) that Riyadh may be cutting them out of their lucrative role as marketers of most of Saudi Arabia's oil." Ibid., 56–57. If so, there would be a rough symmetry with the oil companies' actions. "Corporate relationships with some oil-producing nations are becoming a good deal less cozy," writes the *Wall Street Journal*. "After 50 years of loyalty, [the Aramco partners] last spring walked away from their commitments to buy Saudi oil because cheaper supplies were available elsewhere." *Wall Street Journal*, September 14, 1983, p. 21.

88. Theodore H. Moran, "Transnational Strategies of Protection and Defense by Multinational Corporations: Spreading the Risk and Raising the Cost for Nationalization in Natural Resources," *International Organization* 27 (Spring 1973), 273–287; idem, *Copper in Chile: Multinational Corporations and the Politics of Dependence* (Princeton, N.J.: Princeton University Press, 1974), 119–152.

89. This point is central to Peter Evans's account of MNCs in Brazil and receives support from more general studies such as Joseph LaPalombara and Stephen Blank, *Multinational Corporations in Comparative Perspective* (New York: Conference Board, 1977), 39–42. LaPalombara and Blank offer additional support for the proposition that American corporations are more reluctant to enter joint ventures than are European firms.

90. John M. Stopford and Louis T. Wells, Jr., *Managing the Multinational Enterprise* (New York: Basic Books, 1972), 119–123.

91. Lawrence G. Franko, *The European Multinationals* (Stamford, Conn.: Greylock Publishers, 1976), 120–121.

92. Data from the Harvard Multinational Enterprise Project, as reported in United Nations, *Transnational Corporations in World Development: A Reexamination* (New York: United Nations, 1978), 229. The Committee for Economic Development (CED) says that Japan's higher proportion of minority-owned affiliates is partly attributable to their latercomer status (they may have faced greater host-country pressures on that account) and because their investments are heavily concentrated in extractive industries, an area in which LDCs often insist on domestic majority ownership.

The CED, whose membership is composed of the largest multinational firms, says that these companies offer a variety of reasons for preferring majority or total ownership:

The most important is the desire to maintain centralized management and decision making for the parent system. Other reasons include the desire to avoid the dilution of equity returns, ensuring greater security for technological know-how, and concern about pressure from domestic shareholders for quick returns in the form of dividends when the firm might prefer to reinvest local earnings. Joint ownership is more acceptable to transnationals if they can maintain management control and if potential local partners are established and responsible business firms.

Committee for Economic Development, *Transnational Corporations and Developing Countries: New Policies for a Changing World Economy* (New York: CED, 1981), 35.

93. Yoshino, *Japan's Multinational Enterprises,* 124. Among manufacturing subsidiaries, joint ownership is especially prevalent. In nearly 90 percent of their manufacturing subsidiaries, the trading companies are minority partners.

94. U.N., *Transnational Corporations in World Development,* table III-25. Interview data on policies toward joint ventures are reported in Isaiah Frank, *Foreign Enterprise in Developing Countries,* a Supplementary Paper of the Committee for Economic Development (Baltimore: Johns Hopkins University Press, 1980), 64–70.

95. OECD, *International Investment and Multinational Enterprise,* 33.

96. Robert H. Swansbrough, "The Mineral Crisis and U.S. Interests in Latin America," *Journal of Politics* 38 (February 1976), 20.

97. William A. Stoever, *Renegotiations in International Business Transactions* (Lexington, Mass.: D. C. Heath, 1981); Mike Faber and Roland Brown, "Changing the Rules of the Game: Political Risk, Instability and Fairplay in Mineral Concession Contracts," *Third World Quarterly* 2 (January 1980), 100–119; and several articles in *Mining for Development in the Third World: Multinational Corporations, State Enterprises and the International Economy,* ed. S. Sideri and S. Johns (New York: Pergamon Press, 1980).

98. "Where the Constructors Strike it Rich," *Business Week,* August 23, 1976, pp. 46–56. Multinational investment by service industries such as construction has been studied far less than manufacturing and extractive industries. Yet it is rapidly growing and has far-reaching effects.

99. Kobrin, "Foreign Enterprise and Forced Divestment in the LDCs," table A.1, p. 87. Nine countries have each undertaken between eleven and fifteen acts of forced divestment. A half-dozen more have undertaken much more extensive divestment programs.

100. Paul E. Sigmund, *Multinationals in Latin America: The Politics of Nationalization* (Madison: University of Wisconsin Press for the Twentieth Century Fund, 1980), 170–173.

101. *New York Times,* June 22, 1982, p. 31, plus interviews.

102. Confidential interviews.

103. Sigmund, *Multinationals in Latin America,* 139–147.

104. David O. Beim, "Rescuing the LDCs," *Foreign Affairs* 55 (July 1977), 722.

105. Ignaz Seidl-Hohenveldern, "Chilean Copper Nationalization Cases before German Courts," *American Journal of International Law* 69 (June 1975), 110–119; Charles N. Brower, "The Future for Foreign Investment—Recent Developments in the International Law of Expropriation and Compensation," in *Private Investors Abroad—Problems and Solutions in International Business in 1975,* ed. Virginia Shook Cameron (New York: Matthew Bender, 1976), 166–167.

106. Hawkins, Mintz, and Provissiero, "Government Takeovers of U.S. Foreign Affiliates," table 1.

107. Kobrin, "Foreign Enterprise and Forced Divestment," 77.

108. For a technical discussion of legal claims on nationalized production outside the expropriating country, see Seidl-Hohenveldern, "Chilean Copper Nationalization Cases," and Evrett W. Benton, "The Libyan Expropriations: Further Developments on the Remedy of Invalidation of Title," *Houston Law Review* 11 (May 1974), 924–945.

109. Not surprisingly, the decline of American power has rekindled the Marxist debate over unity and rivalry among advanced capitalist states. A good summary of the contending viewpoints is Bob Rowthorn's "Imperialism in the Seventies—Unity or Rivalry?" *New Left Review,* no. 69 (September-October 1971), 31–54.

110. World Bank Blue Book on bank policy, as quoted in Sigmund, *Multinationals in Latin America,* 154.

111. "Bankrolling World Resources," *Business Week,* April 26, 1976, p. 32.

Chapter Five: The Sources of International Property Rules

1. Richard Lillich, "The Diplomatic Protection of Nationals Abroad: An Elementary Principle of International Law Under Attack," *American Journal of International Law* 69 (April 1975), 359–365.

2. René Albrecht-Carrié, *A Diplomatic History of Europe Since the Congress of Vienna* (revised ed.; New York: Harper and Row, 1973), 416. For a detailed study, see John Chalmers Vinson, *The Parchment Peace: The United States and the Washington Conference, 1921–1922* (Athens, Georgia: University of Georgia, 1955).

3. Robert Legvold, "The Nature of Soviet Power," *Foreign Affairs* 56 (October 1977), 56.

4. Robert Gilpin, *U.S. Power and the Multinational Corporation* (New York: Basic Books, 1975), 19.

5. James G. March, in particular, has pointed out the predictive difficulties associated with what he calls "simple force models." Such models, which rely on measurable indices of power, cannot adequately account for shifts in power or for variations in its use. Drawing on March's account, Robert O. Keohane argues that such models are nevertheless valuable "in suggesting long-term trends and patterns" even if they cannot account well for specific outcomes. Keohane, "Theory of World Politics: Structural Realism and Beyond," in *Political Science: The State of the Discipline*, ed. Ada W. Finifter (Washington, D.C.: American Political Science Association, 1983), 522–523; James G. March, "The Power of Power," in *Varieties of Political Theory*, ed. David Easton (Englewood Cliffs, N.J.: Prentice-Hall, 1966), 56–57.

6. For the origins of the Corporation of Foreign Bondholders, see Leland H. Jenks, *The Migration of British Capital to 1875* (New York: Harper and Row, 1973; first published 1927), 288–291.

7. Neil H. Jacoby, *Multinational Oil* (New York: Macmillan, 1974), 120.

8. *Business Week*, July 28, 1980, p. 83.

9. The importance of this political backing is argued most convincingly by Robert Gilpin and Stephen Krasner. For a succinct statement of Gilpin's views, see "The Politics of Transnational Economic Relations," *International Organization* 25 (Summer 1971), 389–419. Stephen D. Krasner, "U.S. Commercial and Monetary Policy: Unravelling the Paradox of External Strength and Internal Weakness," *International Organization* 31 (Autumn 1977), 635–671.

10. The evolution of postwar trade arrangements is discussed in Charles Lipson, "The Transformation of Trade: The Sources and Effects of Regime Change," *International Organization* 36 (Spring 1982), 417–455.

11. Peter B. Evans, "Industrialization and Imperialism: Growth and Stagnation on the Periphery," *Berkeley Journal of Sociology* 20 (1975–1976), 121.

12. World Bank, *Private Direct Foreign Investment in Developing Countries*, Staff Working Paper no. 348, prepared by K. Billerbeck and Y. Yasugi (Washington, D.C.: World Bank, 1979), 10.

13. Lawrence G. Franko, "What Has Become of the American Challenge," *Challenge* (March-April 1980), 50.

14. Lawrence G. Franko, "Multinationals: The End of U.S. Dominance," *Harvard Business Review* 56 (November-December 1978), 96. Complementary data are presented by Robert B. Stobaugh, "Competition Encountered by U.S. Companies that Manufacture Abroad," *Journal of International Studies* 8 (Spring-Summer 1977), 33–43.

15. Wilkins, *The Maturing of Multinational Enterprise*, 65, 156, 204, 234–236, 260.

16. Wilkins, "The Oil Companies in Perspective," in *The Oil Crisis*, ed. Raymond Vernon (New York: W. W. Norton, 1976), 160–161.

17. Russell Hardin, *Collective Action* (Baltimore: Johns Hopkins University Press for Resources for the Future, 1982), 174.

18. Interviews with executives from regional banks.

19. Theodore H. Moran, "Transnational Strategies of Protection and Defense by

Multinational Corporations," *International Organization* 27 (Spring 1973), 273–287.

20. Robert Swansbrough, "The Mineral Crisis and U.S. Interests in Latin America," *Journal of Politics* 38 (February 1976), 20.

21. Peter J. Katzenstein, "International Relations and Domestic Structures: Foreign Economic Policies of Advanced Industrial States," *International Organization* 30 (Winter 1976), 1–45; Katzenstein, "Conclusion: Domestic Structures and Strategies of Foreign Economic Policy," *International Organization* 31 (Autumn 1977), 879–920.

22. Krasner, "U.S. Commercial and Monetary Policy," 645.

23. These differences in state structure—their sources and consequences—have become increasingly important for comparative policy studies. See, for example, John Ikenberry, "International Change, State Structure and Policy Response: U.S. Energy Adjustment Strategy in Comparative Perspective," unpublished paper, 1983 American Political Science Association Convention; and John Zysman, *Governments, Markets, and Growth: Financial Systems and the Politics of Industrial Change* (Ithaca, N.Y.: Cornell University Press, 1983), esp. chap. 1.

24. William H. Branson, "Trends in United States International Trade and Investment since World War II," in *The American Economy in Transition,* ed. Martin Feldstein (Chicago: University of Chicago Press for the National Bureau of Economic Research, 1980), table 3.8, p. 191.

25. World Bank, *World Development Report 1983* (New York: Oxford University Press, 1983), table 9, p. 165.

26. World Bank, *World Development Report 1983,* table 18, p. 182; John W. Sewell, *The United States and World Development, Agenda 1977* (New York: Praeger Publishers for the Overseas Development Council, 1977), 230, 232, 234.

27. The proposal was made by Paul M. Goldberg and Charles Kindleberger in "Toward a GATT for Investment: A Proposal for Supervision of the International Corporation," *Law and Policy in International Business* 2 (Summer 1970), 295–325. For an extensive analysis of multinational corporations and international controls, see Robert O. Keohane and Van Doorn Ooms, "The Multinational Firm and International Regulation," *International Organization* 29 (Winter 1975).

28. *Wall Street Journal,* November 5, 1982, p. 28; *Business Week,* October 18, 1982, p. 70; *New York Times,* January 18, 1982, p. 23.

29. For a legal analysis of ICSID, see Joy Cherian, *Investment Contracts and Arbitration: The World Bank Convention on the Settlement of Investment Disputes* (Leiden: A. W. Sijthoff, 1975).

30. Charles R. Frank, Jr., and Mary Baird, "Foreign Aid: Its Speckled Past and Future Prospects," in *World Politics and International Economics,* ed. C. Fred Bergsten and Lawrence B. Krause (Washington: Brookings Institution, 1975), 163.

31. IBRD, Operation policy memorandum 1.01 (March 31, 1971), p. 3, as quoted in Edward S. Mason and Robert E. Asher, *The World Bank Since Bretton Woods* (Washington: Brookings Institution, 1973), 746. Mason and Asher later note that expropriation "without adequate compensation can hardly fail to affect adversely the credit standing of the expropriating country." Ibid., 748.

32. Mason and Asher, *The World Bank,* 338.

33. Ibid., 746.

34. Ibid., 157.

35. Ibid., 337.

36. Ibid.

37. The basic policies of the World Bank and the IMF are critically assessed in Cheryl Payer, *The Debt Trap: The International Monetary Fund and the Third World* (New York: Monthly Review Press, 1974), and Teresa Hayter, *Aid as Imperialism* (Harmondsworth, Middlesex, U.K.: Penguin Books, 1971).

38. U.S., Congress, Senate, Committee on Banking, Housing, and Urban Affairs, *Hearings on International Debt,* 95th Cong., 1st sess., 1977, p. 127.

39. Samuel P. Huntington, *Political Order in Changing Societies* (New Haven: Yale University Press, 1968), 12.

40. Frank and Baird, "Foreign Aid," 162–163.

41. Payer, *The Debt Trap,* chap. 9.

42. I wish to thank Robert Z. Aliber for his useful comments on U.S. policy in debt renegotiations.

43. *Wall Street Journal,* September 14, 1983, p. 34.

44. *Wall Street Journal,* August 30, 1983, p. 8.

45. Harold van B. Cleveland and W. H. Bruce Brittain, "Are the LDCs in over their Heads?" *Foreign Affairs* 55 (July 1977), 749.

46. Leslie Rood, "Nationalisation and Indigenisation in Africa," *Journal of Modern African Studies* 14 (September 1976), 435–436. Richard L. Sklar makes a similar point about Zambia's nationalization of Anglo-American Corporation Group's mineral rights. Sklar, *Corporate Power in an African State* (Berkeley, Los Angeles, London: University of California Press, 1975), 36.

47. Tim McDaniel, "Class and Dependency in Latin America," *Berkeley Journal of Sociology* 21 (1976–1977), 75.

48. David G. Bradley discusses these issues and recommends adaptive corporate strategies in "Managing against Expropriation," *Harvard Business Review* 55 (July-August 1977), 75–83.

49. Miguel S. Wionczek, "Mexican Nationalism, Foreign Private Investment and Problems of Technology Transfer," in *Private Foreign Investment and the Developing World,* ed. Peter Ady (New York: Praeger Publishers, 1971), 199.

50. Burns Weston, "International Law and the Deprivation of Foreign Wealth," in *The Future of the International Legal Order,* vol. 2: *Wealth and Resources,* ed. Richard A. Falk and Cyril E. Black (Princeton, N.J.: Princeton University Press, 1970), 177.

51. John Zysman, "The French State in the International Economy," *International Organization* 31 (Autumn 1977), 839–877.

52. Raymond Vernon, *Storm over the Multinationals: The Real Issues* (Cambridge, Mass.: Harvard University Press, 1977), 39–58.

53. *Business Latin America,* October 29, 1970, p. 345; Michael G. Duerr, *The Problems Facing International Management* (New York: Conference Board, 1974), 5.

54. Theodore H. Moran, ed., *International Political Risk Assessment: The State of the Art,* Landegger Papers in International Business and Public Policy (Washington, D.C.: Georgetown School of Foreign Service, [1981]); Stephen J. Kobrin, "Assessing Political Risk Overseas," *Wharton Magazine* 6 (Winter 1981–1982), 25–31; Stephen Blank, John Basek, Stephen J. Kobrin, and Joseph LaPalombara, *Political Environment Assessment: An Emerging Corporate Function* (New York: The Conference Board, 1980).

55. M. Abdel-Fadil, Francis Cripps, and John Wells, "A New International Economic Order?" *Cambridge Journal of Economics* (1977), 207.

56. Edward L. Morse, "Modernization and the New Economic Nationalism," unpublished paper, 1977 International Studies Association Convention, p. 2.

57. Quoted in Tony Smith, "Changing Configurations of Power in North-South Relations since 1945," *International Organization* 31 (Winter 1977), 5.

58. Ibid.

59. Jahangir Amuzegar, "A Requiem for the North-South Conference," *Foreign Affairs* 56 (October 1977), 140.

60. Carlos Fortin, "The State, MNCs and Natural Resources in Latin America," *IDS Bulletin* [Institute of Development Studies, University of Sussex] 9 (July 1977), 51.

61. D. C. M. Platt, "Further Objections to an 'Imperialism of Free Trade', 1830–1860," *Economic History Review* 2d series, 26 (August 1973), 88.

62. Stephen D. Krasner presents and defends this model in "State Power and the Structure of International Trade," *World Politics* 28 (April 1976), 317–347.

63. Weston, "International Law and The Deprivation of Foreign Wealth," 47n.

Chapter Six: Foreign Aid Sanctions and Investment Protection

1. Robert W. Tucker, *The Radical Left and American Foreign Policy* (Baltimore: Johns Hopkins Press, 1971), 21.

2. *Foreign Assistance Act of 1962,* 76 Stat. 260–261, sec. 301 (d) (3) [1962].

3. *Foreign Assistance Act of 1963*, 77 Stat. 386–387, sec. 310 (e) (2) [1963].

4. *Asian Development Bank Act Amendments*, 86 Stat. 57 (1972); *Inter-American Development Bank Act Amendments*, 86 Stat. 59 (1972); *International Development Association Act Amendments*, 86 Stat. 60 (1972).

5. They were right. Foreign investments were remarkably safe during the 1950s, as my analysis in Part I showed. At the time of the Cuban expropriations, there was only one outstanding dispute. In 1959, the Brazilian state of Rio Grande do Sul had taken over the American and Foreign Power Company. Compensation talks had been fruitless, and the dispute festered into the early 1960s.

6. Many academic writers shared this concern; for instance, Frank Tannenbaum, *Ten Keys to Latin America* (New York: Knopf, 1962), 234–235. Representative Henry Gonzalez has said that his anti-expropriation amendments were inspired by Tannenbaum's work.

7. Jacob J. Kaplan, *The Challenge of Foreign Aid* (New York: Praeger, 1967), 181, 303–310. The encouragement of direct foreign investment, and its justification as a powerful lever of development, is a staple of American foreign policy. Only one recent president, Jimmy Carter, has taken a more equivocal position. The Carter administration's position was undoubtedly influenced by organized labor's strong opposition to the international transfer of manufacturing jobs. The Reagan administration, in contrast, has not only resumed the promotion of foreign investment (America's traditional policy), it has made it the very cornerstone of its foreign aid program. The Reagan administration announced this policy at the very outset and featured it prominently in its most important aid package: the Caribbean Basin Initiative. President Reagan reiterated this fundamental policy in September 1983 when he declared a new diplomatic initiative to roll back the proliferating foreign regulations on multinational firms. *Wall Street Journal*, April 14, 1981, p. 48, and September 22, 1981, p. 5; *Business Week*, April 5, 1982, pp. 40, 42; *New York Times*, September 10, 1983, p. 23.

8. Herbert Feis, *Foreign Aid and Foreign Policy* (New York: St. Martin's Press, 1964), 132.

9. *Congressional Record*, 86th Cong., 1st sess., 1959, vol. 105, pp. 12583–12587, 12956–12960.

10. *Mutual Security Act of 1959*, 73 Stat. 252, sec. 401 (a) [1959].

11. Jerome Levinson and Juan de Onís, *The Alliance That Lost Its Way* (Chicago: Quadrangle Books, 1970), 71–73; Edward S. Mason, *Foreign Aid and Foreign Policy* (New York: Harper and Row, 1964), 88–90.

12. Levinson and de Onís, *The Alliance That Lost Its Way*, 144. AID acknowledged that the expropriations had seriously undermined the "climate" for foreign investment in Brazil. According to a 1962 AID report, the outlook for foreign investment there was "not encouraging." U.S., Congress, House, Committee on Foreign Affairs, *Hearings on the Foreign Assistance Act of 1962*, 87th Cong., 2d sess., pt. III, p. 512.

13. A similar, but much more extensive, dispute had occurred in Cuba three years earlier. International oil companies had refused the Cuban government's directive to refine Soviet crude; as a result they were among the first foreign companies to be expropriated.

14. Wilkins, *The Maturing of Multinational Enterprise: American Business Abroad from 1914 to 1970*, pp. 371–372.

15. The companies' economic apprehension was obscured by appeals to anticommunist values. See, for example, the speech by Senator A. S. Monroney, American Petroleum Institute, *1961 Proceedings* 41 (New York: American Petroleum Institute, 1961), sec. I, p. 12.

16. Memorandum for the President from Dean Rusk, Secretary of State, May 27, 1963, pp. 4–5 (President's Office Files, Countries, Ceylon, 1963, John F. Kennedy Library, Boston).

17. Memorandum for McGeorge Bundy from the Department of State, April 5, 1963 (President's Office Files, Countries, Ceylon, 1963, John F. Kennedy Library, Boston).

18. The expropriation dispute in Ceylon was settled only after a new government

was elected in 1965. The dispute had taken a heavy toll. According to a U.S. Department of Commerce publication, *International Commerce*, the expropriations not only cut off U.S. aid, they badly damaged Ceylon's credit from other sources and became "a serious impediment to a flow of capital from Western countries." By early 1965, the country's liquid reserves equaled only one week's imports. All this appears in an article appropriately entitled "Ceylon Has a New Look: New Government Has Given Business Climate a Decided Turn for the Better," by Jackson Hearn, in U.S., Department of Commerce, *International Commerce* 72 (September 19, 1966), 7–9.

19. Raymond Vernon, *Sovereignty at Bay: The Multinational Spread of U.S. Enterprises* (New York: Basic Books, 1971), 46–53; Vernon, *Storm over the Multinationals* (Cambridge, Mass.: Harvard University Press, 1977), 151. These obsolete bargains were radically transformed during the 1970s, often by forced divestments, with disproportionate effects on natural-resource industries. Vernon himself was surprised by the rapidity with which these old bargains were overturned. As he later wrote, "What prevented me (and practically every other scholar at the time) from fully applying the lesson of the obsolescing bargain to the situation of the oil companies was our inability to appreciate that a profound shift in the supply-demand balance was taking place, which might reduce the need of the oil-exporting countries to rely on the marketing channels of the multinationals." This suggests, quite rightly, that historically contingent factors can reinforce (or countervail) the "obsolescing bargain." Vernon, "Sovereignty at Bay Ten Years After," *International Organization* 35 (Summer 1981), 521–522.

20. Theodore Moran, "Transnational Strategies of Protection and Defense by Multinational Corporations: Spreading the Risk and Raising the Cost for Nationalization in Natural Resources, "*International Organization* 27 (Spring 1973), 273–278.

21. Unfortunately, most respondents would discuss lobbying efforts and interdepartmental disputes only if they were promised anonymity. Participants in these interviews were members of the State Department, Treasury, AID, Council on International Economic Policy, congressional committees (members and staff), presidential commissions on foreign aid, and several corporations and business organizations.

One important exception to this norm of confidentiality was George Pavlik, Senator Hickenlooper's aide, with whom a telephone interview was conducted. Asked which corporations had actively worked for the Hickenlooper amendment, he cited the firms listed in the text, all of which were confirmed in confidential interviews.

To some extent the serious scholarly problems presented by confidential interviews can be mitigated by carefully searching the public record. For example, Standard Oil (N.J.) took the most unusual step of praising the Hickenlooper amendment in its *1962 Annual Report*. Harold Geneen's role is discussed by the *New York Times*, May 11, 1962, p. 51, and by Anthony Sampson, *The Sovereign State of ITT* (New York: Stein and Day, 1973), 262. The National Foreign Trade Council (NFTC) openly attacked any social reforms, including agrarian reforms, which did not include "prompt, adequate, and effective compensation." The NFTC Convention Recommendations applauded the Hickenlooper amendment in 1962 and its extension the following year. See National Foreign Trade Council, *Report of the Forty-Ninth National Foreign Trade Convention, 1962* (New York: NFTC, 1963), xx–xxii; NFTC, *Report of the Fiftieth National Foreign Trade Convention* (New York: NFTC, 1964), xliv. Kennecott's role in the amendment's 1963 extension is suggested in the *Congressional Record*, 88th Cong., 1st sess., 1963, vol. 109, p. 21762.

22. Telephone interview with John Newhouse, September 1974.

23. *Congressional Record*, 88th Cong., 1st sess., 1963, vol. 109, p. 2136; *Congressional Record*, 93rd Cong., 1st sess., 1973, vol. 119, p. 26189.

24. *New York Times*, May 13, 1962, sec. III, p. 1.

25. The same corporate and legislative alignments produced a Hickenlooper-style amendment to the 1962 Sugar Act, denying expropriating nations a U.S. sugar quota. *Sugar Act Amendments of 1962*, 76 Stat. 166, sec. 15 [1962].

26. U.S., President, *Public Papers of the Presidents of the United States: John F. Kennedy, 1962* (Washington: Government Printing Office, 1963), March 7, 1962, p. 203.

27. The President's Office Files, Legislative File, 1962–1963, in the John F. Kennedy

Library, Waltham, Mass., show, in 1962, thirteen references to the Hickenlooper amendment, two to the Sugar amendment; in 1963, only one reference to the Hickenlooper amendment.

28. The State Department clearly recognized the amendment's inconsistency with redistributive reform. See U.S., Congress, Senate, Committee on Foreign Relations, *Foreign Assistance Act of 1962: Hearings on S. 2996* [hereafter referred to as *1962 Senate Hearings*], 87th Cong., 2d sess., p. 558.

29. Confidential interviews, confirmed by Theodore S. Brewer, "The Hickenlooper Amendment and Congressional-Executive Relations in Foreign Aid Policy," B.A. thesis (Amherst College, 1968), 59–66. As evidence of United Fruit's successful efforts at building this transnational coalition, Brewer cites interviews with now-retired company officials (named in his paper). See also William S. Stokes, "Honduras: Problems and Prospects," *Current History* 50 (January 1966), 23–24, which stresses the political effectiveness of United Fruit's reduced production.

30. *Congressional Record*, 87th Cong., 2d sess., 1962, vol. 108, pp. 21615–21621. At the same time, the Senate Appropriations Committee issued a report urging strict interpretation of the Hickenlooper amendment. See U.S., Senate, Appropriations Committee, *Foreign Aid and Related Agencies Appropriations Bill, 1963: Report to Accompany H.R. 13175*, 87th Cong., 2d sess., 1962, Sen. Rept. 2177, pp. 22–23.

31. Exploration contracts were held by Standard Oil (N.J.), Union, Continental, Marathon, and Shell; development contracts by Pan American, Tennessee, Astra and Cadipsa, and Cities Service. Abram Chayes, Thomas Ehrlich, and Andreas Lowenfeld, *International Legal Process* (Boston: Little, Brown, 1969), vol. 2, 827.

32. U.S., Congress, Senate, Committee on Foreign Relations, *Foreign Assistance Act of 1963: Report on H.R. 7885*, 88th Cong., 1st sess., 1963, Sen. Rept. 588, p. 291.

33. U.S., Congress, Senate, Committee on Foreign Relations, *Foreign Assistance Act of 1963: Hearings on S. 1276* [hereafter referred to as *1963 Senate Hearings*], 88th Cong., 1st sess., 1963, p. 30.

34. Memorandum [hereafter referred to as "Bell Memorandum"], November 2, 1963, p. 2 (President's Office Files, Departments and Agencies, AID, 1963, John F. Kennedy Library).

35. *1962 Senate Hearings*, 557.

36. Ibid., 558.

37. "Bell Memorandum," 1–2. In a prescient analysis of the Peru-IPC dispute, the State Department also argued that a company's behavior could provoke expropriation and prevent settlement. Even if other corporations considered the proposed settlement reasonable, they could not force the corporation to accept it and, hence, could not prevent automatic sanctions which might damage their own firms. In 1962 this argument was abstract and ineffective.

38. The 1963 additions completed the amendment's foreign aid sanctions. A 1964 addition, the Sabbatino amendment, was directed solely at the U.S. courts' refusal to adjudicate certain foreign investment disputes. Sabbatino is the subject of considerable legal scholarship.

39. *1963 Senate Hearings*, 273.

40. Memorandum for the President from Dean Rusk, Secretary of State, May 27, 1963, p. 1 (President's Office Files, Countries, Ceylon, 1963, John F. Kennedy Library).

41. Though potential sanctions included both bilateral aid and the sugar quota, they were commonly grouped together as the "Hickenlooper amendment."

42. Two contributors to Daniel Sharp's *U.S. Foreign Policy and Peru* reached different conclusions. John Powelson claims that "even IPC has not insisted on the application of Hickenlooper." Sharp, ed., *U.S. Foreign Policy and Peru* (Austin: University of Texas Press, 1972), 147. Charles Goodsell maintains that the company *did* want the amendment invoked. Ibid., 251–252. On the basis of confidential interviews, I would agree with both Powelson and Goodsell that there were important divisions within Jersey Standard, but conclude that the company initially preferred the amendment's use and later changed positions.

43. Paul Sigmund, who has studied nationalizations throughout Latin America,

explicitly rejects my conclusion. "Lipson," he says in a footnote, "sees the nonappli-cation of Hickenlooper as proof of the influence of business on United States policy—a proposition that, in view of the divisions in business attitudes, is impossible to prove or disprove." In his text, however, Sigmund demonstrates no such division in business attitudes. Quite the contrary. He shows that other U.S. companies in Peru had distanced themselves from IPC and opposed sanctions. And he agrees that Jersey Standard was internally divided. That is exactly what I found in confidential interviews with U.S. executives and policymakers. I found, in Sigmund's own words, that other U.S. com-panies in Peru "had no love for IPC, which they considered to have behaved badly in the past. They were reluctant to see the rest of the American business community suffer for IPC's transgressions. Esso itself was divided on the wisdom of applying the Hickenlooper amendment." That is hardly a divisive set of business attitudes. It permits us to make a quite straightforward inference (in terms of the radical hypothesis) that foreign aid sanctions would not be invoked in Peru.

Subsequently, ITT, Grace, and others were also expropriated. Their demands for overt sanctions met overwhelming opposition from most U.S. corporations in Peru. U.S. policy remained unchanged, as does our conclusion.

Sigmund, *Multinationals in Latin America*, 365fn. (first quote), 193 (second quote).

44. Gulf's chairman was once quoted as advocating use of the Hickenlooper amend-ment. *New York Times*, October 31, 1969, p. 63. However, according to interviewees in Congress and the administration, Gulf did not seek to have the U.S. apply the amendment in Bolivia, and later opposed Hickenlooper-type laws.

45. Nelson Rockefeller made this point when he testified that Hickenlooper sanc-tions in Peru would endanger Texaco in Ecuador, an exact reversal of the amendment's deterrent logic. U.S., Congress, Senate, Committee on Foreign Relations, *Hearings on the Rockefeller Report on Latin America*, 91st Cong., 1st sess., 1969, p. 29.

46. Robert H. Swansbrough, "The American Investor's View of Latin American Economic Nationalism," *Inter-American Economic Affairs* 26 (Winter 1972), tables 5 and 7.

47. U.S., President, National Security Council, Memorandum no. 131.

48. Quote is from President Nixon's January "Statement Announcing United States Policy on Economic Assistance and Investment Security in Developing Nations," in U.S., President, *Public Papers of the Presidents of the United States: Richard M. Nixon, 1972* (Washington: Government Printing Office, 1974), January 19, 1972, p. 33. For a knowledgeable analysis of the bureaucratic politics of the President's decision, see Jessica Pernitz Einhorn, *Expropriation Politics* (Lexington, Mass.: D. C. Heath, 1974), esp. chap. 5.

49. Nathan Haverstock, "End to Retaliatory Legislation Sought," *Mexican American Review* 41 (November 1973), 13.

50. Letter to Peter Peterson, Executive Director of the Council on International Economic Policy, from José de Cubas, President, Council of the Americas, August 27, 1971, cited by Einhorn, *Expropriation Politics*, 107.

51. Though the Council later sent Senator Fulbright a letter suggesting opposition to new sanctions, it did not play an active legislative role until the bilateral amendments a year later.

52. U.S., Congress, House, Committee on Foreign Affairs, *The Overseas Private In-vestment Corporation*, 93rd Cong., 1st sess., 1973, Committee Print, p. 18.

53. Because Gonzalez's move was not elaborately planned, the heavy vote in his favor amply demonstrates the House's general ideological preference for hard-line measures. This substitute amendment was not prepared by his staff; according to several sources, it was probably drafted by Washington counsel to a major international oil firm.

54. Council of the Americas, *Newsletter*, December 26, 1973, p. 2.

55. Treasury forced a decision at the presidential level. Nixon supported State and the Council of the Americas, but he also wanted to avoid raising the issue's salience. Thus, his decision was "not for attribution."

56. *Foreign Assistance Act of 1973*, 87 Stat. 722, sec. 15 [1973].

57. Even though the Hickenlooper amendment had been effectively repealed, its approach still had some congressional support. Its final expression was an amendment to the 1974 Trade Act.

One provision in the Trade Act allowed some LDCs to export certain products to the United States under specially reduced tariffs (the so-called Generalized System of Preferences). A Hickenlooper-style amendment was added to block these preferences for countries nationalizing U.S. property or nullifying contracts without prompt, adequate, and effective compensation, or at least good-faith efforts to negotiate such compensation. But this amendment, like the diluted Hickenlooper amendment, permitted presidential determination of all these issues. Thus, it differed crucially from the original Hickenlooper amendment of the early 1960s, which allowed the president no choice about implementation. 88 Stat. 2067 (b) (4).

58. Raymond A. Bauer, Ithiel de Sola Pool, and Lewis A. Dexter, *American Business and Public Policy* (New York: Atherton Press, 1963), Part IV, esp. 421–424.

59. I am indebted to Robert Keohane and Tang Tsou for their comments on an earlier version of this section.

. 60. Einhorn, *Expropriation Politics,* esp. chap. 6.

61. Robert J. Art, "Bureaucratic Politics and Foreign Policy: A Critique," *Policy Sciences,* no. 4 (1973), 472–476.

62. Ibid.; Stephen D. Krasner, "Are Bureaucracies Important?" *Foreign Policy,* no. 7 (Summer 1972), 166–169.

63. See Bruce Andrews, "Empire and Society: Toward a Contextual Explanation of American Aims and Policy in Vietnam," Ph.D. dissertation, Harvard University, 1975, chap. 1.

64. Martin King, quoted in "Reversal of Policy: Latin America Opens the Door to Foreign Investment Again," *Business Week,* August 9, 1976, p. 47.

Chapter Seven: The Development of Expropriation Insurance: The Role of Corporate Preferences and State Initiatives

1. The corollary hypothesis is omitted for empirical reasons: on this issue there were only minor divisions within the executive branch.

2. This problem persists; see U.S., House, Committee on Foreign Affairs, *Hearings on Overseas Private Investment Corporation,* 93d Cong., 2d sess., 1974, p. 35.

3. [Edward Hopkinson and William Machold], "The Development of the Marshall Plan," unpublished paper (December 31, 1947), in Aldrich Papers, Correspondence File II, Box 140, File "President's Committee for Financing Foreign Trade 1948," p. 3, Baker Library, Harvard Graduate School of Business Administration, Boston.

4. Ibid.

5. President's Committee for Financing Foreign Trade, Draft Minutes of Meeting, January 29, 1948, in Aldrich Papers, Correspondence File II, Box 139, File "President's Committee for Financing Foreign Trade, Minutes 1946–1948," p. 3, Baker Library.

6. The most accessible record of these concerns is congressional testimony. Many examples could be cited: the 1948 House Foreign Affairs Committee hearings on the postwar recovery program; the 1949 House Banking Committee hearings on the Export-Import Bank; the 1949 House Foreign Affairs Committee hearings on the extension of the European Recovery Program; plus a number of other House and Senate hearings.

In addition, most major business associations published special reports covering the European Recovery Program or Point IV. See for example, the CED, *An American Program of European Economic Cooperation* (1948); the Chamber of Commerce of the United States, *The Point Four Program* (1949); the NAM, *The Bold New Plan* (1949);

the National Foreign Trade Council, *Private Enterprise and the Point IV Program* (1949), plus the NFTC convention reports and recommendations; the United States Council of the International Chamber of Commerce, *Intelligent International Investment* (1949); etc.

7. The laws are the *Economic Cooperation Act of 1948*, 62 Stat. 144–145 (1948); *Economic Cooperation Act of 1949*, 63 Stat. 51–52 (1949); *Economic Cooperation Act of 1950*, 64 Stat. 198–199 (1950); *Mutual Security Act of 1951*, 65 Stat. 384 (1951).

8. U.S., Congress, House, Committee on Foreign Affairs, *Hearings on the Mutual Security Act of 1954*, 83d Cong., 2d sess., 1954, p. 1196.

9. The NFTC still did not favor the program officially, but it did listen without objection as an aid official explained the program's virtues to the 1958 convention. The ensuing discussion was about practical, day-to-day issues rather than larger objections to the program. See NFTC, *45th National Foreign Trade Convention, 1958* (New York: NFTC, 1959), 230ff.

10. United States Chamber of Commerce, *Spotlight on Foreign Aid* (Washington: Chamber of Commerce, n.d. [probably 1958]), 21–22. Contrast, U.S. Chamber of Commerce, *The Point Four Program* (1949), 15–16.

11. Many of the panels have similar titles, and most are referred to by the name of their chairmen: Paley, Randall, Johnson, Fairless, Boeschenstein, and Wriston. In addition, individual studies were done by Gray, Rockefeller, Grace, and Straus on similar topics, usually at the president's request.

12. U.S., President, Special Assistant to the President, *Report to the President on Foreign Economic Policies* (1950) [Gray Report], 62.

13. U.S., President's Materials Policy Commission, *Resources For Freedom*, 5 vols. (1952) [Paley Report], I: 69.

14. U.S., International Development Advisory Board, *An Economic Program for the Americas* (1954) [Grace Report].

15. U.S., Commission on Foreign Economic Policy, *Staff Papers Presented to the Commission* (1954) [Randall Commission], 126; U.S., Commission on Foreign Economic Policy, *Report to the President and Congress*, 23.

16. U.S., Department of State, Special Consultant to the Under Secretary of State for Economic Affairs, *Expanding Private Investment for Free World Economic Growth* (1959) [Straus Report], 21.

17. John J. McCloy, "Foreign Economic Policy and Objectives," chapters submitted for the consideration of the Commission, U.S. President's Commission on National Goals, *Goals for Americans* (Englewood Cliffs, N.J.: Prentice-Hall, 1960), 347.

18. James Hagerty, Press Secretary to the President, "Press Release, March 2, 1959," mimeographed.

19. U.S., Committee on World Economic Practices, *Report* (1959) [Boeschenstein Committee], 4.

20. *Congressional Record*, 87th Cong., 1st sess., 1961, vol. 197, p. 16204.

21. Memorandum from Don Daughter to Kenneth O'Donnell, "Suggestions for Improvement AID/State Operations," June 13, 1962, p. 10, "A.I.D. 1/62–6/62" Folder, Box 68, President's Office Files, Departments and Agencies, John F. Kennedy Library, Waltham, Mass. Page contains handwritten marginal notes by President Kennedy.

22. U.S., President's Task Force on Foreign Economic Assistance, *An Act for International Development: A Program of Development, Summary Presentation* (revised July 1961 ed.), 106–107. War risk coverage was not mentioned because that had been added in 1956.

23. *Foreign Assistance Act of 1961*, 75 Stat. 429–432 (1961).

24. Investor complaints about AID's administration were voiced repeatedly during OPIC hearings. Strong statements came from the NAM and a senior consultant to the Bank of America. For a restatement of these complaints, see Peter A. Hornbostel, "Investment Guaranties: Bureaucracy Clogs the Flow," *Columbia Journal of World Business* 4 (March-April 1969), 37–47.

25. Quoted in U.S., International Private Investment Advisory Council, *The Case for a U.S. Overseas Private Enterprise Development Corporation* (1968), 2.

26. Ibid., 6.

27. See comments by Senators Fulbright and Church, in *Congressional Record*, 91st Cong., 1st sess., 1969, vol. 115, pp. 38701, 38707.

28. I will continue to equate the terms *political risk insurance* and *guaranty insurance*. OPIC's own terminology is different.

29. *Foreign Assistance Act of 1969*, 83 Stat. 809–818.

30. U.S., Congress, House of Representatives, Committee on Foreign Affairs, *Overseas Private Investment Corporation: Hearings on Title II of H.R. 11792, Foreign Assistance Act*, 91st Cong., 1st sess., 1969, p. 83.

31. *Congressional Record*, 91st Cong., 1st sess., 1969, vol. 115, p. 38700. The Rockefeller recommendation, which Javits cites, is in U.S., Senate, Committee on Foreign Relations, *Hearings on the Rockefeller Report on Latin America*, 91st Cong., 1st sess., 1969, p. 104. The Pearson recommendations can be found in Lester B. Pearson (chairman), *Partners in Development: Report of the Commission on International Development* (New York: Praeger Publishers, 1969), 108–109, 123.

32. See President's General Advisory Committee on Foreign Assistance Programs, Report, *Development Assistance in the New Administration* (October 25, 1968) [Perkins committee], 2, 26–28.

33. *Congressional Record*, 91st Cong., 1st sess., 1969, vol. 115, p. 38699. Many of the groups Javits cited testified before the House or Senate committees. Others, such as the CED, forcefully recommended the OPIC plan in their own publications. See CED, *Assisting Development in Low-Income Countries: Priorities for U.S. Government Policy* (1969) 72–73.

34. U.S., Congress, Senate, Committee on Foreign Relations, *Foreign Assistance Act of 1969: Hearings on S. 2347*, 91st Cong., 1st sess., 1969, p. 164.

35. Testimony of Elliott Haynes in *1969 House Foreign Affairs Committee hearings on OPIC* (see n. 30), p. 42.

36. OPIC's finances are discussed thoroughly in the Church committee hearings and in a 1973 report by the Congressional Research Service. See U.S., Senate, Committee on Foreign Relations, *Hearings on Multinational Corporations and United States Foreign Policy*, pt. 3, 93d Cong., 1st sess., 1973. Also U.S., Congress, House, Committee on Foreign Affairs, *The Overseas Private Investment Corporation: A Critical Analysis*, 93d Cong., 1st sess., 1973, Committee Print, prepared by the Congressional Research Service, Library of Congress.

37. This discussion of the AFL-CIO, like my other analysis of recent guaranties legislation, is based partly on confidential interviews. These interviews were conducted with congressmen and committee staff (on both sides), and with officials in AID, OPIC, and the White House. There are serious scholarly problems in relying on anonymous interviews; this research used them primarily to amplify the public record.

38. The 1974 revisions are at 88 Stat. 763–768. For a statement of OPIC's administrative changes, see U.S., Congress, House, Committee on Foreign Affairs, *Hearings on the Overseas Private Investment Corporation*, 93d Cong., 2d sess., 1974, pp. 20–68.

39. U.S., Congress, House, Committee on Foreign Affairs, *Overseas Private Investment Corporation: A Report*, 93d Cong., 1st sess., 1973, Committee Print, p. 10.

40. U.S., Congress, House, Committee on Appropriations, *Hearings on Foreign Assistance and Related Agencies Appropriations for 1976*, part I, 94th Cong., 1st sess., 1975, p. 936.

41. This point is discussed by Fred Block in "The Ruling Class Does Not Rule: Notes on the Marxist Theory of the State," *Socialist Revolution* 7 (May-June 1977), 6–28.

Chapter Eight: Conclusion: Rule Making and Policymaking

1. This point about the substantive differences between nineteenth and twentieth century property rules follows John Gerard Ruggie's commentary on the different meanings of a liberal international economic order in the two periods. Ruggie, "In-

ternational Regimes, Transactions, and Change: Embedded Liberalism in the Postwar Economic Order," *International Organization* 36, 379–415.

2. There was a debate, however, over the appropriate scope of state-owned infrastructure. To step beyond those limits was to risk categorization as a communist-leaning government in a bipolar world—with all its potential consequences.

3. Charles Lipson, "The International Organization of Third World Debt," *International Organization* 35 (Autumn 1981), 603–631; Lipson, "The IMF, Commercial Banks, and Third World Debts," in *Debt and the Less Developed Countries,* ed. Jonathan David Aronson (Boulder, Colo.: Westview Press, 1979), 317–333.

4. This section draws on several articles, all directed at corporate managers, about strategies to minimize their firms' exposure to risks. Pravin Banker, "You're the Best Judge of Foreign Risks," *Harvard Business Review* 61 (March-April 1983), 158–160; Thomas Hout, Michael E. Porter, and Eileen Rudden, "How Global Companies Win Out," *Harvard Business Review* 60 (September-October 1982), 98–108; I. Mathur and K. Hanagan, "Risk Management by MNCs: The Investors' Perspective," *Management International Review* (February 1981), 22–37; David G. Bradley, "Managing Against Expropriation," *Harvard Business Review* 55 (July-August 1977), 82–83; and a commentary on these strategies by Charles Oman, "New North-South Investment Strategies," *OECD Observer* 112 (September 1981), 13–15.

5. Pravin Banker, "You're the Best Judge of Foreign Risks," 159.

6. Theodore Moran, "Transnational Strategies of Protection and Defense by Multinational Corporations: Spreading the Risk and Raising the Cost for Nationalization in Natural Resources," *International Organization* 27 (Spring 1973), 273–287.

7. P. Banker, "You're the Best Judge of Foreign Risks," 159.

8. This conclusion—that economic sanctions are increasingly difficult to apply effectively—is supported by most studies of sanctions. Robin Renwick, *Economic Sanctions* (Cambridge, Mass.: Center for International Affairs, Harvard University, 1981); Margaret P. Doxey, *Economic Sanctions and International Enforcement* (2d ed.; New York: Oxford University Press for the Royal Institute of International Affairs, 1980); Johan Galtung, "On the Effects of International Economic Sanctions, With Examples from the Case of Rhodesia," *World Politics* 19 (April 1967), 378–416. For a partial rebuttal, see R. S. Olson, "Economic Coercion in World Politics: With a Focus on North-South Relations," *World Politics* 31 (July 1979), 471–494. Olson acknowledges that highly publicized sanctions are usually self-defeating since they stimulate nationalism and effective resistance in the target state (a point I underscored in tracing corporate disaffection with the Hickenlooper amendment). But Olson also argues that more subtle forms of economic coercion can work.

9. Gary Sampson, "Contemporary Protectionism and Exports of Developing Countries," *World Development* 8 (February 1980), 113; Jock A. Finlayson and Mark W. Zacher, "The GATT and the Regulation of Trade Barriers: Regime Dynamics and Functions," *International Organization* 35 (Autumn 1981), 561–602; Bahram Nowzad, *The Rise in Protectionism,* International Monetary Fund Pamphlet series no. 24 (Washington: IMF, 1978); Richard Blackhurst, Nicolas Marian, and Jan Tumlir, *Adjustment, Trade and Growth in Developed and Developing Countries,* GATT Studies in International Trade no. 6 (Geneva: GATT, 1978).

10. Claus Offe, "The Theory of the Capitalist State and the Problem of Policy Formation," in *Stress and Contradiction in Modern Capitalism,* ed. Leon M. Lindberg et al. (Lexington, Mass.: D. C. Heath, 1975), 137. It is precisely because state-run *bureaucracies* are poorly organized to operate as market competitors that state-run *corporations* (in both LDCs and advanced countries) are given quasi-independent status and allowed to incorporate market criteria in decision making.

11. Charles E. Lindblom, "The Science of 'Muddling Through'," in *Politics and Social Life,* ed. Nelson Polsby, Robert Dentler, and Paul Smith (Boston: Houghton Mifflin, 1963), 340.

12. U.S., Department of State, *Point Four* (revised ed.; November 1949), 53.

13. United States Council of the International Chamber of Commerce, *Intelligent International Investment* (New York: U.S. Council of the International Chamber of Commerce, 1949), 8–9.

14. National Association of Manufacturers, *The Bold New Plan* (New York: NAM, 1949), 10.

15. Robert Jervis, *The Logic of Images in International Relations* (Princeton, N.J.: Princeton University Press, 1970), 6.

16. Ibid., 13.

17. My argument is that investment security is no longer closely tied to the specific form of government in the host state (which is *not* to say that the form does not matter at all). Nearly all of my examples have shown that conservative monarchies or bureaucratic-authoritarian governments are now willing to nationalize foreign investments when they find it profitable to do so.

There is another dimension to the same point: socialist and communist countries actively seek commercial relationships with Western firms, holding out the promise of stable, long-term relations based on absolute adherence to contracts. Most deals do not involve equity participation, but some do. In August 1983, for instance, Chinese Premier Zhao Ziyang assured multinational oil companies that they could explore off China's coast without fear of their discoveries being nationalized. Radio Peking quoted Zhao as saying, "It takes a little courage to cooperate with China, but in the end you definitely won't suffer losses." Referring to new exploration contracts with Exxon and Royal Dutch/Shell, he promised that "no matter how the exploration goes, we won't change the contracts. After a big oil field is discovered, it won't be nationalized." That remains to be seen, of course, but the companies seem willing to rely on the contracts. *Wall Street Journal,* August 25, 1983, p. 18.

18. The Soviet Union and the COMECON countries are also an alternative market, but, given their economic problems and sluggish growth, not a very attractive one.

19. According to Galtung's argument, internal measures can offset the effects of external sanctions. These measures, in turn, depend on group cohesion. Galtung's intriguing point is that external sanctions encourage precisely that kind of group cohesion. It would be even more interesting to know in comparative terms how these external effects were mediated by different social structures and political institutions. See Galtung, "On the Effects of International Economic Sanctions."

Index